Books in the Elfquest Saga
by Wendy and Richard Pini

The Big Elfquest Gatherum

The Combined Volumes

Edited by
Cherie Wilkerson
and
Richard Pini

**FATHER TREE
PRESS**

The Big Elfquest Gatherum

ISBN 0-936861-13-4
Published by Father Tree Press, a division of Warp Graphics, Inc.
Publisher: Richard Pini
Design: Cherie Wilkerson
Production: Mary Lou Keenan and Steve Cartisano
First printing: November 1994
10 9 8 7 6 5 4 3 2 1

Printed in Canada

Contents

Publisher's Preface

I'm a bibliophile. I'm one of those irritating types who will cut across five lanes of heavy traffic if I spot an antiquarian bookstore on the other side of the highway. Books are the most friendly concentrations of knowledge and entertainment that the human mind has yet conceived. Oh, to be sure, compact discs read by computers can cram more sheer wordage into a smaller package than any bound, paper book can manage, and multimedia presentations can dazzle the - reader? viewer? experiencer? - with pictures, sound and fury. But nothing else feels like a book that you can hold in your hand, to read in haste or at leisure, in almost any lighting, without batteries or power cords. Nothing else allows the mind and imagination as much freedom to stop and start, to pursue a random thought, to skim the surface or be completely immersed as does a book.

Good books, at least in my world view, do not just come and go. Like the trees from which they're made, good books come into existence, they grow, they change, sometimes they send off shoots from which spring new books. They may go through different editions. The first printing of a first edition may go out of print, and become a collector's item, but the words themselves, the knowledge, the stuff of the book, stays available.

Often, the story of a book's evolution can be found in the introductions and forewords and prefaces that precede the body of the text. Especially in older books, one can find reprinted the Preface to the First Edition, to the Second Edition, to the Third, and so on, down the line to the present incarnation. While not necessary to the enjoyment or understanding of the text, these little slices of history - often personal - provide a slice through the strata of ideas that helped shape the form and content of the book.

That is why this *Big Elfquest Gatherum* is laid out as it is. More than either of the previous volumes, it is an overview of the entire *Elfquest* "tree." It is not only the new and improved, but also the original. The reader will, I hope, find that this collection of elf-iana reads like the rings of a tree, from inner to outer, to give the most complete view of what *Elfquest* is and has been than has ever been collected in two covers. Naturally, this volume can't contain every shred of *Elfquest* knowledge ever written - that would take at least another Big book - but it is a nicely balanced meal as is.

A project of this magnitude would not be possible without the help, past and present, of many people. I thank the following, who worked in different ways - as interviewers, editors, writers - on previous editions of the *Elfquest Gatherum*. They helped provide the building blocks for this one: **Dwight Decker, Deborah Dunn, Jane Fancher, Deni Loubert, Richard Meyers, Paula O'Keefe, Patrick Daniel O'Neill, J. J. Pierce, Ree Moorhead Pruehs, Peter Sanderson, John Weber, and John Wooley.** I'd also like to thank those who collected the words and phrases that went into the Glossary for this and earlier volumes; without these painstaking folks, the flavor of this book would be a little less rich: **John LaRue, Jr., Anne McCoombs, Katerina M. Hodge, Benjamin Urrutia, Vince Mora, Eliann Fensvoll, Brad Johnson, and Linda Woeltjen.**

—Richard Pini

Introduction I

By Richard Pini (from *Gatherum I*, 1981)

Dear Gary (and all the Fantagraphics crew),

The deadline is drawing near for the introduction, or foreword, or whatever you want to call it, to the *Elfquest Gatherum,* and I'm afraid that I'm going to have to send along my apologies instead. Try as I might, I just can't seem to come up with the appropriate words to open this thing.

Which is a shame, really, because if for no other reason, the intro would have been a very good place to acknowledge all the people who have worked on this for the past several months. Wendy and I have of course thanked Dwight Decker personally for doing yeoman's work in editing the book into a coherent, and quite enjoyable, whole—it would have been nice to be able to get those thanks into print. Then too, we'd have wanted to trumpet that we are very grateful to Paula O'Keefe for letting us reprint—with all the extra stuff left in—her excellent overview article; that the insight that J. J. Pierce put into his piece was a joy to discover; that John LaRue's glossary was everything we could have wanted; and especially that Jane Fancher's comments on the art of Elfquest were so right on the mark that *we* learned things we'd never known before! Naturally, this letter gives us the chance to thank you guys again—for everything. After all, the idea for the *Gatherum* was yours in the first place; it's not a project that we would have dreamed up on our own, but now that it's reached fruition, we're glad it exists.

I'd have the chance too, if this were to be a real intro, to thank—feeble gesture on my part—Wendy for everything: for birthing an entire world, for putting up with the insane hours, for letting me put my two cents in—although with current economic inflation I'm not so sure it's that much—for being the better half of Warp.

I guess this is one of the few pitfalls of creating a world that people seem to like to visit a lot: we've gotten a little burned out. Sometime in the next few weeks I, or we, have to do about a half dozen introductions and/or pieces of writing, and there's nothing left at the moment for the one you want. Sorry.

It's a funny thing, mentioning pitfalls. In a sense, I guess we dug one for ourselves when we started telling *Elfquest,* promptly fell in, and have been living there happily ever since. (So, is it still a pitfall then? Good question.) We never planned to have a family, at least not this soon nor this large! But talking about the *Gatherum* as a kind of scrapbook or family album makes the family we've created for ourselves suddenly seem very real. I guess we could say that we don't have the same problems that other families do—we are spared the toilet training and two A.M. feedings—but talk about growing pains for several dozen characters! As well as for the magazine itself! Oy!

You all have been in publishing for somewhat longer than we have; do you get queries from young hopefuls out there who want to get started in this crazy business? If you do, we'd love to know what you tell them. There's so much that's great: the feeling of getting a finished issue back from the printer, the letters that come in telling us that we did good, the rewards both spiritual and financial (hey, we gotta eat, no?) But I wonder. If the hopefuls also had to put up with the bounced checks, the eighteen-hour workdays when the sun is shining, the hassles with the shippers and the mail, the inflexible deadlines, the occasional hurtful letters, would they still want to hang their souls out to dry in front of God and everybody? Then again, no one ever learns about fire without getting burned. We had to get burned a couple of times; we're wiser for it now.

Sure, we'd do it again, knowing what we know. It's a story that really wants telling (it's been inside Wendy's head for years, trying to get out); and what the heck, we've gotten a neat "family album" out of it all, right? Albums are wonderful things, after all; I don't think that anyone would *not* want to be able to look back over some part of their past once that past is gone. We still haul out our own four-color memories here from time to time; the smiles are all still there.

So now we have another album to page through: a kind of growing-up, family, wedding, school, graduation, working, playing celebration all rolled into one. We don't often get the chance to dig into the Warp archives to reminisce over Cutter's growing up or Skywise's rescue from his original death; and you all have put one together for us. It's certainly different from anything we'd ever considered doing, and we're very grateful to everyone involved that it's done.

I just wish I could come up with something—anything—to send you guys for an introduction, but the well's gone dry for now. Well, what the heck, it's the book that counts anyway, right? So I'll just sit back with my figurative pipe and my literal slippers, and enjoy it slowly, one page at a time.

Sincerely,

Richard Pini

Introduction II

by Dwight R. Decker (From *Gatherum I*, 1981)

There's a nifty German word that, like kindergarten, has come into the English language whole because there isn't a really suitable native equivalent: *Festschrift*. The word is a compound of *Fest*, "a celebration or festival," and *Schrift*, "a piece of writing" (descended from the same Latin root that gave us the word *script*). According to Mr. Webster, a festschrift is "a volume of writings by different authors presented as a tribute or memorial especially to a scholar." When it's Herr Doktor Steinheimer's eighty-fifth birthday, for example, his colleagues and associates might write articles and essays in honor of old Steini and contribute them to a festschrift published to commemorate the occasion.

That's pretty much what the *Elfquest Gatherum* is: a festschrift to celebrate the Elfquest phenomenon (although in this case it might be closer to the mark to call it a "questschrift"). Of course, there's no particular occasion being observed here; it isn't Wendy's birthday and it isn't the anniversary of the day Richard got his first telescope. But who ever needed much of an excuse to have a party?

Rather, we're celebrating the triumph of a dream. *Elfquest* has grown from a pleasant little fantasy shared by just two people into a major series with thousands of devoted followers all over the world—and colossal potential for growing even bigger—with a novelized version, a mass-market color reprint, foreign editions, T-shirts and other doo-dads, and much more here now or on the way. Something on that scale deserves a closer look, certainly, along with the congratulations and well-wishing. So we've gathered together a team of articulate Elfquest fans and invited them to put their thoughts and observations on paper, then assembled the result into a festschrift of sorts. If it seems that this or that contributor took the in-depth analysis to the limit, well...no one wanted to give *Elfquest* short Schrift!

The *Elfquest Gatherum* came about partly as an outgrowth of the interview I conducted with Wendy and Richard Pini for the *Comics Journal* #63. As J. J. Pierce commented in a letter to me after reading the interview, "What an *ecology* there is to *Elfquest*, from the influences to the intimacies of collaboration!" Even though the interview was a long one, *Elfquest* is such a rich and complex entity that much, much more could have been said about it.

Meanwhile, Gary Groth, the publisher and editor of the *Comics Journal*, had been considering the possibility of branching out into book publication. An article or interview in the *Journal* can only say so much in the limited space available, but an entire book devoted to a given topic could cover it in as much detail as necessary. *Elfquest*, with all its human interest, colorful story, and snowballing fan appeal, seemed like a natural as a subject for one of the first books. Since I had reviewed the first issue of *Elfquest* for the *Journal* way back when and had done the interview, I had the reputation around the Fantagraphics clubhouse of being the resident Elfquest specialist. When I was asked if I would like to edit the book, my response was an immediate "You bet!" Wendy and Richard Pini are thoroughly delightful people and interviewing them had been such a pleasant experience that I was glad to have the opportunity to work with them again.

In fact, the *Elfquest Gatherum* is as much theirs as anyone's. From the first, Wendy and Richard have aided and abetted work on the book with maximum cooperation despite their heavy schedule in overseeing the rest of the Elfquest empire. They threw open their archives, willingly provided a huge pile of hitherto unpublished Wendy art, and helped me sort through it. Their suggestions, advice, and contributions proved invaluable, and even the book's title is theirs. Although it isn't likely that Warp Graphics (*W*endy and *R*ichard *P*ini) will be replace by Draw Graphics (*D*wight, *R*ichard, and *W*endy), the collaboration was a lot of fun and the *Elfquest Gatherum* came together with remarkable smoothness.

The rest of our gallant band of contributors deserves a vote of thanks, too. Nor can we forget the stage crew: the crackerjack production staff at Fantagraphics who transcribed the interview, set the type, pasted up the layouts, and cheerfully hauled the barges and toted the bales of all the drudge work involved in publishing the book. Everyone is more than entitled to take a bow at this point.

Through it all, one guiding principle was never very far from anyone's mind: Will this book help the reader enjoy and appreciate *Elfquest* all the more? Artwork and features were selected with the idea of answering any questions the reader may have about *Elfquest*, its history, and its underlying concepts. It is our hope that the background information to be found in the *Elfquest Gatherum* will prove welcome and useful, both to the casual reader of *Elfquest* and to the more deeply involved fan.

So here's to *Elfquest!* May its success to date be only the beginning!

—Dwight R. Decker

Wendy edits the editor of the first *Gatherum* (by about a foot and a half and 105 pounds).

The Other Mountain
An introduction of sorts in a personal vein

by Richard Meyers (from *Gatherum II*, 1988)

Elves came into my life early. I was idly wondering, as I was wont to do, what life was like before glasses. Having almost always worn thick spectacles, I couldn't help but wonder what it would have been like had I been born into a time without them. Did you ever notice that characters who *do* live in the era before glasses never need them? Which came first? Glasses or astigmatism?

It's fodder for an observational comedian like Jerry Seinfeld or Paul Reiser. How come nobody from the 1600s back was ever near- or farsighted? That was the question I asked myself, and from that came my first grand script idea. I wedded that casual consideration to my theory that all mythical creations have some basis in fact to come up with a fantasy epic: the tale of a nearsighted, disgraced court jester discovering the remnants of an elfin civilization.

It would be a tragic adventure, I decided, as the court jester fell in love with the female offspring of the only interspecies marriage of elf and human—and this would signal the end of elfin civilization. An angry, envious king would declare war on the elves since they were effortlessly happy and he was consumed with neuroses. The court jester would defeat the king with magic, but the elves' population would be so depleted that they could not survive to modern times.

Although the jester would be heartbroken, his last elf friends would assure him it was just as well—elves could never coexist with humanity. Elves knew how to celebrate life. Humans seemed to need to be miserable. The jester would be left as the elves had found him: alone, in the snow. Still, the audience's tears should've been tempered with joy. The jester had found love, had defeated evil, and had learned something about how to live.

I never actually wrote it, of course. I knew enough about the movie business to know that the script would be hopelessly expensive and impossible to cast. Hollywood elves never looked any good. Besides, my heart wasn't in it. Although I could empathize with nearsightedness, I never liked elves all that much. I had more in common with the evil king: elves were too cute, too uncomplicated...too "perfect."

Sometimes I would tell the story of the nearsighted court jester around a fire at Farm Camp Lowy in Windsor, New York, or on a camping trip, but I dropped it as a viable money-making project. Instead, I started to write articles for *Cinefantastique* and *Starlog*, book proposals for Pinnacle and Charter Publications, and comic book plots for Seaboard/Atlas.

The latter company hired me as assistant editor, where I stayed for a year before moving over to *Starlog* as associate editor. Between the two, I gathered college credits in Bridgeport, Connecticut, and Boston. And somewhere in there I got a package in the mail from Richard Pini.

I had been friends with Richard's brother, Carl, through high school, and we would jump the stone fence behind the Pinis' home to enact fantasy adventures on the adjoining golf course. It wasn't until college that Carl suggested I visit Richard, who was then working at the Boston Museum of Science's Planetarium. The Planetarium? I liked the man already. Here he was, doing what I wanted to do, working with his head in the stars!

We got along fine, and while we didn't do any heavy hanging out together, we kept in touch. So I wasn't exactly stunned when I got the package containing the first two issues (*Fantasy Quarterly #1* and *Elfquest #2)* and a letter. As I recall, the personal missive said that Richard and Wendy wanted to get all sorts of feedback from their friends and fellow professionals. To paraphrase: what did I think?

Well, sir. If memory serves, I had just finished a rough half-year snarling at Atlas Comics where Jeff Rovin was desperately trying to save the dozen comic books he had fathered and nurtured. I had spent this half year watching wonderful work by Michael Kaluta, Howard Chaykin, Walt Simonson, Jeff Jones, Larry Hama, Neal Adams, Pat Broderick, and many, many others being turned into junk for the most petty, ludicrous, and arbitrary reasons by the most short-sighted publishers I had ever worked for.

I had been guided to the top of the mountain then thrown off the cliff. I was going to be a part of the greatest thing that ever happened to comics since Stan Lee. I was going to be one of the innovators in a new line of mature comic books which would set new standards for writing and art. I was going to be one of the ones to bring new depth and emotion to the medium. I was going to be an editor who unlocked the secrets of the form. Me, me, me!

Instead, I toiled over an increasingly degenerating batch of titles that worsened in quality the more the noncreative members of the staff interfered. I was sickened, I was disgusted, I was burned out. At one point I actually walked into the men's room with a pair of scissors and cut off most of my hair. Jeff was not able to sublimate his emotions as well. He nearly had a physical breakdown instead. We were going to do something great and instead were attached to something miserable.

So, maybe my excuse is that the

last thing I wanted to see at that moment was another comic book. Especially one with such beautiful elves. I remember thinking: *look at those chests.* In the words of the comedian, so round, so firm, so fully packed! And that was just the males.

I vaguely remember my answering letter to the Pinis. Too predictable, I said. Too facile. Too pretty. Too pat. As I think about it now, what I was actually saying was that they acted too much like elves! What I wanted to do was make "my" elves more human, more untraditionally flawed. But these weren't my elves, of course, and I should have been stunned and gratified that these two people actually went out and achieved something Atlas couldn't with all its millions. I should have been supportive whatever my personal misgivings were.

But as I said, elves weren't my cup of tea. And after Atlas, neither were comics.

I went away for almost ten years. I watched as Atlas died, its only legacy being to raise artists' and writers' pay rates. After that I couldn't bear to look at a comic book. The grand experiment had failed, killed by the "Golden Rule" (whoever has the former makes the latter). The ultimate tragedy was that Atlas was not killed by competition, but by its own in-house strangulation. Marvel and DC were left to monopolize the business and have the artists dance to their tune.

I wrote books. Nonfiction hardcovers as well as fiction paperbacks. I wrote under every name but my own. I merely touched upon comics again in 1979 when I was the only non-Marvel employee to write a Marvel novel for Pocket Books (*The Incredible Hulk: Cry of the Beast*). I moved forward, without looking back, to enter the science-fiction field with three nonfiction books and two novels. I spoke at conventions.

I ghost-wrote a slasher movie. I worked in television.

Finally I stumbled back into comics. The last, late, lamented Manhattan Empiricon convention had but a single comics panel which needed a moderator. Since most of the panelists were old pals from the Atlas days, I willingly volunteered. Howard Chaykin was in the audience and Walt Simonson suggested I get him up there to talk about his comic which was about to premiere: *American Flagg!* Walt couldn't say enough about it, and the entire experience reminded me of how much fun comics could be.

It also reminded me of the goals I was hoping to accomplish through Atlas. So I took a look at issue one of *American Flagg!* and was hopelessly hooked again. I ignored my existential pain and dove back into the industry—only this time as an observer and an audience, which is really the best job of all.

I continued writing books but read comics voraciously. I got a professional discount at Forbidden Planet, the largest comic book store in the English-speaking world. I became a creative consultant to the Dream Factory, the largest comic book store in Connecticut. I bought comics in Paris, Hong Kong, and Tokyo.

I had come back at the right time. The industry was about to burst wide open. There was about to be an orgy of creativity which would unleash comics' Platinum Age. And once I examined the causes and effects, there was one undeniable fact: if *Elfquest* wasn't the explosive trigger, then it was, at least, the fuse.

Everywhere I went, I saw the effects. *Elfquest* comics, Elfquest magazines, and Elfquest books. Plans for an Elfquest movie, Elfquest toys, an Elfquest television show. But that really wasn't the important thing—not to me, at any rate. The important thing was the effect *Elfquest* had on the comics industry. It wasn't as if Richard and Wendy set out to prove anything to the big boys, to humiliate or embarrass them. The one thing I saw in *Elfquest* was (dare I say it?) love.

Again and again, in my books and magazine columns, I maintain that it takes only two things to make character drama work. Those things aren't good looks or relevance. They aren't marketing and pandering to the lowest common denominator. They are *passion* and *compassion*. Richard and Wendy's passion was obvious in every word and picture. Their characters' compassion was obvious in every panel. This was lush, romantic, engrossing stuff which I was not prepared for or interested in.

But I was an exception. *Elfquest* found its audience in those who passionately and compassionately cared about elves. Sure, I clapped to keep Tinker Bell alive, but I did so reluctantly. Hell, I wasn't going to have the blood of no elf on my conscience! But still, I was more interested in the near-sighted court jester than the race of mythical creatures he was partly responsible for destroying.

Beyond story considerations, however, I credit *Elfquest* for opening up the comics industry because Wendy and Richard proved that an independent comic could not just make thousands of people care, it could make money. Lots of money. So much money that the comics corporations not only sat up, not only paid attention, but paid cash! The companies that had scoffed at the Pinis' chances before, now wanted a piece of the Elfquest pie.

The Pinis had also helped the industry blossom because they had inspired dozens of others to go the independent route, to give life to their own passions, unhindered by the "Dark Side's Golden Rule."

The trick is to care. The trick is to be true to yourself. The trick is to do something for some reason other than just money. The trick is to work hard and finish it. The trick is not to listen to anyone who says it's too predictable and too facile. If you can do that, you can move mountains.

Elfquest has changed the comic world. Without it, there might have been no *American Flagg!*, no *Love and Rockets*, no *Concrete*, no *Elektra*, maybe not even a *Dark Knight* or *Watchmen*. Because the Pinis proved there was a market for something other than just full figures in action. There was a market for words, for deep emotions, for something other than "comic book" art.

It's cold up here on my mountain top. Cold and lonely. I sit here and type without the comfort of elves. They died out of my world many years ago. I must lean down close to the page to see it clearly. I am nearsighted and have no glasses.

In the distance I hear laughter and singing. It's coming from that other mountain, the blue one. I hear the sounds of joy and sadness, of peace and war. I hear life from that mountain.

There is no life here. Only work. But maybe, with time, the elves that live on that other mountain can teach me something. Maybe they can help me see what many others have seen clearly. Work isn't work if you love it. ✧

Leetah offers Nightfall and Redlance the comfort denied the author (at least by elves).

Chronology

For the new reader, and perhaps even for the old, the very first information in this book should be a simple and concise history of the various incarnations of *Elfquest*, for the title and its connected stories have been through sufficient permutations that, without a scorecard, the unwary may get confused.

The chronology is as follows:

• Spring, 1977: The idea for Elfquest is born in story conferences between Wendy and Richard Pini, as Wendy decides to let characters she's lived with for many years out of her head.

• February 28, 1978: *Elfquest* first appears as the feature story in the first and only issue of *Fantasy Quarterly*, an independent comic book by a small Midwest publisher that goes out of business soon after.

• August 1978: Warp Graphics, realizing that self-publishing is the only viable route, releases issue #2 of *Elfquest*.

• 1978–1984: Warp Graphics publishes the independent comic book *Elfquest*—the story of a tribe of elves called the Wolfriders—as a 20-issue, magazine-sized black and white series. *Elfquest* is distributed only through comics specialty shops. These issues are now long out of print and hard to find.

• 1981–1984: The Donning Company publishes *Elfquest* Books One through Four which are colorized collections of the Warp Graphics comics.

• 1981: Fantagraphics Books publishes the *Elfquest Gatherum*, an encyclopedia *cum* family album containing articles and artwork that relate to *Elfquest*.

• 1982: Berkley Publishing releases *Journey to Sorrow's End*, a novelization of the first part of the *Elfquest* saga. Published at first in trade paperback, it is later released in mass paperback, and reissued in 1993.

• 1984: The final issue (#20) in the original *Elfquest* saga is published, and Warp Graphics takes a two-year "vacation" from the elves.

• 1985–1988: Marvel Comics publishes *Elfquest* in a 32-issue series of comic book sized color issues reprinting all of the original Warp Graphics material with the addition of new artwork done specially for this series.

• 1986: Tor Books publishes *Blood of Ten Chiefs*, the first volume in a series of shared-universe anthologies, featuring well-known science fiction and fantasy authors and based on the early world of Elfquest. To date, a total of five volumes have been released.

• 1986: Warp Graphics produces a new *Elfquest* comics series entitled *Siege at Blue Mountain* which continues the adventures of the Wolfriders. *Siege* is a comic-sized, black-and-white series of eight issues.

• 1988: Elfquest is ten years old! Father Tree Press (a "branch" of Warp Graphics) publishes the *Elfquest Gatherum* Volume Two.

• 1988–1989: To celebrate *Elfquest*'s tenth anniversary, Father Tree Press publishes newly recolored and revised editions of the old color volumes, adding new artwork that has not previously appeared in the Donning editions. Over the next few years, Father Tree will collect all available *Elfquest* material into such volumes, providing a dependable source for the stories even though the comic books themselves may be long out of print.

• 1990: Warp begins publication of the third *Elfquest* series, *Kings of the Broken Wheel,* which runs 9 black-and-white issues.

• 1992: Elfquest comics go to full color with the first issue of *Hidden Years.* Over the next two years several new *Elfquest* titles are added to the lineup: *New Blood, Blood of Ten Chiefs, WaveDancers, Shards, Jink,* and *The Rebels.* From time to time the stories in these comics are collected in companion volumes to the original eight (which contain the first *Elfquest* series, *Siege at Blue Mountain,* and *Kings of the Broken Wheel*).

• 1994: Father Tree Press publishes *Bedtime Stories,* a volume of classic fairy tales for younger readers told by and using the *Elfquest* characters.

• 1994: Father Tree Press publishes *The Big Elfquest Gatherum.*

• The Future: Warp Graphics continues to maintain "the *Elfquest* universe" of comic book titles, which collectively tell of the past, present, and future of the World of Two Moons. Berkley Publishing contracts for two more novelizations of Elfquest material, sequels to *Journey to Sorrow's End.* The elves continue to share their stories in ways and in media that no one imagined in 1977.

The tale goes ever on, and the quest never ends...

In the Beginning

The Elfquest
You Never Saw

When *Elfquest* was just beginning, Wendy and Richard put together a package of sample pages and character designs to submit to publishers. The material in the package itself was never published until the first *Elfquest Gatherum*. As you can see, a few details were changed along the road from idea to reality: Cutter originally had two sons, Leetah had a soul name, and oh yes, that's Skywise's first appearance there in the rescue scene.

"CUTTER"

TRUE NAME: TAM, BLOOD-OF-TEN-CHIEFS...

FIERCE, YOUNG CHIEFTAN OF THE **WOLF RIDERS**, A TRIBE OF BARBARIC ELVES WHO DWELL IN THE FOREST REGION OF **HOBSLAND**.

ENEMIES WHO HAVE FELT THE STING OF **NEW MOON**, TAM'S EVER-READY SWORD, KNOW WHY THIS FEARLESS ELF IS CALLED **CUTTER**.

THROUGH PERILS WROUGHT BY **MAGIC**, **MONSTERS**, AND THE NEWLY EMERGING THREAT CALLED **MAN**, **CUTTER** FIGHTS FOR THE SURVIVAL OF HIS TRIBE AT THE DAWN OF HIS WORLD'S TIME!

© W '77

"MORNINGLIGHT"

TRUE NAME: LEETAH, PRINCESS OF THE SUN FOLK... HELD HOSTAGE BY THE WOLF RIDERS BECAUSE OF A MIS-UNDERSTANDING, THIS DUSKY BEAUTY MARRIED CUTTER AFTER A STORMY COURTSHIP.

QUICKBLADE

TOUGH, FULL OF MISCHIEF, THE TYPE OF KID WHO EATS LIVE SNAILS, SHELL AND ALL—THIS SKILLFUL YOUNG SWORDSMAN WILL ONE DAY BE A GREAT WARRIOR, LIKE HIS FATHER.

STARJUMPER

THE GENTLE ONE—A TRUE WOOD SPIRIT WHO UNDERSTANDS THE LANGUAGE OF ANIMALS. HE IS ALREADY ONE OF THE WOLF RIDERS' MOST DISCIPLINED ARCHERS.

© W '77

CUTTER'S FAMILY

The scene as drawn in Wendy's sample in 1977...

Right, the sample page; *and opposite,* how the scene was published in *Elfquest* #6

Did Skywise jump or was he dragged? *Right,* the scene as portrayed in the sample; *opposite,* the scene as published in *Elfquest* #9

THE THIEF FALLS!

BUT HIS ARMS FLY OUT, HIS FINGERS CLUTCH REFLEXIVELY --

--AND HE IS LEFT HANGING BETWEEN LIFE AND DEATH UPON THE COLD LEDGE OF --

--STONE..!

M-MUST HAVE... MAGIC STONE!

NO!! LET GO!!

IT'S MINE!!

SKYWISE!!

NO!

FOR A TERRIBLE MOMENT, HUMAN AND ELF SHARE ONE FEAR --

--ONE FATE--

AND THEN... ONE CHANCE FOR LIFE!

UNH!

Other Days, Other Elves

The elves seen in *Elfquest* aren't the only elves Wendy has in her drawing pen. Here we see some elves of a quite different sort.

Long before *Elfquest,* there were many worlds that Wendy created and sketched. The common thread among these ideas seems to be a love of creatures with pointed ears for, as she has often said, ears with points (as well as large, liquid, slanted eyes) evoke the other-worldly, an animal spirit, a sense of danger. Whether the players in her stories are the winged denizens of *The Ruby Shepherd,* or whimsical, finny undersea beings, they all share the fact that, fins or wings, they are elves.

Just as Wendy's head is full of pictures, so it is brimming with stories. Before *Elfquest,* Wendy wrote a few chapters of *Vaiya, Daughter of Stone,* the adventures of a woman living on a primitive tribal world. In Warp's first, not wildly successful venture into portfolio publishing, Wendy did four plates of warrior women, including one of Vaiya. The portfolio was called "The Barbariennes"—Richard never could resist a pun. The Vaiya plate is noteworthy for the first appearance anywhere in the natural (or unnatural) world of a zwoot.

The Ruby Shepherd.
The bat-winged folk
call to mind an early
version of the shape-
changed elf Tyldak.

Above, Undersea fun with mer-elves. *Right,* Not exactly an elf, but ethereal and mesmerizing all the same—a testament to Wendy's love of Japanese comics and animation.

Kapa Alpha

Happy New Year I'm sure!

WENDY FLETCHER

Another holiday elf: The cover for the January 1970 mailing of CAPA-Alpha (a comics-oriented amateur press association).

Vaiya, Daughter of
Stone from "The
Barbariennes"
portfolio

This page and opposite, sketches of Vaiya, Daughter of Stone

On the Road to Elfquest

As Wendy and Richard worked on their ideas, the character designs and personalities of the elves evolved towards the versions that would finally see print. Here we see some early model sheets that illustrate the development of Elfquest's lead players.

Richard adds: Wendy is one of those artists who almost literally never stops drawing. Whether she is on a nature walk, riding a bus or plane, or just vegging out in front of the tube, she always has a sketch pad at hand. These vignettes (and most of the ones that appear in this book) are the result of her desire never to lose a thought or idea. These character sketches came shortly after the sample pages (see "The Elfquest You Never Saw"); they were done about mid-1977. Already there is a refinement in the look and feel of the major characters of Cutter, Leetah, and Skywise; we also see the first concrete realizations of Redlance, Nightfall, Scouter, and Dewshine.

Opposite, **Cutter and Skywise ponder the mystery (and the promise) of the key to the quest.**

CUTTER

PHYSICAL DESCRIPTION: About four feet tall (average size for a Wolfrider): long, shaggy hair to the middle of the back, part of it caught up in a topknot - hair is beige/white like pampas grass; warm, high-color skin; wears fur vest, deerskin breeches, soft leather moccasin boots; eyes are translucent jewel-blue.

PERSONALITY: What we have here is a young adult elf who became chief of his tribe too soon (Cutter's chieftain/father, Bearclaw, was killed in battle with a magically mutated creature called Madcoil). Consequently, Cutter is a little over-zealous in assuming his responsibilities. He is alert, tense, and rather serious - very protective of his tribe and those he loves. But because he is young he sometimes makes rash decisions. He knows this and relies often on the advice of his uncle, Treestump, and his closest friend, Skywise. Cutter is absolutely unpretentious, guileless and honest. This gets him into trouble sometimes, because he expects the same of others. He is capable of frightening rage, and his skill with a sword makes him a deadly opponent. Against larger enemies he relies on speed and agility. His movements are always quick, graceful and sure. He is sensual and easy with his own body, never self-conscious. In essence, Cutter might be described as a creature of "highs." He can be collapsed in laughter, or snarling like a deadly, enraged wolf. If he were an animal, he would be a bantam rooster or a fighting cock.

LEETAH

PHYSICAL DESCRIPTION: 3' 11" tall (petite among her own tribe, but able to look Cutter square in the eye!); dark auburn hair partially caught up with a crownlet of beaten gold; beautiful golden-brown skin; wears a red, gold and blue color scheme - has several costume changes; has sparkling green eyes.

PERSONALITY: Leetah is gentle and self-posessed and does not like to be unsettled. She is a healer, possessing the power to close wounds, mend bones, and lower fevers through the force of her will. She prefers to be in control of events that affect her. She is methodical and not necessarily imaginitive, but willing to learn as long as she's not pushed. She is the antithesis of the melting, submissive fairytale heroine. She does not like to be dependent or beholden. Nor is she vain. The coming of the Wolfriders forces her to examine the values she has taken for granted for most of her long life (she is at least 600 years old, many times older than Cutter). She is brave, though cautious, and she trusts her own strength. While she appears, at first, to be tempermental and stubborn, this is only due to her resentment of Cutter's uncivil-ized behavior. When she finally accepts him, it becomes obvious that she is independent, not merely snobbish. There is something feline about Leetah. She is light, grace-ful, and eminently pet-able.

CUTTER

CHIEF OF THE WOLFRIDERS;
CENTRAL CHARACTER OF
ELFQUEST; PRIMAL ELF,
VOLCANIC, BUT RATHER
QUIET BETWEEN
ERUPTIONS;
HAIR: PAMPAS GRASS
CLOTHES: BROWN, GOLD
AND FAWN
ANIMAL TYPE: BANTAM
ROOSTER

TM
© WARP

LEETAH

PRINCESS OF THE SUN FOLK;
CUTTER'S LIFE-MATE;
TEMPERMENTAL, SPIRITED
HAIR: MIDNIGHT BROWN
CLOTHES: RED, GOLD, + BLUE
ANIMAL TYPE: CAT

TM
©WARP

SKYWISE

KEEPER OF THE LODESTONE;
CUTTER'S FRIEND AND
CONFIDANTE;
INCORRIGIBLE FILCH;
HAIR: SILVER
CLOTHES: BLUE AND GRAY
ANIMAL TYPE: FOX

KAYEK

CHIEF HUNTER OF THE SUN FOLK;
CUTTER'S RIVAL IN ALL THINGS;
MALCONTENT THROWBACK, ARROGANT,
NEEDS OPPONENT WORTHY OF HIS
                    MAGIC POWERS;
HAIR: BLACK
CLOTHES: RED, GOLD & BLACK
            ANIMAL TYPE: SNAKE

REDLANCE

NIGHTFALL

"THE OLD MARRIEDS"

DEWSHINE   SCOUTER

"THE LOVERS"

Children of the Last Minute

Wendy's original plan had been to give Cutter and Leetah two sons: Quickblade and Starjumper. However, almost at the last minute, she changed her mind, and Suntop and Ember, a boy and a girl, were born instead. Quickblade stayed in Limbo, Starjumper's name was assigned to a wolf, and the story took a rather different turn from what must have been outlined first since the plot starting with issue #8 turns on Suntop's psychic powers—powers neither Strarjumper nor Quickblade seem to have been intended to have.

The sketches shown here illustrate the development of Suntop and Ember from initial doodles to fully fleshed personalities.

Opposite, **the essential Ember, resembling nothing so much as a red-topped dandelion**

EMBER

Upper left, this is the first sketch ever done of Ember. Her character as a rough-and-ready tomboy is beginning to show in her eyes and face, but it isn't quite there yet.

Right, Wendy first visualized the twins as typical Wolfrider children: woodsy and a bit ragged in dress. Further evolution refined them considerably.

**Suntop and Ember
simplified for
possible animation**

SUNTOP—

A YOUNG MYSTIC, VERY
SPIRITUAL—HE'S PO-
TENTIALLY MORE SENSITIVE
THAN THE SUN-TOUCHER.

EMBER—

A TOMBOY, FULL OF
BUSINESS—SHE'LL
BE AN EXPERT HUNTER
AND PROVIDER.

The World of
Two Moons

A Conversation with Wendy and Richard Pini

Since there's nothing like an interview for getting to know someone in print, an interview with Wendy and Richard seemed indispensable for a book like this. On February 21, 1981, a squad of crack interviewers from Fantagraphics arrived in Poughkeepsie armed with tape recorders and cameras, intent on ferreting out the most intimate secrets behind *Elfquest* and its creators. The Pinis weren't facing questions from just Dwight Decker this time; now I was backed up by Gary Groth, Mike Catron, and Peppy White.

With four people on one side of the tape recorder and two on the other, the interview gradually lost its formality and became a casual, relaxed conversation—collapsing now and then into complete silliness.

Afterwards, everyone was close to exhaustion from the marathon gabfest, and we retired to one of Poughkeepsie's finer eateries for nutritional reinforcement. I should say the Fantagraphics crew was exhausted; Wendy and Richard have evidently discovered the secret of perpetual motion and weren't slowed down in the least, even after several hours of doing most of the talking. It's too bad the dinner conversation wasn't recorded; Wendy in particular can more than hold her own in dinner table banter with four slightly demented comic-book buffs and an impressively articulate husband.

So here are Wendy and Richard, chatting in the comfort of their own home, in as close to their natural state as you're ever going to find them when they have company in the house...

—Dwight Decker

DECKER: *Let's start out by talking about one of the concepts behind* Elfquest. *The medieval belief about elves was that while they were essentially immortal and had magical powers, they also had no souls. Thus a note of bittersweet irony: a human being's life might have been nasty, brutish, and short, constantly buffeted by forces of nature he had no control over, living and working in misery and going to an early grave, but he still had something not even the King of the Elves had. When the world ended, the elves would go with it, snuffed out like a candle flame, but a man's immortal soul would go marching on. Is there anything of this in the* Elfquest *mythos? I notice that the humans had a god—Gotara—but nothing has been said about religious beliefs or practices among the elves. Do they have someone they think of as god?*

WENDY: No. No. Part of the reasons for that is that Richard and I are both agnostics and again, that's reflected in our way of life. Well, should I just speak for

FIRE AND FLIGHT
PART I

WRITTEN BY
WENDY & RICHARD PINI
ART BY WENDY PINI

If you join the First Church of Gotara, don't expect bingo parties.

myself or did I speak for you, too [*to Richard*]?

RICHARD: Yeah.

WENDY: Okay. Good.

RICHARD: I mean, you said it nicely. I would have said we're heathens.

WENDY: [*Laughs.*] Yeah, heathens. The world is our religion, I would say. When I get up in the morning and I go out and look at a fine sunny day with a cloud,

man, that's all I need to get a spiritual high.

GROTH: *Was either of you brought up religiously?*

RICHARD: I was brought up in not a strict, but a well-observed Roman Catholic home. I went to church every Sunday for the first fourteen or fifteen or sixteen years of my life and did all the sacraments and the whole thing and all the—

I can't even say I went through the motions because at that age I said, "Well, that's the way it is and this is the way I'm being brought up, so this is the way I'll be." So I simply grew away from it, at the time I don't think through any fault of what it was. It was just that it didn't do anything for me.

GROTH: *Was it gradual or did you at some point simply say...?*

RICHARD: No, it was not a conscious decision: "This week, I am going to stop going to church." It might have been that—in fact, I think it probably was—as I approached going to college and especially when I went to college and living on my own, it just became, "I don't feel like getting up this Sunday until one o'clock in the afternoon so therefore I miss church, and I don't feel too bad."

WENDY: I think your religion is the sky. I think your religion is the stars.

RICHARD: Something like that. But...

GROTH: [to Wendy] *What was your religious education?*

WENDY: Oh, I went to church as long as my grandmother was alive and I was expected to, but when she passed away I didn't go on my own. I was baptized Episcopalian, but I never knew what all the folderol meant, and I went because it was expected of me and not because I believed in it. I believed in God, I very much believe in God, but he's mine, he's not a god that anybody is putting me into or setting rules down about or telling me how long his beard is or anything like that. I don't even know if He's a *he* or an *it* or what. But He's definitely there. He's just mine [*laughs*].

GROTH: *And that's reflected in* Elfquest.

WENDY: Yeah. Definitely.

DECKER: *A thought occurred to me that the elves themselves might not need religion because religion for many people is a way of—*

WENDY:—dealing with death.

DECKER: *Well, no, dealing with nature, one's relationship with nature. Human beings, because of their intelligence, feel alienated from nature, and religion is a way of putting oneself back in tune with the universe. The elves are so close to nature that they have no need of religion. They're already in tune with nature because they're a part of it. They don't feel cut off from it.*

WENDY: Oh, that's excellent. Terrific. I agree with you 100 per cent there. They are—gosh, it's hard to talk about religion. Yes, our humans have religion. They believe in spirits, but in the case of one tribe that was already bugging the elves in the holt, they had a master over the other spirits. It's not that they were monotheistic. It's just that they had one master over all the other spirits they addressed. Gotara is what they called him.

RICHARD: And it was a natural kind of thing, in the same way that early civilizations had gods of volcanoes and storms and things like that. They needed it to explain natural phenomena before science came along, and other religions took over that, and they became a little more sophisticated. It's still a kind of a naturalistic religion, even for the humans. They've given names to the spirits and made a pantheon. It's still a naturalist's kind of religion. They're not as in touch with nature as the elves are.

WENDY: They're a little bit *afraid of*

"**I** believe in God, but he's mine; he's not a god that anybody is putting me into or setting rules down about or telling me how long his beard is or anything like that. I don't even know if He's a *he* or an *it* or what. But He's definitely there."

spirits, too, which is something I'm addressing myself to, which is man's fear of the spiritual side of himself.

DECKER: *Primitive people may feel they have no control over the forces of nature; thunderstorms come, floods come, some other disaster comes, and people are helpless. Religion is one way of trying to appeal to the powers that be for mercy or a favor now and then.*

WENDY: Oh, that goes without saying.

DECKER: *The elves seem to be rather more rationalistic and don't look at it quite the same way.*

RICHARD: Then, too, the elves don't think about death.

WENDY: Our characters, barring disease or getting their brains knocked out, they—

RICHARD: They will live for a long time—or forever.

WENDY: Yeah, they don't have any idea of how long they can live.

RICHARD: So they don't have the need built in within them to desire or hope for a continuance of their identity, of their personality, after death.

WENDY: And they lack one other thing, one other human trait. They lack guilt.

DECKER: *Would it be possible to say that the elves are so innocent in that regard that they've never really known sin, they're never really fallen?*

WENDY: That's right.

RICHARD: They are so honest that they can't feel guilt. If they make a mistake, they know it and they correct it, or they take the consequences of it and go on from there.

DECKER: *Are there outlaw elves, elves who may have somehow committed some crime in a community and were expelled?*

WENDY: Yeah! As a matter of fact, there's a story I want to do about one of the early chiefs who was called Two-Spear and was a little bit mad. He got the tribe into an actual war with the humans and was challenged by his sister. She beat him, won, and became chief. That was Huntress Skyfire, I think, and that's a story I want to do some day if the opportunity arises. He was bad, but he was also a little bit weird in the head [*laughs*].

RICHARD: But still, it was not a case where he had guilt over what he was doing.

WENDY: No, he believed that what he was doing was right. When Cutter kills the thief in [issue] #9, he says—and I had this conversation with Mike Catron when Mike was here to take pictures the other day. We were talking about Conan and the fact that Conan kills about sixty people an issue, average. When Cutter kills this thief—there's only one killing, not sixty—he says to the thief, "You're meat to be wasted, your blood will fall on bare rock and nourish nothing." Now, ordinarily the elves respect life, they don't waste blood, not even human blood—it's part of the flow. But when Cutter utters this curse it takes away all responsibility for that life. The guy becomes dead to Cutter. And so when he kills him there isn't that sense of "I have killed." The curse, in other words, relieves him of any kind of moral agonizing over having to have taken a life without using the meat or the blood as a wolf would. When wolves kill, they use the meat and the blood, you see.

DECKER: *Oh, is that what you meant by that? I didn't really pick that up when I read it, I just—*

WENDY: You just thought it was "You lousy rat."

> "Cutter is expressing the deepest, most irrevocable waste that a Wolfrider can conceive of [to kill someone], because they are like wolves; they put everything to use."

DECKER: *No, I saw it as an expression on Cutter's part of "What a waste it is to take a life that won't serve any purpose. We can't eat this guy. What a waste that it's a life that will amount to nothing."*

RICHARD: In a sense, you've got the right idea, but he is expressing the deepest, most irrevocable waste that a Wolfrider can conceive of, because they are like wolves; they put everything to use. This guy will not serve any purpose. He must be gotten rid of...

DECKER: *"You're not fit to be fertilizer!"* [Wendy laughs.]

GROTH: *Well, is that an out or a rationalization?*

WENDY: I don't know. I had to make a tremendous commitment to kill this character. I am not an advocate of killing as a solution to problems, which is again what I said to Mike. Conan would not say Cutter's little speech to each of the sixty individuals he kills each issue [*laughs*]. But he doesn't even think about it.

RICHARD: It's not clear whether it's self-defense in this case. Is Cutter protecting (a) himself, (b) Skywise, or...

WENDY: He's protecting Skywise, himself, and the lodestone.

RICHARD: Okay, but is it a case of self-defense? Is it kill or be killed?

WENDY: If he did not kill the thief, he could have run away, and the thief would most certainly have bashed Skywise's brains out and taken the lodestone—two terrible things to happen—but I would say...yes, Cutter could have escaped easily.

RICHARD: Could he have wounded him? Driven him off somehow?

GROTH: *In other words, was there an alternative?*

WENDY: I didn't see one.

RICHARD: This gets interesting, like that TV movie about the gun in the house. If you're trapped and you shoot somebody, are you guilty of murder or

is it just self-defense? It might be construed to be a point of contention in this issue of *Elfquest,* what happens here, whether he was justified in doing it. I suppose you could consider it an expression of gray in our own minds.

WENDY: I also had to think about Cutter's nature. He's killed a human before. That old, old hate, which he was just beginning to lose—hardly lost, but beginning to lose—all welled to the surface again. All those defenses, all those prejudices again came to the surface. And I think that was behind that sword thrust. He simply couldn't think gray. He wasn't capable of thinking in gray.

RICHARD: This would be an interesting study in a court of law, but *Elfquest* is not a legal primer.

WENDY: [*Laughs.*] Anyway. Does that cover...? I don't know what started that.

RICHARD: I think to answer your question it's an expression of what either one of us might do under similar circumstances.

GROTH: *So then you must feel—*

RICHARD: Maybe that says something dark about us.

WENDY: We're willing to accept that, though.

GROTH: So then you must feel death is necessary in certain circumstances.

WENDY: Oh, yes.

DECKER: *I'm certain there are people whose loss would be no tragedy.* [Evil, inhuman laughter from all.]

GROTH: *I can think of at least one.*

WENDY: Did you see *A Gun in the House?* Well, that was built around the moral issue of a woman who defended herself against a rapist-murderer. She shot and killed him, and she was arrested for murder, and the whole question revolved around that...

RICHARD: I think it was supposed to follow that—what was it, about a year ago, two years ago, that woman...

WENDY: In Boston...

RICHARD: She shot the guy, she was

trapped, and first they put her in jail, but later they acquitted her, which I thought was the greatest thing in the world.

WENDY: I was cheering through the whole thing. I would have done the same thing, definitely. I wouldn't have thought gray, I would have simply thought "protect me and my child." The whole thing in #9 was such a tense story because that's the first issue they've willingly walked into a lair of humans and confronted their ancient enemies and taken a good look at them. They're trying to tamp down all those age-old prejudices and look at them with different eyes.

RICHARD: It doesn't get done in ten minutes. It doesn't get done in a day. So, suddenly, confronted with this situation, I guess you could say that Cutter reverted.

WENDY: Reverted, exactly.

RICHARD: And does what he feels is necessary under the circumstances.

DECKER: *I was just looking at this panel here that has Cutter in the village looking at the people. Keeping in mind*

Cutter disclaims responsibility for the life he is about to take.

that tooth care isn't quite as good in primitive societies...

WENDY: [*Laughs.*] Yeah, well one of the elements is that the elves...some people have complained that our characters look too much alike, but I think that's only a natural result of tremendous inbreeding.

DECKER: *Something else that just occurred to me is that these elves are technically immortal, or close to it. Paula O'Keefe, in her article—*

RICHARD: Wants more scars—

DECKER: *More scars, and I was just thinking, if the elves are so long-lived, that they probably have very good regeneration.*

RICHARD: It's not regeneration, it's that they have healers.

WENDY: They have incredible healers.

RICHARD: No elf scars—in fact, when we read Paula's article, we said there are very good reasons for that. The reason they don't have many scars is that number one, we humans put more stock in these battle trophies, like the Heidelberg dueling scars: they make us look good, they say that we have conquered an enemy or something, or that we've achieved something and survived it, and this scar is our badge, our mark. Well, the elves are not like that, first of all. They're much longer-lived, so they don't necessarily want to have these reminders of the fact that they could be injured, that they are not invulnerable. At least in conflict with humans, they want to be able to present a complete, a whole appearance. Especially if a human has wounded an elf, the elf does not want the human to know that, or the human to be able to point to that reminder and say, "Ah-ha! I got you!" I imagine that could be a little bit intimidating.

WENDY: Well, our characters rely a lot on the fact that their appearance alone intimidates humans and scares them away quite often. The more potent and unreal and spirit-like they can appear, the better, so they certainly wouldn't want anything that humans can have, like scars.

RICHARD: Or which can suggest to the humans that the elf *can* be injured. They don't put the value on a scar or that kind of mark that a human would or that we traditionally have done in human history, so they would have their healers. The Wolfriders had Rain before he was killed; and ever since they've gone to the Sun Village, they've had Leetah who has even greater powers than Rain. They would have these special elves, these healers, remove the marks, the scars, the wounds, whatever, to make the flesh whole again, to present the whole and complete appearance.

WENDY: Perfect.

DECKER: *Skywise chops off the thief's thumb in issue #9. If that happened to an elf, if he had lost a digit, could the healer regenerate it or would it be a permanent loss?*

RICHARD: I think it would depend on the wound. Now One-Eye, if you look under his eye patch—if he lets you— you will not see an empty socket, you will just see smooth skin covering the whole thing. The eye is gone. Rain the Healer was able to effect that cosmetic repair, but he could not save the eye. The eye was too badly damaged to save. But when we were talking about it, I think we came to the conclusion that the degree of injury would determine whether or not something could be regenerated.

WENDY: Also—we don't want to give away the story—but in about three issues, we are going to deal with that in a different way, that very thing, and I would have to say yes, we have certainly considered that possibility of regeneration and we have approached it in our story.

RICHARD: I think if somebody were to get a hunk of flesh sliced off his arm or leg or something, probably a healer could cause it to come back. A finger, I don't know.

DECKER: *If the healer was on the scene, perhaps the digit could be* put *back.*

WENDY: Oh, I would think so.

RICHARD: Possibly. Because if you remember from #2, where they go back and pick up Redlance, Leetah goes spiritually into him during the healing. She is able to knit the broken bones and to take the injured organs and have them become whole again. Circumstances would determine it, I think, more than anything else, but it's possible.

GROTH: *If an elf were cut in half, both sides wouldn't regenerate.*

RICHARD: No, not spontaneously. But if you had a real good healer and you sort of stuck 'em back together, it might work. [*Wendy laughs.*]

DECKER: *Yeah, how about having each half—*

GROTH: *That's what I meant: grow two Cutters.*

DECKER: *No, no, if you could just cause the wounds on each half to seal over, you'd have two living halves of an elf.*

WENDY: I think we can dispense with such speculation—primarily because I won't *draw* it! [*Laughs.*]

DECKER: *I was looking at that scene of the people in the village. Maybe it's just part of your drawing style, but even though you tried to make the characters different and individual, with some ugly and some attractive and some so-so, they all still look pretty clean.*

WENDY: Yeah, that's a psychological thing. I wanted the readers to look at these humans with a totally sympathetic eye for the first time.

RICHARD: And also, there's no reason for them to be grubby. I mean, they've got an established village, they live by a river, they know what water is.

WENDY: Also, they're all cleaned up because they're greeting the spirits here, you see. They're having a big party, and they're all in their Sunday best.

DECKER: *It might be interesting if they'd had, like many savage tribes, self-inflicted scars, tattoos like—*

WENDY: There's a fellow here [*flips page*] with a scar on his back, a rather large one. It didn't print too well, but it's all down his back. So I did think of that, don't worry [*laughs*].

RICHARD: But again, there is your human putting marks on the body to make it appear more beautiful. And again that's a concept that we personally don't have a whole lot of truck with.

WENDY: I loathe tattoos [*laughs*].

DECKER: *Earlier on, you said that this nameless world is perhaps Earth as it should have been to begin with.*

WENDY: Not as it should have been, but as we would like it. It's a personal Earth.

DECKER: *Yeah, but maybe you're getting something started here whereby your nameless world is going to end up just like this place. There's a line in G. Harry Stine's book about the industrial applications of space flight that, believe it or not, actually connects with* Elfquest. *It was his book,* The Third Industrial Revolution, *Ace, 1979:*

> And in supporting the third industrial revolution (space travel and manufacturing), people may be completing a process started ten thousand years ago at the beginning of the Neolithic age. Before that time, people lived in small nomadic hunting groups and tribal cultures where most children died, where the tribe might perish completely, where people went hungry most of the time, where a person was old and ready for death at the age of thirty years for all his trouble. The big change began when the tribe looked down into a

valley and saw a cluster of dwellings surrounded by tilled fields. The Neolithic age had begun and people started trying to plan for the future, rather than live with the present problems.

That sounds like that scene in #2.

WENDY: Exactly so.

DECKER: *It also suggests that in a few thousand years the elves might be a force to be reckoned with on a galactic scale. Some Star Trek fan might even contemplate the notion that what you've done is recount the early history of Vulcan. The humans will go the way of the Neanderthal and one of Cutter's distant relatives will be science officer of the* Enterprise.

WENDY: We can't say a single word about that because the future is part of the story line, but *that* speculation is wrong.

RICHARD: We are going to address it, although not in prodigious detail. We are going to put some thought into the projected history of what happens.

DECKER: *This is the dawn of time, so to speak, the change from prehistory to history.*

WENDY: Exactly. Our humans are just about to discover metal, so they're coming in. Oh, dear—no, we can't possibly answer that question.

DECKER: *There wasn't a question there, just a comment.*

RICHARD: This is one of those worlds where electricity doesn't work, so we'll never get past a certain stage and everyone will still be riding zwoots.

DECKER: *You can't say that. You've got lightning.* [Laughter from Wendy as Richard, stunned, mulls this one over.]

RICHARD: In another two or three hundred years or a thousand years, or whatever, the Waveries will come and that will be the end of that. [*The Waveries are fictional creatures that eat electricity—*

ed.]

WENDY: [to Decker] You can't beat him.

DECKER: *Okay. Well, steam has to work.*

RICHARD: Steam is fine. But electricity isn't (in this age), and without electricity you don't launch rockets.

DECKER: *Not necessarily.*

RICHARD: Well, gunpowder rockets...

WENDY: [exasperated] Will you cut out the BS! [Wendy laughs as everyone turns to look at her.] That's going to look lovely in the *Gatherum.*

GROTH: *Wendy gets tough.* [General laughter.]

DECKER: *With an arrow pointing to her, labelled "Wendy gets tough," like in the Carl Barks stories. Where were we before we got off on all this? Oh, another notion occurred to me, too. This is getting back to the mythological version of the elves. In the medieval legends, part of the reason why the elves were getting shoved back was because* they were soulless. Specifically, in Poul Anderson's novel, The Broken Sword, what was displacing the elves, the old gods, and the rest of the supernatural was the coming of Christ. Christianity was coming in and the old ways were no longer effective. The new god was displacing all the other ones. In fact, The Broken Sword was a novel about what was happening to the gods and the elves as their time on Earth was coming to an end. So my thought is that perhaps a group of elves and such decided to escape from our Earth at that time and escaped across the dimensions popping into this nameless world.

WENDY: You should write a story about that.

RICHARD: It's wrong, but... [General laughter.]

DECKER: *It's just an idea I had, that originally the elves of* Elfquest *come from our Earth, and—*

WENDY: It's a very good idea. I'm glad it's wrong because it's a good idea, and

thank god we've got something as good.
RICHARD: Better.
WENDY: No, but I think that's what a lot of people are expecting. A lot of people are hypothesizing.
RICHARD: People have written in, in fact, and said, "Yeah, they escaped from Earth and went to an alternate Earth—Earth E," but it's nothing like that.

> "**W**endy has said that Cutter is the expression of her personality with all the human traits removed, and the character of Nonna is the expression of her personality with all the elfin traits removed."

DECKER: *The lady artist and her mate in #8: are they anybody we know?*
WENDY: Huh?
RICHARD: Nah.
WENDY: Who? What? Which? [*Laughs.*]
GROTH: *Got them nailed down.*
DECKER: *Nice cinematic opening to that issue, by the way. I liked that.*
WENDY: Thank you. You're the first one to mention that.
RICHARD: Wendy has said that Cutter is the expression of her personality with all the human traits removed. And the character of Nonna (who is that unidentified artist-lady in #8 and #9) is the expression of her personality with all the elfin traits removed. I think I'm probably a little less easy to pin down than that, but yeah, these are cameos of

WENDY: No.
DECKER: *Now we get nosy and personal. You've said that in some ways* Elfquest *is an allegory of the lives and times of Wendy and Richard Pini.*
WENDY: Gary Groth's ears just grew points and pricked [*laughs*].
GROTH: *And my fangs gleamed.*
RICHARD: He's drooling on the rug.

us.
DECKER: *Other people go to Hawaii for their vacations, but you take up part-time residence on your own fantasy world.*
RICHARD: It's very part time, and we don't intend to make a habit of it.
WENDY: We've finished with Nonna and Adar in two issues.
RICHARD: I guess you could call it an expression: we interact on certain levels just about every day here in Poughkeepsie, New York, with our elves. Now this is an expression of that interaction in the pages of the story itself, of our interaction with the elves themselves.
WENDY: One of the cutest things, I think, is Skywise squaring off with Adar, because it's Richard squaring off with himself. [*Laughs.*] But I very much embrace the elfin side, or what I perceive to be the elfin side of my personality, just as Nonna embraced Cutter without being afraid of him in #3.
DECKER: *Did we cover the matter of the purgative.*
WENDY: [*Laughs.*] I don't think so.
DECKER: *The question is this: if Cutter has what seems to be blood poisoning, or general infection, as a result of the squirrel biting him and getting infected when the wound came in contact with the dirty swamp water, how can what seems to be a purgative—the whistling leaves—do him much good?*
RICHARD: The answer to that question being of course that the whistling leaves are not purgative in that sense. You're thinking of *emetic.*
WENDY: Well, diuretic, actually.
RICHARD: No, an emetic makes you throw up, and that's what Dwight was thinking of.
WENDY: Oh, pardon me. [*Laughs.*] Excuse me.
RICHARD: What these leaves actually are is a diuretic that makes you go to the bathroom a lot. They work through your system, collect all the poisons, filter

them through the kidneys, and from there they become part of the larger universe.

WENDY: Elves have the most incredible kidneys in the world. They have to, because they eat an awful lot of raw meat. As a matter of fact, their whole digestive system is pretty incredible, because you eat a lot of raw meat and you're bound to come up against stuff that could be taken care of by cooking. This is why we eat cooked meat: we got smart.

RICHARD: Tired of trichinosis.

WENDY: Yes, [*laughs*] tired of trichinosis, so the elves have pretty incredible digestive systems.

DECKER: [noticing puzzlement from the Fantagraphics crew] *"Trichinosis is the pig's answer to porcophagy."—Ambrose Bierce.*

WENDY: [*Laughs.*] Anyway, that answered the question. So it wasn't him going out and throwing up, which wouldn't really have any effect on blood poisoning. But as we said, there was no really discreet way to draw that, and time and space did not permit all the gyrations I would have had to go through [*laughs*].

RICHARD: You know, artsy silhouette shots and off panel sound effects...[*Wendy laughs.*]

GROTH: *Sploosh, slush...*

RICHARD: Tinkle, tinkle, tinkle, yes...

GROTH: *Well, could you have clarified that with a word balloon or a caption?*

WENDY: Perhaps. I think I personally just decided to let it go.

DECKER: *You had to do it fast because of dramatic considerations, but it just seems to me that something like that would be an extended treatment over a period of time. Of course, he does come back fairly weak; it does take him time to recuperate...*

WENDY: And Skywise is holding off the humans during that time.

RICHARD: That's the kind of detail

Above, Richard squares off with himself. *Below,* Nonna and Adar. Anybody we know?

that, assuming we continue the series of novels, would probably be easy to go into.

WENDY: Oh, in the novel I would have no trouble with it. I haven't had trouble writing about an awful lot of things we don't put into the comic [*laughs*].

DECKER: *I've got a question about the novel, but I'm going to save that. How thoroughly are the Wolfriders integrated into the society of Sorrow's End? Are they still a separate, nominally independent community co-existing with the Sorrow's Enders or are they merging? If the merger has been complete, what exactly is Cutter's position? He can't be the chief because his father-in-law is the chief.*

RICHARD: Well, you're asking a general question, and you more or less have to take the Wolfriders as individuals.

WENDY: Dwight just said a very interesting thing, though. Why does everybody assume that Sun-Toucher is chief of the village? It's Savah who leads the village.

DECKER: *Really? She just sits in her little house!*

WENDY: That doesn't matter.

RICHARD: There's no leader as there is of the Wolfriders. Savah provides spiritual guidance; Sun-Toucher keeps everybody in touch with the natural force.

WENDY: Yes, but if there's a mass decision to be made—

RICHARD: Then Savah does it.

WENDY: Savah does it. She's the one. But everybody assumes—it's the chauvinistic world we live in [*laughs*]—that it's Sun-Toucher who leads the group.

RICHARD: The question is, is there a

"**I haven't had trouble [in the novel] writing about an awful lot of things we don't put into the comic.**"

tribal entity called the Wolfriders? Well, in #9, we saw that some of the erstwhile Wolfriders, particularly Woodlock and—

WENDY: Rainsong. Eternally pregnant.

RICHARD: Eternally pregnant, yes—have in essence become Sun Villagers. They are perfectly at ease with the life there; they have integrated themselves part and parcel into the life of the Sun Village. Somebody like Strongbow would never in ten thousand years have fit in, which is why he was so eager to go away with everybody else. The tribe that is called the Wolfriders will never be the same as it was. Some of the members have been left behind. They will never again be quite the forest-dwelling, nomadic hunter-type Wolfriders they were.

WENDY: Well, Dart chose to stay and become—

RICHARD: The hunter, yeah, but—

WENDY: Teacher, more of less, of the village—

RICHARD: But the makeup of the tribe of Wolfriders will never be the same as it was in the first few books.

WENDY: No, it never will.

DECKER: *Well, it looks like they may have been searching for something like this to begin with, because after being devastated by Madcoil they were already in a state of flux; their stability had already been pretty well shattered.*

WENDY: Exactly.

DECKER: *You mentioned one elf being eternally pregnant. That was another point that occurred to me* [laughter from Wendy]. *If elves live so long, they probably don't have so many little elves.*

WENDY: Okay, you're exactly right. Rainsong is a real phenomenon, and I think it had something to do with a biological over-reaction to the sudden deaths of so many tribe members—

DECKER: *Like a baby boom.*

WENDY: A baby boom, exactly, and Rainsong is the one-woman baby boom. She really just won't stop [*laughs*]. I doubt that she'll have more than three, but...

DECKER: *It just seemed to be that elves live so long there'd never be very many children.*

RICHARD: Normally, there wouldn't, but we always allow for idiosyncrasies. We always allow for individual characterizations, and whatever seems right for a given character for whatever reason, we'll let that character have those attributes.

WENDY: Exactly. But if you'll notice, I never do draw too many children in the crowd scenes. There really are very few.

DECKER: *That must have effects on, say, elves' children's games, or even the maturation of a little elf, because he doesn't have any peers.*

RICHARD: Well, they become real demons at solitaire. [*Wendy laughs.*]

DECKER: *I would imagine they'd have to grow up fast because they're mostly in the company of adults.*

RICHARD: Well, this gets us into the concept of elf biology that we may have talked about some other time. They reach their sexual maturity really fast, in a few years. And then slide into— what did you call it, the long afternoon?

WENDY: The long, golden afternoon. But for instance, look at Dart. He's being treated as an adult, and he's all of thirteen.

RICHARD: He's being treated as an adult by the Wolfriders, the Sun Folk look on him as a child. Their concept of maturity is different.

DECKER: *Yeah, the Wolfriders would have to grow up fast because they're out in the wild.*

WENDY: Yeah, exactly.

DECKER: *Okay, that pretty much covers that. According to the Elfquest fan club newsletter, Skywise originally had a pretty low life-expectancy* [Richard whistles, Wendy laughs.] *Can you go a little into the influences that snatched him away from the slavering jaws of death?*

WENDY: Richard. [*Laughs.*]

RICHARD: The influence is sitting right here.

WENDY: That's right.

RICHARD: It was in the creation stage of the book. At that point of the evolution of *Elfquest,* Wendy was much more involved in it than I was, because the base ideas were always hers. She was putting down her notes and thoughts and sketches and scribbles and character designs.

WENDY: Not many, though.

RICHARD: Not many, but enough. And we got to talking about some of the characters, and she had mentioned that there was going to be some violence in this one particular scene, which is indeed the scene that happens in the most recent issue, #9, where the thief is responsible—although in slightly different form back then—for Skywise going over the cliff. In the original conception, he was going to go over the cliff and survive just a few moments longer, long enough for Cutter to more or less say good-bye to him. And then he was going to die. And we talked a little bit more about this character; he still wasn't very well formed. We didn't know very much about him.

WENDY: As far as we knew, he was just Cutter's best friend.

RICHARD: And that's it. None of the endearing personality traits were there yet.

WENDY: [*Laughs.*] You supplied those.

RICHARD: And then she made the mistake of telling me that one of his functions in the Wolfriders was to be sort of the first astronomer elf. He watched the stars. He doesn't really have a function as a star watcher, but this was one of the things he did. In essence, this world's very first astronomer. And I was working in the field of astronomy at the time, and it has always been one of my great

Portfolio Outtake:
"He's an astronomer, he's my elf, I take charge of him, I take possession, and you're not going to kill him"—Richard

loves and still is, although I'm not working directly in it now, and I looked at her sort of out of the corner of my eyes and said, "Astronomer." And she said, "Yeah." And I said, "You're not going to kill him." And she argued with me and discussed it with me—

WENDY: Oh, I had this dramatic death planned.

RICHARD: —and debated it with me and the whole thing, and I said, "You're not going to kill him. He's an astronomer, he's my elf, I take charge of him, I take possession, and you're not going to kill him." And it was really no more complicated than that when it came down to it. I was just not going to give in on this point, so we kept him around.

WENDY: Sometimes I wonder if in the very innermost recesses of my mind I didn't do that deliberately to get you so involved in this damn thing that you couldn't possibly let go.

RICHARD: If that's the case, then you are a more subtle, sneakier, incredibly more devious son-of-a-gun than I ever gave you credit for. But that's how Skywise got saved: she made the mistake of telling me he was an astronomer.

DECKER: *Does he do things like weather predictions?*

RICHARD: No. He is at the stage that if there is such a thing as precession of equinoxes on this world, he will be able to detect it because he'll live long enough himself to see it. But that's getting technical.

DECKER: *I wonder if he'd be able to keep track of dates just by being able to tell the seasons.*

WENDY: We're very vague about that in *Elfquest.*

RICHARD: We're very vague about time. We measure time by days, moons, and seasons. Skywise is at the point where he looks at the sky and he's able to perceive patterns, and maybe he's beginning to think about stories to tell

along with the pictures that he sees. He does know that there are wandering stars. He doesn't know that they are planets the way we do, but he does know that there are "stars" that move against the background of fixed stars.

DECKER: *Issue one: "See, Cutter..? The great wolf chases the human hunter across the sky. He's clumsy, that hunter! One day, he'll trip and the wolf will get him." Cutter replies, "You see all that up there, Skywise? Strange...I just see stars." It looks like the constellations must be the same there as they are here, since that sounds like Orion and Canis Major—the Great Dog—behind him.*

RICHARD: No, that happens to be a coincidence. Yes, on Earth we do have a hunter called Orion. Yes, we do have a lot of animals in the sky.

WENDY: Yeah, but most humans are hunters on this world, so Skywise would naturally—

RICHARD: He would pick images that meant something to him, and images that would mean something to the elves are images of humans and images of wolves.

DECKER: *If the constellations are different, are there different planets in the star system?*

RICHARD: Without going into the technical aspects of it, we're assuming, offstage, that this is a realized world, a possible world, and as such this solar system could have other planets that he'd be able to see.

DECKER: *It has two moons, I notice.*

RICHARD: Yes. It's a very physically real place we're dealing with here.

DECKER: *Hard edges.*

RICHARD: Yeah.

GROTH: *I had some questions about your working relationship.*

RICHARD: Stinks. [*Wendy laughs.*]

GROTH: *I figured that, but—*

RICHARD: What dirt do you want to dig?

GROTH: *One thing I'm interested in is*

Identifying constellations

have to say that aside from the mutual interest in comics—and there were differences there too, because I was very much the collector, buying every title, the whole thing, and Wendy was—

WENDY: I was a dilettante.

RICHARD: Wendy would buy a favorite title or two, or whatever. But I think another difference would be that I grew up more science oriented whereas Wendy grew up more fantasy-world oriented.

WENDY: Except I scored real high on that aptitude test in mechanics. I do have a pretty good mechanical mind, it's just that I haven't exercised it much [*laughs*].

RICHARD: It's not that there were really differences, objective differences, but rather differences in emphasis in what our interests were. Because I still liked movies of fantasy and she liked things having to do with the natural world.

WENDY: Oh yeah, I was reading Ellison before I met Richard.

RICHARD: I'm talking about the natural world and you talk about Harlan Ellison. Where'd that lead [*laughs*]?

WENDY: I just meant that Harlan is science fiction.

GROTH: *Shh...don't tell him that* [laughs].

WENDY: Do you mean he stopped loving science fiction?

GROTH: *He wants to divorce himself from the label.*

WENDY: Ohh...pardon me, Harlan. When I read him at the age of seventeen or eighteen, Harlan was science fiction.

RICHARD: His early stories were more science fiction, hardware, than they are now. But aside from that...I think we both had a lot of interests in things visual. The overlap might have been more not in what we read, but what we saw: movies, we would have both gone to the same types of things, seen *Fantasia*, seen the Harryhausen films, seen whatever fantasy films came out...

how your interests converged. Because obviously you didn't grow up in a similar environment. You didn't really have...well, your interests weren't that similar. You were both interested in comic books, to a certain extent, but...

RICHARD: That can provide a lot of common ground. No, not really. I would

WENDY: Well, you were impressed by art at the time, I remember. The first letter I wrote him I sent him a sketch of one of the Marvel superheroes and—

RICHARD: I freaked out. It was the most incredible thing I'd ever seen. And so—I think it's that there were minor differences. There were a lot more similarities when we finally got together that were just easy to...

WENDY: And huge differences.

RICHARD: What were the differences?

WENDY: I loved opera.

RICHARD: That's got nothing to do with *Elfquest*.

WENDY: [*Laughs.*] Yes it does, in a way. After we got married is when we actually discovered the differences between us, more than when we were courting, shall we say.

RICHARD: It was difficult to get into those things through letters, so you sort of have to—

WENDY: When you're courting by mail, you tend to want to show your best side.

GROTH: *Well, when you're courting in person you also want to show your best side.*

WENDY: True, but I think a lot of barriers get let down when courting in person.

RICHARD: You can slip in person.

GROTH: *Yeah, right.*

RICHARD: You can let defenses slip, whether deliberately or accidentally; you can show a bad side. Living in each other's sweat tends to be different.

WENDY: But we were pretty honest. We saved our letters and we look at them from time to time. We were pretty honest because we were looking to communicate in so many ways.

RICHARD: "The Elfquest Letters."

WENDY: Ahhhh! [*Laughs.*]

GROTH: *A new volume.*

WENDY: No, there are certain Elfquest stories and certain writings that Richard and I have done that nobody will ever see [laughs]!

RICHARD: No, but it will be published posthumously. Shock the daylights out of everybody. [Wendy laughs.]

GROTH: *We'll have to kill 'em to do it. From what I remember of the interview Dwight did for the* Journal, *you got married very soon after you met. Is that true?*

RICHARD: No. We "met," if you want to call it that, through the mail, as a result of that letter in *Silver Surfer* in the early part of 1969, and we got married in the summer of 1972, so that's almost four years, three and a half years.

GROTH: *How much of that was spent corresponding and how much was spent together?*

RICHARD: There was a sum total of six weeks spent in actual contact before we got married. I would go to California or, once or twice, I think you came to the East Coast—

WENDY: The first time I came I took every cent I had in the bank. When I came back I didn't even have a dime to make a phone call [*laughs*].

RICHARD: —for at most two weeks, and then we'd have to get back to what we were doing. I was in college—

WENDY: True love. Oh, God.

RICHARD: I remember one month I got a phone bill for seven hundred dollars, and I said, "This is bull. I can't live this way."

> "There are certain Elfquest stories and certain writings that Richard and I have done that nobody will ever see."

GROTH: *You could fly out there for that.*

RICHARD: Yeah, back then? Are you kidding? Three times you could!

WENDY: My parents were wondering where this boy could get the money to call me every night.

DECKER: *I was wondering that when*

you mentioned it in the first interview. Where did you get the seven hundred dollars for the phone bill? [Wendy laughs.] *What did you have to sell to raise the money to pay the phone bill?*

GROTH: *Dealing cocaine from time to time...*

RICHARD: Well, this is Cambridge. There are a lot of ways to make money in the Boston–Cambridge area.

WENDY: He sold himself [*laughs*].

GROTH: *Few people knew that Richard was a male prostitute.*

RICHARD: That's right. "Seventy-five dollars and twenty-five cents, who gave me the twenty-five cents?" "All of them did!" No. You see, it was one of the college phones, so I took out a loan from the college and paid that back gradually. The phone company didn't care, they just wanted their seven hundred dollars, but I was able to pay back the college in small installments.

DECKER: *As I said in the other interview, I was just amazed that you could run up that much of a phone bill. It would be difficult to run up a seven hundred dollar phone bill now, even as high as phone rates have become.*

WENDY: It was so easy [*laughs*]. So, to answer your question: Yes, we got married after four years of corresponding and on the phone and such.

DECKER: *What about the working relationship?*

GROTH: *Yeah. What exactly are the steps you go through when you put together an issue of* Elfquest?

RICHARD: First there's a story conference; we both know the whole story from #1 to whatever. We know where it's going, how it's going to end, where it's going to end. Little details will probably be changed, modified, added, subtracted as we go along, but the overall thing, we already know that. We knew it before we started publishing. We'll have a story conference for a given issue, and usually that takes place—it helps to

relieve the boredom— on long automobile drives.

WENDY: What about restaurants?

RICHARD: Restaurants, at least you're doing something creative. You're interacting with a pizza. But in a car there's nothing to do but watch the road. So we'll talk about #9 or #10 or whatever, and usually what will happen is that Wendy will start outlining the finer detail that she sees going into this issue, and she'll be going along, and perhaps I'll say, "Wait a minute, that's not consistent, this happened back then, how do we resolve this action? How do we resolve this motivation, there's no motivation there?" and we'll go through this whole thing and hammer down what is a pretty finished plot. Then Wendy will sit down and write the actual script.

WENDY: Stage directions and everything.

RICHARD: She will put the words on paper. She'll give that to me and I'll go over it from an editor's point of view, to see how the rhythm of it reads, how it feels.

GROTH: *How much editing do you do on her script?*

RICHARD: That's a hard question to answer, because—

WENDY: I edit what he edits [*laughs*].

RICHARD: Yeah, it goes back and forth and I can't say, "Well, I edit 40 per cent or 60 per cent." I can't put a numerical value on it.

WENDY: Because he may edit what I've written and it's just lovely, and then I go to put it in the panel and it won't work.

RICHARD: I would say, to answer it as best we could, there's a little bit of something done just about on every page. Sometimes there's more, sometimes there's not as much. I think that everything she does is subject to it, and I think to a greater or lesser extent just about everything she does gets touched a little bit.

GROTH: *Okay. What kinds of things*

do you edit? Do you edit out whole balloons because they're superfluous, do you edit words...

RICHARD: It's not at the point where we can edit out a balloon and I can explain why. When I get the script, I may think that a sentence is too wordy, so I'll condense it. I may feel that there's action happening here and I want the words to reflect the action, short sentences as opposed to long sentences—

WENDY: Or a caption may not be necessary because the action—

RICHARD: Right. But that comes later, because after the script gets finished she'll take it and she'll start doing the layouts, pencils, and placing of word balloons within the panels and the words within the balloons. She'll draw something and we'll then both look at it and say, "Oh my god, this facial expression says it all; you don't have to use this caption." So I may have edited a caption or left it alone, and it turns out we don't even want it. A certain number of sentences may not fit comfortably into a word balloon, so then we've both got to sit down, and "let's think of a way we can say this with fewer words." We do it together—what I do is sort of an initial editing, I guess. I will try to make the decisions like "This interrupts the action, let's see if we can say it more economically," or "This isn't clear to me, here's maybe how we could try saying it." Then when it goes into the art, there's another editing in terms of making it all come together as a whole.

WENDY: And often, just as I'm doing the lettering, I'll call him up from downstairs and get his approval on a change in an entire sentence that I will decide to make.

RICHARD: Because the way she draws a pose, a face, a movement may change what the words need to say.

WENDY: You can't always predict what's going to happen.

RICHARD: And so that all happens as it's going along.

GROTH: *Do you edit the art?*

WENDY: He provides a sounding board.

RICHARD: Yeah, I provide a sounding board, a second opinion. I may look at something she has drawn in a face and say, "Wouldn't it be better, or more meaningful, or more amusing, or whatever, if you changed that expression just a little bit?" or "That perspective doesn't look right to me." A lot of these are things she sees, but I know it happens to me and I know it happens to her: you sit working on something for days and hours on end, and you can't see it.

WHITE: *It takes a different perspective.*

RICHARD: Right. Which is why we are continually editing what each other has edited until the book is finished. We are changing things almost literally until the last minute. So that's how it works. It really is a continual rehashing until the book gets to the printer.

GROTH: What do you think Wendy's strengths and weaknesses as a writer are?

RICHARD: Her strengths are that she has the imagination. She can construct the world. She can people it. She can create the images. She has them in her head. And she can get them pretty effectively down on paper. I know that I've heard from other people who've tried to write, "I've got the images, I just can't find the words to do it." But she can do that. I think her only weakness is that she's not as trained in the use of words, in the facility to use words, to construct sentences, to put blocks of words together

> **"We both know the whole story from #1 to whatever. We know where it's going, how it's going to end, where it's going to end. Little details will probably be changed, but the overall thing, we already know that."**

as I might be because I've had more practice at it.

WENDY: Since we've been working on the novel, I think I've improved, but I would agree with Richard's assessment.

GROTH: *Why did you have more practice? What were you doing?*

RICHARD: What I was doing for nine years of my life was working in the planetarium field and spending a lot of time writing the programs that people would come and see. I don't know if you've ever been to a planetarium show, but you go there and somebody is speaking words that mean something. Somebody is expositing on some facet of astronomy. And it was always my de-

sire to say things as clearly and as excitingly, as economically as I could. Other people had other approaches. I have always loved the language, I have always loved to read, I have always enjoyed reading the way people worked with words. Shakespeare did certain things with words and Joyce did other things with words and the writers of pulp stories use words in a certain way, and I've always been fascinated by the English language. So I made it a point to tutor myself, always to use words to their best advantage, to show them in their best light. This is where I think my contribution to the writing comes in. Wendy can provide me with a skeleton.

WENDY: And a good deal of the flesh.
RICHARD: Yeah. She has the ideas. I don't have the world inside my head as she does. But I can take what she writes and I can firm it up, I can make it read a certain way. If you want a certain mood, I can put that into it just by manipulating the words.
WHITE: *She gets the bones and the flesh, and he puts the skin on.*
RICHARD: Whatever. There are any number of—
GROTH: *But you require a skeleton.*
RICHARD: I can put together something of a technical nature. I can write a planetarium show, because that's my background, that's where my imagination lies. But for this—
GROTH: *But with fiction, you require a structure.*
RICHARD: I would have to say, I have not tried writing something from a whole plot of my own experience, and I have not felt the need to. I don't know what the result would be like.
GROTH: [to Wendy] *What was your writing experience before* Elfquest?
WENDY: Writing? Goofing around. There's about seven unfinished novels stacked up there in my studio. Really, just goofing around. I never had anything I had written published professionally, and I never thought I would be a writer.
GROTH: *What writers have most impressed you?*
WENDY: Shakespeare. Oh, gosh, it's awful hard to say off the top of my head. Ellison, certainly. Moorcock impressed me a great deal at a very impressionable age.
GROTH: *I'd say Ellison's influence is not evident in* Elfquest.
WENDY: No, no, no. Certainly not his style, perhaps just his honesty. Maybe just that.
RICHARD: That's a difficult question, because neither of us, especially now,

have a whole lot of time for outside reading. I think I have a little bit more than Wendy does, but I don't think either one of us has sat down to read deliberately.
GROTH: *Did you ever read somebody you were so impressed with that you wish you could write—*
WENDY: You mean, where you look and say, "Damn, that's *written!*"
GROTH: *Yeah.*
WENDY: Dickens, Kipling, people who can write things in such a way that if you could say them yourself, that's how. You'd do it, but you couldn't in a million years come up with it that way. They put the answer right in front of you [*laughs*].
GROTH: *I think we're most impressed with things we're totally incapable of imagining ourselves.*
WENDY: Well, that's interesting. I'm not incapable of imagining...do you mean in terms of story or in terms of structure?
GROTH: *No, in terms of sheer poetic expression. Things you simply wouldn't do for one reason or another.*
WENDY: I think it's more in terms of *couldn't do* [*laughs*].
GROTH: *Yeah, that's what I mean: things you couldn't do.*
WENDY: The great, great writers speak to your heart and soul instantly and you vibrate with it, but who of us could imitate genius?
GROTH: *That's what makes it genius.*
WENDY: Exactly. Well, for instance, we received a tape from Christy Marx today. It was an hour of her playing her beautiful harp, and I just sat there going "Ohhhhh," and the tears were coming down. It's because this is something extremely pure and extremely whole and you don't listen to it wondering if a bad note's going to be hit, it's just there [*laughs*]. And I couldn't play a Celtic harp in a million years. So to listen to

that and just be in awe of it is a wonderful feeling. Or the way Ellison puts words together, or Shakespeare, or Dickens, or...

GROTH: *To use two basics* [laughs]. *Harlan and Bill.*

RICHARD: Yeah, but you see, like Shakespeare, there's the controversy that he really didn't write the plays, so maybe we'll find out that Harlan didn't really—

WENDY: Well, what does it matter if he did or not?

DECKER: *Somebody had to.*

WENDY: The point I was leading up to is I think it's wonderful to have idols, not necessarily that one aspires to be like, but in the sense that one can just sit

"**I think it's wonderful to have idols, not necessarily that one aspires to be like, but in the sense that one can just sit back and say, 'Yes, they exist in my universe and isn't that wonderful.'"**

back and say, "Yes, they exist in my universe and isn't that wonderful."

GROTH: *Yeah, they're inspirational. Guideposts. You said that you* [Richard] *were more involved with comic books and you* [Wendy] *were more involved with fantasy and so forth. How did you learn the idiom of comics? I mean, obviously you read some, but did you sit down and study them before you put* Elfquest *to paper?*

WENDY: It's interesting; ever since I was a little girl, I've drawn my own comics for my own amusement. I think it's in the other interview about a roll of paper towels—I would just use each towel for a panel. I also used to watch "Winky Dink" on TV—you know, where you could draw right on a plastic sheet over the TV screen. I never had the plastic sheet though—made a real mess on the television! I've always connected words and art. This probably has to do with my fascination with animation, because animation is art that talks, and...

GROTH: *I was thinking of some of your visual storytelling, which is purely conventional comics, and which you can't learn from animation, except I suppose, by extrapolating from it. You can't learn by reading prose. And you seem to do a lot of that stuff extraordinarily well, to my mind.*

WENDY: Thank you. I'm sure I picked a lot of it up from my early fascination with Jack Kirby's work and Don Heck. The first Marvel I ever read was an issue of the *Avengers* that Don Heck had drawn and it blew me away. I was about fourteen years old, and I said, "This is different!" I really glommed onto the *Avengers,* and then I began to read some of the other Marvel line, and got introduced to Kirby's art, and that made a very strong impression on me, the dynamics of it, the grace—believe it or not—of his figures is just...well, it's been put into words a million times, I don't need to say it. I was a true Marvel fan, even though I didn't collect many of them. I couldn't afford to, but there were just certain titles I would not miss. I like to think they were the best of the line: *Thor, Fantastic Four, X-Men, Sub-Mariner* was wonderful for a while when Buscema was drawing it, and this was my introduction to the nitty-gritty of how to tell a comic book story, certainly it was. And now that I think of it, I read the *Casper the Friendly Ghost* series quite avidly when I was a little girl. Or as often as I could get hold of it.

GROTH: *You seem to have refined all of these early influences substantially. Your approach isn't like Kirby's, which is very direct and immediate, because you do a lot of multi-panel things, small progressions, which work really well.*

RICHARD: I think you have to take into consideration the last three years, the monstrous learning experience. You could study and read about and look at what other people do in comics for the rest of your life, but the act of actually doing it in an intensive way for three years is the only way to really learn. When you go back and look at #1 and compare it to #9, it's amazing.

WENDY: Some of the stuff you will see in the pile we have amassed of early stuff I think shocks me, and I bet it would shock you too, at the literal ineptness of some of it, and that was only three years ago. Now I consider myself, with #9, to have made a quantum leap in style to the point where everything clicks very well. Number nine is the first issue I've done where I haven't really worried about it, and I think it shows. There's another thing that distresses me. Nobody else can draw the characters. We get a lot of unsolicited art from cartoonists and fans. No one has even come close. And I don't know why. To me, they don't seem that difficult to draw.

DECKER: *You'd have to be Wendy Pini to draw them.*

RICHARD: Or else have practiced it 'til

you can do it.

GROTH: *Well, there are imitators, but they don't have—*

RICHARD: The spirit, the spark.

WENDY: I guess so, but one would think someone could at least come close. The bodily proportions are all shot to hell, the faces are all wrong.

RICHARD: That's because they're not trained as artists.

DECKER: *You're getting stuff from amateurs.*

WENDY: We've gotten a couple of things from people who have a more than amateur skill, I think, but still have not been anywhere close. The closest we've seen is the animation. It's about a minute's worth of pencilled animation of our characters, and taken individually the drawings don't look that much like our characters but when they're in motion, you go "That's them!"

RICHARD: There is this interesting illusion that takes place.

WENDY: Oooh, it's really something. There's a wonderful shot of Cutter bursting through the bushes and looking like this, and saying, "Yeah! Yeah! That's the way he moves!"

GROTH: *Did you have formal art training?*

WENDY: No.

GROTH: *So you're basically self-taught.*

WENDY: Very basically.

GROTH: *How did you go about solving formal art problems, like deep space and spatial relationships?*

WENDY: Well, perspective was a huge problem to begin with. I think it was simply just blundering ahead. Like I explained to you before, there wasn't too much preliminary art done before I started putting pencil to paper on the first issue, and I simply blundered right into it.

RICHARD: Also, it's not a case of working in a vacuum where you had no references at all, because there were comics to look at. You might say, well okay, this particular artist feels that a broken panel layout has this effect, maybe that might work with modifications here or there. I can adapt that, I can learn from that.

WENDY: Well, remember, #1 was incredibly simplistic in terms of layout. It was just panel, panel, panel. I was feeling my way along, and I think #1 is 99 per cent inspiration and 1 per cent skill. Number one just kind of trots along; it's a satisfying issue, satisfyingly drawn, simply because I didn't challenge myself too much. I just told the story and kept the pace fast, and it works even though there are a lot of obvious elements of amateurishness in it, at least to

me now. Just as the series itself progressed and the story got more complex and more refined, so did the artwork. It was just a learning process.

GROTH: *Okay. If you didn't have formal art training, how did you approach color in your work?*

WENDY: Instinctively. I've always been good with color. It's just one of those things. I think Berni Wrightson may be another instinctive colorist. Fabulous stuff. But I've always loved working with color and I have never really had any problems with it.

GROTH: *Did you study painters?*

WENDY: Classical? Yes. I remember that one of the most wonderful things that ever happened to me was that when I was eight, my cousin—my big cousin, he was a grown-up [*laughs*]—gave me a volume of Leonardo da Vinci, and in the inscription he put, "To one who would not be overpowered by it." Now that's something to say to an eight-year-old and it stuck with me my entire life. I pored over that book. Oh! And I remember copying DaVinci's drawings and trying to find out what he found, trying to solve what he solved, trying to see what he saw, and I remember paying a lot of visits to art museums, the DeYoung museum in San Francisco, here the Metropolitan Museum, in Boston the Museum of Fine Arts; classical art for color certainly had a very strong influence on me. Then too, animation—the coloring I use varies from earth tones to very bright, almost garish colors, and I think it depends on which way I'm leaning, toward my animation or toward my classical influences.

GROTH: *You have a big project in the works, a colored version. How are you approaching that in terms of color? First of all, technically. You're painting black and white...*

RICHARD: We've taken the original art, which we are not going to color, and made very high quality Xeroxes.

WENDY: There are some streaks that can be fixed very easily, but they are very bright black...

RICHARD: And all of the fine-line work is there. This paper takes watercolor very nicely, so she will be painting with watercolor dyes, and probably watercolor felt markers.

WENDY: I don't think markers.

RICHARD: Not at all?

WENDY: No. Probably just the dyes.

RICHARD: Right over these pages.

DECKER: *You used a lot of fine linework to add tones and depth. Are you whiting some of them out before you add color?*

WENDY: Some, definitely. Especially in #1.

RICHARD: But there will actually be not so much of that, because with the right application of the right color, you get the same effect as if you had toned it in that color, but in reality you've left the fine black linework do the tone.

DECKER: *I was thinking of the Abbeville Press edition reprinting Mickey Mouse newspaper strips where color was applied directly over the benday patterns* [Benday is a technique to give a print the appearance of tone by putting a texture screen directly onto the printing plate rather than on the artwork itself as with Zipatone—ed.] *The result was pretty murky.*

RICHARD: No, no, no. First of all, benday is a difficult thing to work with. In

YES...

The interlude behind the rocks. Note the rare use of Zipatone for the texture of the rocks.

color, the book will probably resemble the Prince Valiant Sunday pages in the way the color is used. Especially looking at the reprint books, the Nostalgia Press ones. They have a very nice pastel feel to them and it's just color laid down over black and white. I think we can achieve the same thing here.

WENDY: I'm certainly going to pay a lot of attention to toning, different shades of the same color, and introduction of a totally unexpected color into a color that tends to give depth. For instance, flesh tones. People are surprised at how much blue you use in a flesh tone.

RICHARD: I think they're also going to be surprised at how much darker the Sun Folk are than the Wolfriders.

WENDY: One of the things that unfortunately we weren't able to stress in black and white, is that the Sun Folk are quite dark.

DECKER: *There's a comment that Leetah's children are as tan as she is.*

RICHARD: Yeah! There are indications throughout the book, but I think that people tend to either gloss over those or forget them.

WENDY: I remember a black guy, a fan I guess, asked me if we were going to have any Blacks in *Elfquest* because

everybody was white, and I said, "Wait 'til you see it in color." [*Laughs.*]

GROTH: *You don't use shading screens in* Elfquest.

RICHARD: No. No mechanicals.

GROTH: Why not?

WENDY: Superstition [*laughs*].

RICHARD: Actually, there was one issue in which Zipatone was used, and it was in #5 where they go have their little interlude behind the rocks. The mottling, the texture of that rock, was done in Zip—

WENDY: Although there was linework over it.

RICHARD: But it's—you've always said it's too mechanical.

WENDY: I have a superstition against it. It's like my wedding gown. I made my wedding gown entirely by hand. I wouldn't let a sewing machine touch it. I don't know why. There was just something pure about doing it all by hand.

RICHARD: She's very much a primitive.

GROTH: *Do you have an aversion to technology?*

WENDY: In a way.

RICHARD: A couple of years ago I went up to Canada to see the eclipse of the sun. For me as an astronomer, it was

Speech bubbles in image:
-- AND SOMETHING WHICH ONE AS *BRAVE* AS YOU CAN FORGIVE EVEN LESS --

--*FEAR!*

I WAS *AFRAID* TO GO WITH *CUTTER* --

-- *AFRAID* OF THE UNKNOWN LANDS BEYOND THE DESERT!

TWICE IN MY LIFE I HAVE SEEN THE SUN TURN INTO A BLACK DISC, HALOED ALL AROUND WITH RAINBOW STREAMERS OF LIGHT.

THOUGH MY FATHER, THE *SUN-TOUCHER*, PATIENTLY EXPLAINED THAT IT WAS BUT THE GREATER MOON'S *SHADOW* PASSING BEFORE THE DAYSTAR -- I WAS *FROZEN* WITH FEAR - EVEN WHEN THE LIGHT RETURNED!

Leetah's fear of the eclipse

one of the high points of my life to be able to do this. We talked about it and I asked her, "Do you want to come along?" And she said no. I said, "Why?" She did not want to see the sun get blotted out: "You can explain it, and I understand it totally, it's simply a chance juxtaposition of the moon in front of the sun. However, I think if I see it I'll die." Which is fear of the eclipse.

WENDY: That went into *Elfquest* #8, by the way.

RICHARD: She has a primitive aspect to her personality, and I certainly don't want to run roughshod over it. It's part of what makes *Elfquest* as real as it is.

WENDY: Yeah, I'm a primitive. It's not that I'm against technology, but the world I would create for myself would not have beer cans and cigarette butts, and that sort of thing.

DECKER: *Would it have antibiotics?*

WENDY: Sure. They grow all around.

DECKER: *Central heating?*

WENDY: Well, wear skins! [*Laughs.*] I don't know. The thing I have against Zip is that it becomes less the work of my hands, and—

RICHARD: And it also looks unnatural. I think you have to have a real skill with it to make it look like it belongs. I think Wally Wood has that skill. I think a couple of other people—

WENDY: Oh, Woody does incredible things with Zip that—

RICHARD: Occasionally other artists. I'm trying to—

WENDY: Palmer!

RICHARD: Tom Palmer has that skill, but it's very difficult.

WENDY: Did you see the cover I did for the *Buyer's Guide?*

GROTH: *No, I don't think so.*

WENDY: That was almost all Zip. It has a very commercial look for the work that I do. But that answers your question, I guess. In some cases, I think some people would consider it a flaw that I didn't use Zip with my rendering.

RICHARD: But still—I always point this

out—this is how *Elfquest* started, and if it looks crude by comparison, it looks a little amateurish, I don't want to change it, because when people look back they can easily trace that evolution. And that's part of the charm for me.

GROTH: *There was a lack of weight and volume in the earlier issues.*

WENDY: Definitely. Definitely. I think I'm coping with black a lot better now. I've always had an abhorrence for solid black, especially in the sky, but I'm coping with it a lot better now [*laughs*]. It was always color in my mind, and I'm just so thrilled that we're going to get a color volume.

DECKER: *You mentioned that scene with the rocks, the love scene, the big payoff in #5. Now this reader in #9 writes in—*

WENDY: [*Laughs.*] I knew we'd get around to that.

DECKER: *It's something of a nutty letter anyway, but I think he does have a point. He says, "Another example is #5. After all the multi-issue build-up, you delivered the big, heavy love scene. What a letdown! After all that development I expected some real soul-rattling love-making that would have made Aleister Crowley drool with envy. And what do I get? Rocks! That's what I get: rocks! What's a comic book for if it ain't got pictures?" Well, I do think he has a germ of a point in that you spend several issues on the courtship of Leetah and Cutter, and the payoff is pretty much accomplished in one page. It's nicely done—I'm not faulting it—but I'm wondering, why did you decide to do it in one page like this, instead of going on for some pages with, oh, say,*

full-page panels of symbolism, a dream sequence with, say, poetry, something lyrical...

WENDY: That's a bunch of schlock. That's a bunch of B.S. [*laughs*]. This says all that needs saying. Dream sequences and flower petals and thunder and lightning...sheesh!

RICHARD: Number one, it's a terrible cliché.

WENDY: It's a terrible cliché. Number two, Cutter and Leetah aren't even in love yet. This is a very private scene that's happening here. It's something they're giving into and they're not even in love yet.

WHITE: *They did say that a couple of pages before.*

DECKER: *"I don't even like you very much."*

WENDY: She says that. They have a biological drive that they're giving in to, and it may be fun, but they've still got a lot of work to do on their relationship. Why have a big love scene when it's not a love scene per se? I mean, that would have been dishonest. It's a sex scene, which we choose not to have people...

RICHARD: Gape at.

WENDY: Gape at [*laughs*].

RICHARD: It is the acceptance of Recognition. What's happening here, in fact—one of the interpretations of that last little "yes"—is that acceptance, but it's an acceptance of that one particular thing, it's not an acceptance of the whole package. In fact, we have gone into this in the novel. The point is that it takes a while for love to come into fruition.

WENDY: Well, we even did that in #6 when we said that Leetah doesn't know quite when love took the place of Recognition.

RICHARD: Yeah. But I think we're a little bit more explicit in the novel.

WENDY: There was no logical basis for a love scene here because they are not in love yet. They are simply accepting

> "We will have a love scene coming up between Cutter and Leetah very soon that I think will satisfy a lot of you flesh-mongers."

the curse, if you will, of Recognition.

DECKER: *"Well, let's get it over with."*

WENDY: No, not at all.

RICHARD: It's pleasant.

CATRON: *It's purely physical then.*

WENDY: Right now it is. That's why Leetah was acting like such a bitch the whole time. That's why she says, "To me, Recognition is more than mere blind instinct." She wanted it to be more, but she finally had to reconcile herself to it. No, Recognition is not more than mere blind instinct.

RICHARD: Recognition is really blind instinct, and if you're lucky and if you're good, you do get along with the person you're Recognized to.

WENDY: We're going to be dealing later on with a Recognition where both parties actively dislike each other. And that's going to be...

RICHARD: There's a lot of conflict involved in that. But this, they've come to the acceptance that such a thing can be pleasant. That's when she's smiling. She no longer hates him; she no longer thinks of him as this brutal force that wrecked her life.

WENDY: She knows he's not going to dominate her, take away her independence, destroy her in any way, and so she's open to a new experience. Her relationship with Rayek has gone absolutely nowhere, and it's not going to go anywhere, so she's open to this new experience, but it ain't love yet.

RICHARD: And what the letter I suspect really wanted was not a love scene, but a sex scene, and there are other places for that.

WENDY: And it's none of his business [*laughs*].

RICHARD: *From Here to Eternity*: on the beach there, when they pan up into the clouds. That's a classic; that's what we did.

WENDY: There couldn't be a more sensual scene. You had a "but" there, Dwight. You wanted more pictures.

DECKER: *Well, all right. I do think he has a point, though. After all these issues, all we get is rocks...*

GROTH: *Dwight wanted to see some flesh.*

DECKER: *No, not flowing juices or...just something symbolic going on for two or three pages to really make the point.*

WENDY: No, I'll argue with you about that forever. I think it says all that needs saying. We will have a love scene coming up between Cutter and Leetah very soon that I think will satisfy a lot of you flesh-mongers [*laughs*].

DECKER: *Wait a minute, you've misunderstood me—*

WENDY: No-no-no, of course I haven't. I know exactly what you're saying.

RICHARD: The point is, also, that you're again operating from a very personal point of view. So is *Elfquest*.

WENDY: You see, this was just the beginning. You're going to see the whole range by the time the story's ended—if you know what I mean [*laughs*]. You know, we're not going to be coy.

RICHARD: We have positions to take, but we'll take them at those times down the road when it's best for the story to take them. It's not that we're adverse to taking them, it's just that we're not going to take them before they're right.

WENDY: We will brew no wine before its time—or whatever [*laughs*]. Good ol' Orson.

DECKER: *Okay, I think we've taken care of that. One of my correspondents, John C. LaRue, Jr., read the interview we did for the* Comics Journal, *and had this to say about one of Wendy's statements. She said, "Yes, there is a prejudice against elves." John replied, "This is pure hyperbole. I think what Wendy means is that there is a widespread dislike against anything cute, anything that arouses emotion, that forces people—men especially—out of their cool. Fear has always had many faces, the Pinis said back in #1, and the fear of*

being thought soft with all that it implies has resulted in a great deal of property damage over the years, to say nothing of worse crimes." In context, of the interview itself, I think you pretty much made the point John makes, but do you have any comments to add?
WENDY: No. He said it.

"**The reason so much writing in fantasy and in the comics seems almost like an ingrown toenail is because that's precisely what it is.**"

DECKER: *I bought a copy of* Elfquest #8 *in a comics shop—that was the issue with all the big-eyed moppets on the back cover. A friend of mine, who's a peripheral fan at best, was with me at the time, and when he saw all the cute little elf-children, he said, "Do you really like that stuff? Icky-poo!"*
WENDY: [*Laughs.*] Elf-children are entitled to be cute. Human children are cute. There is nothing wrong with it.
RICHARD: Afterward he went looking for his issues of *Casper* and *Little Audrey.*
WENDY: No, it's all part of the whole universe we've built, and some of our characters are perfectly well entitled to be cute. There's nothing wrong with it. I don't perceive most of our adult char-

Elf-children are entitled to be cute—Wendy

acters as cute, I really don't. Some others may, maybe because of the large eyes. I think one of the reasons our characters appeal so much is that every human being has an instinctive urge to protect the young. This is one of the instincts that has not, fortunately, been bred out of us yet.
DECKER: *All mammals seem to have it, too. Pet dogs and cats are more tolerant of abuse at the hands of human babies than from human adults, for example. They seem to know cubs are to be treated patiently.*
WENDY: So do we. We instantly respond to large eyes, large heads, small bodies, soft hair, soft skin [*laughter from Groth*]—really, we do. We have this protective urge toward that, and I think this is why people fall in love with our characters so easily, because they have that protective urge toward our characters. And we have made our characters victims, which just reinforces that. It's a grabber [*laughs*].
DECKER: *I was just thinking about John saying being thought soft has led to all sort of crimes. I think what John means is that, for instance, the other gang members want to go out and smash windows or something, and the little guy says, "But I don't want to do that." The others reply, "Ahh, are you a chicken?"*
RICHARD: That kind of thing, or it is unmanly to cry or to be sensitive in any other way because that's what women are, and men don't do that.
WENDY: In order to write about something honestly, you have to have experienced it, and this is something I've noticed about myself more and more. I can write about prejudice because I've felt prejudice, I can write about characters who overcome fear, because I've been very cowardly in many ways in my life. I think one of the reasons I identify with Cutter partially is because I want to identify with him, and he's becoming

braver, more authoritative, as he gets older, and I've become an awful lot more courageous in my dealings with people since I started this whole thing.

RICHARD: Issue nine more or less represents that. That letter that Dwight talked about, I don't know if we would have been prepared to answer it or to print it earlier on, when we were still developing, when the characters were still...

WENDY: Well, even then I was afraid at first to print that letter, because I thought in a sense it might pollute the gestalt [laughs] of that particular issue, but then I said, "No, there comes a point where you've got to take a stand."

GROTH: *Do you really think it's necessary to experience something before you can write about it?*

WENDY: No, but I think I can only say that as an artist and a writer, I have to know what it feels like before I can with any kind of authority set it down.

RICHARD: I think it's necessary to have experienced maybe the pieces out of which you can create, whether or not those pieces were gained in similar situations. Nobody has been into space beyond the moon, and yet we can draw wonderful pictures about what it must look like and we can write stories about what it must feel like.

WENDY: The reason so much writing in fantasy and in the comics seems almost like an ingrown toenail is because that's precisely what it is. People are not drawing on their own experiences, they're simply drawing on "well, this character did this in this story."

GROTH: *They're drawing on abstractions.*

WENDY: Precisely. And it gets weaker and thinner the more you do it.

DECKER: *Well, an example of creation from different experiences I heard about in my college classes was Stephen Crane with the* Red Badge of Courage. *Crane wrote a novel set in the Civil War, about what it means to be a coward and what it means to be brave, but he had never been in a war; he was born in 1871, between the Civil War and the Spanish–American War. He had apparently just listened to veterans talking about their war experiences and cobbled the book together from what he'd heard and from his own experiences that could translate into what it's like to be on the battlefield, even though he had never actually been on the battlefield.*

RICHARD: Well, that's it. You have to have the pieces. It doesn't matter, really, where you get them, as long as they're honest.

WENDY: That is true, but there has to be some kind of foundation.

DECKER: *Ah! And what of the novel?*

WENDY: Ah! [Laughs.] What of the novel?

RICHARD: [in Sigmund Freud voice] Ah, vot vud you like to know, eh, vot uv de novel?

WENDY: [in little girl voice] It ain't for widdle kids [laughs].

DECKER: *Well, converting pictures and dialogue into prose must be a headache. Adaptations from one medium to another are fraught with peril because different media have different requirements for mood, setting, pacing, characterization, and plotting.*

WENDY: Yes-yes-yes-yes [laughs].

DECKER: *Novelizations of movies seem to be more successful the less they try to be exact transcriptions of what's on the screen. Adaptations of prose into com-*

> "We instantly respond to large eyes, large heads, small bodies, soft hair, soft skin. I think this is why people fall in love with our characters so easily. And we have made our characters victims..."

ics form don't really work because of space requirements, A 32-page Classics Illustrated, five panels per page average, would have 160 panels to do The Count of Monte Cristo. *The result is wordy captions, abrupt scene-shifting from panel to panel—*

WENDY: Wait a minute. Wasn't *The Count of Monte Cristo* already written [*laughs*]?

RICHARD: No, he's talking about going from novels into comics.

WENDY: Oh, I see...

DECKER: *And so the result is wordy captions, abrupt scene-shifting from panel to panel, overblown dialogue just to get too much dialogue in too few pages. Ideally, the artist and writer should be one individual and the comics story should generate itself, the result being a natural product of the artist's knack for smoothly flowing scene-by-scene progression and logical panel breakdown. But you're going the other way now, you're going from comics into a novel, which would have presumably entirely different requirements.*

RICHARD: Yes. Well, it's a case of where the writer and the artist are one individual—even though there's two of us sitting here. That goes back to our working relationship. I guess we're lucky that way or else we're very, very good at it.

DECKER: *You do have an advantage. If I were given a comic book story and told to adapt this comic book into a novel, I'd be hampered because I wouldn't feel I had the right to go beyond anything that's already there, whereas Wendy and you have the story in your minds already, you can feel free to add and expand.*

RICHARD: Well, that's exactly what's happening with the novel. The comic book now is acting as the skeleton for the novel. When you read the novel you will recognize everything that happened in the comic—

WENDY: And the dialogue.

RICHARD: The dialogue is changing very little. It is changing a little bit. In the novel we have the opportunity to—

WENDY: Totally new scenes.

RICHARD: —put new scenes, new dialogue in that because of space limitations weren't in the comics. Just for one example, one that comes to mind is in #2. The Wolfriders have to leave Redlance and Nightfall out in the desert because Redlance can't go on. He's too badly injured, he's too weak. And we devote, I think, two panels to the leave-taking and three panels when we come back to them. But in the novel we have the opportunity to go into a whole deep interaction between the two of them that there is just no hint of in the comic—

WENDY: With Redlance and Nightfall alone in the desert.

RICHARD: He is slipping away and she is trying to reach him and there's interaction on the sending level and on the—she is having things interact within herself, her own thoughts, and her own feelings, and it's all true. It all happened. It couldn't go in the comic because there wasn't any space, but it's all ours and there's nothing that we're making up that isn't already...

WENDY: In other words, people will read it and say yes.

RICHARD: "Yes, that happened. I didn't see it in the comic, but that's the way it must have been."

DECKER: *It's all canonical.*

RICHARD: And again, like you said, if you were given something somebody else had done, you wouldn't feel necessarily comfortable about doing it.

GROTH: *Unless the other were dead. Then you can do anything you want.*

WENDY: [*Laughs.*] That's right.

GROTH: *You said something earlier, at the beginning of this—if I'm reconstructing right—you said there were things in a novel that were easier to do than in a comic. Can you elaborate on that? What*

kinds of things were you talking about?
WENDY: I can give you a specific example. Right now I'm doing a scene that did not appear in the comic. I'm working on a scene right now where Leetah is taking her first good look at Cutter. Now, this never appeared in the comic, as a matter of fact: the Wolfriders are all bathing in hot springs. She's getting her first good look at him. And I talk about the tremendous vulnerability and actually sometimes physical danger she undergoes as a healer in

entering an injured body and knitting it all back together. She compensates for it and bestows a little reward upon herself—she knows every secret there is about the body, and everybody in the village knows she does. And she can, when she chooses, unlock these secrets and give them to whomever she favors—and I think you know what I mean by "unlocking these secrets." She knows as much about pleasure as she does about pain.
RICHARD: Oh-h-h.

GROTH: *A-ha-a-a.*

CATRON: *Oh, those secrets...!*

WENDY: [*Laughs.*] To couch that in perfectly, let's say just raw, lay-it-on-the-line language would take some of the poetry away from it, which I don't want to do, so in a sense I'm not spelling it out. I'm saying that Leetah, being a healer, knows the very favorable sides of the physical, too, and her relationship with Rayek has gone about as far as it can go in that direction. They've explored a great deal. But Cutter is a whole new thing to her, and his innocence, his very animal-like innocence, attracts her in a way in which she's never been attracted to Rayek. Now this is pretty sophisticated stuff for little kids to read. As a matter of fact, I would recommend that parents screen the novel before they read it to their kids. "Oh, Mommy, there's *Elfquest!*"

RICHARD: By the same token, I would be willing to bet though, that unless the parent were the kind of parent who just said, "No, you can't read that, it's not good for you," having read the novel, probably wouldn't feel funny at all about reading it to a child or letting the child read it.

WENDY: I don't think we're doing anything in the novel that would traumatize a little kid. As a matter of fact, some of it would go right over their heads and they wouldn't realize what is being talked about.

DECKER: *Exactly. Junior wouldn't know what you meant if you just said that Leetah and Rayek had in the past explored the heights of rapture and the depths of pleasure and let it go at that, and didn't quite specify the actual technique—you know, Kama Sutra position #22...*

WENDY: No, there are other ways to say it than "the heights of rapture" and all that. There are plenty of ways to say it.

DECKER: *Well, you just write around it. Don't go into the plumbing.*

RICHARD: Exactly.

WENDY: We're not doing a Gothic romance here. It's—I don't know what kind of flavor you would describe it as having. It's a romantic story, but it's not a Gothic romance. It may be something totally new. I'm excited about the possibility that this may be something totally new in fantasy. However, it's very realistic, too. We're postulating certain things that don't happen in real life—we're postulating sending and certain uses of energies in the form of magic—but in many ways it's extremely real and extremely human. This may be a different kind of direction for fantasy to take, I don't know.

DECKER: *In your world, how does magic really work? You have sending, you have the various forms of magic.*

RICHARD: This is going to be a necessarily vague answer, because (1) we haven't thought about it and (2) we don't intend to. Magic in our world is not a nuts-and-bolts thing. It's not something we feel like getting into, the nuts and bolts of explaining. The closest we would want to come to it is saying that it is a natural force to the elves, a form of energy. Not something supernatural, but a type of energy to them.

WENDY: And a manipulation of it.

RICHARD: Yeah. Well, we can manipulate energy, we can manipulate electricity or heat energy, so these elves can manipulate this, which we will call magical energy. Sending is no more, really, or less than a psychic telepathy. Rayek's—in #3 was it?—being able to levitate the food at the banquet was just a type of telekinesis. Savah's astral projection is just manipulating that energy to form an image of herself. The

"**L**eetah knows as much about pleasure as she does about pain."

only other time that magic has been looked at is in the creation of Madcoil, and if you can postulate that magic is a type of energy, you can postulate that if it gets used it can remain—somebody said like a battery...

WENDY: Yeah, well, that was in Paula O'Keefe's article. As a matter of fact, she looked at that pretty extensively.

RICHARD: If energy can be used, it can be stored. It can be left in places. And so if the early elves on this planet used energy, some of that energy might have remained around, and it could have been changed from a good type of energy that they might have used to light a fire, to a bad type of energy that would create mutants.

DECKER: *Maybe magic would be a form of living energy that would spoil with the passage of time?*

WENDY: That's a nice way to look at it.

RICHARD: You don't even have to consider it as living to say that it'll spoil. I mean, iron rusts. It undergoes changes.

DECKER: *It degenerates or decays with the passage of time.*

WENDY: Much of the magic used in *Elfquest* is a variation of psychokinesis. There's no real difference between a healer and a treeshaper except one works with living wood and one works with living bodies.

RICHARD: It's variations on a theme, but again the main point I think that you're getting is that...it's not...we're not calling on the dark dimension to do this act, to perform this feat.

WENDY: [*Laughs.*] The dark lord...

DECKER: *No imps, no—*

RICHARD: No imps, no evil Maxwell's demons, no. None of that stuff. It's just

the manipulation of a type of energy that we don't have here on Earth.

DECKER: *It just seemed to me that when you rationalize by calling it telepathy, you're just explaining the obscure by means of the even more obscure.*

"I find my characters to be very sensual and certainly an expression of my own sexuality. And I'm not claiming to be hot stuff or anything, it's just that everybody has this element within them and I'm not afraid of it."

RICHARD: We're calling it magic for the same reason that we're calling them elves.

WENDY: 'Cause we wanna!

DECKER: [Laughs.] *That's about the most rational response I've heard yet.*

CATRON: *So this world doesn't have electricity, but it does have magic?*

RICHARD: Apparently it has electricity, because Dwight says there's lightning.

CATRON: *It's your world.* [All laugh.] *Maybe this lightning isn't electricity.*

WENDY: That's possible, too.

DECKER: *We need a Ben Franklin elf to find out.* [Wendy laughs.]

RICHARD: We've got the key. All we need is a kite.

WENDY: That's right. One key in all the world.

GROTH: *I have a question that I suppose could be construed as a personal question—*

WENDY: That's okay.

GROTH: *—but since you're an artist, anything goes.*

WENDY: [Laughs.] Well!

GROTH: *You said earlier that Leetah has pretty much experienced everything there was to experience with Rayek. She was going to move on to—*

RICHARD: This is a work of fiction, you know. [*Wendy laughs.*]

GROTH: *Informed by fact, I think.* [General laughter.]

WENDY: [*laughing*] Oh-oh, I'm afraid of what's coming.

GROTH: *But am I interpreting that right so far?*

WENDY: Mm-hmm...

GROTH: *"Mm-hmm." Ah-ha, we've got her on the run.* [General laughter.] *Well, how do you feel about that in relation to your own life?*

WENDY: In relation to life? You mean...?

GROTH: *Just that attitude—*

RICHARD: Human life. Is it a mirror image?

GROTH: *—that she has experienced everything there is to experience physically.*

WENDY: She's six hundred years old.

GROTH: *Oh, I see a loophole here.* [General laughter.] *No, honestly...*

WENDY: Okay. Okay. Give me a second.

GROTH: *I'd like both your opinions.*

WENDY: Yeah. I think you should answer it too! [*Laughs.*] I think that artists, writers, poets, whatever, often give themselves the vanity—and maybe it's not such an untruthful vanity—that their experiences are extremely intense, and I can imagine six hundred years worth of explorations [*laughs*]. Is that enough?

GROTH: *Hmmm...* [Laughs.]

RICHARD: It's not what he was looking for...[*General laughter.*]

WENDY: Sometimes I feel...well... [*Laughs.*]

CATRON: *Wait a minute! Let her finish this! This is not a bad subject either! Let's get finished with this one.*

WENDY: I have vivid recollections and vivid expectations [*laughs*] and...

RICHARD: And I'm just going to sit here with a smug smile on my face and you all can...(*General laughter.*)

WENDY: Leetah is...Cutter and Leetah are almost like animus/anima to me.

Cutter is certainly the male half of me, and Leetah—the way they're drawn, I mean, Cutter has exaggerated male traits, the exaggerated pectorals, the sharp cheekbones, the hardnesses, and Leetah by counterpoint is all femininity and soft curves, and I'm extremely aware of this. Most women are certainly not built like that [laughs]. But it's sort of a solidification of the intensity of experience I'm drawing upon and impressions I've received and things like that. I find my characters to be very sensual and certainly an expression of my own sexuality. And I'm not claiming to be hot stuff or anything, it's just that everybody has this element within them and I'm not afraid of it, I'm happily married [laughs], and I turn it over to you.

DECKER: *One point just occurred to me. There is one thing Leetah hasn't experienced by the time she runs into Cutter. She apparently hasn't been a mother yet. Is there any reason why she held off on that for six hundred years?*

WENDY: She hasn't Recognized Rayek, she hasn't Recognized anybody.

DECKER: *But you don't have to Recognize anybody.*

WENDY: You don't have to, but I think in Leetah's case she...there's almost a kind of element of fate in her and Cutter getting together. I really doubt that she could have conceived before she met him.

DECKER: *I can just imagine her father talking to her: "You're such an old maid! You're almost six hundred and you haven't gotten married."*

WENDY: They don't have that concept of time. They really don't. [*to Richard*] All right, your turn. You're on the spot.

RICHARD: For what? Hey, I'm not the one who draws these. [*General laughter.*]

GROTH: *A-ha! A-ha!*

CATRON: *I love it.*

WENDY: You're not going to make any commitments [*laughs*].

GROTH: *I was just wondering how relevant that attitude expressed in the book was to your own.*

WENDY: About...

GROTH: *Well, about exhausting physical attraction.*

RICHARD: You mean, do you think it's possible for two people who have spent a lot of time together to have that happen to them?

GROTH: *Right.*

WENDY: Oh, sure.

GROTH: *I mean, obviously it does, but...*

RICHARD: It happens to us every now and then.

WENDY: Sure, we get sick of each other. But now you're getting into the concept of lifemates, I suppose, that there's just kind of a core or bond that cannot be destroyed no matter how much the outward surface is disturbed.

GROTH: *This segues nicely into something else I wanted to ask you, which is of a personal nature, and that is, how integral or important is your creative*

Beauty—and sex appeal— is in the eye of the beholder.

collaboration on Elfquest *with your marriage and your relationship?*

WENDY: You should have caught us yesterday [*laughs*].

RICHARD: You're a day late.

WENDY: In other words, if we weren't working on *Elfquest,* what would be doing?

GROTH: *No, not exactly. Let me see if I can phrase this any differently. How does it relate to your personal life? How important or integral a part of your marriage, your relationship, is working together creatively?*

WENDY: Right now, *Elfquest* is everything.

RICHARD: I think that if and when *Elfquest* comes to an end, in whatever form, I think we will have discovered something that would remain missing had we not done it. It's almost forced us to be able to interact with each other on more levels than we were prior to working on this project. We could interact on whatever levels two people who are married to each other can interact—I don't even want to delve into that can of worms because it's different for everybody— but this is a new aspect. It's a professional working relationship, and I think we would be the poorer for not having it.

> "**S**ure, we get sick of each other. But now you're getting into the concept of lifemates, that there's just kind of a core or bond that cannot be destroyed."

WENDY: I think we've gained greater respect for each other in a lot of ways. One of the most difficult things is to separate our husband-wife relationship from our business partner relationship. That's extremely difficult and it often leads to arguments because he deals with me as a business partner when I wish to be dealt with as a wife, and vice versa. Particularly in the past three months I have been practically unavailable during the day—

RICHARD: Night. Evening.

WENDY: Morning. No, I really did put in seventeen-hour days on #9, and [*muttering*] that cover for the *Journal* was one of the reasons [*laughs*].

GROTH: *Don't tell your Elfquest readers that. We'll be lynched.*

WENDY: But it's as if everything had happened at once: the color volume, the novel, #9—which was a much larger issue than others we've done, twelve pages longer than our usual story—of course, the *Gatherum,* too. Everything seems to be happening all at once, and it's a great deal to have on one's mind. And it certainly caused some friction and almost some growing apart occasionally, and this is something we were dealing with yesterday. We simply got out of the house and got to know each other again.

RICHARD: Which is a problem, because living here is where *Elfquest* lives.

WENDY: Look around you. Everything is related.

RICHARD: She certainly can't leave her work at the office and come home.

GROTH: *Right. I know that feeling.*

RICHARD: Right. So sometimes we have to get out.

GROTH: *It almost seems as though you have two intense relationships whereas most couples have one. You have a marriage and you also have a very intense close creative collaboration.*

WENDY: It's almost like making a baby.

DECKER: *But we've all known couples who don't interact on any level except the husband-and-wife relationship, and they have very little else in common. He goes out bowling on Tuesday night and she has the club meeting on Wednesday, and they have very little to really talk about except for the homey affairs of day-to-day running the house. It*

seems like you've got something more involving than just...

WENDY: We've been very lucky.

GROTH: *I'm not sure what point I was trying to make. There did seem to be a greater intensity to your lives.*

WENDY: There may not have been a point, but I think there's something very good to bring out. It's like I was telling you earlier, I especially, and Richard, too, suffer a great deal from the strain. I've been living on the edge for the past couple of months, and...

GROTH: *I can't think of any other husband-wife collaboration that's quite as close as yours in comics. And offhand I can't think of any other art.*

DECKER: *I can think of a few in science fiction. C.L. Moore and Henry Kuttner wrote stories together as Lewis Padgett and it was impossible to tell where one had started and one left off. Edmond Hamilton and Leigh Brackett were also*

a married couple, but that was more distant as far as writing went than the Kuttner/Moore partnership.

RICHARD: Kelly and Polly Freas—although she does not do art.

WENDY: Well, I really think Kelly and Polly Freas's situation mirrors ours to a certain extent because Polly has Richard's role and I have Kelly's role. It's kind of reversed: Polly is the business person, and she acts as sounding board for Kelly's work.

DECKER: *In L. Sprague de Camp and Catherine de Camp's* Science Fiction Writer's Handbook, *they go so far as to say that if you're a working writer, male or female, and married, the best thing you can do is get the spouse involved. Don't leave him or her alone at night when you're going out to give a lecture at a club meeting.*

WENDY: There's no question.

DECKER: *In fact, in the de Camp rela-*

tionship, Catherine de Camp became business manager for the partnership and got to be such an expert on financial affairs that she has written several books on the subject on managing personal finances. And that keeps the spouse from feeling left out.

WENDY: That's marvelous. But I find it interesting—and of course you have the same thing with the Frazettas: Mrs. Frazetta does all the business dealings—very few women are in the position of being the artists and creators with the husbands being business manager and co-creator. I feel that Richard and I are in a fairly unique situation. There are all of five women I can think of off the top of my head who are involved in comics at all, and I feel...I feel if I were to get run over by a truck tomorrow and lose both my arms, I could lie back and feel that I had really made some kind of mark here already even just in three years because—

DECKER: *You could still keep it up even if you did lose both your arms. Did you see that movie* Joni?

WENDY: I just think that as a woman—not too many people have stressed this—but as a woman I feel pride that I've created this and kept it going. It certainly couldn't have been done without Richard. His creative input is...

GROTH: *He's bored silly by this.* [Wendy laughs.] *Do you ever feel there's a danger of becoming obsessed with your creative involvement?*

WENDY: Oh, absolutely.

GROTH: *That it might overwhelm other aspects of your life?*

WENDY: Well now, this is interesting. Maybe I had better not say "absolutely," because it hasn't gotten to that point now.

RICHARD: I think there was a greater danger of that earlier. I think early on in the marriage when she was working on her Stormbringer project—

WENDY: Oh, that was a mistake.

RICHARD: That was a massive thing—you have some of the art from it.

WENDY: Elric ate, lived, breathed, and slept with us. I mean, he was—

RICHARD: It was a lot of artwork, it was going to be a massive project in terms of time and everything else, and she was obsessed. As she said, the spectre of Elric was living with us and sleeping with us, and I got tired of having a third person in the bed.

WENDY: I got to the point where I wanted Richard to become Elric. As a matter of fact, we entered one of the world science fiction convention masquerades and he did Elric, and my god, the girls were flappin' around him—taught me a lesson.

RICHARD: Didn't mind that at all. That aspect I could get along with any day of the week. But it was too much and we had a blowup over it, and she chucked the whole thing, more or less, lock, stock, and barrel.

WENDY: I ripped up some of the art and tipped my worktable over, and sealed off the room. It was really a scene.

GROTH: *That leads to an interesting question: do you have a temper?*

WENDY: [*laughs, speaks in little tiny voice*] No. No. Of course not. [*Laughs, resumes normal voice.*] Yes. Yes, I do. I have a temper, but I'm a very good angry person. I don't get irrational. I get mad as hell. Will you bear me out on this?

GROTH: *But you did tip over your drawing board and tear art apart, which isn't the most rational response.*

> "I feel if I were to get run over by a truck tomorrow and lose both my arms, I could lie back and feel that I had really made some kind of mark here already."

Portfolio Outake: Wolfriders being good angry people - do not interrupt them in the middle of dinner!

WENDY: Okay. But that was the end of an obsession. I have not had an obsession since.

RICHARD: Mostly that's true.

WENDY: Will you bear me out? Am I a pretty good angry person?

RICHARD: By your definition. [*Wendy laughs.*]

GROTH: *What do you do when you get mad?*

WENDY: I talk. I talk in very angry tones.

GROTH: *You've been mad all night?* [General laughter.]

RICHARD: No, that's one thing we do that we don't observe a lot of other couples doing. We talk about every problem, and thereby solve it or at least understand it.

WENDY: We're not afraid of each other, which is important, and I think an awful lot of couples don't communicate because they're afraid of letting too many barriers down—revealing something about themselves. But we're not afraid of each other. I yell at you any time I want, right?

RICHARD: And I ignore you.

WENDY: [*Laughs.*] That's right.

GROTH: *It's a good relationship.*

DECKER: *We've talked about obsessions, this thing becoming an obsession. What about the other side of the coin? What happens when it becomes just a job? Is there ever any risk of the sparkle vanishing? Suppose some toy company wants to put out an Elfmobile and they want you to have Cutter and Skywise drive around in an Elfmobile?*

RICHARD: If the price is right, you're going to be able to get an Elfmobile for Christmas. [*General laughter.*] No, that's one of the reasons that *Elfquest* as projected does have an ending somewhere between #15 and #20, somewhere in there. The story that we are now involved in will have a very definitive and, we hope, satisfying conclusion.

DECKER: *But I did notice that when you edited the transcript of the first interview, where you originally said you were going for fifteen issues, all the fifteens got changed to twenties.*

RICHARD: I think we picked twenty because it was a number to pick rather than changing the interview to say "open-ended."

WENDY: It's likely it will be twenty. Twenty sounds pretty reasonable at this point.

RICHARD: We don't intend to be pegged down. If it turns out to be nineteen and that's where it ends, we're going to be very nasty. "But you promised us twenty issues!" We'll reprint #1 and send it to them. [*General laughter.*] That's one of the reasons this series has an end. If at that time—and doing #9, there were times when I felt, "Oh, lord, I'm sick of doing this"—and if we both said this, "It's becoming just a hackwork job," and—but luckily that feeling is born of desperation rather than reality.

WENDY: I'll tell you what keeps me very optimistic is that whenever I finish an issue I don't want to look at pointy-eared people—I need at least a week to get away from them—but I always find myself saying, "Gee, I'm excited about doing this, this, and this in the next issue."

RICHARD: When that stops, then we worry.

WENDY: But that hasn't happened yet.

RICHARD: The reason for having the series end is so that if we find that maybe for the last couple of issues it's beginning to wear thin, we can fulfill the obligation and it will have finished. If we are hot to trot for the next forty issues, we can go on from there. But we're leaving ourselves that possibility. We will never continue this series if we don't want to do it. We wouldn't let it become a hackwork job for us. We wouldn't let anyone else take it and let it become a hackwork job. ❖

Another example
of the use of
Zipatone: Ember
grown up.

Recognition
How loud is *your* reptile?

by Richard Pini

One of the more commented upon of the phenomena that have been introduced into the stewpot of fantasy through *Elfquest* is that of *Recognition*.

At first it seemed that Recognition was little more than a particularly elfin form of love at first sight (or what Mario Puzo referred to in *The Godfather* as "the thunderbolt"). And admittedly, when it happened to Cutter and Leetah in *Elfquest* #2, there was not much else given in that issue to explain that Recognition was anything more. The word itself is not used until *Elfquest* #3 when Treestump attempts to explain what is wrong with his chief, and only a cryptic thought by the Sun-Toucher late in *Elfquest* #2 hints that what has happened between Wolfrider and Sun Village maid might be something of some import.

Then, as events progress—through "The Challenge" (issue #3) and "Wolfsong" (issue #4), to the resolution in "Voice of the Sun" (issue #5), and beyond into issue #6, "The Quest Begins"—various bits of Recognition lore come to light. Recognition, it seems, creates in the pair of afflicted elves a strong urge to mate with each other; the imperative is so powerful that to deny it is to court sickness and perhaps even death. Also, Recognition ensures that the mating will result in offspring (elf children are quite rare otherwise) and further, that those children will express the best genetic qualities of both parents. In later issues (the sequence in Blue Mountain) it comes out that Recognized couples need not stay with each other, as long as the sexual and generative imperatives are attended to. Dewshine and Tyldak just do not like each other, but they are able to reconcile their differences sufficiently to meet Recognition's demands. Thus freed, Dewshine continues in her relationship with Scouter.

Since the end of the series with *Elfquest* #20, other facets of Recognition have been thought out and examined, and some conclusions have been drawn. A couple that has Recognized does not necessarily stay together for life; lifemating is a decision of choice, whereas Recognition is imposed. This is not to say that Recognized couples can't lifemate—Cutter and Leetah seem to be well into that category—but it is not necessary. Given that, it is also possible that the partners in Recognition may, after a suitable period of time (something normally on the order of scores to hundreds of years), experience Recognition again with different partners. It is possible that one of the partners may die, either before or after the act of procreation. If the partner dies after, the surviving elf can Recognize again, and there will be no (or few) ill effects following the loss of the partner—at least from the point of view of Recognition. If one of the elves dies before Recognition is consummated,

Recognition strikes!

Dewshine and Tyldak meet halfway, as each sees the shape of the other's inner being.

the survivor will not die but will experience that "sickness" that comes from the unfulfilled urge. However, he or she will recover as it is not the function of Recognition to kill elves.

All of which is well and good. Recognition then seems to be at its basic level a genetic "device" to produce high quality elf children. It is selective and irresistible. It always works. But *why* is it?

The answer lies in two qualities possessed by the original "High Ones" even before they left their homeworld to explore the cosmos. (To avoid terminological confusion with the elfin High Ones who came out of the castle in issue #1, they shall henceforth be called "the Coneheads," for obvious reasons.) These beings were both essentially immortal (meaning that they lived at least a very long time; for all practical purposes, anything over ten thousand years equals infinity), and they were telepathic. With immortality came great reductions in the urges, both physical and social, to bear young. (Which is not to say the folks were ascetic; they had the opportunity to do away totally with physical form and yet chose to remain "clothed in matter"

because, simply, it felt good. They still enjoyed sensation, but sex itself and its attendant pleasures seem to have fallen into disuse.) With telepathy came the ability to know another mind on as deep a level as the sender and receiver desired.

The Coneheads were also shapechangers, which is to say that over long evolutionary time their psychokinetic powers of matter manipulation became so finely tuned that they could shape the very stuff of which they were made. This power operated down to the genetic level; if a Conehead changed into a toad, he or she could mate with toads and produce offspring (the partner would have to be a very big toad, however, as mass is conserved). The mind of the shifter would retain its "Coneheadedness," although the longer the change was in effect, the blurrier the memories and thoughts of the thinker would become. After a while the Conehead/toad would think and respond to stimuli very much like a real toad and likely would forget how to change back. (The severity of this problem is in direct proportion to the psychological difference between Conehead and imitated being; i.e., it's

WE, FOR I EXISTED BY THEN, LEARNED TO SEND OUR SPIRITS "OUT." THESE LITTLE DEATHS TEMPTED US TO ABANDON OUR BODIES ALTOGETHER, FOR IT IS VERY PEACEFUL WITHOUT FLESH AND THE SENSES.

BUT WE CHOSE **FORM** AND ALL THE PLEASURES AND PAINS THAT GO WITH IT! WE CHOSE AN IMMORTALITY SEASONED WITH **CHANCE** RATHER THAN TRANQUILITY.

THERE WAS NO NEW GROWTH OR KNOWLEDGE TO BE HAD ON OUR FINISHED WORLD, SO ONCE AGAIN WE LOOKED TO THE STARS...AND TO A NEW GOAL--

--EXPERIENCE!

The Coneheads make the choice that will define their nature for all time.

more dangerous for a brunette Conehead to change into a gnat than into a blonde Conehead.)

Take all this, put into a pot, and stir. The Coneheads went into space to explore the myriad worlds to be found. One group chanced upon the World of Two Moons during its so-called middle ages when elfin mythology was rife. The Coneheads, desirous of learning about the human culture they observed, shapeshifted into elfin form, the better to learn from the (ostensibly) superstitious natives. They *were* elves at that point, as their "magic" would have altered their genetic material elfwards.

Then the trolls rebelled, the castleship (which the Coneheads had also reformed to resemble the structures they saw on the world below) crashed, and the (now) High Ones found that, for whatever reason, they could not muster the power to shift back (or indeed to do much of anything they were used to doing—note issues #1 and #20). The High Ones were stuck. And the need for something that would turn into Recognition began.

One theory concerning the structure of the human brain is that it consists of three "layers," arranged like the layers of a wrinkly onion. The deeper one probes into a brain, the older or more primitive one finds the feelings and functions of that portion of tissue. The innermost layer is the limbic or so-called reptile part of the brain, responsible for basic territorial and reproductive urges; the middle layer is the "mammal" brain, which gives rise to the urge to take care of young; and the outermost, most recent layer is the "human" brain or cortex, wherein higher cerebration and the writing of articles takes place.

It is thought that, even though Homo sapiens on Earth represents to date the pinnacle of cognitive evolution, he still functions in large part according to the dictates of those earlier brains he carries within his skull. In particular—overlaid with motherhood and conscience though it may be—down in the bottom of the brain there is a drooling reptile who wants sex. Period. This may be simplistic, but it goes a long way to-

Recognition ✦ 87

ward explaining Recognition.

Even though they may have been vastly further along their evolutionary scale than man is along his, the Coneheads still started out in the same places: the primordial soup, the swamp, the reptile-infested jungle. No matter how subdued the early brain's impulses

the primitive humans who attacked them (issue #1) and were forced to attempt survival in a hostile environment. Even though they were still technically immortal (their shapeshifting would not have affected that), they soon discovered that there were plenty of ways in which the world could kill

Leetah plays hard to get, and Cutter feels the effects.

may have become by layer upon layer of high-level cortex, they must still have existed. Though the primitive reptile's shout of "Want sex! Want to reproduce!" was probably reduced to a mere whisper, subordinate to the massive conscious mentation of the rest of the brain, it was not silenced. It still spoke, though on a subconscious level.

And the Coneheads were telepathic.

When the castle-ship crash landed upon the World of Two Moons, the Coneheads were essentially trapped in the elfin form they had taken before the accident that stranded them. They were now the High Ones of Wolfrider memory-legend. They were scattered to the four corners of the compass by

them. And deep down in the basements of their minds, the reptiles were remembering what the minds themselves had forgotten: that one kind of insurance against death is progeny.

So the reptiles started yelling for all they were worth, "Hey, you up there, either you start getting it on or we're all going to die! You hear me?" Now, had the High Ones not been telepathic, nothing more would have happened and there would have been no *Elfquest* because all the High Ones would have died thousands of years before Cutter was born. However, as mentioned in the Elfquest novelization *Journey to Sorrow's End,* the High Ones managed to relearn, by watching animals and indigenous humans, what sex was all about. They began to experiment, goaded subconsciously by the reptile brains within them. "Yeah! It feels *good,* doesn't it? You can do it, you *want* to! You know you do!" And because the High Ones were telepathic, and because the reptiles could "pirate" a bit of that communication between individuals, the experimentation was hastened:

Reptile John: "Hey! Anybody out there? I'm horny as hell and this yo-yo doesn't know the meaning of the word."

Reptile Sue: "Hello? I thought I just heard something...nice."

Reptile John: "Do you mean I'm not alone? Come to papa! I'll get this big lump to cooperate if it kills me! Hey, upstairs! You got the parts, now *use* them!"

And two High Ones, who probably had not thought about sex in untold centuries, rediscover the joy inherent in trying to create little High Ones.

Natural selection takes a hand in the development of Recognition as well. It is easy to imagine that the reptile brains in certain of the original High Ones either had stronger "voices" than did others or else were able to cast more of these voices onto the telepathic "carrier wave" generated by the High Ones' subconscious minds. Whatever the method, those stronger reptiles were able to get their host bodies to participate more often in producing offspring, which thereby had the effect of concentrating the reptilian ability to shout "I want sex!" and be heard by a receptive mind (and where the mind *goes,* the body follows), which made the shouting louder and the receiving easier, and so on.

Eventually, things would have gotten to the point that the reptiles, while still operating on a subconscious level (though loudly to each other), would be able to communicate more than

The exception that demonstrates the rule? Kahvi and Rayek discuss the fine points.

just the desire for sex. They would have some kind of understanding of the genetic makeup of their hosts. (Remember, the conscious minds of the Coneheads could manipulate the matter of their own bodies down to the genetic level, so the potential for understanding this makeup must have permeated those minds.) At some point, an individual reptile would have started shouting, "Hey out there! I'm horny! Not only that, but I'm good looking, with great eyes. Only trouble is, the ol' hearing's not so hot. Any available partners out there with fantastic hearing? We could make a heck of a kid, with *good* eyes *and* ears. How about it?" And if there were a receptive reptile in the area whose host filled the bill, the two would start talking and pretty soon, bingo. It was the equivalent of the Personals column in the local swingers' newspaper. And it began creating elves with increased genetic potential.

From this point it is only a small step to Recognition as it is known in the Elfquest saga. As the reptile brains became more and more communicative, constantly shouting their genetic requests into telepathic ether, competition and natural selection would continue to favor those who could make the best connections the fastest. Eventually, the reptiles would stop *asking* the hosts to participate and would start *demanding*. (This may be taking anthropomorphism to the limit, but if it works, use it.) Reptile John XXIII might see in Reptile Sue XVIII some attractive genetic potential and yell to his host, "Go get her or I'll make you *so* sick, I promise!" The elfin maid's reptile is making similar unsubtle, non-negotiable demands of her landlady. Thus Recognition. From a certain point of view it is the natural result of increasingly successful sexual blackmail on the part of each reptile brain over its host. However, the overall effect has been to strengthen the elf race on the World of Two Moons to the point where it can be considered out of danger of extinction. And in at least some cases, having a wonderful time doing so. Ask Skywise. ✥

Timmain, first mother of the Wolfriders, shape-changes out of the form she took to survive on the World of Two Moons, a shape having far-reaching consequences.

Getting Bent:
Thinking Like an Elf

by Wendy Pini

Opposite, according to the Scroll of Colors, the history of the High Ones

The ease of creating an alien race that is humanoid but definitely inhuman is directly proportional to the degree that the aliens deviate from human norms. Even in a crowded subway, a fellow with three eyeballs will tend to stand out—moreso if the eyes are at the end of stalks. This is the easy way to indicate a character's alienness. But when the physical differences between human and alien are very subtle—say, an acceptably normal human appearance that masks infrared vision and a sense of smell comparable to a bloodhound's—communicating those differences becomes trickier. Even more delicate is the task of revealing the alien emotional and psychological makeup, which must differ in significant ways from the corresponding makeup of a human, and yet be capable of producing "events" identifiable as thoughts and feelings.

The elves of *Elfquest* are not mythological creatures. They are evolved, shape-shifting aliens whose adopted elfin traits breed true because of the high survival rate/value of all who possess those characteristics. The progenitors of this elflike race, who have been nicknamed the Coneheads, were slender humanoids with elongated limbs and somewhat conical skulls. The Coneheads evolved from humble beginnings, through a period of high technology and space travel, only to return to their biological and spiritual evolution.

The Coneheads discovered and perfected the use of the "magic" which slept within them. Their powers included various forms of psychokinesis, self-

THE HIGH ONES CAME HERE FROM...ELSEWHERE.

THEIR WORLD, LIFELESS NOW, LIVED LONG AS WORLDS GO AND BORE MANY YOUNG AS WORLDS DO.

THE EARLY HIGH ONES DEPENDED ON THEIR LAND FOR SURVIVAL, UNTIL THEY TAMED IT, AND MADE IT DEPEND ON THEM. THE GIFT YOU CALL MAGIC SLEPT IN THEIR BODIES, BUT THEIR TOOLS AND WEAPONS GAVE THEM SO MUCH POWER THAT THEY DID NOT LOOK INSIDE THEMSELVES--

--FOR OTHER SOURCES.

IN TIME ALL THEIR LANDS AND WATERS WERE NOT ENOUGH TO SUSTAIN THEIR NUMBERS.

SO SOME FOUND OTHER WORLDS TO DWELL ON, AND A STAR'S LIFETIME PASSED BEFORE DESCENDANTS OF THOSE TRAVELERS WENT BACK TO SEE THE HIGH ONES BIRTHPLACE.

THE RETURNED ONES CHOSE TO STAY AND AID THE USED-UP WORLD THEY FOUND.

IN DOING SO THESE CARETAKERS AWAKENED THEIR INNER MAGIC. IT TOOK THE PLACE OF TOOLS AS THEY EASED THE AGING LAND THROUGH THE LAST OF ITS LIFE.

BUT PURPOSE CHANGES WITH TIME. THE HIGH ONES BECAME ABSORBED IN EXPLORING THE LIMITS OF THEIR POWERS.

DEATH AND BIRTH HAPPENED TO THEM LESS AND LESS OFTEN. AND EVEN SHAPE AND SUBSTANCE LOST MEANING FOR THEM--

--FOR BOTH, THEY LEARNED, COULD BE CHANGED AT WILL.

THEN CAME THE CHOICE — THE CHOICE WHICH, ONCE MADE, DEFINED THE NATURE OF THE HIGH ONES FOR ALL TIME!

BEFORE HE CAN SPEAK FURTHER, SUNTOP SAGS TO HIS KNEES.

mutation down to the genetic level (shape disguise), astral projection, and manipulation of energy fields. It was, by then, a short evolutionary step to the complete abandonment of physical form, resulting in existence on a purely cosmic, spiritual plane. But the Coneheads chose not to take that step. They retained their physical bodies, highly mutable though they were, and proceeded to become planet-hopping voyeurs, changing shape to blend in with the creatures on the inhabited worlds they visited.

All moral judgments aside, the Coneheads were not infallible. The Elfquest story is an intimate and detailed chronicle of one of their mistakes and its far-reaching consequences. The earthlike World of Two Moons is our stage. Its indigenous, intelligent inhabitants are, for all practical purposes, human beings, and the flora and fauna are only slightly different from those which existed during Earth's prehistory. (Some poetic license has been taken. For example, although most of the animals seen in *Elfquest* resemble their terrestrial Pleistocene counterparts, there are still a few large saurian leftovers from earlier eras. It makes for intrigue.) As revealed in *Elfquest* #20, the Coneheads had intended to visit the double-mooned planet, disguised as elves, during its fairy lore–minded "middle ages."

Although the indigenous, intelligent inhabitants of the World of Two Moons are, for all practical purposes, human beings, and the flora and fauna are only slightly different from those which existed during Earth's prehistory, some poetic license has been taken.

But the trolls, servants to the Coneheads, rebelled and caused an accident which hurled the castle-ship back in time to the planet's Paleolithic era. The High Ones' frail elfin bodies— it's at the point when the ship crashes that the Coneheads start to be referred to as the "High Ones"—were ill-suited to the harsh environment then prevailing. The atmosphere, for reasons as yet unexplained, had a draining effect on all their "magic" powers. Unable to propel their ship back into space, the High Ones, as elves, were stranded.

The subjects of the Elfquest saga, the tribe known as the Wolfriders, are the product of many adaptive changes made by the High Ones and their descendants over untold generations. The Wolfriders exist in their world's Mesolithic era. Like the wolf packs they emulate, the Wolfriders hunt and roam the large territory they have claimed; but like certain human tribes, they require a "home base," in this case, the holt. Over countless turns of the seasons, the Wolfriders have had many different holts, but they have lived in their current one (that is, current to the beginning of the Elfquest tale) since the reign of Goodtree who founded it.

The Wolfriders haven't much changed their life-style since Huntress Skyfire ousted Two-Spear and brought her tribe to an awareness of *The Way,* a loose code of behavior that stresses harmony with nature. It may safely be assumed that events in *Elfquest* #20 will precipitate irreversible changes in the Wolfriders' attitudes and in the tribal culture (though when and how these changes show up is still terra incognito). But Bearclaw dealt with much the same problems and conflicts as did other chiefs before him. Though the Wolfriders have never been a stagnant society, neither have they been truly progressive until Cutter's rule.

Elfquest elves have certain obvious

physical traits—the equivalent of the aforementioned three eyeballs—that differentiate then immediately from humans. However, since the story focuses on characterization, it is far more important to examine that indefinable "bentness" which makes elf-think different from human-think. Emotionally, the elves' makeup is similar to ours. The characters laugh, cry, know anger, fear, and hatred. But their thought processes are, by human standards, skewed. Their logic goes so far in a straight line and then bends.

Humans tend to think in terms of time. *How long will this take? When do we eat? How long will I live?* We are fully aware of our own mortality and spend most of our lives trying to cram all the living we can into the hours allotted us. The Wolfriders, too, are mortal. But they can live a very long time— several thousand years. Therefore, the line between mortality and immortality is fuzzy at best. But fear of death from any cause is not at the forefront of most Wolfriders' conscious thoughts. Whatever sense of urgency they experience is derived from immediate circumstances and not from general angst about a fleeting life span. A Wolfrider will worry about the possibility of dying if there is a long-tooth nearby; he will *not* worry about dying of old age. (Also, general awareness of the Wolfriders' lifespan—which is shorter than that of a pure-blooded elf—did not come until Cutter's time; until then, the tribe pretty much assumed that life was short because death was always premature and unnatural.)

In their emulation of and actual mind-to-mind contact with wolves, the Wolfriders have developed a state of consciousness known as *the now of wolf thought.* In this state, which when taken to extremes is like a trance, an elf can go about his regular activities with no anticipation of anything beyond the

The Wolfriders' view of mortality— blissful ignorance...

moment, untroubled by hope or fear. The Wolfriders regard it as a practical and desirable way of existence during periods of non-crisis.

While they can communicate telepathically to a certain extent with their wolf friends, the Wolfriders avoid doing it, primarily because lupine body language is so clear in its meaning and also because a "wolf send" is brain-breaking hard work! When an elf does enter a wolf's mind via telepathy, he receives only impressions; the sending between Cutter and Nightrunner is not to be taken literally. Wolves do not think in complete sentences or in anything like a linear pattern.

and eyes opened.

Elves are capable of cause and effect rationalization, but when confronted with the unknown, they tend to be as curious (and often, because of the now of wolf thought, as short sighted) as wolves. They may attack something too big for them or they may flee from something harmless. Depending on how much time has passed between similar learning experiences, Wolfriders repeat mistakes just as wolves do. They forget quickly.

Probably the most significant area in which elves differ from humans is in their social and sexual interactions. Although they revere their ancestress Timmain in legends, the Wolfriders have no religion and no moral code beyond The Way. Their attitude toward sex goes beyond any "free love" concept since elfin sexual relations cannot be anything but free. Even those who choose monogamy (in its biological, rather than social or religious sense) are free because mutual fulfillment inspires them thus.

Depending on how much time has passed between similar learning experiences, Wolfriders repeat mistakes just as wolves do. They forget quickly.

The one fly in the idyllic ointment is Recognition, explained in depth elsewhere in this volume. A male and female elf who do not, for some reason, get along with each other might find themselves trapped in this irresistible genetic bond; in which case mating must take place and pregnancy must result. That is what Recognition is for.

Fortunately, Recognized couples have, as all elves do, the advantage of being able to send. It is very hard not to like someone when his/her soul name is revealed and deepest thoughts and feelings are completely open. Deception and manipulation are impossible. And since with elves, liking is just a short step away from loving, nearly all Recognized couples remain close throughout their lives, long after their children have grown and flown. However, since the deep urge of Recognition fades once mating has taken place, the possibility exists that (1) an elf may Recognize a second partner some time after the first Recognition—this may lead to various and intriguing living arrangements; and (2) an elf could conceivably mate with or even Recognize his or her daughter or son many years after the child's birth, since over long times the relative age difference between parent and child all but disappears and genealogical connections are forgotten. This situation, however, would almost always arise only in response to the absolute unavailability of other potential mates.

"Lovemates join for pleasure and lifemates join for life, but Recognition...ahh!" There are some good points to Recognition. Because of the intense spiritual as well as physical communion, the pleasure quotient is higher in the sexual relations of Recognized couples than in lovemates (which, because of sending, is already higher than we poor humans can know—*sigh*). The term *lifemate* indicates that lovemates have pair-bonded; Recognition is not necessary for lifemating to take place. The pair may or may not opt for monogamy, but it is not a conscious decision based on possessiveness or jealousy. Lifemating is a "marriage" without ceremony or the need for sanction. It can happen any time, even (rarely) between the very young before sexual activity begins. If one member of a lifemated couple Recognizes a third elf, that elf may be incorporated into the bond to make a three-way union, but lifematings are for life and do not break up except under extraordinary circumstances.

Children belong to and are parented by the entire tribe, although the child will not forget who sired and bore him until many hundreds or even thousands of years have passed. Family units share and know each other's soul names. Child abuse is unheard of, as is spoiling and coddling. It is important that "cubs" learn as quickly as possible the laws of nature and the rules of forest survival. Elf children are encouraged to be brave but taught to be cautious. They are raised with a sense of self worth and are not loaded down with unrealistic parental expectations. They are allowed to be who they are and to develop whatever talents they possess at their own pace. While elfin parents may have certain hopes that the child may be the vessel of one of the "magic" abilities that elves are known to express, there is usually no pressure for the child to "get out there and perform." Redlance's treeshaping powers showed up rather late as such things go; Rainsong knows her cub will be a healer like his grandfather but does not know how or when the power will mature.

In humans, possessiveness, jealousy, and the need for control are all products of insecurity. Insecurity stems, in large part, from the inability to communicate with others. Among the Wolfriders, communication is a fine art; the tribe's number is never very large and each member is vital to the survival of the tribe. Within the tribal system there are fights, challenges, and disagreements, but once resolved, there is no aftermath of resentment. Like wolves, the Wolfriders squabble and then forget it. Unlike wolves, they are not ruthless about picking on *omegas* (low members on the totem pole—which raises the question: *are* there any

low members, and if so how are they determined?) Capable of compassion and empathy, the elves do not coldly weed out the weaker or less effectual members of the tribe.

Another aspect of the vastly increased potential for communication afforded by sending is the *soul name,* a construct necessitated by the individual's need to maintain *some* part of himself as private.

Since it is possible that a telepathic conversation between two elves could leave both minds scoured of those things that make each elf unique, the soul name is a word/ sound/concept belonging to (and almost sacred to) each individual. When two

or more minds are in telepathic union, each can sense when he is approaching another's soul name and "pull back." Also, each can tell when another is getting close to his own soul name, and each can close off the communication. Only a dark and depraved psyche (like Winnowill) would knowingly invade the mind of another, perhaps even to the point of discovering the soul name. Among Wolfriders, the privacy of thoughts—and especially of soul names —is never questioned.

Ultimately, the key to understanding elf-think (particularly Wolfrider-think) is an awareness of how three factors would affect life as humans know it: a sense of immortality (or lack of a sense of time pressure), an ability to live in the perpetual present, and the ability to communicate intimately with another mind/soul.   ❖

Of course, there will always be some for whom elf-think is easier than for others. There is no problem so great it can't be ignored.

A Day in the Lives

It has been said that one should take one's work more seriously than one takes oneself. It has also been said that one should not take anything *too* seriously. There were times during the telling of the original Elfquest series that the work and the world seemed to get very serious indeed. Since Wendy and Richard had long maintained that it was so easy to tell the elves' story because the little folk actually lived with them, perhaps it was only natural that cartoons chronicling the "real-life" adventures of Cutter and crew started appearing in the back pages of the comics. The "Day in the Lives" vignettes certainly helped to keep things in a kind of perspective and provided a gently humorous safety valve for when the pressure got high. In addition, Wendy and Richard (as well as some of the creative folks they work with) have discovered the joys of cartoon notes between and among each other, as well as the insanity that can result during fax wars! All in all, it's generally in good fun. Except...the neighbors can be heard, now and then, muttering, "It's only a comic book; it's only a comic book..."

"I'D LIKE TWO HUNDRED POUNDS OF WOLF CHOW, AND ALL THE SHORT LEASHES YOU'VE GOT!"

Revenge is sweet...

Sharp-eyed readers
caught a minor(?)
mistake on
Clearbrooks's left
hand...

The artist's view of the publisher, and some advice to same...

SNORT! SNORT! SNORT!

THIS IS A FUN COMPANY!!

WE LAUGH AT OUR SELVES GODDAM IT!!

HEY LISSEN, BOSS... ALL WORK AND NO PLAY— Y'KNOW?

Wendy finally hears from a long-silent friend, and a fax war follows...

BIG BROTHER... BIG BROTHER... HMMM... NOW WHO..? LESSEE... I USED TO KNOW THIS GUY... KEN... KENNY SOMETHING..? GOOFY GUY... NUTS ABOUT CARS AND TRAINS... BUT HE DISAPPEARED... STOPPED RETURNING CALLS. I THOUGHT A CROC' ATE 'IM!

ANYHOO, IF THAT'S YOU, MOM'S GOT HER BUTT PARKED AT THE COMPUTER ALL DAY AND CAN'T GAB ON THE PHONE. SO FAX HER A LETTER, YA B_____! WHY YI OUGHTTA.... SHE'S GOT HER OWN MACHINE NOW. MOM'S A FAXIN' FOOL!

YEAH! I KNOW — (BUTT) YOU BETTER FIX YOUR FAX

OH MY— I'M TALKING OUT OF MY BUTT—

Better check your Backbone Placement, kids.

C.C. CHANGE THE BOOK TO ELF RUMP?

T. RYWHE THIS IS ...

SO WHAT'S WRONG WITH MY FAX? FIX YOURS! IT CUT OFF YOUR LAST SENTENCE!

AS FOR TALKING OUT OF MY BUTT... NOPE... NOPE... WON'T SAY IT... TOO NASTY.

Afterword

by Wendy Pini

This afterward originally appeared in the first volume of the *Elfquest Gatherum*. While the date mentioned, June 1981, is long past, the sentiments Wendy expresses toward *Elfquest* readers are still valid.

—Editor

A year. A solid year of nonstop, non-negotiable, up-to-our-asses-in-alligators work.

And it's finally done. On Friday, June 19, 1981, Richard typed "The End" to 130,000 words of *Elfquest—The Novel,* and I put the last dab of paint on 160 pages of stats of the artwork for the *Elfquest* volume. Behind us, already in print for the year, we have issues seven through ten of the black-and-white comic, a color portfolio, and an eight-page featurette for Marvel Comic's *Bizarre Adventures*. All that in 365

days—say it fast and it sounds easy! How the hell did we manage it anyway? I don't even remember.

As Dwight said in his introduction [Introduction II], the *Gatherum* is a celebration. It's very appropriate that such a scrapbook *cum* elf family album should appear at this time, for now is certainly a time of reflection for Richard and me; and for you readers who have taken this whole long, bumpy ride with us from the beginning, who are now finishing this book, it is a time to realize that you are a part of the family in this album. You are a part of the quest.

As you read this, Elfquest is entering the mass market arena as an elaborate full-color volume, as a novel, and soon we hope, as a full-length feature animated cartoon. But I think Richard and I will always reserve our warmest feelings for the simple black-and-white newsprint comic that we continue to publish. Because that's how we started. It's Elfquest's most basic and most intimate incarnation. The charm of any comic book lies in its immediacy. This holds especially true for Elfquest in its black-and-white format.

As I look over this past year I am touched most by memories of the little and not so little things Richard did to help us both survive. He is a frighteningly efficient and capable person, possessed of a solid business sense and a sharp creative wit. He doesn't just manage Warp Graphics, he conducts it like an orchestra, perfectly harmonizing the string section of his artistic output with the brass of his business dealings. He is indispensable and he knows it. It's a good thing I don't know it, or he'd be insufferable!

The bunch who produced the *Gatherum* have already been thanked and will be again—many times. But I feel that those for whom this book was published should be thanked as well. You, who loved *Star Trek* and *Lord of the Rings* and *Star Wars* and *X-Men*, thank you for being flexible enough to love *Elfquest* too. Thank you for making room. I don't know how you do it.

During one of my early conversations with Gary Groth, he asked me what some of my favorite comics or fantasy books were. He was slightly perplexed when I replied that I seldom read that sort of thing. You see, I'm basically full up. When you carry a whole world and the fates of dozens of characters around in your head, it's very difficult to become involved with anyone else's fantasies. At least I find it difficult. That's why fans amaze me. Their capacity for incorporating world upon world into their own private universe seems endless.

I'm very glad that Cutter's nameless world has been allowed to establish its own orbit in so many hearts. ✧

" I don't know that it's right to follow the same set of rules all your life. You just ought to like yourself."

Further Conversations with Warp

Interview by Peter Sanderson

This interview took place in late 1984 in Poughkeepsie. The original Warp *Elfquest* series had recently ended, and the Marvel Comics reprints had yet to start up. Mingled feelings of "postpartum" depression and optimism about new titles and animation ran high.

PETER SANDERSON: *Do you see* Elfquest's *success as a spur to the creation of more comics in the fantasy genre?*

WENDY PINI: We're surprised that there haven't been more already. *Elfquest* took eight years to be told. And we thought that perhaps we'd see more elves and fairies pop up, but they didn't. I think it's because a lot of creators still don't identify with the genre and would rather do something they're more comfortable with.

RICHARD PINI: It's a notoriously difficult genre to work with because it's so easy to abuse. Even superheroes, by whatever ways they get around them,

still pay a kind of homage to the laws of physics and so forth. In fantasy, if you are undisciplined, you can create a world and very quickly get tangled up in its lack of laws, its lack of internally consistent logic. And I think this is probably what scares most people off. It seems very easy, but as soon as most people try it, they find it's very difficult. But again, I think that *Elfquest* has already had some effects on the attempt to do fantasy in comics. I think there are a couple of fantasy comics out there that certainly weren't out there before *Elfquest* and perhaps might have been inspired into existence by *Elfquest*'s success. We had a good laugh over the ads for *Grimwood's Daughter* 'round about the time *Elfquest* 19 or 20 was coming out. One ad said, "The elves are dying," [*Wendy laughs*] and no one at Fantagraphics will ever convince me that wasn't a little aside at *Elfquest*.

WENDY: I think an even more astringent aside was "Elves like you've never seen before." What, Vulcans? C'mon! Punk Vulcans! [*Laughter.*]

RICHARD: Jan Strnad is a fine writer.

WENDY: Yeah.

RICHARD: I've liked everything he's done so far.

WENDY: Jan has soul.

RICHARD: He does have soul. Whether or not *Grimwood's Daughter* is an attempt to come in through the door *Elfquest* has opened, or whether it's absolutely independent—"I have this idea and I've wanted to do it for a long time and it wouldn't have mattered if *Elfquest* had never existed"—I think in some ways you will see more fantasy because of *Elfquest*. But I also think people will discover how difficult it is to do well.

SANDERSON: *Do you think it's necessary to have a personal vision in the work*

to do fantasy whereas superheroes to some extent can be done by rote?

WENDY: I think anything good is done with a personal vision, and if anything is done by rote, it's going to show. Any genre, whether it's superhero, western, fantasy, or science fiction, has to have a personal vision to lend it the substance and structure it needs to fly, to continue.

RICHARD: You look at Frank Miller's *Daredevil*. He took a character that was going in seventeen different directions and suddenly stamped upon it in large letters "FRANK MILLER'S VISION," maintained it for the period he was doing it, and then went away. People are trying to follow that lead now and not succeeding nearly as well as Frank did. It's interesting to read—but not the way it was.

WENDY: I think we can go back to the example of *Weirdworld*. Elements were introduced into *Weirdworld*—Black Riders, dragons, elves, wolves—all the things your average fantasy and science fiction reader is accustomed to seeing. These are cliché symbols of fantasy. But in my opinion there wasn't enough of a new twist added onto it to give it any substance. So you had all these wonderful little clichés floating around and nothing to hold it all together, no direction for it to go in. You have to have something to say, no matter what you're doing, and then you pick the symbols with which to say it, because comics is a visual medium as well as a writer's medium. You have

> "**Y**ou have to have something to say, no matter what you're doing, and then you pick the symbols with which to say it, because comics is a visual medium as well as a writer's medium."

to combine the two. Both areas of the medium have to have a vision. You can have terrific artwork, but if the script is soulless and dead, it's going to be felt. You can have a terrific script, but if the artwork is soulless and dead, it's definitely not going to fly.

RICHARD: And if you don't have a vision, you had better be one excellent craftsman because in a sense you have to fake it, to make it look as if you are very much involved with what you're doing. It's just that the majority of creators can't or don't.

WENDY: And again, you have this steamroller of scheduling, which is that this *has* to be *out this month*, y'know? [*Laughter.*] And when creativity comes up against something like that, then it becomes a real grind, and my admiration goes out to anyone who can rise above that grind and make a statement the way Frank Miller did.

SANDERSON: *To what extent did* Elfquest *turn out at the end as you saw it at the beginning? Did the plot and characterizations change from what you had originally intended?*

WENDY: Well, our formula for doing *Elfquest* was initially to plot the whole thing out. Even before we did our first promo package back in 1977, we knew how it was going to end.

RICHARD: I have to jump in here with an amendment to that. The overall plot did not change. But you [*Wendy*] and I had a number of discussions on points. The whole of issue twenty, I think, was more vague in our minds at the beginning than it came out being, when we finally got around to putting that issue out.

WENDY: Well, we always knew that the elves were going to reach the castle and that they were going to discover their origins.

RICHARD: True, but I'm referring particularly to the whole idea of "what does death mean?" So we had to give some thought to and make some decisions about what death and after-death are to these characters. We were faced with a little bit of a dilemma in that we didn't want to say in every case that first death happens and then *this* happens, because we wanted the readers to think about what things like life and death mean, not only to the characters, but to themselves as readers.

WENDY: I will readily admit that up until issue 19 we debated about whether One-Eye was really dead, or whether we would revive him. Richard loved him and wanted him back, and I felt for the integrity of the story he had to die. And during the course of our debates, we came upon the chilling third alternative, which is only doing justice to the nature of elves, which is not the same as the nature of humans. We established early on in the story that the elves have the capacity for astral projection, that is, the spirit existing outside the body. So why wouldn't it follow then, that the spirit would continue to be a force after the body has died? And as we began to talk about this more and realize that death, in our minds, probably isn't the same thing for elves as it might be for humans, we realized we had to deal with this as a story concept, and have the other characters deal with it. Clearbrook calls out to her mate's spirit; the spirit doesn't respond. Usually, in a fantasy story, when someone's love calls out to a spirit, the spirit returns, and everyone lives happily ever after. Why didn't this happen in *Elfquest*? Because not only did we want the characters to think about it, but we also wanted the readers to think about it. Maybe dying isn't as bad as we've been led to believe. Maybe death is another state that you don't necessarily want to come back from.

RICHARD: And we weren't about to make that choice, certainly not for the readers. We didn't want to impose whatever feelings we had on them by saying, "The reason One-Eye does not answer Clearbrook is that he's out there in the Elysian Fields having a grand old time with all the other characters who have died." And so, by leaving it with a big question mark in that respect, I'd like to think we have very subtly forced the readers to think about the concept of living, the concept of dying, the concept of spirit, the concepts of after-life and nonexistence.

WENDY: It is something that's not really focused on with any kind of consistency in superhero comics. Particularly in the Marvel Universe, resurrection is the rule of the day. If enough readers write in and say, "I miss that character," they'll find some way to bring him back. Therefore, the fans get this idea, "We have the power of life and death over the characters we like; therefore, we shouldn't really take death seriously when it happens in a story."

RICHARD: They want what they're used to. They don't want to think they have no power over One-Eye. At the World Science Fiction Convention someone said, "When are you going to bring One-Eye back?" And we looked at this

> "**M**aybe dying isn't as bad as we've been led to believe. Maybe death is another state that you don't necessarily want to come back from."

person in the audience and said, "One-Eye's story is told. You have to relate to it however you want." And this person sort of sat in his chair and went "Ohhhh...." [*Wendy explodes in laughter.*] And that's the answer we had for them. They have no power over the characters, and therefore, they are getting a more truthful experience in the reading of the story.

SANDERSON: *They are being forced to recognize the reality of death.*

RICHARD: They've been forced all through *Elfquest* to accept the reality of the various and sundry things we've put in there. The reality of death. The reality of—

WENDY: Sex.

RICHARD: Of sex. The reality of love as an emotion and what it means. The reality that you can think differently from the way I think, but that doesn't make you wrong and me right, or vice versa; and we can still get along. I hope it's been a subtle manipulation, but not an unkind one.

WENDY: Let me make a point about the fans which I think is very important. They are often put down by people in the industry because of the tendency they have to say, "This character died, but I want him back," and all that. It is the industry itself that has created the belief in fans that they have that power. If someone says, "No, this is the way it's going to be," I maintain that most fans are intelligent enough and respectful enough to say, "Oh, okay. Hey, this is something different." And they'll like that. They really like to be treated with respect.

SANDERSON: *You must have felt a great deal of pressure to keep the series going.*

RICHARD: Oh, heavens, we generated a lot of that pressure ourselves. Most of our readers, when they wrote in to comment on issue 20, said, "I am very sad that *Elfquest* is ending; it's been a part of my life. But you did good, you wrapped it up, and I'm happy for the experience and for having known it." We still get letters saying, "Oh, please, please, please don't let it end. Please continue." But most people were quite understanding that way. I'm sure in the back of their minds, they kind of hope we'll continue. We even created some of that pressure ourselves. Here we've got the best selling independent comic going at the moment, and we're cutting it off. After eight years of doing the same thing under very intense conditions, it was absolutely necessary that we take a break. We've said repeatedly that the characters are not dead. They're not even in limbo for very long. We have other plans. But they're other plans of ours, and not a response to the pressure coming from outside.

WENDY: In other words, the next *Elfquest* you see will come out when it's time for us to do it, not because there's a lot of screaming. Although, I confess, I hope the screaming continues, because that means the interest will still be there.

RICHARD: If the screaming continues, it will be because of the Marvel reprints, because that incarnation will be the one that bridges the gap as far as comics output is concerned for the next three years.

WENDY: And hopefully, by the end of that three years, we'll also have the film coming out, and then who knows what kind of demand there'll be for *Elfquest*? If the film's a success we've already discussed the possibility of opening up a subgenre of *Elfquest* aimed almost exclusively at children but with the same kind of quality we've been putting into the adult-oriented *Elfquest*.

RICHARD: It's almost going to be a Star Comics version of *Elfquest* specifically for very young readers.

WENDY: We will leave the controversial stuff out, but not the questions we ask. We want them to think. We just won't deal with certain things.

SANDERSON: *When you speak of new plans for* Elfquest *in the future, are you talking about new stories?*

RICHARD: Oh, yes.

WENDY: The next thing that will happen will be a graphic novel, which will be a self-contained story.

RICHARD: We're tentatively looking for it to be two years down the line, in autumn 1986, as a hundred-page graphic novel in the color volume *Elfquest* format. It will be a new story that picks up the characters where we left off at the end of issue 20. We deliberately left things unanswered. We knew there were more stories. There will probably be three or four new graphic novels over the next few years.

WENDY: At present I can see only two. The next graphic novel will have everything to do with where we left off. What effect has the knowledge of their origin had on the Wolfriders, these primitive little creatures suddenly confronted with the universe opening up?

RICHARD: We've said for years that *Elfquest* is a novel with twenty chapters. It has a beginning, a middle and an end. True and false. It's completed, it's done, but as Wendy has said, there are other adventures. Ultimately, however, there is an absolute brick-wall ending beyond which there is nothing else. And that is eventually going to show up in a graphic novel, as say, two or three or four down the line.

WENDY: When Arthur Conan Doyle wanted to kill off Sherlock Holmes, he had done what he could with the character, and he was tired of it. And the fans forced him to bring him back, and it was never the same. That is never going to happen to us.

SANDERSON: *What about the previous generations of the Wolfriders?*

RICHARD: That's the project we're calling *Blood of Ten Chiefs*, which is a shared universe anthology series. For

the last several years Bob Asprin and Lynn Abbey have been editing a very successful series of anthologies based on a concept called *Thieves' World*. Bob and I were sitting around one day, and I mentioned to him an idea Wendy and I had for a storybook called *Blood of Ten Chiefs*. There'd be a little story on each one of the chiefs, and Wendy would do illustrations. Bob suggested, "Why don't you have other authors involved in this?" This was an intriguing idea. So

for the last six months to a year, we've been getting together all the pieces of paperwork that are necessary. This is a monstrously complicated administrative thing to do. We're at the point now where we have an agent who is making a pitch to publishers for the books, and we have a list of authors, and the four of us—Wendy and myself, and Bob Asprin and Lynn Abbey—will co-edit. We're very excited about it because it represents an infusion of imagination beyond what we two are able to come up with on our own. It's easy at this point to feel burned out about the characters. But somebody who hasn't been living cheek by jowl with the story

for the last eight years can manage to come up with all sorts of new things.

WENDY: We've had to be very careful in how we've guided the other hands that have become involved in the perpetuation of the Elfquest mythos. For instance, the Chaosium Elfquest role-playing game is doing very well. Of necessity, new additions have had to be made to the Elfquest universe; for instance, the concept of Prairie Elves and the concept of Sea Elves, which I myself had never dealt with in the story and never would have dealt with in the story. But for the game it's good to have other characters who can be met along the road. But when the fans write in and say, "Do these also exist in Wendy and Richard's universe?" we have to say a very firm "no." Nothing really exists in *Elfquest* until we put it down on paper ourselves. Also, for the fan fiction that comes in we publish in *Yearnings*. When a series, such as "Star Trek," stops, fans have a tendency to want to keep it going by doing their own stories and artwork; and eventually, if the series is long enough away, the fans begin to think of their own fiction as being The Thing. And they get confused. So that's why we're trying to keep as much of a handle as possible on the fan fiction that's done, and to continually keep it in their awareness that this is fan fiction.

SANDERSON: *Will the* Blood of Ten Chiefs *stories be officially part of the canon?*

RICHARD: We are going to be very careful about what goes into *Blood of Ten Chiefs* in terms of making sure it is consistent. I think right now we've come to a decision that it will be part of the Elfquest story. We stand behind what these authors will do in *Blood of Ten Chiefs*. We will not stand behind what someone rolls the dice for in the role-playing game or what somebody writes as a piece of fan fiction.

WENDY: When I was a fan, I thought as a fan, I behaved as a fan; but when I became a professional, I put away fannish things [laughter]. That's essentially it. We can get behind these professionals; they're top storytellers in their field.

SANDERSON: Would you allow other writers and artists to deal with the characters in Elfquest itself?

WENDY: Absolutely. In fact, I'm looking forward to the possibility of a collaboration with a young woman who has worked as an animator on the West Coast. She's the first person who has ever given original drawings of my characters to me that have contained facial expressions exactly as I would do them, but not traced. She's got a feeling for the characters like no one else I've encountered. And I'm hoping that perhaps she can become an assistant penciller on the graphic novels, because if everything goes well, for the next three years I'm going to be up to my neck in production of the animated film. And if we have to have a graphic novel out in two years, not all the work can be mine.

RICHARD: I think a general answer to that question would be that aspects of any given project might be given over to others, to a greater or lesser extent. But I can't imagine a creative project that we would simply turn over lock, stock, and barrel to some other team of people to write, to create, to draw, to do everything else, without our involvement on some level.

WENDY: That's precisely because of what we were saying about fantasy before. It's too easy for it to get out of control. It's so tempting to say, "Let's haul in a dragon or a unicorn" [laughter]. And the more people who become connected to the Elfquest universe, I think the more temptation there will be to say, "Let's pull out all the stops. We can do anything. There are no rules."

SANDERSON: Did simply the fact that Elfquest took eight years to do change it in any way?

WENDY: Yes. I started the series when I was twenty-six years old, and that was all the living I had done, and now I'm thirty-three, and oh, boy, the living that Richard and I did during those eight years! Really smart readers will watch the relationship between Cutter and Skywise and get an indication of some of our changes in attitude as the story went on, since those are the two characters we identify with the most. I found very early on I identified very strongly with Cutter, but towards the end of the series he became almost too masculine for me to get as close to as he was before. He really grew up. I think it's probably easier for women handling male characters to handle younger characters. But as Cutter matured through the story and asked deeper and deeper questions, I began to step back from him, sort of to retreat into the Kahvi character [laughter] who was a female I could relate to a lot easier than to what Cutter had become. All the characters grew. They all changed. All the characters resolved something in their own hearts. In the first five issues I don't think that was ever in our minds, the depths to which the characters would go.

RICHARD: There was no need for that at the beginning because those first issues were establishment, and then let's get on with the quest. As things progressed, we knew we were going to have to deal on a gritty, realistic level with war, with love, with sex, with life, with death. It became necessary to devote more and more space to each of these things because they are inherently complex things. There were times when we wondered, because of things we were thinking or feeling, whether a character would do A or do B. We might have planned A way back at the beginning, but because of our own growth and our own experiences over years of time, we had to ask is it still reasonable to expect A or is this character going to do B?

WENDY: Winnowill was a character who surprised us because the series would have been fifteen issues long if it hadn't been for her. We had originally planned only the fifteen issues. I think issue #11, where she was introduced, was the turning point for the depth of the story to increase. She turned it into a character that I found fascinating. She is so subversive and so subtle in what she does. She never comes out and does violence until the end of her part in the story. Just watching her little spider web break thread by thread became a very fascinating thing. The darker quality of the story began to come out at that point.

SANDERSON: *How did the Elfquest animated film project come about?*

RICHARD: It was in 1981, in the fall, that we got a call from the Nelvana studio up in Toronto. They were interested in doing *Elfquest* as a full length animated film, which was our goal. We tried to work with them for almost two years, during which time it became increasingly obvious that these were not easy people to work with, because although their studio was capable of spectacular animation, they did not have a feeling for what *story* is, how to tell a story. We became more and more frustrated with the things they were trying to tell us should be in the animated film. Then *Rock and Rule* came out and failed, and they decided that animation was not the way to go, and presented us with a treatment of the film that, at the time we received it, we didn't know was meant for live action. It was just a bizarre amalgam of *Elfquest* and *The Wizard of Oz* and *Herself the Elf* and *Peyton Place*. When we went back to them and said, "What is this?" they said, "Oh well, we want to do it live action." I said, "Say what?!"

WENDY: I got on the phone with one of the directors and said, "We've got four-foot elves who ride wolves. How do you propose to do that?" And he said, "We'll put children in costumes on trained wolves," which shows how much he knew about wolves.

RICHARD: So, anyway, it took us another several months after that to get the property back. It was under option, and we had to acquire it back legally, and we did. We went looking for another studio. We had done our homework and decided we didn't want any of the big animation studios—Disney, Bluth, Filmation, Hanna-Barbera, Ruby-Spears, Rankin-Bass—we just didn't want any of them to do it. We didn't like their style of work. So we focused on smaller studios and found a smaller studio on the East Coast, and they turned out not to be as businesslike as we would have liked. So by a great stroke of luck we connected up with a number of people over the last seven or eight months who were able to allow us to consider the absurd alternative of starting our own studio. Fortunately, somewhere in there, it was suggested that maybe we'd want to approach an animation studio that's already established, but that we'd raise the funding for the production, have it in hand, and approach a studio from that position of power. Hold the purse strings and you have control over your project. So in essence that is what we have been

> "**I**t [the Elfquest film treatment] was just a bizarre amalgam of *Elfquest* and *The Wizard of Oz* and *Herself the Elf* and "Peyton Place." We went back to them and said, 'What is this?'"

doing for the last several months. We are working as closely as we can with a studio down in New York City. We are still in the process of acquiring the financing and should have that tied up within a couple of months, at which point Wendy goes on staff to that studio as creative director, designer of animation, and six other things, because she's the Source.

WENDY: We're also working from a screenplay which probably won't remain intact [*laughter*], but at least it's a structure to work from.

SANDERSON: *You expect someone will rewrite the screenplay?*

WENDY: No, I expect we'll have a story conference in which the key animators and the directors get together and from the basic structure we will pick the thing apart and find out what will work cinematically and what won't. That's a process that could take up to eight months.

RICHARD: So Wendy goes on staff with them. I become—in essence, if not in fact—what you would call executive producer because I will be shepherding, as I have done with the *Elfquest* comic, the business aspects and the financial aspects of the film, and she is shepherding the creative aspects of the film.

WENDY: The whole thing is suddenly on a much larger scale. This is national and international. I am looking forward to it, and I cannot wait to get to work on this film. It's just going to be the next step, and one that we've been hoping

for for so long.

RICHARD: And something else: despite any statements to the contrary, when *Elfquest* was optioned three years ago, that was the first instance I know of a studio optioning an independently owned and creator-controlled comic book series.

WENDY: Unless you count Richard Corben's *Neverwhere*. That appeared in the *Heavy Metal* movie.

RICHARD: That's true. The reason I mention this is the news releases saying that *The DNAgents* being optioned for TV represents a breakthrough for creator-owned comics and creative control over the product—but we were there three years ago. And in fact it was our exercise of our creative control that caused us to leave Nelvana.

SANDERSON: *What is the studio you're now working with?*

RICHARD: The studio is Zander's Animation Parlor. They have done many animated commercials. They also did the CBS-TV special "Gnomes."

SANDERSON: *Jack Zander used to work on "Tom and Jerry" at MGM in the 1940s.*

"**R**ichard is going Where No Richard Pini Has Gone Before. He taught himself to be a publisher and editor, and now he's teaching himself to be a movie mogul."

WENDY: He'd be very pleased that you know that. He thinks that nobody knows what he used to do [*laughter*]. I hasten to point out for any of the readers who have watched "Gnomes" that that's not the kind of animation that will be in the Elfquest film. If everything goes through as planned, there will be a look to the Elfquest film that hasn't ever been seen in an animated feature film before, because the coloring will be done at a studio in Brazil, where they do some spectacularly good airbrush effects.

Wendy's version of The Palace of the High Ones...

They intend to airbrush each cel, where it's appropriate, so you will have a roundness and a fullness to the figures that has never been seen before.

SANDERSON: *I take it this will be full animation.*

WENDY: Absolutely. No rotoscoping. This is a real cartoon. We are not trying to imitate or to mimic live action. We are trying to create movement on a fantasy level, larger than life.

RICHARD: So that's what's happening with the animation, and it's tremendously exciting for me because it involves talking with people on a level that very few people on the creative end of things get to do in comics.

WENDY: Yes, it's not every day you get to call up Roy Disney [*explosion of laughter*].

RICHARD: He's one of the individuals we have had to speak to in the past with regard to trying to set up distribution and so forth and so on of a film. And there is marketing, there is publicity, there is licensing, there is a myriad of ancillary things connected with making a film.

WENDY: My part of the film will be essentially what I'm accustomed to, but Richard is going Where No Richard Pini Has Ever Gone Before, and it amazes me how he's holding up through this. Again, he's doing what he's done before: he taught himself to be a publisher and editor, and now he's teaching himself to be a movie mogul [*laughter*].

SANDERSON: *How much of the story will the film cover?*

WENDY: It will cover the quest proper, from issue 6 through issue 20.

RICHARD: That section of *Elfquest* is a good adventure story. It will need to be pared down tremendously. Certain things will need to be condensed or whatever, but it will survive as a rollicking good adventure story with the values of *Elfquest* intact.

WENDY: What may shake fans of *Elfquest* up a little bit is that events in the story have been condensed, squashed. Certain scenes just won't be in there because cinematically they don't work; they drag. Some characters will be eliminated.

SANDERSON: *Because of time limitations in the film.*

WENDY: Exactly. The animators are going to have to move seventeen Wolfriders through the story, which means that rather than having the tribe constantly on screen, we're going to be focusing on individual characters. For an animated film, it's still going to be a very rich and complex story. The approach that Zander's studio wants to take is to aim at an older child-level family audience. I suppose you could call it around the level of PG-13. They really take the story seriously. They want to tell a story that's going to be talked about both in the sense of filmic storytelling and cinematic inventiveness.

SANDERSON: *How did you get into publishing other people's comics?*

RICHARD: Well, round about issue 14 of *Elfquest*, I was at a convention. I was shown a portfolio of artwork by Colleen Doran, who is doing *A Distant Soil*. I said, "This is very nice; send me some Xeroxes." And the next year at the convention I saw her portfolio again, and there was more artwork, and there were sample comic pages. I said, "This looks like it belongs to a story," and I asked her to tell me the story. By the time issue 17 of *Elfquest* had come out, and it was very much on my mind that in a year I was going to be a publisher with nothing to publish because *Elfquest* would be done. So I asked Doran if she'd like to do a book in the *Elfquest* format, and she said yes, and we worked out a contract. Then *Mythadventures* came along in a conversation with Bob Asprin. We were sitting around at a

table at yet another convention, and he was expressing a desire to see his books translated into comics form, and it began to appear to me that properties were sort of floating my way. This takes us up to just within the last year. We've started to expand in the sense of gaining new personnel. I'm trying to build a support staff of people. It occurred to me that two titles or three titles is still not very much of a comics publishing company. And it's not that I want to go into the ring and slug it out with First or Eclipse; I just want to be a presence in the independent publishing market. We were a presence with *Elfquest* because *Elfquest* was such a phenomenon. But now it appears to become necessary to act like every other company: have five, six, or seven titles that come out on a regular basis, monthly or bimonthly. No more of this three or four months in between because it takes a

...and Nelvana's version.

very special book like *Elfquest* to maintain the interest necessary to wait four months for the next issue. That's where we are right now: we've got *A Distant Soil*, we've got *Mythadventures*, we've got *Thunderbunny*, we've got three or four other titles under consideration, and I would like by the middle of this year to have those half dozen titles coming out bimonthly.

WENDY: But you're branching out into other things as well.

RICHARD: Yeah. We're branching out into doing books. I intend by the middle of next year to have at least two "book books" under Warp Graphics' belt. One of them will be an art book on the work of Alex Schomburg, a wonderful man: all his comics covers for Timely and all his science fiction artwork. And the other one will be a book of Wendy's artwork that she did for a project based on the Michael Moorcock fantasy novel *Stormbringer*.

SANDERSON: *You* [Wendy] *said in the previous* Journal *interview that you couldn't see yourself working in a big corporation.*

WENDY: I was thinking of Marvel. Quite frankly, I couldn't see myself doing that on a regular basis.

RICHARD: It's a different work environment. It's a different pressure environment. Yes, Warp Graphics is expanding, and in the next year or two, three, five, we may take on another two, three, or five employees. I think of all the independent comics companies, First Comics is the one that people look at when they want an example of how something is being run well. And I've been to their offices, and I think they have fewer than ten people there. I don't get any impression of *quote* large corporation *unquote* about First Comics. It's still very comfortable. And I think we would be able to maintain that situation so that neither of us nor anyone working for us would feel "I'm

a cog in the big machine." I'm very cautious about Warp Graphics' plans for growth and expansion because I've seen how one can grow too fast, and I don't want that to happen.

WENDY: It's not so much growing fast as overextending yourself.

SANDERSON: *Do you two see yourselves as staying in comics indefinitely?*

WENDY: I'm still committed to trying to explore the extent of what I'm capable of doing, and that will probably take the rest of my life. Now that *Elfquest* is done, and I've admitted in public I'm elfed out for a while, I want to teach myself how to draw all over again, because having been a cartoonist for eight years, my sense of proportion is all skewed, and whenever possible lately I've been drawing and sketching from life. Cartooning is caricature, but you have to understand the rules before you can break them; and I'm sort of losing my grip on the rules, and I want to go back and find out what the rules are. That's why I want to paint and draw more. That ambition still remains: to paint, to draw, to be a serious artist.

RICHARD: If Wendy is a creative talent, I seem to be an exploitative talent [*muffled burst of laughter from Wendy*]. And I say that with a certain pride because it's necessary. It took both of us to get *Elfquest* going and to make it grow, and I find I enjoy the role of facilitator, if you will, very much. It's what I am going to be doing with respect to the movie; what to whatever extent the other comics and book properties will allow me to do, I will do with them. The concept of finding the right market, or finding the right person to talk to, or finding the glue that holds two pieces of something together, of making it work—the phrase that is put in quotation marks all the time is "wheeling and dealing." That's what I like doing, and I think I'll be doing it for a long, long time. ✧

Portfolio

In 1980, Wendy and Richard Pini put out a portfolio of scenes from *Elfquest*. Since this was a limited edition of twelve hundred signed and numbered copies, it is rather hard to find. Even the reprint that appeared in the *Elfquest Gatherum* Volume Two is now out of print. So here it is once more. (Hang onto this copy.)

Plate One — "The Lure"

Plate Two — "Blood of Ten Chiefs"

Plate Three — "Troll King"

Plate Four — "Recognition"

Plate Five — "War Chieftess"

Plate Six — "Festival of Flood and Flower"

The Conversation Continues

Interview by John Weber

This interview, the third of four, took place in late 1987 in Philadelphia. The new Elfquest tale, *Siege at Blue Mountain,* had been running for about a year, Wendy and Richard had been around the block several times in an effort to turn the story of the Wolfriders into an animated film, and Warp, the company, had undergone its own bout of expansion and contraction. In the three years since the Sanderson interview, "Further Conversations with Warp," the general mood has changed, as has the overall state of the comics market.

JOHN WEBER: *Tell me first how you guys met. It's a great story!*
WENDY PINI: Well, let's see—you told it last time.
RICHARD PINI: I told it last time.
WEBER: *Whose turn is it?*
WENDY: It's my turn this time. This is such an oft-told story, it's become apocryphal by now. As teenagers, we both read and collected comics, specifically Marvel Comics, and...let's see,

I guess I was about eighteen, a senior in high school, and I wrote a letter in to the *Silver Surfer* comic. And, much to my surprise, they published it, along with my address. So I started receiving letters from all over the country, from boys who were interested in meeting a *girl* who read comics [*laughs*] because back at that time—
WEBER: *It was* Millie the Model, *that's what girls were reading.*

RICHARD: Well, also, there weren't that many female fans, and that there was, was a rare and wonderful thing.

WENDY: Conventions were just starting to get off the ground, and everything. Back in the late Sixties, the situation was really primitive [*laughs*] compared to now. So, as I said, I got letters from all over, and one of these letters really intrigued me because, rather than telling me everything about himself, the writer said, "If you want to know more about me, you have to write me," and that was a letter from Richard Pini at MIT. I got curious, so I wrote, and he wrote, and I wrote, and he called, and I called, and we exchanged photos, and I sent him some drawings, and he sent me some of his writing. We got to know each other, and by the end of that year [1969] we were pretty well certain that this was *it*. We tried to meet off and on in the next four years, while he was finishing college.

RICHARD: From my point of view: I was nineteen, and I was hauling my load of comics back home to my dorm room every week, and I was reading this issue, and I was struck by the letter. It was a wonderful letter, it would have been a wonderful letter no matter who wrote it. But the fact that it was by a *female* was doubly enticing [*laughter*], so I was motivated on two levels to respond: the intellectual and the hormonal. And we saw each other about once a year for the next four years. Those were our "dates."

WENDY: They were very intense dates!

RICHARD: And then, finally, in 1972, I graduated and Wendy moved east. We got married.

WEBER: *Did you meet halfway, in the middle of the country?*

RICHARD: Oh, no. I wrote that first letter in January of 1969, and by August, we pretty much knew we wanted to meet each other. So she was enrolling at a school in Los Angeles, and I was at MIT in Boston. I got into a little Renault, and sixty hours later, I was getting out of the car in Los Angeles.

WENDY: He didn't eat, he lived on Vivarin and Life Savers; and he went straight across the country!

WEBER: *We're lucky you're here today.*

RICHARD: Yes, yes. I never even saw the town of East Winslow, Arizona, where I got stopped for speeding [*laughs*].

WENDY: Eighty miles an hour through a town that he didn't see! So...yes, he arrived at my college, and I came out of my dorm room, and there he was down at the end of the hallway, and we sort of did a Clairol ad [*laughs*], slow-motion towards each other, we recognized each other, and the rest is history.

> "The fact that the letter was by a female was doubly enticing, so I was motivated on two levels to respond, intellectual and hormonal."

WEBER: *So some Marvel editor out there somewhere is responsible for all this?*

WENDY: Marvel Comics takes full credit for it. In fact, we were used as characters in the *Ghost Rider* comic book written by Tony Isabella some years back, which means that Marvel Comics owns us as copyrighted characters. Therefore, we cannot reproduce with-

Art imitates life— sort of. The creators of Elfquest host the Ghost Rider. © 1975 Marvel Comics.

out Marvel's permission [*laughs*]!

RICHARD: I don't know, I just dread having to ask permission.

WEBER: *It could be a great legal case. Front page of the* National Enquirer, *I think! Anyway, let's talk about* Elfquest *and the whole notion of it. You had the idea way back when, in some form—*

RICHARD: Wendy's always been a storyteller. She's always had pictures and words going around up there. I guess the ingredients of *Elfquest* have been in her mind for a long, long time.

WENDY: In one form or another, the characters have always existed. My cartooning style is highly influenced by Japanese comic books, which I discovered in my early teens. As I began to develop my cartooning style, the characters began to take on more solid form and began to seem more like themselves. I've always drawn little elfin cartoonish figures. In 1977, the time seemed right to bring the book out.

RICHARD: Nineteen seventy-seven

was a watershed year for all of us in science fiction, fantasy, and comics because of *Star Wars.*

WEBER: *How tough was it in the beginning?*

WENDY: Not as tough as it is now.

RICHARD: Back then, there was almost no independent comics market.

WENDY: There were only about three hundred direct sales shops.

RICHARD: Well, we don't even know what the number was. It was a small number compared to now. There was almost no direct sales market. There were only two distributors, Bud Plant, Inc. and Seagate Distributors, distributing to this fledgling market. That's all there was. We started out with a loan from my parents, not knowing how to publish, not knowing where to go, going to the Yellow Pages and looking for a printer because there was not the network of information that there is today. We printed up ten thousand copies of *Elfquest* and then went to Bud Plant and Phil Seuling and said, "Will you take our print run?" They said yes, and the rest is history. But because we were about the only kids on the block with a comic—*Elfquest*—at that time, acceptance was very easy. There was no competing product. Nowadays, my god! You have to have the hide of a rhino to get into this pool!

WENDY: It's not necessarily any harder now to get your product accepted if it is a really exciting new concept, or if it really grabs people in some way. And there are people starting out just exactly the way we did. What comes to mind right now is *Teenage Mutant Ninja Turtles*. They [Eastman and Laird] started out exactly the way we did. They decided to publish it themselves, went through the Yellow Pages and looked up a printer, and it just took off from there. So history does repeat itself, certainly. I think the great difficulty now is in having staying power. Distributors are on very shaky ground right now; they're dropping like flies. Retailers are also losing their stores, and nobody's paying anybody adequately. And everybody's in debt to everybody. So having the ability to hang in there and get your series past four or five issues is very, very difficult.

RICHARD: There's a problem in that a lot of small publishers seem to be looking at things in a skewed way. Some of these publishers may be young kids who are still living at home. They don't have to pay rent, they don't have to buy their own food. They don't have the expenses of a business. So they might feel fine that they're selling two thousand copies of their magazine. They think they're a success. By that standard, I suppose they are. By the standards of the wider industry, that's not true. That same product to a larger publisher would be a failure because it wouldn't be carrying its own weight. It's been a complex, bizarre market for the last year and a half.

WENDY: Yeah, I think it's only just now beginning to start to steady itself. In that steadying, I think we will see a lot of dropping away of the get-rich-quick efforts that have popped up in the past couple of years, and the titles that do have the staying power are the ones that we're going to see continue on the stands.

WEBER: *Comics have, I guess in the last year or two, really entered the mainstream, I think, what with the* Superman *revamping,* Dark Knight, *things like that, that are being publicized in the national press. Waldenbooks is carrying—*

WENDY: Well, the reason Waldenbooks carries graphic novels at all is because of *Elfquest. Elfquest* was the first graphic novel to be accepted and—

RICHARD: To penetrate that market.

WENDY: In this country.

RICHARD: In a certain sense, you're right. *Dark Knight*, the *Superman* revamp, the *Watchmen* collection, these are all PR coups. Warner Communications went out and they got a lot of interviews in magazines and papers like *Rolling Stone* and the *New York Times*, and TV shows, and so on and so forth. That's still superficial. Comics are still looked at in this country as children's literature, even though you will find *Rolling Stone* talking about the hard grittiness of *Dark Knight*, or whatever. Until there is a section in the Waldenbooks store, for example, devoted to graphic novels—right now, there are probably only three or four, maybe a half dozen graphic novels worthy of the name available—until you have a section of these things that people will go into and browse the way they browse the romances, the way they browse the mysteries, the way they browse science fiction, comics are not yet mainstream.

WENDY: But I agree with you that they are beginning to edge their way in.

Boom" catches attention, and it's been used for years to immediately associate the audience's thinking with comic books; and of course, that's not what *Dark Knight* and some of the other things are all about now. There is just an incredible lumbering slowness in changing people's thinking about comics.

RICHARD: There's another thing, and it's very subtle, I think. You're *not* seeing "Pow Zap Crash" with *Dark Knight* and *Electra: Assassin* and *Watchmen.*

WENDY: Or *Elfquest*, really.

RICHARD: But what you *are* seeing with those other ones is, *"These are the New, Dark, Gritty, Nihilistic Comics for Armageddon, Comics for Adults."* It's a different kind of "Pow Crash Bam," and it is, in its way, just as bogus. Because it's a PR hook. It's not really a reality yet. It's a hook, it's a label, it's a pigeonhole.

WENDY: That term, *hook,* is a deadly one to me. I'd like to throw it up and skeet-shoot it! Hook is a term we hear quite frequently, in terms of marketing a property to the mainstream, and we heard it in the context of *Elfquest* in trying to deal with CBS last year. They had trouble finding a hook for *Elfquest*, they had trouble pigeonholing it as a boys' show, a boys' action show, or a girls' fluffy-cute show. "What age group is this aimed at?" they asked. We kept saying this is for everybody, everybody can get something out of it. And they were not able to deal with that concept.

RICHARD: You don't have hooks for mysteries or cookbooks—unless it's a gimmick book—or romances. They're there! They're part of the literary foundation, or brickwork, or whatever, of this culture. What we need is to have comics become one of those bricks.

WEBER: *Do you think it can happen?*

RICHARD: I think it's got to! It has happened in Japan. It has happened in Europe. There is not the perception in

WEBER: *What drives me crazy is that, every time you see an outside article on, say, the Batman character, you see the "Zap, Pow, Boom" sound effects in the headline. I don't think I've seen a mainstream article that didn't do that.*

WENDY: Well, there's a tremendous amount of inertia, as Richard pointed out, in the way comic books are looked at in this country, and the "Zap Pow those countries of comics as "kiddie literature," said with a sneer.

WENDY: But I hope what happens in this country doesn't happen like what has happened in Japan, in the sense that because of the overcrowding of the society, people tend to do a lot of living through the comics. They do their little beehive routine, going to work every day, and getting home, and it takes them two hours to get to work and two hours to get home. Of course, we have that here, too. But once they get home, to a very small apartment in which a family of twelve is living or something, they live through the adventures in the comic books. Out of that, you get comics like *Rapeman* and stuff with incredible violence in it that, I suppose, gets all the day's troubles out of the reader in a catharsis. But I certainly hope that it never goes that far in this country.

RICHARD: But again, I think comics need to become widely accepted as a kind of literature, unless comics want to stay stuck in this little hundred thousand, two hundred thousand, maybe five hundred thousand readership, this tiny little cubbyhole. That's really all the comics fans/readers there are in this country. Whereas you have a lot more people reading John D. McDonald or, god help us, Barbara Cartland.

WENDY: Or L. Ron Hubbard.

RICHARD: Or L. Ron Hubbard [*laughs*]. Well, science fiction has managed to become more mainstream. You find it on the *New York Times* best seller list with fair regularity.

WENDY: Since the mid-1970s, it's become very respectable because it makes money. Anything that makes money is very respectable in this country.

WEBER: *It's the bottom line, for any business.*

WENDY: Right.

WEBER: *Marv Wolfman, in the introduction to the first volume of Elfquest, writes that he envies both of you because you can do whatever you want with the characters; you created them, you publish them. But the more successful Elfquest gets, I imagine there's more pressure to keep a certain status quo or to get conservative.*

WENDY: No, at least not in the very seminal part of the book as we publish it. Currently, we're doing the *Siege at Blue Mountain* series, which is done in the same way that we

> "That term, *hook,* is a deadly one to me. I'd like to throw it up and skeet-shoot it!"

did the original twenty-issue series. We're publishing it in black and white first ourselves. Then we'll be going on to collect it into two color volumes, just as the other color volumes were. And *Siege at Blue Mountain* has absolutely no input into it whatsoever but Richard's and mine. We're taking the characters exactly where we want to take them. We get outraged letters from fans who don't like the direction that we're taking them, or we get highly encouraging letters from people who like what we're doing and want to see more. We don't care either way. The story's ours. We're taking the characters where they have to go right now. Yes, we still have that luxury.

RICHARD: On the other hand, you have raised a good point: the demand for *Elfquest*. Our readers are very voracious. They are very hungry. Wendy and I—particularly Wendy, because she is the artist, she is the goose that lays the golden eggs—can only do so much in a given period of time, and no more.

WENDY: I like how you put that.

RICHARD: To ask for more is to kill the goose. Nonetheless, we have made the decision that *Elfquest* is large enough, it is a large enough universe and a large enough concept to admit other stories.

WENDY: Absolutely.

RICHARD: And if we can have those stories done in a way that makes us comfortable, if they're good and we're happy with them, then, yeah, we do want to produce them, and it raises the task of having to get other people to produce them. That's why, for example, we have the *Blood of Ten Chiefs* anthology series. These are short stories, prose stories, written by other well-known science fiction people like C. J. Cherryh and Piers Anthony and Robert Asprin and Lynn Abbey. There's a goodly long list! We are in close contact with all of these people, and they are writing about characters in the past. First of all, these characters don't directly intrude upon what we're doing. And they're also characters about which Wendy and I can't really write because we don't have the time we'd like, we don't have all the ideas in our minds that we'd like to express that these other people do. It's fresh material. It's a new way of looking at *Elfquest*, and we're very excited about that. But it does require that we look elsewhere if we want *Elfquest* to grow beyond what two people are physically and creatively capable of doing.

WENDY: I had an interesting conversation with a couple the other day at a convention. The husband asked me, "Doesn't it bother you the way the fans trivialize your characters in their own writings and drawings? Doesn't it frustrate you?" He pointed out that their ideas don't seem to be very innovative, that they seem to be very imitative and they're not using their imaginations as much as they could. And I felt compelled to remind him that these were very young people who hadn't done a lot of living yet! There wasn't a lot of life experience to draw on, so much of their experience comes from reading other people's stuff and getting inspired by that. But, moreover, the fact that they're out there doing anything at all, the fact that they're using all of that creative energy for something besides shooting up dope or bashing each other's brains in, I think, is fabulous. I would do anything to encourage that. And possibly, out of that, can grow some people who can actually and truly contribute to the Elfquest mythos someday.

RICHARD: Or not even to the Elfquest mythos. Let's say that there's a thousand kids out there who are writing, you know, what to us would be juvenile or trivialized stories. Maybe fifty or ten or five or whatever of those will decide that they like writing so much that they're going to keep on writing, so they will keep on writing. They will practice, they will hone their talent and skill and become writers.

WENDY: Really, we both came up through the ranks of fanzines and mimeograph and stencil. Our first exposure to having people read our work and comment on it came through fanzines, and I still think that's a very healthy way to go. But, you know, an ironic thing right now is that I think many fans have been trained through peer pressure to look down on fanzines because of all these little basement publishers who are able to do five hundred issues of *Frogman Versus the Tree Giants*, or whatever, and the distributors *buy them* [*laughter*]! So, very often, stuff that is of

> "**W**e and the ones who have lasted, and the ones who are good, have paid a certain amount of dues. A lot of the kids who are [self-publishing] now haven't yet. There are very valuable things to be learned in the process of paying dues."

fanzine or lower quality ends up on the stands, so that important intermediary learning ground of the mimeograph and the little low circulation fanzine is lost.

RICHARD: And the criticism of your peers, even though you may not look at them as that, is gone. You miss the interaction of working with a bunch of people on a fanzine. Whereas if you sit and do your own comic, you tend to think, "Wow, I'm right up there along with *Elfquest* and any other professionally produced independent comic," and it's a false comparison. I don't want to sound judgmental, but we and the ones who have lasted and the ones who are good have paid a certain amount of dues. A lot of the kids who are doing it now haven't yet. There are very valuable things to be learned in the process of paying dues.

WENDY: Yeah, I think greed has propelled a lot of these kids faster than they really should be going, you know, and the greed of the—well, I won't be all that specific, just greed in general has started a vicious circle in motion. Properties that really aren't well developed have been put out there on the stands. The consumers see the comic on the stands, and it might be the first issue, so they buy it anyway, even though it's junk, and they sock it away—

WEBER: *And they sell it at a convention for ten dollars because it's a first issue.*

RICHARD: Or more often, the dealer, the retailer, buys a bunch of these, hoping, in a month or two, to sell them for ten dollars each, and finds he's not able to do so. So he's stuck with this

inventory that he's either paid for or not paid for, but he can't sell it. If he hasn't paid his distributor for it yet, he's not likely to. The distributor has lost that revenue, so perhaps he doesn't pay the publisher. And it becomes a vicious, dirty circle. And everybody hurts. There's an amazing lack of business professionalism in the direct comic sales market. And that is one thing that's got to change. Along with the public perception of comics in this country.

WEBER: *Another problem, with something like* Teenage Mutant Ninja Turtles, *is that given all of the variations of that title, the original gets pegged in with the imitators. It all becomes distasteful, imitative. You can tell by comparing quality, but if they're all lined up there in one row...*

RICHARD: Somebody who doesn't know, but who has only heard that there are a dozen adjective-adjective-adjective-noun titles won't pick up the *Turtles* because that person doesn't

know that this was the precursor, this one has quality. And that's bad. The ones that deserve to die will die, but the ones that deserve to live can be hurt.
WENDY: Even *Elfquest* has run into that, in terms of parodies that have been done over the years, and you know, our characters have been lumped in with the Smurfs and so forth, and it's a complete misconception of the type of fantasy that we're doing. Fantasy itself is very, very difficult to do as a sustained series in comic book form. And I really don't think, apart from *Elfquest*, it's been done in another series that has lasted as long. Fantasy really is such a personal, subjective thing that you have to be able to sustain your vision and your commitment to it over a very long period of time. That's awfully hard to do, especially in the mainstream comics, where the pressure is on to either have a blockbuster, or it's out. With *Elfquest*, we were very lucky. We started at a time when it was possible for us to grow from humble beginnings and to build a following, an extremely loyal following, so that we were able to stop in 1984, at the peak of *Elfquest*'s popularity—for which we were told by any number of people that we were absolutely insane. And we were able to pick up again in 1986 right where we left off and our readership followed right along with us; and the people that we used to know who read the original twenty issues are now reading *Siege at Blue Mountain*. But it was our ability to sustain the vision and keep our commitment to

> "**T**here's one underlying, fundamental, rock-bottom problem with [animation] —whether it's done in Japan, Los Angeles, New York, or Poughkeepsie: money."

Elfquest, I think, that keeps the fantasy whole. Because we really haven't been bullied by the pressure of sales or the Comics Code or any of the things that many other creators have to deal with.
WEBER: *You talked about* Elfquest *getting too big for two people, and maybe having other people handle it at some point. I read the review by Paula O'Keefe* [The World of the Wolfriders] *about the personal involvement and how that makes* Elfquest *work: personal involvement between the two of you, the characters and you two, the characters, and the readers. Can that be maintained?*
WENDY: To varying degrees, it can. Certainly we've had our high and low periods of interest in *Elfquest*. Certainly there have been times when it seemed that it was dominating our lives. We had to take a breather from it for a while, as I did in 1984. For two years, I really didn't do that much with it. We were talking about this in the car on the way here, as a matter of fact. The fact that *Elfquest* does have a life of its own. It does now exist in the great "out there" apart from us, in some ways. It continues to be carried along by its own momentum. We just feel that we are the guiding spirits behind *Elfquest* now. The vision is ours, and whoever handles it, whether it be in animation or when we start up a juvenile line of Elfquest stories aimed specifically at a younger audience—we'll have other writers and artists working on that—we will still be where the buck stops. And that's how the story will maintain its integrity and how the characters will not go afield.
RICHARD: You might have asked the same question of Walt Disney. He started back in the 1920s, I think, in his garage, and he was drawing cartoons. Now Walt Disney Productions became a big company, and it produced some mighty fine films. There was always—whatever Disney was like as a person—there was always the Disney stamp.

We talk about it today, how it's missing. We look fondly back at *Snow White* and *Pinocchio* and *Sleeping Beauty* and all of that, and we say they're not doing it like that any more. So it *was* possible for a singular vision to either infect or affect a lot of other people who could carry that vision through while one person or two people oversaw it. And we think the same thing is possible now. Maybe the world has changed a little bit, and maybe things are more complex today than they were thirty or forty years ago. But we believe very strongly that the same sort of thing is possible.

WENDY: For instance, we've never lost our belief that, eventually, and hopefully within a very short period of time, we will connect up with a production company and an animation studio that will cooperate with us and give us the kind of creative control that will make us feel comfortable. Certainly, in working to make a film, there comes a point where the studio has to feel that the project belongs to it. They have to feel like the parent and that this is their child. Otherwise, they can't be committed to it. And we firmly believe that we are going to be able to find such a unit that respects our vision and *shares* it and then can run with it. The search has been a long one, we've been looking for about six years now, and we've been connected up with this studio and that studio. In each case, the problem has been that they've wanted to take the creative control away from us and to tell the story their way. Rankin/Bass would have done *Thunderelves*. Nelvana would have done a combination of *The Wizard of Oz* and *Rock and Rule* [*laughter*]. This we found out as we worked with them and listened to their version of Elfquest. But we know that somewhere out there [*Wendy suddenly sings "Somewhere Out There" from* An American Tail]—and it may be [Don] Bluth, who knows? [*laughter*]—is the someone who appreciates that *Elfquest* would not have been the success it was but that we made it so. We created it and it went its way with our vision, and that's what made it the success it was, and there'll be someone out there who will respect that.

WEBER: *You took the first step: you created it and published it and took care of it for ten years. You ever thinking of taking it the next step yourselves?*

RICHARD: Oh, yeah [*laughs*]! We got as far at one point in this "filmquest," we got as far as scouting out locations in the Poughkeepsie, New York, area to locate and build an animation studio. We were looking at buildings. There's one underlying, fundamental, rock bottom problem with all of it—whether it's done in Japan, whether it's done in Los Angeles, whether it's done in New York City, or whether it's done in Poughkeepsie: money [*laughs*]. Whether you're gonna build a studio and hire people, or whether you're going to hire an existing studio, or whether you're going to guarantee something, you need mucho dinero. For an animated Elfquest, we've had different people say different things to us, but let's just say we need anywhere from five to ten million dollars to do a production correctly.

WENDY: Yeah, that's not even as much as some of the films that are out now have cost. *The Black Cauldron* cost twenty-five million dollars. It was a total bomb. They could have fed Ethiopia with that.

RICHARD: It's kind of obscene when you think about it. But that money has to come from somewhere, whether it's a bank, an investor, a toy company, a studio—which then for its investment wants to own the property—a distribution company—who in return for its investment wants to be able to have input into the making of the movie. It's very convoluted. And what we have seen before us, and what we see before us, is many, many different paths. It's like a spider web: you can go down many strands, and at different points, there are crossed strands, and you can cross from one path to another, depending upon what you think is the right thing to do. And so, we're staring down these glistening strands of pathways, and working every day, following leads, talking to people, and about the only thing we know is that it's going to happen someday. *Elfquest* could be a Saturday morning series, it could be an afternoon cartoon series, it could be a prime-time special, it could be a prime-time miniseries, it could be a theatrical film, it could be so much, and we're pursuing all of it.

WEBER: *Is it a problem sometimes, your being involved with the characters, being too close to them? Does it handcuff you sometimes?*

WENDY: No, not any more. It used to be, particularly when we were getting towards the end of the series in 1984. That's all our lives were about at that time. I lived in my studio, I ate, breathed, and slept *Elfquest!* I was working against horrendous deadlines because not only was I working on finishing the series by a specific time, but we specifically had to have it out to premiere at the World Science Fiction Convention in Anaheim, California, that year. We were having a big premiere party there. I was also working with my assistants on getting the fourth color volume colored. I was literally working around the clock. My health was failing. I was so involved with the characters and what was happening to them, because that's a very violent part of the story where we lose some favorite characters and so forth, that emotionally, I was pretty much of a wreck. I really was not thinking logically, and I don't know if I couldn't have done things in better

proportion. That's how it happened. It's an experience I never want to go through again, and I think I can do work equally good without killing myself for it. But I think that happens when you're involved with too many things at once. Sometimes you can forget about yourself and let yourself be consumed, and your project sort of takes over.

WEBER: *If you, say tomorrow, had to hand over* Elfquest *to people in the industry, are there people you would like to see do* Elfquest?

WENDY: Not right now.

RICHARD: Well, the answer to the question is basically no. But we have had the opportunity from time to time to work with some people who have demonstrated a sensitivity to *Elfquest* that we have found pleasant or refreshing. I don't think that we would be comfortable entrusting the entire thing to them, say, "Here it is, go, run with it," without being able to look over shoulders or check in from time to time.

WENDY: I've had particular trouble finding people who can draw the characters. I can find people who can draw bits of them. For instance, there are a number of women artists that I know that can do the facial expressions rather well. But their figure drawing is weak. They don't have the sense of chunkiness and mass that the characters need. There are some male artists that I know, and one of them has been my assistant, Joe Barruso, who had a very good feeling for animation and the chunkiness and mass of the characters. But the facial expressions weren't very subtle. To find an artist that has that combination, so far I haven't been able to come across one. There's either a weakness in one area or the other.

WEBER: Siege at Blue Mountain: *when is it coming?*

RICHARD: Well, the first four issues are out. Issue #5 will be going into production real soon now.

WENDY: Within the next month, I would guess. It's at the inker's right now.

RICHARD: All of it?

WENDY: All except four pages. Those are mine.

RICHARD: It should be out within a month. There are a lot of extenuating circumstances that have befallen the schedule of *Siege*, and where we used to agonize terribly over scheduling during the last series, for a lot of reasons, we're not agonizing over it this time. As Wendy said, there are ways to kill yourself, and there are ways not to kill yourself. And we really don't choose to kill ourselves, which is not to say that we deliberately want to go and be irresponsible. But, especially with the state of the market, not all of the reason for *Elfquest*'s slowness is up in Poughkeepsie. For example, if we don't get paid by the distributor for the previous issue, then we're not motivated terribly to get the next issue out on time to that distributor so he can fail to pay us again. Meanwhile, the printer wants to be paid for both. So there's this debilitating give-and-take.

WENDY: It's a tough time to be doing a series right now. It's a tough time to be emotionally involved with your baby right now. There are a number of independent companies now who are putting out a great quantity of product. And we watch various series die after four or five issues and hear "Oh well, that's all right, we'll go into another one," and I suppose that's one way just to keep yourself out there on the stands. But it's kind of a throwaway way to look at the material you're producing.

RICHARD: It's also another reason why the only comic series coming from us is *Elfquest*. Now we're also doing books because we're in the process of publishing trade books, and a book is a one-shot project. Even if it's a series of books though, you don't have the pressing monthly or bimonthly deadline. It's

scheduled, and the book comes out on this date, and then you get involved in another really different project. There's a certain ease to be had from working that way as opposed to a continuous, grinding deadline.

WENDY: I've been talking to a number of people in the industry who are beginning to feel the burden of, say, having been ten or twelve years in that grind and wondering, "Is this all there is?" We have discovered that you can go just so far in the comics field. And there comes a point where you can't really take your format any further. *Elfquest* has done everything it's possible to do with a comic book. We started out as an innovative, independent series, black and white, self published. We gained a huge readership—by the time we finished the twenty issue series, we were up to a circulation of one hundred thousand. We were the first independent series to be licensed and reprinted by a mainstream comic company, Marvel Comics. We were the first graphic novel series produced in America to be marketed through Waldenbooks and B. Dalton's. There isn't any farther that *Elfquest* can go. All we can do is repeat ourselves. That's not what we want to do. In fact, my plans for the future, as far as working on *Elfquest*, are that I don't intend to do a series in black and white, in chapters, and have it come out five months later or whatever any more. The next *Elfquest* story that I do

> *"We have discovered that you can go just so far in the comics field. There comes a point where you can't take your format any further. Elfquest has done everything it's possible to do with a comic book."*

to having the luxury of doing the work that way.

WEBER: *Can you give a little preview of what's to come?*

WENDY: You mean not just *Elfquest* projects, what else we've got going? Well, one thing I'm very excited about right now is *Law and Chaos*, which will be out in late November, early December.

RICHARD: Second half of November. This is a Father Tree Press book. I mentioned doing books earlier. In fact you've got one of our books right there, the *Gatherum*. We published that. Our first book was called *Chroma*, which was an art book

This page and opposite, three scenes from Law and Chaos

will be a nice, big, fat graphic novel, complete in its entirety, before anyone sees it. And I'm going to enjoy that much better! However long it takes to produce, I don't have to worry—

WEBER: *It'll be ready when it's ready!*

WENDY: Exactly. And it'll be very well loved by me, and I'm looking forward

dealing with the art of Alex Schomburg, who's a science fiction/comics illustrator. Well, in November, we will be doing *Law and Chaos*, which is another art book—and it's the account of Wendy's involvement with a project to single-handedly [*laughter*] animate the Michael Moorcock novel *Stormbringer*, which is

about his character Elric—I guess Elric is really the first sword-and-sorcery anti-hero.

WENDY: He was the antithesis of Conan the Barbarian. Moorcock's intention was to do a character that was the complete opposite of Conan.

RICHARD: Anyway, Elric is an archetype. Wendy was involved with the character, a very moody, philosophical character.

WENDY: I read the book when I was sixteen years old, and even before I had met Richard, I had written

to Moorcock and asked his permission to adapt it as a film project. I worked on it for about five years.

RICHARD: We've been talking here about the difficulties of doing animated films, seven million dollars, and she wanted to do one by herself [*laughs*]!

WENDY: Nobody told me I couldn't [*laughs*]!

RICHARD: Well, anyway, it turned out to be impossible to do for a number of reasons, which are gone into in the book. Wendy has provided the text. There are some hundreds of illustrations that she did that were never used but that have survived to this day.

WENDY: Full color, every page.

RICHARD: We pulled out about 120–130 of the best of these, and the book has these illustrations plus Wendy's text. It's going to the printer next week, and we're very excited about this book. People have been looking forward to it for a long time.

WENDY: It's the most personally revealing thing I have done because, in the text, I talk about—well, just as I spoke to you about the difficulties of getting the Elfquest series done, *Elfquest* was nowhere near, has never been, the kind of obsession with me that *Stormbringer* was when I was a teenager. I had literally dedicated my life to this project; this was my mystical ovation to Brahma or whatever [*laughter*]. You know, that was way back in the flower child era, and my mind was expanded, and I just thought this was great. And so everything that I did was built around

getting this film done. And I talk a lot about obsession and what that has to do with creativity and what kind of energies you channel, and what you lose when you get into the grip of an obsession. I've never talked about this in public.

RICHARD: So that's November. Next year is *Elfquest*'s tenth anniversary. The first issue of *Fantasy Quarterly* appeared in February of 1978, so 1988 is our ten-year bash, blowout, kickoff, whatever. And we've got a lot of things planned. Volume Two of the *Gatherum* will come out in 1988, around springtime. We are planning to do all future *Elfquest* color volumes ourselves. We are planning to revamp the existing *Elfquest* color volumes and publish them ourselves. So '88 looks like a very busy, very exciting year.

WENDY: And who knows, by then the film might be in production [*laughter*].

WEBER: *Which film, the Elfquest one, or—*

WENDY: The Elfquest one [*laughter*].

Stormbringer, I think someone else will do [*laughter*]. I fantasize that someone will pick up *Law and Chaos* and flip through it and say, "Why, here are our model charts, let's go"—you know, just make the film [*laughter*].

RICHARD: In which case I say, "Let's talk." [*Laughs.*]

WENDY: I think they'd better talk to Michael Moorcock first.

WEBER: *Then there'll be* Law and Chaos II, *based on...*

RICHARD: If they use your models, they talk to us.

WEBER: *I should have been a lawyer.*

WENDY: It's fascinating, isn't it?

RICHARD: Lawyers are the only ones who win anything anyway.

WEBER: *What comics do you guys read, when you have time? Any that you follow?*

RICHARD: I guess I speak for myself here—I don't follow anything. We both used to be fans in the mid and late 1960s. That was a wonderful time to be a comics fan because, particularly, Marvel was just beginning to feel its oats, and it was the new kid on the block, and it had the fresh Stan Lee–Jack Kirby–Steve Ditko feel to everything. In the early Seventies everything seemed to stagnate, and there have been ups and downs, and ups and downs, and now comics, at least as far as I'm concerned, have gotten so commercial.

WENDY: Cynical.

RICHARD: Cynical. There's such a pressure to have blockbuster hits, to create knockoffs of what the other guy's blockbuster hit is, that the good stuff is few and far between. I think that, again, for myself, I got caught up in Frank Miller's *Daredevil*, I got caught up for a while in Walt Simonson's *Thor*. I enjoyed Frank Miller's *Dark Knight*. I can say I enjoyed it without saying I agreed with it. I think I can do that. I'm kind of following to see what John Byrne does with *Superman*.

WENDY: We tend to follow what our friends in the industry do. We tend to keep up and see what they're doing. Personally, I'm thrilled right now that First Comics and Eclipse Comics are bringing out *Lone Wolf and Cub* and the *Kamui* series because, particularly the *Kamui* series, the artwork of Sanpei Shirato, was a very strong influence on the look of *Elfquest*. And *Siege at Blue Mountain* in particular is my tribute to the look of the drawing in the *Kamui* series.

RICHARD: Wendy was plowing through that series in the original Japanese *years* before Japanimation became popular in this country.

WENDY: After I'd moved back east and married Richard, I think it was in '74 or '75, we met a guy who had been living in Japan for some time. I think it was a military connection. He had a large collection of Japanese comics. Among the things he had for sale was this enormous volume, with a beautiful red cover, of the *Kamui* comics. And that was the first look I had at it. Bought it right on the spot. Didn't know what the story was about, but the tremendous cinematic storytelling! So the fact is that *Kamui* and *Lone Wolf and Cub* are available now for readers to get a really good taste of Japanese storytelling—

This page and opposite, the Japanese influence from the early adventures of Kamui.
© 1988 Viz.

for the Japanese. You see, a lot of readers are exposed now to Japanese comics and animation and movie-making that is aimed at a Western audience. And as such, that sort of stuff is very self-conscious and not really true to the Japanese mentality or to their own basic, historical way of telling the stories. *Lone Wolf and Cub* and *Kamui* are integral to the Japanese philosophy of life. Very *bushido* [*laughter*]. The translations seem to be extremely faithful, very simple, very beautiful, very tasteful, and I just think it's wonderful that these books are available in this country and so true to the Japanese philosophy.

WEBER: *And they're being accepted in the Western world.*

WENDY: They seem to be. I have no idea what the sales are, but I'm hoping.

RICHARD: Sales are probably good. The only possible fly in the ointment is that the fans of Japanimation are picking these up and seeing, only superficially, that they are a ninja story, or a samurai story. And they're not seeing the thousand of years of culture that are behind this way of storytelling and these stories. If they miss that, then they might as well not buy it, and they might as well look at *Star Blazers* again.

WENDY: To truly appreciate Japanese comics, there is so much for us to learn from their style of storytelling. You have to understand what a hand gesture means because they're different for men and women. It's almost like Kabuki, like watching a Kabuki play. Once you've learned that subtle second language to the artwork, it makes it all the more fascinating.

WEBER: *We were talking about the independents and the commercialism of comics and you're familiar with the Jon Sable soon-to-be TV series, and I understand that they're taking the comic, ending the run, and retitling it, just calling it Sable (like the TV series will be)*

and starting with #1. That sort of bothers me that they would do that. I understand the reasoning behind it...

RICHARD: Rick Obadiah is a businessman, and a good one. I've sat down and shared conversation with him. He's very savvy. I'd be willing to bet that the decisions he has made, is making, will make, are good for some aspect of the commercialization of the Sable property. Aesthetically, I don't know. I have different feelings about that. I might say, "He's going with what somebody behind a desk at a network headquarters is requesting that he do." Is he selling out? I don't know. I mean there are those who would say he is, there are those who would shrug their shoulders and say, "Who cares?"

WENDY: In the long run, it all depends on what it looks like when it gets on screen. Will Eisner made no secret of the fact that he detested *The Spirit* special [*laughs*].

RICHARD: What we hope is that we do not get to that point. When we were dealing with CBS, they made a lot of requests of us to change the concepts and feeling of *Elfquest*. Some of those requests, with the help of some good writers, we were able to accommodate. And we felt what we came up with was true. Some of the later requests, where they wanted us to go further and further and further away from what we had originally created, we finally had to throw up our hands and say, "We can't do this!"

WENDY: No, we couldn't countenance that.

RICHARD: We just can't stomach it, really. And so we didn't. That's one of the reasons why we're not on CBS Saturday morning. There's artistic rigidity, there's artistic flexibility, and then there's selling out. I think the two extremes are not good. But I think that middle ground—there's a way to stay integral to what you have, and yet work with other people to achieve an agreed-upon goal.

WENDY: The term *selling out* is a very subjective thing. We were accused of selling out simply by having Marvel reprint *Elfquest* [laughter]. In some areas, some fans were very disturbed that we didn't remain "pure."

RICHARD: That's because those fans hate Marvel.

WEBER: *And also, those fans want to be kind of cultish—it's theirs, it's their book.*

WENDY: It belongs to them.

RICHARD: And I can understand that because, back when we were reading Marvel, when it was, as I said, the new kid, the number two, "we try harder," we felt a certain betrayal, whether or not we were entitled to feel that, by Marvel's viewpoint. We felt it when they

got successful, and they started wearing their success. Now there are fans who feel about *Elfquest*, you know, "we discovered it," "you and us against the world"; but the fact that they feel that would never stop us from attempting to get *Elfquest* to a wider audience, which is why we signed the deal with Marvel.

WEBER: *One more item about commercialization and we'll go on to a couple of other areas. Have either of you seen the new* Batman: Son of the Demon *graphic novel that just came out?*

RICHARD: Yeah.

WENDY: I haven't seen it yet.

WEBER: *There's a scene in there, and maybe it's because I grew up on DC—I picked up Marvels, too, but it was mainly DC—a scene where Batman literally disrobes and goes to bed with Talia. I don't have any rational explanation for it, but it really disturbed me, even though I'm an adult and—*

WENDY: That's probably the little boy in you that grew up with Batman.

WEBER: *To do that with a character—*

WENDY: I don't see anything wrong with it [laughs].

WEBER: *I really don't either, but I can't separate the discomfort I felt—*

RICHARD: Possibly the source of that feeling is that for years and years and years and years, Batman has been a shadowy figure, mysterious. I mean he's gone through periods of being very camp and very silly, but if you go back to the origins, the idea of the Batman is a terrifying, dark figure of night. And perhaps somewhere in that mind that we all had when we started reading comics, we think that there are some things that we are not meant to know. You don't see Captain America sitting on a toilet!

WENDY: Well, I think it's also the nature of the superhero himself. If you stop to think about it, even the costume of a superhero is a closed unit. I think the Silver Surfer is the ultimate expres-

"The costume of a superhero is a closed unit. The skin-tight costume is a very enclosing kind of thing. It's constricting. And you don't tend to think of the character as flesh and blood. You think of the costume as being the character."

sion of that. He cannot have sex because he's coated with silver [*laughter*]. But the skin-tight costume is a very enclosing kind of thing. It's constricting. And you don't tend to think of the character as being flesh and blood. You think of the costume as being the character.

RICHARD: There's not a man in there. There's a foreskin there. And you know that Bruce Wayne wears a three-piece suit, and you see him walking around talking to Commissioner Gordon. But with the Batman— it's not quite Bruce Wayne in there, there's an elemental kind of force which again, going back to *Dark Knight*, that's, I think, one of the main things Frank Miller was examining. This mythological force that transcends flesh-and-bloodedness. And that may be the source of that discomfort.

WENDY: We've often gotten letters, and even with *Siege at Blue Mountain*, we get letters from people who are disturbed when we show nudity or eroticism of any kind with the characters. "I can do without it," they say. "It's okay for you to show everything else, but I can really do without all that mushy stuff." And let's face it, our society is still repressed when it comes to sexuality. We have no problem with showing blood and violence. I was just going to say about the Batman character that Batman has *bled* for us over the years many, many times [*laughter*], and in situations that could be considered subliminally erotic. Maggie Thompson and I got off on a kick, an interview that we did once, that touched on the subject of how women respond to violence and how underneath it all—

RICHARD: Suffering.

WENDY: —and suffering, as an erotic stimulus. So the Batman has done that for us, in spades, over the years. So what is really disturbing about his actual sexuality being depicted?

WEBER: *The answer is, there really isn't anything. And I wouldn't write and say, "Take it out," or I wouldn't skip that page.*

WENDY: Yeah, but you had that little twinge [*laughter*].

WEBER: *I did, and I couldn't believe I was seeing it, and I went back and checked again, and you're right, that is okay, but—*

RICHARD: We grew up and we have these impressions imbedded. I have no idea what impressions are being imbedded in the minds and creative souls of kids who are starting to read comics now, because we started back then, and you started at a certain time. You never let them go. They're always there. So if the Batman was dark and spooky and not quite human, to see him as ultimately human might be bothersome. We're friends with John Byrne. We go and eat dinner at his house, and he comes and eats dinner at our house, and I think he's a wonderful talent. But I don't know if I'll ever quite accept his *Superman* the way I fondly remember *Superman* from the late 1960s. The Weisinger stories, which are absolutely absurd and silly, but nonetheless, they represent an essence of Superman that is very important to me.

WENDY: You don't even analyze why it's important. I mean, ultimately, if you try to analyze why it's important to you, those wonderful, childish love affairs, they fall apart [*laughter*].

RICHARD: [*in a big voice*] Ah may not know comics, but Ah know what Ah like [*laughter*].

WEBER: *Let's talk about, quickly, children's entertainment. What is good on TV, what's bad, what's being done right?*

RICHARD: What's good on TV is a statue that I brought home from a flea market. It sits right on top, and it's very pretty. That's what's good on TV.

WENDY: What he means is, he bought

a nude lady with a clock in her stomach, or the equivalent [*laughter*]. What's good on TV is anything that has to do with real human experience. One of the things that I wanted to say on the radio interview earlier that I didn't get a chance to was that we don't believe children should be protected from anything. We think that everything, in proportion and in perspective, is appropriate in children's storytelling, even unto violence and eroticism.

WEBER: *When you say this, do you mean children's storytelling, or...*

WENDY: Well, storytelling for all ages, actually, but storytelling that is accessible to children. *Elfquest* is not aimed at any particular age group. Our audience tends to be in the high school/adult age group.

RICHARD: But it is accessible to everyone.

WENDY: It's accessible to children, and they interpret it on their level. We don't feel that any element of life is inappropriate in the telling of a good yarn. Whether it's dealing with questions of morals, responsibility to society—

RICHARD: Love, life, death.

WENDY: Love, life, death, all of those things that are universal experiences are appropriate for children to handle, and they can handle it, provided that it's done in proportion, with perspective, with guidance. We give our younger readers some difficult things to deal with sometimes. For instance, one of

> "**W**e don't feel that children should be protected from controversy; we don't feel that children should be protected from thinking. And any storytelling that prevents you from thinking is not good storytelling."

the major themes in *Siege at Blue Mountain* right now, in a very subtle way, is child abuse. And it's done in such a way that different age groups can perceive what we're saying about child abuse at different levels. And what we are hoping is that this sparks discussion among people who trust each other, whether it's parents and children, friends and friends, teenagers among themselves, whatever. We don't feel that children should be protected from controversy; we don't feel that children should be protected from thinking. And any storytelling that prevents you from thinking is not good storytelling.

RICHARD: Unfortunately, that's most of what's on television, whether it's prime time, Saturday morning, weekday afternoon, or you name it.

WENDY: The toy companies don't want you to think. They want you to buy. So Filmation does "Marshal Bravestarr" or Rankin/Bass does "Thundercats." And they do stories with heavy-handed morals as a sop to the parents. And after the story's done, the characters come out and tell you what the moral was, even though the child at age two is smart enough to get what the moral message was. It's all a sop to the parents so that they will say, "Oh, that's good stuff, I'll go out and buy the toy. It's okay." Antithink.

WEBER: *Is there anything on TV you would let children watch? You don't have any children.*

RICHARD: We do not have children, and again, for myself, I watch very little television. So I couldn't tell you. Honestly, I'd like to be in the position of helping to get *Elfquest* on, and I could point to that and say, "Yeah, I think that's good." [*Laughs.*] I'm only being half-egotistical here. There are shows, I guess, that are highly praised by people, perhaps "The Cosby Show," which deals with a family situation. Or

"Family Ties," which deals with, from time to time, issues that face kids. I guess perhaps I'm cynical, though, in that I think if a child—and that can be anywhere from three through eighteen—receives a half-hour dose of something that could be considered good once a week, that's not enough. It doesn't stick. It doesn't last. Unless it simply reinforces what's already in that person's life. There's a family structure, or some kind of support structure: *that* reinforces.

WENDY: And the kids, as inarticulate as they sometimes are, are telling the producers and creators, just as they've been telling us all these years that we've been doing with *Elfquest* exactly what they want. I think more interaction of parents with children, more conversation, will make kids more trusting and more able to say what they want without worrying about getting slapped in the mouth. But kids write to us, they write to other comics creators and tell people what they like. They like the feeling of family and belonging. They like the feeling of a value system.

They like the feeling of a direction. They like the feeling that a character might grow and learn after making a mistake and that there isn't a punishment for all time. They really do relate to that. That's what they want.

WEBER: *Here's a scary thought. Is that—the value system and the feeling of family—is fantasy the only place the kids can get that?*

WENDY: Sometimes. That's why they become fantasy junkies. You go to a convention, you know who they are: the "moonshots," the ones that drift around with that look in their eyes. You can spot them a mile away. They are the ones who live through fantasy because life is simply too unbearable for them. They get addicted to it. It's like a drug. And I really feel bad when creators put down fans and talk about them as, you know, lump them all together into that moonshot class. I feel very strongly for these lost ones, as irritating as they can be, as much as they can get on your nerves, I feel very sorry that this is their only source of feeling that they belong to something,

Two-Edge: Child abuse on the World of Two Moons.

that they live in fandom because they don't have family at home, or an ability to talk to friends, or whatever.

WEBER: *It becomes their family.*

WENDY: It becomes their family. The Star Trek junkies, the Doctor Who junkies, the Elfquest junkies, they're all out there. And they are all sucking off something that's giving them a sense of purpose. I don't think this is healthy. I don't think this is right, and I speak from experience because I went that route with Elric when I was a kid. I wouldn't encourage any kid to become an Elfquest junkie, or any other kind of junkie. Proportion is what we're talking about. We were just talking about that earlier. Proportion in all ways, in storytelling; any story that has an ax to grind is going to burn itself out eventually, like the nihilistic comics that Richard was talking about earlier. Any ax to

THE RIDDLE WAITS, GROWS MORE PROFOUND THROUGH THREE TURNS OF THE SEASONS.

THOSE WHO WILL HELP TO SOLVE IT KNOW NOTHING, YET, OF THE ROLES THEY WILL PLAY.

While some parents felt that the violence was all right, eroticism, as in the above scene, was taboo.

grind eventually has its limits. Human experience doesn't.

WEBER: *I also wanted to ask you about the labeling/rating controversy. I think I have an idea where you stand.*

RICHARD: Well, I think the whole flap that happened when DC announced its rating system has been done to death. Basically, my feeling on that is, I'm in agreement with the people who walked out, who said that they walked out not because there was a rating system being considered, but because it had been considered and imposed without any input from them. In other words, their work was going to have this thing done to it without any input from them. That was wrong. I think ratings are a silly idea because I don't see how the heck they can be consistent. I have a difficult time envisioning a title like *Spider-Man* having a consistent rating. To borrow the movie ratings, let's say *Spider-Man* is assigned a PG-13. That

means that every story must fall within the bounds of a PG-13 comic book story. That means you can't have a gentle, G-rated *Spider-Man* story, and you can't have something grittier that would gain it an R. You can't do it with a series. I have absolutely no problem with advisories. We used advisories once on *Elfquest*. An advisory is just a little note that says this contains such-and-so and such-and-so. This contains violence, this contains some scenes of nudity, this contains adult themes, however you want to word it: some bit of communication from publisher to consumer. That doesn't bother me in the least. Ratings—I don't think it's ever gonna happen in the comics. You see books now that say "for mature readers," but that's an advisory. That's not a rating. The ratings thing is mostly hot air, and it's going to dissipate before we're really aware it was an issue. You watch. ✧

Kings of the Broken Wheel

Interview by Patrick Daniel O'Neill

The Hunan Balcony East is one of my favorite restaurants in the lower midtown area of New York City. So when Richard and Wendy Pini agreed to meet me outside Marvel Comics' offices on Park Avenue South just a few blocks away, we set out for this Chinese restaurant for our lunch and interview. After ordering, while waiting for the food to arrive, Wendy showed me the make-readies for her second Beauty and the Beast graphic novel from First Comics. Hence, the interview begins with a discussion of that project.

PATRICK DANIEL O'NEILL: *Since we've just finished looking at the Beauty and the Beast graphic novel,* Night of Beauty, *let's start there: You say you started this before the TV series aired its first episode of the final season in which Catherine died.*

WENDY PINI: It was interesting. Ron Koslow, producer of "Beauty and the Beast," was very satisfied with *Portrait* of Love, my first graphic novel. There was about a month that went by while I was involved in other things, and then First and I began to talk about doing a second graphic novel. Within a couple of weeks, I submitted a story which was sort of a standard "Beast and robbers" kind of story. Koslow was sort of lukewarm about it. "If you want to do this, you can," he said. Then I spoke with him and he told me, in some detail, what was going to happen in the third season and needless to say, I was stunned.

I was able to see, however, a copy of the teleplay of the movie in which Catherine meets her end. Out of that grew this story. Essentially, it's Orpheus in reverse: Vincent goes into the after-life to see Catherine, but his motives are quite different: instead of bringing her back, he has to send her further in. It's a great sacrifice, a great love story. Ron Koslow was very happy with it, and I was given total freedom with it, once he accepted the script. I flew with it as though they were my own characters.

RICHARD PINI: He also gave you a hell of a compliment there; he said he wished he had the money to do this as the movie instead of what they did.

WENDY: No, not instead of—he wished they could have made a two-hour movie out of this to sort of put the cap on Vincent and Catherine's relationship.

We had an unlimited budget with the graphic novel for special effects. [*Laughs.*]

O'NEILL: *That's one of the wonderful things about doing sf and fantasy in comics. You never have to worry, "How much is it going to cost to peel away someone's skull or put wings on a horse and make it fly?" It costs the same as it costs to draw anything else: however much pencil and ink you use!*

WENDY: In the afterword that I wrote for *Night of Beauty,* I described the phone call from Ron in which he said, "I wish we could do this one," and I wheedled, "Can't we scrape together a few million dollars?" And he cracked up, saying it would cost considerably

more than a few. [*Laughs.*]

O'NEILL: *Well, if anyone ever wants to do a big-screen version of "Beauty and the Beast," you've got the script.*

WENDY: I think nobody wanted to watch Cathy die. The feeling I had doing this story was that maybe it would help some people who were deeply affected by it to mourn her. You'd get to see her one more time and say goodbye.

RICHARD: I think it's good that it comes out after the show has gone off the air because on one of the computer bulletin board systems, someone made the comment that not only did they not want to see Cathy die, but they didn't want to see her do it week after week, because it's in the opening. I think this writes a very nice *finis* to the series.

O'NEILL: *Particularly since the producers didn't get to write one of their own.*

WENDY: No, Linda Hamilton wanted

The Palace awakens: Timmain is called home (from *Kings of the Broken Wheel*).

to leave the show; she had her baby, and from what I've heard, everything's fine there. I guess they were expecting her to do a few more episodes than she eventually ended up doing, so they really had to make a major shift for the third season and put Cathy out of the picture within that one film. There was a lot of scrambling going on last sum-

The Beauty and the Beast: Catherine and Vincent.

mer in the "Beauty and the Beast" offices.

O'NEILL: *Let's move back to* Elfquest.
RICHARD: What's that?
O'NEILL: *Sure, a strange topic to be discussing with Richard and Wendy Pini. I'm clear on this because I've known you people for a long time, but I think a lot of readers are not clear on the fact that Elfquest is a joint project, that it's not just*

Wendy Pini who does Elfquest.
WENDY: Really?
O'NEILL: *Yeah, when I talk to people about it, they say, "Oh, that's Wendy Pini's book." And I have to correct them, "No, it's Richard and Wendy Pini."*
WENDY: That's interesting because Richard travels a great deal more than I do and makes more appearances at conventions than I do. I tend to get the impression that he is now the voice of Elfquest.
O'NEILL: *He's the spokesperson, but they see you as the person whose work is visible, I guess.*
RICHARD: You do the work and I exploit it.
WENDY: Let's set that record straight in this interview! [*Laughter.*]
RICHARD: We're having a great deal of fun with this new series [*Kings of the Broken Wheel*]. We worked closely together on the first series; we were not able to work so closely together on the second series [*Siege at Blue Mountain*] because there were things happening outside of—but connected to—*Elfquest* that had us both under a lot of pressure. Now we're back to having a whole lot of fun working together.
WENDY: It's so nice to have Richard back. If people don't realize that it's a joint effort, I can't stress too strongly how important he is to the plotline, because his feedback makes it go in directions I never would have thought of.
O'NEILL: *Do you see a difference in* Siege at Blue Mountain *because Richard was less involved?*
WENDY: Yes, for that reason, and for many others as well. *Siege at Blue Mountain* was a team effort. My inker was Joe Staton, my letterer was Janice Chang, and that was unusual in itself, since I did the lettering and inking myself in the first series, with occasional assistance. And, of course, Richard was very much occupied with other things. We still had our story

sessions, and he still edited each chapter as it came out.

But *Siege* was a very different effort, because it was an eight-part story, not open-ended or very long like the first one. It had a specific goal: We were essentially doing a story about child abuse and we had eight chapters in which to tell it. It was much more tightly focused on a single topic than we had done before.

RICHARD: With the original series, we had the luxury of letting the number of issues expand to take up whatever story we came up with. Way back, we had originally announced it as fifteen issues; it grew to twenty. We had the luxury to do that.

Siege at Blue Mountain was announced as a particular length. Each issue of *Siege* is very jam-packed, because we had a certain amount of story to get into eight issues. This is unlike both the first series and the new series.

O'NEILL: *So it's not quite as leisurely.*

WENDY: Absolutely. One of the elements I think some people missed was individual characterization. *Elfquest*'s following has different favorite characters, and they demand that each of these characters get his or her moment in the spotlight. We weren't really able to do that as much in *Siege* as we were before or will now.

I go back and look at *Siege* and I'm very happy with a great deal of it; it was great to work with Joe. He has a feel for cartooning that very few inkers who also do realistic work have. He has a nice fluid line; it's uncluttered and organic, which is something I've always appreciated in his work. Add to that, that he did a scathing satire of *Elfquest* for another company.

O'NEILL: *Wasn't it on First's version of* E-Man?

RICHARD: Issue #7.

O'NEILL: *Marty Pasko wrote it, didn't he? He wrote all those scathing satires in the early First issues of* E-Man.

RICHARD: "Smeltquest" was the title.

O'NEILL: *He mixed them with the Smurfs, right?*

WENDY: Most people do when they satirize *Elfquest*.

Working with Joe was tremendous; he really knew what he was doing. What I found was that our energies combined, because we're both very energetic artists and our work is very vigorous. The two combined was so... the word I guess I'm looking for is "explosive"... that it just spills all out of corners. [*Laughter.*] I tended to change my drawing style a little bit because I was in tune with Joe's. I think he tended to change his inking style.

> "**W**endy does the work and I exploit it."

O'NEILL: *I know people who normally ink their own work have a tendency to leave some of the drawing for the ink stage. Did you find yourself putting those in again or leaving them out and having them come out differently in Staton's style?*

WENDY: It got to the point where if I forgot something in the pencils, Joe would remember to put that detail in when he inked it. It must have been a heck of a job for him because we had thousands and thousands of characters in that series. He took it on like a trouper.

O'NEILL: *He inked the Avengers at one time; it can't have been any worse.*

RICHARD: That's true.

WENDY: I think the thing that made the artwork in *Siege* the most different from the art in the original series was the quality of constant movement. There was almost no resting place: constantly energetic and very frantic.

O'NEILL: *How did you come to call it* Kings of the Broken Wheel?

RICHARD: We've already had one person ask, "Are you gonna get Gene

Autrey to do the music?" [*Laughter.*] I suppose it does sound a little bit like a Western, but the subtitle is drawn from clues we scattered throughout *Siege* and the original *Elfquest.* When we were setting up those plot elements, Wendy was talking about the things she wanted to have happen in the first issue, and my reaction was, "Wait a minute! We don't have a boundary; I think maybe there are too many things happening in the first issue. If we remove this one and just concentrate on these, we can do some wonderful things with development."

WENDY: I had to shift mental gears and realize we're doing an open-ended series again.

O'NEILL: *The change, from an open-ended series in* Elfquest *to a limited series in* Siege at Blue Mountain—*do you see that as a response to the changes in the direct sales market? I see the direct sales market as having become more structured, with the people who do the ordering looking for a set number of issues, etc.*

WENDY: Hmmmmm...

RICHARD: To a certain extent that's true.

WENDY: Do you think it might have been almost a subconscious response?

RICHARD: I think it was at least partly conscious. At that time, there were a lot of four- and six- and eight-issue series. That single digit number type. It was at the time we started *Siege* that the connection between Warp Graphics and Apple Comics began, because Warp just wanted to create comics and Apple was going to be the entity which published them.

> "**W**e've already had one person ask, 'Are you gonna get Gene Autrey to do the music [to Kings of the Broken Wheel]?'"

We were talking in a business sense about a given period of time in which things should happen. I think those two factors, taken together, dictated an eight-issue concept.

If we had discovered halfway through that it wanted to be ten issues, we might have gone to ten, but it wasn't going to grow like Topsy after that.

WENDY: Once again, *Siege* had a very specific goal. It had a simple plot, a villain to defeat, and a baby to get back—all in eight issues.

RICHARD: I guess we owe the Poughkeepsie Galleria Mall a certain amount of credit for the genesis of the idea that *Kings* is a big story that's going to go on for a long time. We had some ideas about *Kings of the Broken Wheel,* and we go to this mall often because they have good fast food. We'll walk up and down the corridors and bounce ideas off each other.

We were doing that one evening when one or the other—or both of us—suddenly got a wild idea. We looked at each other and started "what iffing" all over the place. The story went from quart size to 55-gallon–drum size. We realized we had a tiger by the tail—and it was a very exciting one.

WENDY: What's gotten me the most excited about this is that I've fallen in love with *Elfquest* all over again, but on a grander scale. Whatever it is or was that people like about *Elfquest,* they're just going to get more of it this time. It's gonna be more lush, more emotional, more dramatic, more humorous.

O'NEILL: *That brings up an interesting question: How do you, after almost eleven or twelve years of working on this one basic concept, maintain your own enthusiasm?*

WENDY: It's like a marriage. Like they say in The Four Seasons, "You have your peaks and you have your valleys." [*Laughter.*] There are times, of course, when you have to work through a writer's block or an artist's block because you have a schedule to meet, and that's hard. But—how can I put this?—it seems like I can't remember a time when we weren't doing *Elfquest* together. It's like having a child. There have been times when we've been tired of it or not in tune with it, but the kid's home and we're delighted. Right now, we're just in love with all the possibilities.

RICHARD: Again, from late '85 to late '88, there were events surrounding *Elfquest* of a legal nature that were very draining of energy. It's difficult to do any work under circumstances like those we found ourselves in. Now, we own *Elfquest* lock, stock, and barrel; we're working together; we have our mechanism set up for printing and distribution. It's all done but the doing. All of that stuff being set up allows us to just focus on telling the story, which is a lot of fun.

WENDY: I find what's happening with the artwork in the first chapter is that there are a lot of silent panels in which we just take advantage of the characters' facial expressions or actions. That goes back to the leisurely idea of letting the reader absorb at his own pace what the character might be thinking or feeling, without spoon-feeding it to him.

RICHARD: Also, there's a return to the "business."

I can go back and read *Elfquest* now, years later, and find things that Wendy drew in there that I missed the first 150 readings. Now that I'm doing it for the 151st time, I look and say, "Oh!"

And I'll go to her and ask, "Did you do that on purpose?" And she'll smile at me like I'm some sort of chimp, saying, "Just figured that out now, did you?" [*Wendy laughs.*]

O'NEILL: *I can remember being in an English lit class and asking the instructor, "Did the author really mean to put that in there so we'd remember it when we get to page 127?" Sometimes the instructor would say, "Yes, of course he did," and other times he'd say, "That depends. Give him the benefit of the doubt."*

WENDY: I have to confess that sometimes Richard finds things and asks if I did it on purpose, and I answer, "No! I don't even remember doing that!"

RICHARD: Note to the transcriber: We are taking a fried dumpling break.

O'NEILL: [*through a mouthful*] *Since I'm undoubtedly the transcriber, that's not necessary.*

WENDY: [*noticing that the restaurant is playing Bette Midler's "Wind Beneath My Wings.*] How did this song ever win a Grammy? I hate the ending; I wish she would just stop!

O'NEILL: *She does drag it on forever, doesn't she?*

Getting into the business side a little, Richard: We delayed this interview because you were on your way to the West Coast to talk about other things that were going on, that might affect not only Elfquest in other media, but even Elfquest in print. What can you make public?

RICHARD: I was spending several days hanging my nose over the shoulders of people who were demonstrating very powerful new computer colorizing systems to me. If anyone is at all familiar with Macintosh color computers or Commodore color computers, they know that there are programs that allow you to draw and paint color illustrations. This software has gotten tremendously powerful—witness Ted Turner and colorization. Whatever you may think of it, it's a powerful piece of programming.

We are working with a producer on the West Coast who will take the existing artwork from the original *Elfquest* series and turn it into four storyteller-type videos, the first of which will be ready in June. They will be distributed through video stores.

LATER...LONG INTO THE NIGHT...

Kings of the Broken Wheel—a time of loss...

O'NEILL: *So this will largely be still pictures, fading in and out?*

RICHARD: We're not trying to say to anyone that these are animated cartoons. That's why I use the phrase "storyteller." If you go into a video store, you can find tapes that consist of narration over illustrations from a book, with some manipulation of the images, along with music and sound effects.

This is a large and growing market—"kideo video"—and if we can tap into that, we achieve two goals: We get Elfquest as a concept recognized by a much larger audience than we now have and we open that audience to the idea of other Elfquest things.

In order to do this easily, they are scanning the artwork into the computer memory and then manipulating it with these powerful programs—taking out the word balloons and putting in color. Once that's done, they can do anything they bloody well want with it.

WENDY: They can even do a little bit of animation, which is really exciting.

O'NEILL: *Yes, I've seen some of this done: they can isolate a piece of the picture and make it move. They can't do anything very intricate, but they can certainly make an arm move from waist to shoulder level.*

WENDY: They can do marvelous things with color. They can fade a daytime sky to a nighttime sky; they can do reflections in water—things like that.

That part of the visit is fairly straight forward. These people are working on this right now. They also wanted to know whether or not it would be possible to scan Wendy's art from *Kings of the Broken Wheel,* colorize it in computer, and then print out separations—film negatives—to send directly to the printer. All rather than coloring the pages in the traditional manner, photo- or laser-separating them in the traditional manner, and then sending those negatives to the printer.

We went back and forth on that for several days. While the coloring effects are quite amazing and very beautiful to look at, we decided against—at least at the present time—doing it that way, because even at a fine scan resolution, you get a dot pattern that will wipe out some of the very fine detail work Wendy does with brush and ink. We couldn't have that.

So, for at least *Elfquest Book Seven*, the first four or five issues of *Kings of the Broken Wheel*—which we hope to have out in November or December—we'll have the coloring done right here in New York by Chelsea Animation, who did the work on the first six [*Elfquest graphic novels*].

O'NEILL: *DC is using some kind of a computer coloring system on some of its books, notably Doom Patrol. I don't think they're scanning the artwork to create the black plate—that's still being shot from the artwork in the traditional manner—but they are scanning it in to do the coloring on computer and spitting out the other three plates as direct film negs.*

RICHARD: There are systems available now that make it borderline economical to do coloring in that way. It was not economically feasible for us to do *Elfquest* in that way because Marvel and DC mostly use a fairly limited palette.

For *Elfquest* we have a much broader spectrum.

WENDY: We're looking for subtle shadings.

O'NEILL: *I'll point out that the palette on the books DC is computer coloring is considerably broader than that on its hand-colored books because they have a greater range of screens available.*

WENDY: Let's face it, it's still more or less an experimental process. I don't think everybody knows that the last scene of *The Little Mermaid* was the first animation colorized by computer.

O'NEILL: *I knew they had animated a good deal of* Mermaid *on computer as they had* Great Mouse Detective.

WENDY: But the last scene of *Mermaid*—with the big crowd scene which would have taken painters a long time

to paint—is colorized by computer. It's not noticeably different from the rest of the film, but it is still experimental. There's a long way to go with it.

RICHARD: Of course, when you're Disney and you have—

O'NEILL: *Deep pockets.* [Laughter.]

RICHARD: *Very* deep pockets, and Mickey Mouse bucks to burn, you can do that. If we had an unlimited budget, I'd say we'd do it that way.

WENDY: I wouldn't be so quick to say we would brush Chelsea Animation off. I was very happy with the job they did, and I love the look of animation colors on the *Elfquest* artwork.

It simply reinforces the thought that *Elfquest* was always done with animation in mind. People keep asking us, "When are you gonna come out with a film?" and our answer has always been, "When we can find a studio that will not take it and change it into "Elf Mutant Ninja Turtles," or "Thunder-Elves" or whatever and keep its integrity! Until that time, we think these videos are a nice stepping stone. People will have the artwork that they love and are familiar with, and something very close to the original story.

RICHARD: Kevin and Pete, nothing personal!

WENDY: We love you, Kevin and Pete! [*Laughter.*]

O'NEILL: *I take it the videos will be done with actors doing the voices of the characters, someone reading the narration along with music and sound effects.*

WENDY: Won't that be fun?

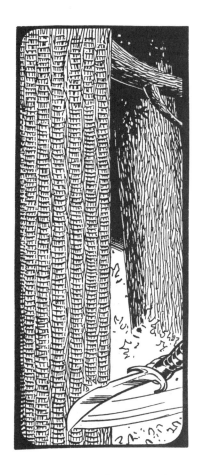

...And a time of long waiting.

O'NEILL: *Do you have a time frame for the release of the first of the videos?*

RICHARD: The first one will be out no later than June 1st. We're looking to have all four out by year's end. We'd like to have the first new video—taken from the *Kings of the Broken Wheel* material—out sometime around the release of the color book.

WENDY: One thing we didn't tell you about *Kings of the Broken Wheel* is that we are breaking away completely from *Elfquest's* traditional landscape. In *Kings*, we're not only going to play with different locations on this world we've created, we're also going to play with time, so things will be happening not only in faraway places we've never seen before on the World of Two Moons, but also at different times.

This is done, of course, with the possibility of *Elfquest* expanding into other media. But I'm excited about it because I get to draw some wonderful new things and put the characters in wonderful new costumes and have them deal with stuff they've never, ever dealt with or even conceived of dealing with.

RICHARD: Basically, the idea behind *Kings of the Broken Wheel*—which you're going to have to abbreviate "KOBW: 99.9 FM on your dial"—is "Guys, you think you know what it's like to be on a quest; you don't know nothin'!"

O'NEILL: *Let's talk about your other project, Richard, adapting Piers Anthony's Xanth novels into comics form. What led you specifically to those as a project?*

RICHARD: I am very skeptical of adaptations. I've seen, as have we all, hundreds of them done and, in my humble opinion, very few of them have been done really well and effectively. A lot of them have been all right; some have been done poorly. But I'm generally skeptical of them because, if something works well in one medium, the chances of it working well in another are inherently slim.

We did the Mythadventures adaptations, and we had a lot of fun doing that, but ultimately it sort of just petered out. Xanth is a series I've been reading for a little while, and of all the science fiction and fantasy that I have read—at least recently—these stories *feel* the most like Elfquest feels. They are to a large degree written for a juvenile audience; grownup readers can enjoy the heck out of them, but I think they're written for a juvenile audience, and so is Elfquest.

WENDY: Young adults.

RICHARD: Young adults.

I've known about Xanth for a long time, and I've known about Piers Anthony for a long time, and I've felt like Xanth is like Elfquest for a long time, but it wasn't until recently that those pieces of thought came together.

I met Piers Anthony about five years ago at an American Booksellers Association show, and we chatted for a few minutes about this and that. I knew about his work and he knew about Elfquest. His daughters were big fans of Elfquest. At that time, he mentioned—just off the cuff—the idea of Xanth in graphic novel form the way Elfquest is in graphic novel form. I said, "Yeah, wouldn't that be a wonderful idea" and promptly forgot about it.

About three years ago, I contacted him to do a story for us for *Blood of Ten Chiefs,* the Elfquest anthology series, and again didn't follow up on the Xanth graphic novel idea. Then last fall, I got a letter from him, asking permission to incorporate some Elfquest elements into his newest Xanth novel, *Isle of View.* If you know anything about Xanth,

> **"I**n *Kings of the Broken Wheel* we're not only going to play with different locations, we're going to play with time."

you know it's a pun-filled world. Say that fast and it's "I love you." He needed to have an elf character who could move around. In Xanth, the elves can't move around much because the further they get away from their elf elm trees, the weaker they get; this elf needed to move all over the world.

The reason he needed this character is because he'd gotten a letter from the mother of a twelve-year-old girl who'd been badly injured by a drunk driver. He entered into a correspondence with this girl—and the fact that she was and is a fan of Xanth and Elfquest and was getting letters from Piers Anthony really helped in her recovery. I should say "has helped," because she has a long period of recovery left.

Piers decided to put her into the next Xanth novel as an elf. But, since he needed that elf to go all over the world, Xanth elves wouldn't do. He reasoned, "She also loves Elfquest, maybe I can make her a visiting Elfquest elf." He wrote to us, and we said we'd love to, please feel free.

So, the new Xanth novel, out in paperback in November, is actually an Elfquest-Xanth crossover novel.

In the course of our correspondence about this, I mentioned that I was enjoying the Xanth series, wouldn't it be wonderful if they were in graphic novel form, and Piers said, "Don't you remember...?" And he also paid us a very high compliment when he said, "If anyone were going to do the Xanth graphic novels, I'd want it to be the Elfquest people."

He twisted my arm, and I said I'd love to do that; then it was just a matter of putting together the team. I'll tell you—I knew I wanted to try and get Dennis Fujitake, because I'd seen his work on *Dalgoda* and *Retief,* and he has a wonderful, fresh, lively, fluid style that I thought would work perfectly with the young adult nature of the Xanth

stories. So I contacted him, and he said he'd be happy to do it. He lives two blocks away from Gary Kato who's doing the coloring, and wheels are turning; it's a wonderful project and a lot of fun.
WENDY: I just saw the first few pages of the Xanth graphic novel last week and felt tears coming, because the artwork is absolutely charming—and absolutely in tune with the level of the stories.

I have to admit Dennis surprised me. When Richard said he was getting Dennis, I tended to think of him more in terms of his *Dalgoda* work.
O'NEILL: *Which is sort of technological.*
WENDY: But he does have what I would call—and I hope he's not offended by this—a feminine sensibility that applies very well to the organic nature of fantasy. It's coming through beautifully in his first Xanth novel. I'm excited; I can't wait to begin reading this.
RICHARD: We'll adapt *Isle of View* in three volumes, the first out in June. That excites me no end because I think even Xanth fans who are not comics fans will be attracted to this, because it's the first installment of the new book that they won't get to read in prose for another five months. I'm hoping to attract a lot of people who are not comics aficionados into comics—at least appraising, if not buying—with this.

The second volume will be out around about the time the paperback comes out, and the third next spring.

Then we have a wonderful option open to us: We can continue to adapt the new books Piers is writing, always

"**I am very skeptical of adaptations. If something works well in one medium, the chances of it working well in another are inherently slim.**"

staying a jump ahead of the paperback publication; or we can go back and adapt the earlier novels; or—god help us all—we can try to do both!

It's very exciting, and it's good for

Chex Centaur and Jenny Elf size each other up for the first time (in the Xanth Graphic Novel #1: *Return to Centaur*).

Warp Graphics because it feels like Elfquest, and I don't want to do lots and lots of projects. I will limit the things we do to those projects that feel comfortable. If we can be said to have a company outlook or feel, it's characterized by Elfquest and Xanth. I wouldn't want to do big robots.

WENDY: If you think about it, there really aren't too many fantasy comics out right now. I think it's fortunate that Warp Graphics has made itself known to generally non-comics readers through *Elfquest,* whether through *Blood of Ten Chiefs,* the graphic novels, or someone passing on the comic series to someone who has never read a comic book before.

A great deal of *Elfquest*'s audience is in among the science fiction and fantasy readers, who don't generally frequent comic book shops. They will find out, through information in *Elfquest* and through talking to people who read *Elfquest* regularly, about the other things that Father Tree Press is doing. And because of the association with Piers Anthony, it will again be among the realm of people who don't usually read comics.

The same thing happened with Beauty and the Beast. Most of the people I'm getting feedback from, most of the letters First is sending on to me, are from people who never picked up a comic book in their lives. They happen to like the TV show and gave the book a try. They say, "I had no idea that comic books could be like this."

O'NEILL: *I want to go back to the video project for a moment because something occurred to me as you were discussing the young adult target audience for both Elfquest and Xanth.*

What do you see as the audience for the Elfquest videos? Young adults or the pre-school through first grade audience usually attracted to that kind of thing?

RICHARD: I think it's the younger audience: six to eight, six to ten years old. I'm terrible at trying to parse people the way.

O'NEILL: *The way marketers do?*

RICHARD: Right. The videos are geared for young kids. That's good enough for me—5 $\frac{1}{4}$ to 5 $\frac{3}{4}$? [*Laughter.*] If *Elfquest* as published equates to *Batman* as it...as published in the 70s, then these videos—and this is not pejorative—equate somewhat to "Superfriends," as Batman was portrayed on Saturday morning TV. We don't have anything to equate to *Dark Knight*.

That's the shift. The videotapes will certainly make reference to the existence of the books.

WENDY: And the books will be noted to be young adult reading.

RICHARD: I think people will understand that Elfquest does exist on a variety of levels, in terms of the maturity of its presentation.

O'NEILL: *I remember during the original publication of Elfquest, a couple of times you got letters from people who were upset because this was a story they had been reading to their children, and suddenly there was an element they found inappropriate to expose their children to.*

WENDY: And it was *very* interesting what they found inappropriate. The violence was fine with them. It was the sexual things that bothered them.

O'NEILL: *Have you thought at all about the need to edit the story for the videos because of that problem?*

RICHARD: The videos will be edited. Consider that we're taking twenty issues worth of material and putting it onto four half-hour videos. These youngsters, who are coming upon these tapes for the first time, will get the entire story of Elfquest from start to finish—but I'd say we have pared as much as two-thirds of the subplots out of this treatment for the videotapes.

They will be perfectly geared to that age audience.

WENDY: Characters' motives will be portrayed as much simpler, much less in shades of gray than in the published version of Elfquest. Trolls are bad because they're trolls; there's no more explanation needed.

RICHARD: The die-hard Elfquest fans will probably shriek bloody murder for a number of reasons, one of which being, "but you cut so much!"

WENDY: Don't be too hard on the die-hard Elfquest fans; they're a pretty intelligent bunch.

RICHARD: Well, whoever it is that will scream bloody murder will do so—and you know that someone will. The point being that whoever protests will not understand what is necessary to take it from the comic format into the video format.

But we are satisfied with the adaptation. It serves its purpose well.

O'NEILL: *What are your working methods like on Elfquest?*

WENDY: We have it down to a pretty simple system.

RICHARD: Actually, it's different now.

WENDY: Yes, because of the computer, there's quite a big difference.

RICHARD: We've gone high-tech. [*Laughter.*]

WENDY: We both have Mac Pluses that talk to each other. The traditional thing we still do is go to a shopping mall or on a long drive and have our plotting sessions. After that's done, I sit down and write the script. That goes into Richard's computer, he edits it, we discuss it. Then, very simply, I print out the edited script and begin to do breakdowns and pencils.

I do a page a day, penciled and inked. I'm barely penciling; I go directly to inks, practically. I can draw these characters in my sleep by now.

If we discover that there is some artwork that tells the story and dialogue is not needed, that will be shaped out of the script afterwards.

> "It was *very* interesting what [people] found inappropriate [for their children]. The violence was fine with them. It was the sexual things that bothered them."

O'NEILL: *Do you find as you're drawing that there are sometimes scenes that should have been included in the script that were not? Does the path of the story alter as you draw it?*

RICHARD: That would happen, probably, during the plotting/scriptwriting phase. It hasn't happened yet, but we're still working on the first issue. It

Cutter and Petalwing get acqainted.

certainly could. That's one of the very nice things about being able to have linked computers.

WENDY: I do recall discovering what I thought was a plot hole. I called Richard and said, "Why is this character here? Why doesn't he do *this* at this point?" We had to discuss it and figure it out; it was vital to the scene. As it turned out, it's important that that character do nothing at that point, to bring forward his particular problem in the plot.

O'NEILL: So, *unlike the way most comics are done, you're inking before the lettering is done. Richard, you're now lettering on computer?*

RICHARD: This is wonderful! Last year at the San Diego Comics Expo, before the convention, I got to talking with David Cody Weiss, who is working at Disney. He had developed comics lettering typefaces; he had this whole system by which he could overlay the balloon, with the lettering, onto the scanned artwork. He could place the balloons anywhere he wanted, move them around, and then print out just the lettering and balloons.

He could then cut the balloons out and paste them to the finished art or give the page of balloons to the printer with the art with instructions to combine them to make the black plate.

I was just amazed at how good it looked. So I asked if it was available to we mere mortals. He said yes, so I licensed the software from him—it's proprietary, he owns it—and I've been learning how to do comic book lettering.

I can't letter worth beans by hand, but on the Mac I can do it and it looks professional.

O'NEILL: *I believe he does lettering for DC and I heard mention that he was working by computer. On one of those computer networks we discussed before, Jim Massara, a letterer, was talking about something like this as well. He said once you have the letter forms in the computer, it's much simpler to just type the words in than to have to sit and carefully use a pen.*

WENDY: And you never have to worry about correcting blobs of ink or misspellings.

RICHARD: There's a spell-checker built in. Anybody with the right software, could create his or her own distinctive lettering and use it. David has done this very well; he has two different styles of lettering.

WENDY: Here's something we haven't talked about: Janice Chang created the ultimate preserver lettering. Is there any way to incorporate that into the system, or do we have to go back to Janice for that?

O'NEILL: *Is there a way to scan a new font into the system?*

RICHARD: Now, *that* is an interesting question.

O'NEILL: *That's one of the things that people talked about on the computer net. Is it possible to do an alphabet by hand and then incorporate it into the software? So that, for example, by hitting the right function keys, you'd be operating in the preserver alphabet?*

RICHARD: There is at least one program with which you can do that now.

WENDY: If you scan artwork, why can't you scan lettering and then reproduce on a Xerox?

RICHARD: Because in a computer you hit the *A* key and it goes into memory and makes the image of an *A* on the screen. If I scan that *A,* it says, "Here is a picture of an *A.*"

O'NEILL: *You have to have some way of taking that picture and making it come out when you strike the* A *key?*

RICHARD: Right. Right now, it's just a block of artwork, the same as any other picture is.

WENDY: I'm saying you could use Xerox. You could have one printout of the alphabet and use the copies.

O'NEILL: *You could even go to some-place like Letraset, which will make up special transfer sheets from your samples.*

RICHARD: Transfer sheets means going back to doing it by hand and very slowly.

WENDY: I'll tell you something: *I* ain't doing the preserver lettering! [*Laughter.*]

RICHARD: Is there any preserver talk in the first issue?

WENDY: Yes.

RICHARD: Damn it! [*Laughter.*]

WENDY: I'll make sure there is!

O'NEILL: *The problem is that computers are actually inherently stupid. All of them are, as someone said, merely a whole bunch of light switches that have*

been programmed to turn off and on in a particular fashion. When you strike a key on a computer, you are telling it, "Turn on this set of lights and turn off that set of lights." That creates the pattern. You'd have to have a program that says, "This set of switches creates this pattern." On a Mac there are different fonts built in.

RICHARD: I know the software I need. I suspect it's a variant of what David used to create his own lettering; I could have done the same thing with the time and the inclination. It looks like I'm going to have to, now.

I'm beginning to understand why Cutter feels the way he does about the preservers. [*Laughter.*] Damn bugs!

WENDY: [*looks at Richard's plate*] You didn't eat your veggies.

RICHARD: I had some of my veggies.

O'NEILL: *I had some of mine, too.*

WENDY: Look at both of these men! They're not eating their broccoli!

O'NEILL: *Red meat! Red meat! We're men, Wendy!*

WENDY: This is why we have wars.

O'NEILL: *Or at least arguments between men and women.*

[*Note: The preceding exchange occurred two weeks before President Bush's well-publicized pronouncements on the subject of broccoli—O'Neill.*]

RICHARD: Getting back to the lettering: This is a step that Wendy doesn't have to do—or have done—between the penciling and inking. So when she sits down to a blank sheet of paper, she can buzz right on through at whatever speed she wants without interruption.

O'NEILL: *You do have to say, at least in your head, "This is where the balloon goes."*

WENDY: Yes. I've developed an in-

"**I'm beginning to understand why Cutter feels the way he does about the preservers. Damn bugs!"**

stinct for that. I do have to compose the panels with the dialogue in mind.

With the simplicity to the approach to *Kings of the Broken Wheel,* there will be many silent panels. And very little in the way of captions—the reader will understand through the artwork. That's my favorite kind of storytelling, where someone can read along and say, "Ohhh, I know what that means."

O'NEILL: *Wendy, do you find it useful as an artist to be able to go to a non-Elfquest project as a break, a respite?*

WENDY: Absolutely. Beauty and the Beast was a dream from start to finish. It was a created project; we had to do a lot of convincing with Ron Koslow that the world needed a Beauty and the Beast graphic novel. He's not a comic-book reader, even though his first cousin is Steve Gerber. (It's a small world, isn't it?)

Once he saw that we were going to be true to the TV show and that Vincent was not going to be dressed in skin-tight tights and a cape [*laughter*], he realized there would not be any loss of integrity in translating from one medium to another. He was very happy about it. We were given almost total freedom on the second graphic novel once the script had been accepted.

For me, I began to look at light differently. First of all, I was working in color; second of all, I wasn't doing cartooning. I was doing realistic illustrative art with accurate portraits of the characters, being aware of lighting in quite a different way from *Elfquest.* It was thrilling. Some of the effects that came out I look at and say, "I didn't know I could do that!" It was a revelation.

Some of this is being carried into *Kings of the Broken Wheel.* The art is richer and more lush for having had the experience of a year and a half on Beauty and the Beast.

RICHARD: She had to learn how to draw elves again.

WENDY: I'd been doing the human proportions and had to work to get back to the stretch and squash of cartooning.

O'NEILL: *I fondly remember the issue you did of* Jonny Quest. *Like many of your projects, it had a gentler aspect than the general run of* Jonny Quest. *Much as we all loved the action-adventure...*

WENDY: Part of that was due to Bill Loebs. We were doing the origin of Race Bannon. Race was my hero when I was sixteen; I wanted to be Jezebel Jade, live on a junk in Hong Kong, and have adventures! Getting to do his origin was really a kick!

Bill did this tender story about Jonny's mother dying and brought Race in as the companion to complete the family again. It was very moving, very simply told, and very easy to draw because it was all right there.

While I was working on it, Bill and I sort of linked psychically, and I would give him art that he hadn't indicated in the script, and he would call and say, "That's just what I wanted." It was the kind of story that happened that way.

O'NEILL: *Did you find it interesting working from a model sheet of characters that were not your own?*

WENDY: I have been drawing Jonny since I was a kid. C'mon! I learned how to draw people from Jonny Quest! One of the most exciting things that ever happened to me was meeting Doug Wildey at San Diego Con. After that, I got a package in the mail a few weeks later. He had sent me his very first study of Jonny. It blew me away—a nice smudged pencil drawing. You could tell it had been through the wringer, but

> "**I** have been so fortunate in my career because everything I have done has been a labor of love. I feel guilty about this."

this was his very first model study of Jonny. That is a treasure!

I used to draw the Jonny Quest characters in high school, and the teacher would come by and rip the page out of the notebook. [*Laughter.*]

O'NEILL: *I remember things like that, too.*

RICHARD: Somewhere we have—

WENDY: Oh, please don't tell!

RICHARD:—comics pages that she did back then. The show came out in '64 and '65...

WENDY: I wasn't even sixteen!

RICHARD: She was enamored of it. There had not been anything like it on TV.

WENDY: It was inspiring.

RICHARD: So she set about doing her own funny books—a trend which was to continue.

WENDY: Richard loves to rag me on this. I did, back when I was a teenager, a page of Jonny and Dr. Quest in the lab and Jonny's looking at a bubbling, glowing flask, and Jonny asks, "What's this, Dad?"

RICHARD: The answer is something like, "Balonium 37...and phosphors." [*Laughter.*]

WENDY: What did I know? It glowed!

The Jonny Quest project was a labor of love, and when I look back, I have been so fortunate in my career because everything I have done has been a labor of love. I've never had to hack anything out. I feel guilty about this.

O'NEILL: *Let's wrap this up with an attempt at prophecy or clairvoyance on your parts.*

RICHARD: I knew you were going to say that. [*Laughter.*]

O'NEILL: *Where do each of you see Warp Graphics, Father Tree Press, your own work in five years?*

WENDY: What we'd like to see, or what we can realistically expect?

O'NEILL: *Either way or both.*

WENDY: I'd like to see Elfquest break out of the graphic novel ghetto in Waldenbooks and see it in some other medium—film or TV—with most of its integrity intact. That is still a dream we both share. As for my work, I think it will be very much what it has been; I'll continue doing *Elfquest* and other projects that I love on the side.

RICHARD: I'm looking at a plan—a combination of realistic and wish-dreaming—that within a year or two allows me to sell off the publishing rights to everything Warp Graphics has done: at this moment, Elfquest and Xanth. I have been a publisher for the last dozen years; it has been fun, constructive, infuriating, educational, eye-opening, depressing, elating, and several other adjectives. I have found though in just the last few months, that I enjoy the heck out of working, doing the Xanth adaptations, working with Wendy on Elfquest. I like it a lot.

I think I'd like in the next five years for some larger company to hold the license to publish what we produce or package. We might still be doing Elfquest; I hope still to be doing Xanth. But instead of me being on the phone to the printer and distributors and all the other players in the publishing game, I just put the thing together and give it to this other entity.

O'NEILL: *That's almost what you tried to do with Apple Comics.*

RICHARD: In a very embryonic way, but I'm setting my sights much higher this time around.

I could even see myself as the liaison between that publisher and the printer...but not the one actually responsible for getting it done and paying the bills and so on and so forth.

WENDY: Underline paying the bills.

RICHARD: *I hate paying the bills!* I think for someone of my temperament, what I've described would be a wonderful way to spend the next several years.✧

Visitors to the Elfquest Universe

A Touch of Stardust

by Dwight R. Decker

One of the first reviews of *Elfquest* to appear in the fan press was this one, published in the *Comics Journal* #42 (October, 1978). Wendy and Richard had sent me a review copy of *Fantasy Quarterly* #1 and the package of sample pages and artwork they had submitted to publishers; and as the breathless quality of the review shows, I was a bit overwhelmed. Even though I'd known one or the other of the Pinis for years, I hadn't known they had this kind of thing in them.

Although my review alerted quite a few people to the existence of *Elfquest* (John LaRue, co-compiler of the glossary in this book, was one), I can't really take any credit for helping make *Elfquest* popular. Reviewers don't have that kind of power. Oh, they can tell you about a book or movie that you might otherwise have overlooked and make you interested enough to follow up on the information, or by their silence allow you to miss out on something you might have liked if you had only known about it—but at the bottom line, a product sells itself. No amount of overheated praise would have made *Elfquest* a success if it hadn't been worthy of it.

In more ways than one, I'm glad Wendy and Richard suggested that we reprint my review here. Contrary to popular belief, a lot of writers don't strut around with their chests puffed out like a pouter pigeon when they see their work in print—no, they cringe and groan and moan and gnash their teeth because there's nothing like the cold fixity of a printed page to make all the grammatical mistakes

and clumsy expressions and inappropriate choices of words that went unnoticed before suddenly stand out in all their glaring (and unchangeable) horridness. In this case, I managed to say things like "they charge to the rescue wreaking havoc in their wake." I also suffered from a bad case of "Increase Your Wordpower," describing Wendy's maiden name as what "she was yclept before her nuptials." I'd always wanted to use the word *yclept* in a sentence, but obviously this wasn't the place to do it. Now, at last, I can polish up the stylistic infelicities and present the review the way it should have been written in the first place.

—Dwight

Elfquest is the most gorgeous thing I've seen come out of comics fandom in the eleven years I've been here. I don't think I've ever seen even a professional comic done as well.

Elfquest is the story of a band of elves searching for a new home after being driven from their old one. And it's *beautifully* told. The drawings on every page sparkle with verve and life, the story grabs you by the lapels and won't

Can a musical interlude be effective in a silent medium like comics? Some would say yes, but the author of this review seems to agree with Picknose.

let go until you've read it all, and the characters are living personalities you get to know and care about. *This* from a young woman whose major claim to fame heretofore was going to comics conventions in a chain mail bikini and performing as Red Sonja?

It certainly is. It was just about ten years ago on the button that I first heard of Wendy Fletcher, as she was known before her marriage. Not only was she a female comics fan at a time when Maggie Thompson was the only other femme-fan out of some two thousand-odd active hobbyists, she was also a remarkably talented artist. Wendy was still a teenager then, but her art was already near-professional, combining a girlish charm, a joyous sense of life, a dash of wit and humor, and an artistic discipline that belied her years. Those of us who knew her were convinced that the girl had a magnificent talent, a spark of genius if you will, and would undoubtedly be heard from in the years to come.

One criticism is that the human beings are depicted as brutal savages. It struck me as a little odd because Wendy once took Marvel writer Stan Lee to task for his less than complimentary portrayal of the human race in general.

It took her a while, with a few diversions like her marriage to Richard Pini, a few covers for *Galaxy Science Fiction,* and her Red Sonja act popping up along the way, but with *Elfquest,* Wendy has finally arrived.

The tale begins at the dawn of the world—or perhaps of *a* world and not necessarily this one, since two moons can be seen in the sky. Men are still no more than half a step above the animals. When a castle full of gentle, highly civilized, pointy-eared elves crashes through a ruptured dimensional wall, the first confrontation between Man and Elf is brief and violent. Only a few elves are able to escape alive into the forests.

Wendy's natural history of elves still has a hole or two to be filled in at this point: the first elves on the scene are quite as tall as the human beings, but their direct descendants (with whom the bulk of the story actually deals), are considerably shorter. Their pointed ears, however, seem even larger. Grotesque, warty trolls, who also figure heavily in the plot later on, are evidently the much-mutated offspring of some cute little midgets seen briefly with the tall elves when they first stumble out of the castle.

In the generations since the arrival of the elves, relations between them and the humans have not improved. In the very first scene of the story, a tribe of men has captured an elf and is about to sacrifice him to Gotara, the god of the humans. A grisly exhibit of skills shows that this elf is not the first. (The elf skulls, I noticed have a prominent ridge of bone where the ear would be. Besides making the dramatic point that these *are* elf skulls, the ridge of bone is necessary simply to support ears the size of those the elves have. Or so Wendy explained it to me when I asked her about it.) The other elves are not standing by helplessly while one of their number is sacrificed; they may have shrunk over the ages, but they've also gotten a lot tougher. Mounted on semi-domesticated wolves, they charge to the rescue, wreaking their own inimitable brand of havoc. The humans respond by setting fire to the forest in which the elves live, and the elf chieftain, Cutter by name, perceives that this is clearly time to relocate. Unwisely, he appeals to the trolls for help,

Even denied the use of color for this scene, Wendy grits her artistic teeth and pulls it off anyway.

and the rather unpleasant trick the trolls pull on the elves is the basis for the first issue's cliffhanger.

There's much more to it than this: Wendy and Richard have thoroughly worked out the details behind their created world, and it lives and breathes, yet without ever bogging down in background. The telling of the tale is remarkable in its economy; most non-professionals (and too many professionals) in comics overwrite their scripts, filling each panel with wordy captions and balloons that look as though they are about to burst. Wendy, on the other hand, seems to have an almost instinctive knack for knowing how much is too much and when to let the illustrations do the talking. Words and pictures mesh to complement each other, and the story tells itself—seemingly without effort. This is a professional piece of work in every sense of the word.

My criticisms of the story are few. One in particular is a complaint that the human beings are depicted as brutal savages. It struck me as a little odd because Wendy once wrote a letter that was printed in an issue of the *Silver Surfer* comic book, taking Marvel writer Stan Lee to task for his less than complimentary portrayal of the human race in general. However, a letter from the Pinis to me reports that "there are going to be good humans as well as bad elves. The Silver Surfer Syndrome does *not* live!" My only other criticism is that a sequence in which the elves sing does not work terribly well, but that is only because songs in a silent medium like comics simply cannot work as well as in a movie. Music has to be heard to be effective.

The real flaw in the ointment, however, is the production of *Elfquest* itself. The editorial by the publisher hints at innumerable problems in getting the book to the press. For example, the original intention was to publish it in color, and Wendy drew the story with color effects in mind. The book was finally printed in black and white, so several pages of the story, such as the scene of the forest fire, fall pretty flat. For a publishing operation not much above a fanzine level (i.e., a hand-cranked spirit duplicator in the basement), such foulups are perhaps to be expected, but it's less forgivable for a project this major. The book is further hurt by an overall look of cheapness and sloppy amateurishness in the way it was formatted and put together. Matters may improve in future editions of *Elfquest;* just before this review was completed, I learned from the Pinis that they are looking for a new publisher for the second and subsequent issues.

The second issue, incidentally, has been completed, and if anything, the artwork is even more beautiful than that in the first. The Pinis sent me photostats of some of the pages for *Elfquest* #2, and at a recent comics convention in Chicago, I showed them to comic book writer Marv Wolfman.

He was surprised beyond measure: "I thought Wendy just went around as Red Sonja! I didn't know she could draw!"

Well, now he knows. Now the whole world knows.

Overall, Elfquest is startling because its tone is different from that of most other comic books throughout their forty-odd year history. Too many comics have been tasteless or vulgar or senselessly violent or gruesome, appealing to the lowest common denominator of the public taste (or to whatever the editor considers the twelve-year-old male mind to happen to want), and a comic book done with care, taste, sensitivity, love, and even a touch of stardust is almost a shock. A few scattered laborers in the comic book vineyards stand out because of their determination to tell *good* stories in the comic book form and raise the level of the field, if not to that of a sophisticated adult, at least to that of the best of children's literature: Carl Barks, Walt Kelly, John Stanley, Bob Bolling.

To their exalted ranks may be added Wendy Pini.   ✦

The World of the Wolfriders

by Paula O'Keefe

Elfquest has been around long enough that it has become regarded as almost as much a permanent part of the comics scene as Spider-Man. In the fan press, longer and more analytical essays about the series have begun to appear in place of short reviews. That's just one more indication of *Elfquest*'s popularity and importance.

Of the various analyses to date, Wendy and Richard liked this one best, so we obtained permission to reprint it here. It originally appeared in the *Comic Times* #4 (January 1981) with slightly different editing. Naturally, any and all conclusions are Paula's own and are not necessarily canonical, but the Pinis think she came pretty close to the heart of the matter in more than a few places.

—Dwight Decker

The weaving of the world of Elfquest began many years before its first drawings were set on paper. In interviews, both Wendy and Richard Pini, co-creators of the series, have discussed Wendy's long-standing affection for elves, and Richard remarked in the original printing of *Elfquest* #1 that "the elfin-folk have been part of her life since the beginning....The ideas for our stories go back awhile, even before Wendy and I met." That was in 1969; they married in 1972. Apparently, only a feeling that elves had "been done," that there was nothing new to add to the body of elfish tales both folkloric and fictional, kept Wendy from telling any such stories of her own. That is, until she was inspired—or as she put it, given a "kick in the motivation."

That kick was Ralph Bakshi's animated film *Wizards,* which provided the revelation that new variations on the ancient theme could indeed find a home in the 1970s. After considering a comicbook adaptation of *Wizards* or a sequel, Wendy and Richard decided to create instead an original saga, using elfin characters Wendy had been sketching for years. The first issue of the newborn series was published by the equally newborn Independent Publishers Syndicate comic *Fantasy Quarterly,* in March of 1978.

While fan reaction was enthusiastic, the Pinis were not entirely delighted with the resulting work. The publisher had promised four-color printing, but at the last moment—a few weeks before publication—he had resorted to black and white except for the cover. The artwork, carefully planned for color reproduction, hardly appeared at its best in this format. So, when IPS, like its predecessor Power Comics, went to an early grave, the Pinis were left with a not entirely unpleasant decision. Should they let the well-received but poorly presented series fade away, or take the plunge that its warm reception seemed to warrant and attempt to publish *Elfquest* themselves—this time to their own exacting specifications?

Their decision, of course, is comics history. *Elfquest,* now at its ninth issue as a Warp Graphics publication, is among the most acclaimed independent productions. The first issue has been reprinted and reworked with glossy covers to match the format of its suc-cessors, and neither the storyline nor its quality shows any sign of failing. *Elfquest* has clearly found an audience and a home in fantasy fandom.

So what of this saga that has attracted such attention? Well, once upon a time...

Tall, elegant, medievally lovely elfin aliens descended upon a Paleolithic world. Their palacelike home sank through a "hole in the sky" and landed among terrified savages who brutally massacred the newcomers. The surviving elves fled in panic into the forest of the primordial planet, their magic powers weakened in its strange environment; and under its two moons they embarked on the eon-long devolution that was to produce Cutter's Wolfriders.

Smaller than their ancestors (they are about four feet tall, weigh about sixty pounds, and have four-fingered hands), the Wolfriders are a seventeen-member elfin tribe that skirmishes endlessly with the hostile humans near their forest home. They are commanded by a chief or chieftess, a hereditary leader who holds the position for life. Cutter, son of the former chief Bearclaw, is the current chief. Forest dwellers and shy by

Once upon a time, tall, elegant, medievally lovely elfin aliens descended upon a Paleolithic world. Their palace-like home sank through a "hole in the sky" and landed among terrified savages who brutally massacred the newcomers.

daylight, they have apparently been peaceably settled in their current holt (or woods) for some time. They have an uneasy truce with the local trolls, providing them with herbal medicines and meat, and bartering furs and leather for the troll's forged weapons and other metalwork.

The most notable tribal feature of the Wolfriders is their alliance with the forest wolves. The elves literally ride the wolves in a loving, working partner-ship. Much more than mounts or hunting dogs, the wolves are kin to the Wolfriders; they share food, shelter, and telepathic communication. Like their furry kindred, the elves relish raw meat and howl celebrations of pack history by moonlight. With their wraith-like, eerie standing in folklore and warm family relationships in reality, wolves are a perfect choice for this elfin pair-bond. They lend Cutter's tribe some-thing special: speed, nocturnal mobility,

and a touch of weird guaranteed to make superstitious humans dread every shadow through the trees.

Which the local humans do. Convinced their deity Gotara intended the land and its game solely for human use, they burn at the stake any "wolf demon" they catch. When Redlance, the Wolfrider's best tracker, is captured, the elves kill a human in rescuing him, and the humans retaliate by torching the forest. Fleeing to the troll caves, their only hope of sanctuary from the inferno, the Wolfriders are betrayed and trapped in a caved-in cavern that leads only into scorching desert. With no provisions or water, forced to leave the injured Redlance and his mate Nightfall behind, the exhausted elves make their way across the waste—where, to their amazement, they find another elfin settlement.

Here live the peaceful, civilized Sun Folk of Sorrow's End: farmers and gatherers, as settled and daylight loving as the Wolfriders are wild and nocturnal. Like the Wolfriders, their ancestors crossed the desert to make a home here in long ages past; one ancestor, ancient Savah, still lives among them. The Sun Folk are so sequestered from the rest of the world that they consider humans a legend and can hardly imagine a deliberately inflicted wound. Only one of them, Rayek, is a hunter.

The Wolfriders raid the village for food and water. Cutter, however, all but runs over the settlement priest-leader's daughter Leetah and falls squarely into one of the elves' emotional heritages: Recognition, the instant knowing of one's lifemate. He impulsively abducts the maiden and is pursued by Rayek, who considers himself Leetah's intended.

These three make up the conflict that takes up the next three issues, with Recognition at its core. Recognition is

hard to define in human terms, being neither love at first sight nor lust—or at least not exactly. Elves can and do pair without it, but when two elves do Recognize each other, a lifelong match is a foregone conclusion; it means instant realization that here is your lifemate, your other half, sexual match, and (eventual) only love.

That is, it's supposed to. But civilized Leetah, too sensible to simply jump when instinct whistles, finds feral Cutter a barbarian and Recognition a nasty mess. Likewise, though fond of Rayek, she bristles at his arrogant assumption that she will inevitably be his. The rivals challenge, duel, and struggle it out; and Cutter and Leetah finally join to the joy of most concerned. Defeated, Rayek leaves the village and strikes out on his own.

Years pass. Leetah delivers twins into the world: tomboy girl Ember, destined for chieftess rank, and brother Suntop, inheritor of his mother's healing powers and other magical abilities. A skirmish with human wanderers convinces the Wolfriders that even here they are not safe, and Cutter determines to set out and locate other scattered elf tribes, helping to unite them against the human enemy. With his friend and advisor, Skywise, he's off...to trolls, kindly humans, and who can say what more.

This summary raises a bookful of intriguing questions—Where *did* the original elves come from? How far have they ranged and how many tribes have sprung from that landing party (or par-

The Sun Folk are so sequestered from the rest of the world that they consider humans a legend and can hardly imagine a deliberately inflicted wound.

Panel text: LEETAH TURNS FIRST TO RAYEK, HER LIFELONG FRIEND WHOSE MAGIC POWERS ARE SURPASSED BY NONE SAVE SAVAH...

AND WHOSE RESTLESS, BROODING NATURE IS AS COMPELLING AS AN INTRICATE PUZZLE.

THEN--

--SLOWLY--

--ALMOST AGAINST HER WILL --

Panel text: LEETAH'S EYES ARE DRAWN TO CUTTER'S. HE IS RAYEK'S OPPOSITE IN EVERY RESPECT — ARTLESS, FRANK HEARTED, WILD AS A BEAST OF PREY.

AND YET...

The conflict that sparked the early Elfquest stories. Leetah is torn between her lifelong friendship with Rayek and her Recognition of Cutter.

ties)? And how have some of their powers survived and others died out?—among others.

There is no doubt that their ancestors were aliens. Skywise, the aptly named, is the link to them, an astronomer who sees constellations where Cutter can only pick out stars, who is fascinated by the magnetic meteorite held sacred by the trolls (of which he now owns a chip), and who divines the sunhood of stars from a chance remark by Leetah's father, Sun-Toucher. (It is interesting that this feeling for stars shows up in both tribes, nocturnal and diurnal; even the Sun Folk call their sun the Daystar.) The "hole in the sky" through which the elves' castle fell could well be some sort of warp, linking a universe where magic works to one where magic apparently was not found before. Why the elves fell, and how many of them came, are harder ques-

tions, though the presentation of the scene (*Elfquest* #1) suggests deliberate migration rather than accident. Only time and the Pinis will tell.

The magical heritage of the High Ones, as the elves call their ancestors, is more ambiguous than the otherworldly heritage. The power of magic has been largely lost on the new world and is only selectively carried by a few elves. The hunted, secretive Wolfriders make extensive use of telepathic "sending" and of "treeshaping," a sort of telekinetic Bonsai-craft, while the Sun Folk, far from human enemies to overhear them and having no forest to cope with, have all but lost both arts. Both tribes need, and so have retained, the power of empathic healing. Leetah, for example, is the village healer; she heals the wounded Redlance when the Wolfriders arrive. Leetah can also send but only when in healing rapport or, it is

182 ❖ **The Big Elfquest Gatherum**

suggested, sexual communion. Savah, the Sun Folk's ancestress, is apparently the only member of either tribe capable of casting her awareness, voice, and image great distances. Like the Wolfriders, she can communicate telepathically with animals. Rayek has mastered such powers as levitation but needs a strong emotional impetus to send. The magical powers seem to touch here and there at random unless called for in survival.

But these benign magicks are only half the picture. The early attempts of the elves' stranded ancestors to use their powers on the new world, with its dense atmosphere and unknown variables, barely helped them survive. They could hardly know what dark results their innocent struggles brought about, results their descendants fight with still. Unknown to the elfin aliens, something about the world of Elfquest holds magic in pockets or loci, like Yoda's treehole with the Dark Force, and places where they used their power held the magic like batteries for generations. Presumably, these spots could have good *or* evil effects when tapped, but the only one we know of produced catastrophe. Struck by lightning, the magic locus fused two savage beasts into the monster Madcoil which slaughtered many Wolfriders and wolves—orphaning Cutter— before being killed by the tribe. Though they themselves ended Madcoil's bloody career, the elves are still held responsible for it— and possibly other such mutations—by the humans, who

claim malicious elfin sorcery bred the destructive beasts to bedevil them. This horror has left such a scar that Cutter still blanches at the notion of loosing "evil magic," even from Skywise's harmless meteor chip (*Elfquest* #2).

The other clear remnants of their forebear's culture that the Elfquest elves bear are soul names and Recognition. Soul names have parallels in human cultures, such as the secret name given children in some American Indian and island tribes, or the coven name chosen by a new witch. The soul name is your true name, known only to your parents, yourself, and your Recognized mate.

The conflict ignites an open challenge, and the scene at the window is played for the first time.

(Leetah knows Cutter's instantly when she Recognizes him though he does not speak it to her at the time and she does not know what the word means.) It contains the essence of your identity and self, and aids as a telepathic beacon to your presence.

Little has been said about the use of

Rayek departs, and Savah regrets.

soul names among elves, but the interesting point has been made that the Sun Folk do not have them or even know what they are. Leetah, for example, deeply imprinted with Cutter's soul name and the knowledge that it *was* a soul name, still had no idea what it *meant;* she desperately asked Nightfall of the Wolfriders, "What is a soul name? I must know what it means!" and Nightfall stood stunned at the idea of an elf not knowing. Like their general lack of telepathy, this lack of soul names is probably attributable to the Sun Folk's unthreatened, enemy-free life. Open and candid, with no one to hide anything from, they therefore have nothing to hide, thus have no need for the secret of a guarded name. If the Wolfriders follow human pattern in this instance, the soul name is vulnerable and not used aloud except when secure. The telling of it is a gift of trust and the finding of it by an enemy a grave

threat; hence the Wolfrider custom of tagging on descriptive names that are mostly nicknames: Cutter, Scouter, Clearbrook, Dewshine—names that are safe to use. The Sun Folk fearlessly use their real names, the only names they have.

Recognition is the mysterious and powerful pair-bonding of elfin mates. Exactly what purpose it served their ancestors was unclear until it was explained as a means of genetic selection linking the best genetic pairs and preventing damaging inbreeding in the always-small elfin population. Its meaning has been lost in the long course of evolution (if it was ever deliberate or consciously understood), and even now it is more exception than rule. It does not necessarily include love, though it is to be assumed that a Recognized (i.e., perfectly matched) pair will eventually develop emotional devotion toward each other. Little Dewshine's airy remark that she finds love "far more pleasant" than Recognition (she and scamp Scouter are enamored), and the fact that Leetah and Cutter only come to love each other some time after they're officially life-mated, leads one to speculate that a couple might Recognize despite mutual indifference, active dislike, or lovers elsewhere. This sort of biological imperative—since whatever it is not, it *is* emphatically sexual—is easily understood as having evolved to insure reproduction, traditionally infrequent in elves, whether romance was present or not. Rainsong and Woodlock, one Wolfrider pair, have two children—remarkable for an elf family—and Leetah and Cutter's twins bear out Savah's prediction that theirs will be an exceptional match. (In this context, it is intriguing that the unRecognized couple Redlance and Nightfall, though the longest-mated pair of Wolfriders, are childless.)

The Elfquest cast is a volatile, compelling, and fascinating mix. Any discussion of the characters has to begin with Cutter. Six years an orphan when the story begins, he had independence and chiefhood dropped on his young shoulders in one bundle when Madcoil struck the tribe. He carries both well, though on the surface he would seem to have learned more from his crafty, roistering father, Bearclaw, than from his gentle and diplomatic mother, Joyleaf. Savah, amused, termed him "a fighting cockerel," and indeed he has more than his share of swift tem-

per, fierce devotions, and black moods. But that is an uneven description, missing his best points. He is honest, direct, and clear as fresh water, without a scheming fiber in his body. He is also a creature of integrity, dignity, and—when he uses it—a great deal of common sense. Further, he is an excellent battle tactician, yet capable of great gentleness with his children and tribespeople, grimly willing to accept any trouble or punishment for their sake. And not only that, he is patient enough to endure the trials he goes through to win

The scene at the window played again—with happier results.

Skywise flattens Cutter's ego with impunity when called for.

Leetah, with only a few verbal explosions, and so unswervingly respectful of her right to free will that he steels himself to lose her rather than physically forcing her hand. Not your average hothead.

His handling of the Leetah matter, in fact, is a good index to him. Seized by Recognition, he does kidnap her on sight but returns her to her village without a murmur of protest; tolerates Rayek's jealousy with remarkably even temper; navigates the complicated challenge rite Rayek demands and Leetah agrees to, and *still* does not attempt to push his suit past one angry confrontation when his victory doesn't convince her. Humans would have sunk to rape and murder for less, and his father probably would have just slung the lady over his wolf and been away, but Cutter tries reason and plain old waiting long after one would expect his patience to snap. Partly, of course, this is due to his complete belonging to her, since they are Recognized, but his willingness to

Humans would have sunk to rape and murder for less, and Cutter's father probably would have just slung the lady over his wolf and been away...

let her see for herself something that a Wolfrider woman would have accepted utterly on the spot speaks volumes for him. He is much more his wise mother's son than he seems to be.

He also has the advantages of an excellent advisor, Skywise, his right-hand (left-hand?) partner. They are a solid combination, with Skywise's calm reason, insight, and slightly mystical perception making a neat balance to Cutter's frequent impetuosity.

Skywise is a stargazer, inseparable from his troll-filched chip of meteorite, which he fancies is part of the North Star. "There is nothing evil in the stars...or in anything that comes from them," he assures Cutter, probably as much from racial memory as personal conviction. He is also a bit light-fingered and a flirt, having recovered from Madcoil's killing of his ladyfriend Foxfur to the point of socializing with the desert elf lasses by the time Cutter takes up the quest. He seems unlikely to settle down though; care and steering of Cutter are probably his main responsibilities for the foreseeable future.

He is certainly not a jealous friend. He sets his diplomatic talents to smoothing the way between Cutter and Leetah as soon as he sees what is afoot, and he becomes a trusted friend of both. Neither is he a flunky; he flattens Cutter's

ego with impunity when called for (*Elfquest* #4 shows a perfect example). Practical in a crisis, he is still fundamentally his name—a startracker, mythmaker, storyteller, peering over the edge of magic into science. He may know his constellation legends, but he also knows the stars are suns.

Rayek of the Sun Folk is a moody, smoldering type. He has some of the elfin powers lost to all the desert elves but Leetah and matriarch Savah. At first seeming just the "heavy" of the tale, with his heavy-handed possessiveness of Leetah, arrogance to his tribespeople, and belligerence to the newcomer Wolfriders, he gradually becomes more sympathetic. As Leetah's lifelong friend, for example, and only possessor of the old elfin powers who is her contemporary, he naturally assumed he would be her choice of mate. How can he accept her sudden link to a stranger, a crude barbarian chieftain from a foreign place?—especially one

whose arrival came as a stunning shock in the slow, riversmooth life of Sorrow's End. Too, he was the only hunter of the village, fiercely proud of his status as a magician and protector, suddenly jarred from this position by the coming of seventeen hunters who impress the Sun Folk enormously. (In fact, it is interesting to consider how like the Wolfriders, and unlike his own people, he is: a proud, temperamental hunter among peaceful farmer-gathers he scorns as "dirt-diggers," a user of powers they've long lost. He defends them, but in a way a human might fence in his sheep, and is long used to thinking of himself as solo and superior.) All the same, he might have gotten over the shock, and treated them with something like civility.

But he cannot and does not because there is a black streak in Rayek. He uses his skills to paralyze and give painless death to game animals but also to stun a Wolfrider into a blank-

Cutter and Leetah are culturally dissimilar, yet alike in strength of character.

Rayek uses his skills to paralyze and give painless death to game animals.

eyed trance and nearly hurl Cutter from a dizzy height, even when owing him his life. He is a brooding vindictiveness that cannot forgive. He would never make a tree-shaper, powers or no; he is a thing of subtle force that too easily turns unsubtle: a tamer and a breaker. But one cannot help thinking that he would make a star of a Wolfrider (if he could swallow his pride), creature of cool shade and mystery that he is.

He did leave one odd chance for the future when last seen bearing for points unknown: a little smile, sphinx-like, when Savah telepathically wondered whether a three-mate marriage of Rayek, Leetah, and Cutter was so unthinkable. (It *has* been done.) Yes, unthinkable, he said, but he *did* smile...

And what about the center of all this controversy? Leetah, daughter of the tribe's leader, has something of the princess about her. Dignified and spirited at once, utterly civilized, she holds an ironclad determination to choose her own course. She is over six hundred years old, still young for an elf, but much older than Cutter, and has spent those years in peace, healing and doing the small, steady work of the com-

munity. She probably thought she would one day give Rayek the nod he craved, some day in the long stream of days.

Then the Wolfrider's arrival strikes into her life like lightning, and all plans are changed. How she handles the situation speaks volumes for her enormous inner strength, perhaps never called on before. Consider the shock: suddenly Recognized to and by a stranger, a savage who kidnapped her on sight. She does not *want* it, and struggles, with all her reason and logic, to retain sane choice in the grip of a spiritual and biological finality as definite as thirst. There should be more to uphold a life-mating than one eye-locked moment, Leetah believes, and she struggles determinedly toward it for what must be endless, painful weeks. Her loyal fondness for Rayek never dims—her best friend, secret and fascinating in a way frank Cutter cannot be—and she finds it hard to even *like* Cutter, a raw-meat–eating, cave-and-tree–dwelling companion of wild animals. She flashes out in anger at both of them when they presume on her next word or act, partly because she hardly knows them herself. But, like the intelligent person she is, she holds aside prejudice to study Cutter fairly, and no display of his true personality is lost on her.

It is Dewshine's injury in a zwoot hunt (zwoots are the large pack beast domesticated by the Sun Folk) that finally turns her, so it is worth noting in some detail. Leetah is startled to see Dewshine head out with the Wolfriders to turn the stampeding herd, exclaiming that "it is not a maiden's place." Dewshine chides her and rides gaily off. This is striking; for all her insistence on freedom, Leetah has probably never imagined that freedom is anything more than the ability to be taken seriously at her "yes" or "no," certainly not risk or danger. Dewshine has the full freedom of a Wolfrider, "to run and hunt with the pack as she wills," even if it should mean her death. Leetah sees this clearly. Her spirit and fire would be wasted in the placid village whose people are content to take refuge in the caves and let the beasts trample through, and at the end of her long life she might well feel she had missed what would have filled it—and that does not just mean Cutter. She darts under the hooves of a furious zwoot to save Dewshine, almost as if proving herself. This realization—that in turning to Cutter she is surrendering no independence at all, rather buying it in full—is surely what convinces her to face the longing of Recognition and change her mind. (And remember, they are not in love, and will not be for years. Call it a truce.)

An odd knot we have here: Cutter and Leetah so culturally dissimilar, yet so alike in strength of character; Rayek and Cutter unalike ethically, yet with a primal, predatory cord in common; Rayek and Leetah two complex, gifted individuals in an ordinary tribe, too strong to be happy together since neither could dominate, but the best mates for each other had no one else come along. A fine complementary triad.

And we should consider ancient Savah, the eldest elf in the tale. "Mother of Memory" to the Sun Folk for her remembrance of history back to its foundation, she is the nearest thing to a High One we have seen. A wonderful creature, tall and elegant, she is a model of benign humor and gracious wisdom. Her height is due to her great age, as she is much closer in ancestry to the tall original elves than to her descendants at Sorrow's End, though as she says, the High Ones were long before even her time. Her function is mainly to provide counsel and smooth paths, but what she is, is more important than what she *does:* she is a physical link to the elves' past, a repository of their great powers. She and her mother were the founding mothers of the Sun Folk, and she remembers the desert crossing and the endless war with the humans before the settling of the place they hopefully named Sorrow's End. Just as clearly, she sees some of the future. A sort of elfin Sybil, she is a figure of eternal elf nature in a beset and changing world, with a touch of Madonna.

There are any number of other personalities present here, too: Nightfall, Redlance's defiant mate; genial, stalwart Treestump, Cutter's uncle and the eldest Wolfrider; mystical little Suntop and spunky Ember, Cutter and Leetah's twins; Strongbow, the tribe's best archer, sullen and so taciturn he prefers sending

It is interesting to consider how like the Wolfriders, and unlike his own people, Rayek is: a proud, temperamental hunter among peaceful farmer-gathers he scorns as "dirt-diggers," a user of powers they've long lost.

Leetah darts under the hooves of a furioius zwoot to save Dewshine— and to prove a point.

to speech; and flirtatious, dryadlike Dewshine, Treestump's daughter and thus Cutter's kid cousin. They are all distinct—much more so than the Sun Folk, of whom only six or so stood out at all—and this is the series' strongest point: characterization and the workings of interpersonal feeling. The Pinis' character handling is subtle and compassionate in every situation, and in fine detail. Bearclaw, for example, is a tough-hearted old rogue, but the loss of his beloved mate strikes him so deeply that from his first certainty of her death, he never speaks again. Nightfall stands staunchly by her Redlance, pelting vultures with stones as they face their fate in the desert. One-Eye, an-

other tough fighter, is seen smoothly braiding his mate Clearbrook's long hair. And so on. The love of mated couples and parents, the faith and loyalty of the tribe for chief and chief for tribe, jealousy, and racial hatred, have all surfaced here and are evenly and realistically treated. The characters have reality and depth, something that has certainly helped endear them to their fans.

Also of interest are the scenic backgrounds which are rendered with fine affection for the flora and fauna of both forest and desert. Artist Wendy has claimed an impatience with backgrounds, so this careful detail might be an exercise in patience, but it works. The character art is graceful, strong, and expressive.

However, it might be a little too pretty—which is a weakness of the series, or at least a point that puts off some fans of other comics. The elves are undeniably pretty, with large, liquid eyes, smooth muscles for the males, and graceful curves for the females. The exceptions—stocky Treestump, slender Dewshine, stately Savah, and

The careful insistence that the saga is not happening on our earth cannot carry much weight beside so many customs and behavior patterns we recognize as our own, two moons or no.

tall Clearbrook—are not really enough compensation. The style is not unpleasant, but it does cloy in large doses. I would like to see more scars.

There is also the one-sided treatment of humans to a fault. Before issue #8, the local equivalent of Homo sapiens were painted as relentless enemies of the elves—and religious bigots to boot—with barely a flicker of sympathy. Surely in all these ages they cannot have all been bestial any more than all elves can have been good. The Pinis promise to see to this, though, and with issues #8 and #9, a wider variety of humans, some good and some bad, have been featured.

The last is a clinging problem; the elves just don't seem as alien as the Pinis would probably like and neither do the humans. The careful insistence that the saga is not happening on our earth cannot carry much weight beside so many customs and behavior patterns we recognize as our own, two moons or no. The savages who slaughter the original elves could easily be Neanderthal-period humanoids, and by the Wolfriders' time, they could have logically advanced to Cro-Magnon. In flora and fauna, the world could easily be Terra, with the exceptions of zwoots and dreamberries (somewhere between wine grapes and peyote, elf-style). As for having elves, trolls, and magic, who is to say old Terra does not have those too? They go back to our deepest memory and figure in some stories the Wolfriders would probably find familiar.

All this, however, does not really explain the phenomenon of *Elfquest*'s popularity. This little elfin band, in a mere nine issues at the hands of two creators, has acquired the character credibility and affectionate audience that major characters of the long-established companies have taken years and crews of writers to claim. How does it work?

One of the Wolfriders' main advantages is the leisurely pace they are

Humans, both bad and good

allowed to keep. Unlike the superheroes of overground comics who are hobbled by convention into slam-bang fight scenes month after month, the Elfquest formula generally presents one central scene of dramatic action—by no means necessarily a battle—per triennial issue. The rest is personal development, character interaction, and elfin history in a comfortable, even-paced blend. There is enough time to know the Wolfriders as individuals, and there is something to know about each of them, though much varies from elf to elf. An overground comic would not reserve space to show that Rainsong is a devoted mother or that Leetah's sister Shenshen is a little tart about Rayek.

The Wolfriders have the fortune of remaining in one set of hands, those of their creators, who know them intimately enough to claim to live with them. "They steal the cereal and cut notches in the furniture," Richard claimed.

The severe, dramatic editing of overground comics is not applied, giving *Elfquest* a full and rather peaceful quality as befits a story not happening against a background of urban crime or science fiction warfare. Time is an important factor here; character development, though much more highly regarded in overground comics in recent years than in their past, is still mostly limited there to love affairs and maybe a dash of past personal history, because the present story is what will sell the issue. The elves, by comparison, have ages of racial history behind them. That history is basic to *Elfquest;* ages and ages of slow-paced time, yet full of the conflict between elf and

human that fuels their current adventure. Events happen as much as a result of the past as because of present events. The seemingly all but immortal elves' long memories keep that past in firm link with the present.

There is something attractive about this lack of contemporary hurry and haste, this sense of continuity back to ancient days, as can be seen all around us in things like the fascination with genealogy and family histories, groups like the SCA (Society for Creative Anachronisms), the communal movement, Dungeons & Dragons, and even the popularity of historical novels. People can feel an affection for it that is not as easy to feel for the contemporary setting of most other comics.

Also, they *are* elves, and elves, like dragons and unicorns, are a major point of the recent fascination for things medieval. Partly this is linked to the interest in things of older, slower days, and partly because they are *magical*. The twilight, ancient magical quality of elves that fascinated Yeats, Dunsany, and Tolkien holds just as many hearts today, I'd venture, as it did when elves haunted folk belief. The Wolfriders are deliberately non-ethereal, and their magicks are pared down to the utilitarian. But Savah and the first-arrived elves in *Elfquest* #1 have a real magical prowess. The first-born, wisest of all, the Tuatha De Danaan and Liosalfar of Irish mythology, live on in those elegant creatures.

Wendy Pini compares the appeal of *Elfquest* to that of *Star Wars* in one interview. Though *Star Wars* plays the arena of science fiction rather than that of historical or medieval fantasy, it is certainly in its heroism, imagery of knights and princesses, and great visual beauty, a magical movie.

Another aspect of their appeal is the consistency of the elves as individuals. Throughout the Cutter–Leetah–Rayek confrontation, there is no doubt at any time why any of them act as they do. Not all the elves are treated quite as three-dimensionally. For example, Strongbow is presented simply as a surly, grim human-hater who loves his wife. But *Elfquest'*s main characters are well rounded enough to be understandable in almost any mood. Compare this to the lesser lights of popular overground groups like Colossus of the X-Men or almost all of the Micronauts except Bug and Acroyear. With a standing cast of seventeen Wolfriders and scores of supporting characters, the Pinis have achieved an excellent personality-to-nonentity ratio in contrast to overground comics with fewer characters.

Of course, overground characters have problems in remaining consistent, especially in retaining one writer/artist team over any appreciable time span. No major company character seems to have this kind of luck for long with perhaps the exception of Marvel's Conan and Dracula. This incessant changeover invariably leads to differences in approach with different weight given to this or that aspect of the character, or entirely new aspects being invented. Also, the writer or artist may not especially like the assignment, which can reflect uncomfortably on the character. All in all, it is inevitable that with changes in fashion (mysticism, relevance, etc.) and execution, overground comics (as the property of a company) shift the handling of their characters and make them slightly different people from now to then.

Compare this to the Wolfriders, who have the fortune of remaining in one set of hands, those of their creators, who know them intimately enough to claim to live with them. "They steal the cereal and cut notches in the furniture," Richard claimed in the intro to *Elfquest* #1.

There is no way they could fail to handle the Wolfriders as real folk. Would that more overgrounders had such luck!

I can recall Frank Thorne claiming to have a rapport with Red Sonja to the extent that he heard her voice and consulted with her on story points, and Denny O'Neil holding such a fondness for Fritz Leiber's Fafhrd and the Grey Mouser that he admitted to fearing their intervention if he handled their regrettably short-lived DC vehicle, *Sword of Sorcery,* poorly. These are the rarities, as is Steve Gerber and his relationship with Howard the Duck and Man-Thing, but it is notable that these are all characters handled by no one (or almost no one, in Sonja's case) before the artists mentioned. No one had meddled with them much.

And maybe that is the reason for it all: plain personal involvement, affection, and love—personal involvement between the Wolfriders themselves; the Wolfriders and their inventors; and the Wolfriders, their inventors, and their audience. A scarce enough element in entertainment these days, it certainly helps make *Elfquest* the wonder and pleasure it is. It is not there to shock and scare or cliffhang you or feed your violent tendencies; it is there to do something as old as elves: tell you a story. And in trying to do something they were not sure could be done—find a new, enthralling format for the ancient people of the Hills—the Pinis have done something just as new and appealing for the form of comics. ✦

An overground comic would not reserve space to show that Rainsong is a devoted mother or that Leetah's sister Shenshen is a little tart about Rayek.

The Art of Elfquest

by Jane Fancher

Along time ago, in a living room far away from Poughkeepsie, New York, a tiny human by the name of Wendy Fletcher sold her soul to a little pointy-eared fellow of questionable parentage. It's the only rational explanation for how she can do what she does so much better than anyone else.

Actually, as much as one would like to be able to account for it in so easy a manner, the pages of Elfquest are the culmination of years of hard work and study, a strong case of common sense coupled with excellent powers of observation, and a good stiff dose of gut feelings and intuition. The consistent, beautifully conceived and executed organization of her Elfquest world owes nothing to formal training in either the arts or sciences, and from that lack of formal training comes some of her greatest strengths and weaknesses. Those years of work and study did not take place at an art school or even at a university but were rather a long period of trial-and-error experimentation with her own capabilities. During that time, she was exposed to the talent of comics artists such as Jack Kirby and John Buscema; the animation and characterization techniques of Walt Disney, Osamu Tezuka, and Chuck Jones; and the glorious, exotic beauty of the Oriental art style. All of these influences come into her work but none is overpowering. When combined with a strain of independence to tell *her* story *her* way, the results are uniquely Wendy.

The drawback to such an approach to learning is the wasted time involved. One can spend many times longer discovering how best to achieve the result desired if one must rediscover the process by oneself. However, by learning on her own, she was not and is not bound by the prevailing styles taught in schools, and as a result she has been able to present to the public something that cannot be described by the terms *comic* or *novel*. *Elfquest* is something delightfully new and different. It will be very interesting to see how much influence her particular combination of techniques will have on the next generation

Fig. 1. Model sheet for female elves' faces. As an example of Wendy's care in making the elves distinct personalities, note how each has a uniquely shaped face.

of comic illustrators. In the meantime, her techniques deserve a closer examination.

When Wendy and Richard first approached me about writing an article on the art of Elfquest, my initial reaction was one of positive enthusiasm only to discover, on further consideration, that they obviously had a secret wish to see me stashed away in a padded cell deep in the caverns of the trolls. Never has the old adage "I could write a book" been more appropriate. There are literally dozens of angles from which a proper analysis could and should be approached in order to do Wendy's abilities justice. As this is physically impossible to do in the space available, I will limit myself to a few of the aspects I consider outstanding and leave the joy of discovering others to the reader.

A magazine as well rounded and complex as *Elfquest* makes it all too easy to dismiss the artwork as "technically well done," "beautiful," or even "too cutesy" and proceed to expound at length about the significance of Cutter's chieflock or some such. Without trying to belittle the plot and character lines, I feel it is extremely important to note how much of the "deep, hidden meaning" and character development is accomplished without a single word being spoken (at times making any narration as may exist almost painfully redundant). The development of the

Fig. 2. Cutter compared with Skywise.

character and plot that is so central to the unique quality of the story is the result of very effective "visuals": casting; makeup, costume, and set design; camera angles and lighting—in short, the artwork. Most such director/producer aspects are not found solely in Wendy's work. In perusing old comics, I found virtually all of these aspects were used at some point or other with varying effectiveness. One of Wendy's outstanding talents is the frequency and skill with which she incorporates them into the panels.

The Casting

The most obvious aspect of the art is the exotic appearance of the elves and the amazing individuality endowed to each and every one of them. It is rare in comics to be able to differentiate one main character from the next. Take all the heroes and heroines that a single artist has drawn, shave their heads, and strip off their costumes, and the result would probably be two batches of clones: one male, the other female. There seems to be a basic "look" required for the superhero that each artist establishes early on in his career and rarely, if ever, varies from. Only villains and minor characters seem exempt from this rule. Otherwise, it is appalling how much the artist comes to depend on a hairstyle and costume to differentiate the characters. There is a rationale behind the tendency, for it takes much hard work and time to establish individual appearances and to stick with them month after month. Wendy, however, preferred to go to the extra trouble to keep her characters individualized, even though she faced an even more difficult problem in making her elves not only unique unto themselves, but also doing this within a set of parameters that made them unique as a species from humans. As if that were

A

B

C

Fig. 3. The five ages of Cutter: *A*, as a child; *B*, as a young hunter; *C*, the hunter six years later; *D*, centuries after that; and *E*, very old age.

D

E

not difficult enough, she is also dealing with a cast of main characters not merely one or two strong, but composed of seventeen Wolfriders and at least five major members of the Sun Folk tribe. She has given characteristic features, expressions, body types, and even stances to each one (figure 1).

In the case of Cutter and Skywise, for example, Wendy has an excellent opportunity to draw two characters who are very similar (figure 2). They have the same cultural background—both are of the physically oriented tree-dwelling tribe—and both are in top physical condition so they could have adopted similar habits. Both appear so frequently in the panels that a common facial and body style would certainly be easier for Wendy to use. But they are singularly unique.

There is, of course, the ever-present difference in hair: Cutter's is long and silky (though horrendously cut), while Skywise's pouf of silver mane must be kept confined by his headdress. Under those shaggy locks lie very different features. Skywise has a touch of the Romanesque to his nose; a soft, Cupid's bow mouth; and a squarish chin. The young chief is characteristically seri-

Fig. 4. Cutter is still recognizable whether drunk or ill.

ous and intense (even when drunk, he tends to glower), while his second-in-command looks out at the universe from under a skeptic's raised eyebrows. Even in the midst of a crowded panel, Cutter's outthrust chest and firmly planted feet would never be mistaken for Skywise's slender, relaxed figure. The same type of analysis can be made using any two characters in the book, and it is made possible because of constant and conscious consideration of each and every one in panel after panel. Each time the reader sees a character, no matter how small the character appears, it is immediately apparent who that character is. Wendy jokes about "typical Pini poses," but the scope of these poses is so broad that a pose could just as easily be called a typical "Leetah" or a typical "Shenshen."

Wendy's conceptualization of her characters is so thoroughly worked out, in fact, that she has been able to show Cutter at five distinct stages of life, as well as in varying stages of health, and he has been easily distinguishable in each (figure 3). Issue #4 shows him first as a child with his father, then as a very young hunter who loses both his parents and is thrown almost too early into a chieftain's role. The rest of the first five issues takes place six years later; an additional seven years are added between issues #5 and #6; and finally, there is the sketch of him as an old man in the reprint of issue #1. We have seen him drunk on dreamberry wine (issue #7) as well as haggard and ill (issue #8; figure 4), and in each appearance he is undeniably Cutter. The youthful roundness in issue #4 holds the dimensions of the face to come just as the elderly, wisdom-lined face retains the bone structure that his seven years of married life honed from the still soft lines of the young chieftain. Subtle changes in overall expression also mark the passage of time. The rather foolhardy bravado in the first five issues is replaced, for the most part, by a more quiet confidence in the wisdom of his own decisions from issue #6 and on. (It does not necessarily indicate he is less foolhardy, only more sure of his own right to be a fool.) While the other characters are not so

Fig. 5. The eyes have it.

Within the image panel:

FOR ALL THEIR AGE-OLD AND JUSTIFIABLE RESENTMENT OF HUMANS -- THE "TALL ONES" WHO ARE SO STRANGELY DIVERSE IN APPEARANCE AND SO VIOLENTLY UNPREDICTABLE IN TEMPERAMENT --

--CUTTER AND SKYWISE OBSERVE THAT A SMILE IS A SMILE AND A TOUCH IS A TOUCH AMONG HUMANS AND ELVES ALIKE.

Fig. 6. Elves and humans find common ground.

fully represented, the same kind of growth can be seen between issues #5 and #6 in the faces and figures of the young children and adults. Though costumes change abruptly and new characters are added without any formal reintroduction, we are never in any doubt about whom we are seeing.

Oddly enough, some of the aspects of Wendy's artwork that promote such uniqueness of character are the very ones that most often come under attack from her critics. When criticisms are made regarding the art, the phrases "too cute" or "too pretty" are often heard. Are these valid complaints, and even if they are, does it matter?

To answer the second part first, I think the complaints are basically irrelevant. The art style is an integral part of the Elfquest world that Wendy has created. Wendy's work is unique, consistent, and well conceived. Purpose lies behind every stroke of the pen. She is not making an attempt to put across someone else's concepts, and therefore she needs to answer only to herself. Just as the introduction of more explicit sex and violence that a few readers have requested is totally inconsistent with the Elfquest approach, so too would be an *elimination* of the innocence and humor that contribute to the "cuteness."

However, the complaints do deserve to be more seriously considered, for they are made sincerely and serve to bring out some good points as well. Since the humans are, if anything, depicted too harshly at times, and the trolls are blessed with faces only their mothers can truly appreciate, any such

FEAR HAS ALWAYS HAD MANY FACES...

Fig. 7. Picknose's ancestors arrive with the elves.

complaints must be aimed at the elves alone. The apparent excess of beauty and cuteness in the elves owes more to the story's intrinsic qualities and its approach than to any aspect of Wendy's artistic capabilities.

By virtue of the physical specifications for the species, the elves are destined to be labeled by our standards as cute or beautiful, and it all centers around their enormous, slanting eyes (figure 5). Eyes have been a fascination, in fact a fixation, of human culture since its beginning; and large, luminescent eyes have been an accepted basis for youthful innocence and beauty. Therefore, no matter what is done to them, those elfin eyes are going to register as beautiful to us. The narrowest-, beadiest-eyed elf of the lot would appear to have unusually large eyes to us, whereas to one of his own species,

he might appear mediocre to ugly.

In addition to the eyes, the elves' long middle age means we rarely, if ever, see an elf with a lined face. In our youth-oriented society, youth is also a sign of beauty; therefore, the youthful tendency also increases the effect of "cuteness." When a child apes adult expressions, we tend to laugh rather than accept them seriously. Pini elves are comparatively small, delicate creatures with enormous eyes, all of which we humans tend to extrapolate as young and innocent. As a result, there is often a feeling of the precocious child in their expressions that, in adult humans, would not be at all "cute."

The humans in the story are, if anything, almost too blisteringly realistic. In the early issues, the difference in actual art style between the simple, cleanly linear work used for the elves and the rather strained, over-worked style used for the humans made a somewhat discordant note at times. There is not a single human, however, who falls into the "too pretty" look-alike trap of other comics. It was as if Wendy knew what she wanted the humans to look like but was still straining to achieve that effect; whereas with the elves, the defining factors of face and body were long since secure. As time went on, and especially with the introduction of Nonna, Adar, and Adar's people, Wendy appears to have become more comfortable with the difference between elves and humans and is able to depict the humans with the same clean lines and efficiency she uses with the elves (figure 6).

Another aspect to consider is the overall emphasis of the book on characterization and interpersonal relationships. The unrelenting intensity seen in most comics is missing, making the cartoon-like nature of comic art in general seem more noticeable. This is not to say that Wendy's style is any less realistic than that of other comic artists, only that her characters themselves and her emphasis on expression and interaction make it appear so in contrast to the single level of intensity of other comics.

A valid point that is sometimes brought up is to liken her work to Walt Disney characters. It may be due to the fact that she stresses character and the individual's actions and reactions to situations both serious and humorous, rather than to any conscious copying of the Disney style. So many comics refuse to include humorous interchanges that when we do see emotion, it is always in regard to intense, highly dramatic situations. The Disney style of animation, along with that of Chuck Jones, is one of the few that explores the wonderful visual nuances of facial changes in humorous situations. There-

fore, when Wendy includes them as part of everything else in her work, it is only natural to compare her with Disney. Perhaps it is high time other comics started taking themselves less seriously and included some of the wonderful, humorous exchanges that are part of the close working relationships and that usually take place in the most nerve-wracking situations. It can only be accomplished by artists with the same sense of human expressions the Disney studio cultivates—artists like Wendy.

Makeup, Costume, and Set Design

When I asked Wendy about the reasons for the overall "look" of the elves, I was surprised to learn that she had never consciously studied anthropology, for the developments (both physical and cultural) she shows taking place can be beautifully explained in scientific terms. These qualities she gives her elves stem, not through an awareness of existing theories, but through an uncanny ability to observe and correlate. But theory exists to her support her every move.

Picknose's name can explain the reasons for these changes. He was given the name in honor of the distinctive shape of his nose and not because of any social habits he may have.

Physical changes are always the first to be noticed in hindsight (though they are not generally the first to take place). With the elves, the evolution into a shorter, tougher breed is probably the result of a more limited food supply and more exposed mode of existence, and the relatively larger ears indicate an increased dependence on their natural

Fig. 8. Wolfrider clothing contrasted with Sun Folk fashions

senses. The pale skin and hair of the Wolfriders would appear to be less effective for their precarious coexistence in the deep woods with the wolf-hunting humans than would be the better camouflage of dark skin and hair. However, their early association with the wolves and their obvious abilities to protect themselves in other ways make another, more subtle evolution-ary factor take precedence. Their skin color is probably due to a vital chemical reaction similar to the production of vitamin D in humans. This is a reaction catalyzed by sunlight that takes place in the lower skin levels. All things being equal, a darker skin absorbs less sunlight. Therefore, the less sunlight received, the lighter the skin color must be in order to absorb the amount of

Fig. 9. Troll creativity in home furnishings

sunlight necessary for production of vitamin D. The only other source of vitamin D for primitive humans was sun-dried meat. Since the Wolfriders live in the wood and eat raw meat, they would evolve into a basically light-skinned race. The more exposed Sun Folk, on the other hand, need a higher average level of pigment in the skin to protect them from the ultraviolet radiation and so are darker.

The evolution of the trolls is even more fun to consider because they are victims, not of environmental pressures, but of social ones. Living deep in the caverns, safe from wind, rain, and humans, and with necessities supplied by the elves in exchange for metal goods, the trolls have changed from the charming, stubby little creatures we saw disembarking from the castle (figure 7) to the big-nosed, pompous troglodytes typified by Picknose and Oddbit. The source of Picknose's name

can explain the reasons for these changes. He was given the name in honor of the distinctive shape of his nose and not because of any social habits he may have. The trolls are a mining folk and find large, pick-shaped noses singularly attractive and desirable.

Technologically, matters are equally interesting, and more important, they are always internally consistent. The Wolfriders are a tribe of hunter-gatherer elves who use either troll-made metal tools or self-made stone ones. The Sun Folk are more advanced with agriculture, well-developed metallurgy, and distinct

The evolution of the trolls is even more fun to consider because they are victims, not of environmental pressures, but of social ones.

Fig. 10. Picknose's bow and Old Maggoty's woven robe

Fig. 11. Elf-shaped interiors

labor specialization. This fundamental difference in the economies of the two tribes leads to all the wonderful costume and architectural differences between them, and yet, due to their common ancestry, they retain a haunting similarity that sets them apart from the indigenous humans.

The Wolfriders live on the same economic basis as the humans in their vicinity, but the humans entered that state from a less civilized one, while the elves were once extremely civilized. The humans' clothing is very simple, composed basically of tied-on skins, strings of bones, etc. There is no knowledge of worked metal. The ancient elves' highly civilized knowledge of metal could not incorporate well with the living forest surrounding them, but they retained a source for metal in the

form of the trolls who lived underground. Thus, the elves still have a certain amount of metal tools and decorations which they augment with feathers and tiaras of flowers. The difference in materials used for decoration is fascinating. The conceptual desire for decoration exists in both cultures, but the ability to utilize the more delicate items differs drastically. The humans would most likely destroy any feathers or flowers in their attempts to wear them simply because they have not yet developed the necessary delicacy of workmanship.

The elves used not only skins, but softly tanned hides carefully tailored into clothing that still retains some of the lines of the ancient ancestors' clothes. The tunic style with the pointed "wings" over the shoulders is still there, even though the tunics are universally short due to their tree-dwelling/wolf-riding way of life and the wings are reduced due to simpler styling and softer materials. The clothing is also simply designed, easy to put on and keep on. Even though the Wolfriders'

Fig. 12. Centuries pass between the two panels.

ancestors must have had knowledge of woven cloth, the idea died an early death, for they did not have the time, the facilities, or the need to re-create it in a forest home. Growing fibrous plants is difficult in a forest glade, but softly tanned hides are plentiful and durable.

In apparent opposition to the hunter-gatherers are the Sun Folk (figure 8). Agriculturalists, with many people and much time, they have exquisitely woven fabrics and complex clothing. For example, they wear long skirts, full-sleeved shirts, and robes such as are never seen in the Wolfriders' styles, and yet are still reminiscent of the Old Ones, as befits a people who spend most of their time outdoors. The more sedentary lifestyle of the Sun Folk makes long skirts possible, but even so, the only full-length garments are those worn by the ancient Savah and the priestly Sun-Toucher.

The costume design is truly one of the most refreshing aspects of Wendy's work, for her costumes are not only attractive and accurate in their use of materials, but the designs are also functional and realistic, an unusual state in this age of skin-tight clothing in superhero comics. Full-figured women are finally given clothing that could not only be worn, but worn comfortably; and the feat is accomplished without sacrificing beauty or sexual appeal. The major disadvantage is that soft shirts and gathered materials are much more difficult and time-consuming for an artist to draw than are tights (which essentially require only that the artist draw the clean lines of the human body) and are therefore relatively impractical for the production-line comic.

The costumes of the other groups are equally well conceived. The first humans introduced are cave dwellers who wear scant clothing with no tailoring at all and whose decorations are composed only of strung bones. Adar's people appear to be somewhat more sedentary, living in carefully constructed huts. Correspondingly, their clothing is slightly more complex with definitely more time put in on their decorations on which complex knotting and beading designs are beginning to show. They still have no real tailoring, not even the leather stitching that begins to show in Nonna's clothing and the garments that she has made for Adar. Adar's people have not yet reached the stage of agriculture, as they are seen gathering berries, and the offerings made to the "spirits" consist of hunted and gathered materials. Nonna's people seem to be even more advanced, for she and Adar wear distinctly more tailored clothing than the other humans. It would be interesting to find out if this is solely the product of Nonna's own inventive mind or if it is indicative of the level of development of all her people.

The trolls are delightfully disgusting creatures who live an underground, completely mechanized existence. They retain metallurgical skills and are probably the most creative of all the tribes. They are at that marvelous stage of development where practically everything they make has a spirit of its own. From the dreamberry wine mugs to the bellows over the forge, everything has a carved, cast, or forged face (figure 9). Their clothing is simple and composed of leathers derived from the forest elves, but their decorations are all elaborate metal work. There are two exceptions at least to this general rule that must be relegated to the "mysteries to be answered later" file: Old Maggoty's robe, which appears to be of woven material, and the bow Picknose wears in the end of his beard. The bow is a double mystery. Not only does it appear to be made of something other than leather or metal, it is also the only bow in the entire epic (figure 10).

In addition to makeup and costume design, Wendy excels at designing sets. Again, there is an undertone of a common background. The retention of a close association with and affinity for nature is displayed in the architecture of both elf tribes. The Wolfriders are tree dwellers whose living homes were shaped in their growth to form the tree's natural contours into familiar and comfortable rooms. Even the steps are formed of massive burls curling down inside the trunk. The fascinating thing is that the interior design of the Sun Folk's houses displays the same type of ordering, as does the inside of Nonna and Adar's cave (figure 11). All have rounded, vaulted rooms in which all windows, nooks, and crannies are also rounded. Staircases always curve, as do pathways. There are never any straight lines or square corners except on the woven and embroidered wall hangings. The tree-formed houses of the Wolfriders look basically like the surrounding trees but are much more massive of trunk and rather "cultivated" in appearance. The same can be said of the homes of the Sun Folk. Their rounded, piled-up shapes are controlled versions of the surrounding

Still visibly of the same race and with the same goal of protecting their people, Cutter and the ancient leader approach the problem with opposing attitudes and capabilities.

Fig. 13. Time control through multiple panels

rocks. Whether this is a "Pini-ism" or a consciously conceived similarity of style is unimportant, for it still lends the sense of common roots so vital to the story.

Lights, Camera...Action!

Although all the design characteristics mentioned so far are noteworthy, we will now consider what must be the most outstanding aspect of Wendy's work: her ability to control the direction of the reader's attention. Her use of slow motion, zoom lighting, camera angle, close-ups, and even the focus of the character's eyes all serve to take the reader in hand and force him (very politely, of course) to read and experience the book at *her* pace, noticing those things she wants the reader to see.

The usual approach for comic art is to tell much of the story with a more or less straight-on view accompanied by occasional close-ups. The pictures are relatively evenly spaced in time and serve to give the reader a basically omniscient viewpoint of the action in the story. The technique works relatively well because of the emphasis on action rather than characterization. In *Elfquest,* however, it would be fatal, as Wendy instinctively realized. Her work instead occasionally throws the reader into the reference frame and viewpoint of one of the characters, lending a strong feeling of empathy for that character and actively involving the reader.

Lighting is one of Wendy's most potent tools. She sometimes sacrifices strict accuracy for the effect a powerful backlighting can give. The silhouette effect with the luminous elf eyes focuses attention on those eyes and so to their expression and direction. At the same time, it emphasizes the attitude of the body overall and so can add an ominous or deeply sorrowful mood to the scene.

Wendy is very talented at controlling the reader's sense of time through the number of panels devoted to a given topic. This ability is demonstrated

Fig. 14. Focussing the reader's attention with reflections in a character's eyes

Fig. 15. Wendy manipulates time and space.

drastic the changes that have taken place in the elves have been. The potent effect of placing them on two separate lines is difficult to pinpoint. Presented this way, Cutter and the ancient chief are directly juxtaposed as are Skywise and the ancient's second, making a direct correlation more effective. It also serves to convey the elapsed time between panels. Panels on the same line are interpreted as directly sequential, whereas there is a subconscious break that can occur between distinct lines. Be that as it may, these two panels show the reader at a glance the physical and emotional changes that have taken place. Still visibly of the same race and with the same goal of protecting their people, the two leaders approach the problem with opposing attitudes and capabilities. The ancient ones must cower in the bushes, hiding from the humans, while Cutter avoids detection only as long as it takes him to plan his attack. The slender, delicate ancients in their exotic clothing shake in fear and clutch empty fists in useless frustration, while the chunkier, larger-eared Cutter and Skywise snarl with determination, and the sword New Moon gleams with deadly warning. Even the jewelry depicts the changes that have and yet have not taken place. The leaders both wear neckbands, the seconds both have headpieces. The shapes are similar, but the delicate skill that wrought the ancients' accessories has either been lost or perhaps no longer appeals to the rugged, earth-bound elves. The conceptualization of the two panels is masterful, the execution clean and elegant.

The other side of the time-manipulation coin is the multiple panel, slow-motion effect that extends the time it takes the reader to absorb a scene that may take place, physically, in a fraction of the time the previous single panel required (figure 13). This places

in the very first issue which includes possibly the most informative two panels in the history of comics (figure 12). Because of the apparent simplicity of design and the immediate action of the previous and following panels, one is not at first glance aware of how much he has learned from these two pictures. However, by making them essentially the same picture with just a change of characters displayed, and placing them on the same page, one over the other (as opposed to side by side), Wendy makes the reader immediately aware of how much time had passed and how the reader into the same stepped-up time frame experienced by the protagonists. In a comic like *Elfquest* in which time does not flow smoothly for its inhabitants but is composed of long periods of sudden action, the technique is remarkably effective.

Another effective way of focusing the reader's attention is the reflection of an object in the eyes of a character. This grants us momentary access to that character's mind so that we share Cutter's horror of the burning forest highlighted in his eyes and Rayek's obsession with the relationship developing between Cutter and Leetah (figure 14). An important aspect of this concept is the use of the close-up in general. Wendy uses the ingenious trick of inserting a close-up of the main point of action over a regular wide angle pan shot of a scene. Whether it centers around the handle of New Moon striking the trolls' door or looking over Cutter's and Savah's shoulders across a long and very narrow span at the Sun Symbol, it serves to give the reader a double perspective of the action taking place. Not only is the overall action displayed, but the center of action—or the effect the action is having on a particular character—is displayed at the same time.

The most effective and subtle of the possible techniques available to an artist or film director, and the one most frequently ignored, is manipulation of the viewpoint from which the action is being examined. This is accomplished using very careful placement of the "camera." Properly done, it can place the reader immediately into the brain of one of the characters in the scene, increasing the emotional impact of the action immensely. Too often used, it can give a warped point of view of the entire story since one does not see all of the action taking place. Also, there is a fine line between an effective, artsy

angle and a viewpoint angle. Generally, the difference may simply mean the inclusion of the character's hand or foot in the picture, but more generally, it is a focusing on a part of a picture or character rather than simply a closeup view at an interesting angle. The difficulties inherent in this type of work is why the most common viewpoint in comics is the omniscient one. The action must be portrayed above all, and the risk is present, using this technique, that it will not be. However, Wendy dares to use it, and it is perhaps this trick that sets her work apart.

Wendy forces involvement with the characters; whether consciously or unconsciously, she recognizes the importance of it in telling of her deeply personal story. If the reader is not right in there struggling with the elves, the book loses all meaning and impact. It thrives not on dramatic, slam-bang action, but on long periods of character development with sudden, highly dramatic pieces of action that almost make the reader feel the sword in his own hand.

A good example of all the above techniques that deserves careful consideration is a scene in issue #9, page 27 (figure 15). In it, Wendy takes the reader in hand and masterfully controls his sense of time and space.

From an omniscient viewpoint, we see Skywise, relaxed and quiet, walking through the bushes, unaware of the eyes of the thief marking his passage. Zooming in, our attention is centered on three things: the lodestone, Skywise's relaxed hand by a sheathed blade, and the thief's eye and reaching hand. Time slows as we see more and more of the action taking place. The quick overview puts relative positioning in perspective and makes Skywise's actual drawing of his blade blindingly swift (between panels 5 and 7, he has gone from a relaxed posture to whipping around samurai-style, his blade drawn). Panels 7 through 9 are once again through the thief's eyes. As for Skywise, his emotions are carefully delineated for us; we see him bringing the blade around as his body turns a complete circle. We feel the thief's frustration as "our" hand comes back with agonizing slowness in comparison to the quicksilver movement of the elf. We see his blade flash down and then the blackness of shock in panel 10. We don't even see our thumb graphically hacked off; we don't even really feel it—yet. We scream more from shock than from pain. Then as we, the reader, turn the page (a very important piece of strategy, for we don't really know what has occurred until we have performed this physical act), we are released from the thief's mind and allowed once more to watch the actions of all the people involved. This is not a unique instance

Fig. 16. A Pini elf encounters a Bakshi elf, and the differences in style are obvious.

of Wendy's work, but it is certainly one of the best.

But What About the Art?

We have seen that as an artist, Wendy makes a great film director: she has the appropriate instincts and knows how to use them, and she has the necessary dedication and love of her subject to put in sixteen hours a day on it. In addition to these talents, however, she utilizes a tremendous amount of skill as an artist, making each and every panel a tiny work of art, and the overall story is held together with repetition of design and theme much as a painting is held together with line and color. Her skills as a portrait artist have already been alluded to, her eye for detail is phenomenal, her subtlety at drawing parallels is unsurpassed, and her sense of humor is irrepressible.

Wendy's mastery of subtle expression is extremely valuable in *Elfquest*. While the comic has been likened to *Star Wars* in its production of an epic of heroic, yet fairy-tale stature, there is an additional parallel that I have yet to hear anyone mention, one that struck me forcibly in the recent re-release of the motion picture. One of my favorite scenes has always been the segment that shows Luke standing against the double sunset, showing the tiny expression changes from frustration to longing to a sense of wonder. A similar scene occurs when he goes back to his uncle's farm and sees the destruction that has taken place. In that phenomenal scene, much is said without a word being spoken, all through Luke's wonderfully mobile face. His questioning look as he comes around in his landspeeder changes to one of shocked disbelief as he realizes what has occurred. He lowers his head as though unwilling to accept what has taken place, then raises it again with a look of utter determination and dedication. As I watched the movie this last time, I felt a shock of déjà vu that owed nothing to the film itself. It was almost as though I were reading a Wendy Pini comic. She is the only artist I have ever seen utilize the technique so effectively, and she is able to do it only because she is so extremely good at drawing expressions and showing inner turmoil and decision. These are so well done that any narration is redundant. One of the improvements in the overall story has been an increasing awareness of how well these sequences stand on their own and an elimination of excessive narration.

In addition to being an excellent portrait artist, Wendy is able to take on the extremely difficult challenge of dealing with seemingly dozens of characters in a single panel and still having a distinct center of attention and purpose in the panel. In issue # 1, page 15, there is a total of seventeen Wolfriders on the page who are desperately organizing an evacuation. A glance at the panel gives the feeling of a totally organized retreat due to that rather small central character calling out a few basic instructions. All the lines, both static and in motion, converge on Cutter. The trunk of the tree down which Strongbow is handing Dart to Moonshade leads to Cutter as does the perspective line formed by Treestump, his wolf, and Dewshine, Scouter, and his wolf. Woodlock and his family are running toward Cutter, and even Clearbrook and One-Eye far in the background focus attention on Cutter by looking at him.

All too often, once the newness of a strip has worn off, the artist takes on an increasingly production line quality to his work: characters lose individuality, and each panel is designed like the one before it. One of the best aspects of Wendy's work is the way it has grown and continues to grow. For instance, Wendy's elves have all too frequently been compared to the elves in Ralph Bakshi's animated film *Wizards*. While they had come into being and the story was outlined long before *Wizards* came along, it is undeniable that the first issue or two of *Elfquest* was decidedly more *Wizards*-like in style than subsequent issues. There is a very good reason for it. Just before *Elfquest* #1 went into production, Wendy toyed with ideas for a comic version of (or sequel to) *Wizards*. Accordingly, she drew a large number of samples in Ralph Bakshi's style of animation. Therefore, when actual production of the Elfquest saga began, traces of the Bakshi look remained.

In time, they gave way to Wendy's own natural style which is more graceful and oriental in appearance than *Wizards* (figure 16). It is great fun to hear her talk about this period because, while the story of Elfquest had long since been established, all the characters were still unformed. Consequently, when sketches for *Wizards* were done, the background elves were clamoring for center stage. It was as though the two worlds were competing in her brain.

Fig. 17. Leetah's affections symbolized by her necklace

Fig. 18. "Negative"
white on black

As it happened, Wendy's elves won out and evolved into the various members of the Elfquest cast, giving readers and movie-goers two unique experiences.

The detail Wendy notices in every facet of living adds tremendously to the overall story. The stances she gives children, the natural feeling of the way the riders move on and off the wolves, the active changing of the pupils in the eyes to reflect fright or excitement, all show not only a commendable ability to retain detail of the world around her,

but also the ability to reproduce it at will. It is this type of detail that adds to the ultimate feeling of watching real people.

Wendy's eye for detail often takes another route to expression. It seems that each time I reread an issue, I find new parallels hidden somewhere in the panels. Wendy is consistently finding new ways to remind us of previous issues or to connect one character with another. There are the obvious ones like the scene in issue #3 in which Cutter goes to Leetah's window and strives to get her to listen to "reason." The scene ends with Rayek's infamous challenge. However, it is repeated in issue #5 with quite a different ending. And there are the little things, like the emblem on Ember's tunic which is taken directly from her grandfather Bearclaw's necklace, or the XXX on the dreamberry juice. One of my favorites is Leetah's necklace. Made for her by Rayek, it is composed of three teeth hung with gold beads and suspended from a simple gold neckband. Then in issue #6, we see that her necklace is now just a slightly more delicate version of Cutter's (figure 17).

Last, and probably most important, is that marvelous Pini sense of the ridiculous and the sublime. From the wolf cubs chasing their tails to a father's gentle goodbye caress of his sleeping son's cheek, from Skywise licking his chops over a possible treasure chest to a tear in a proud young chief's eye, *Elfquest* is one joyous and heartwrenching experience after another.

As each new issue arrives, I am always anxious to compare it with the previous one, for Wendy is always trying out new ideas. In issue #6, there is page 3 with its "negative" white on black (figure 18) and page 7 with the panels delineated entirely in black. She has become steadily more adept at handling the pen-and-ink techniques available to her as well. Her improvement ranges from big things, like an ever-growing awareness of differentiation between background and foreground by using heavier lines and more detail at the point of focus, to little things, like the shading of the iris of the eye using radial rather than parallel lines. But these are really rather minor technical points that grow with her continued experience.

Possibly the key to the art remaining alive and fresh, if it can be pinpointed to one source, is Wendy's ability to approach her work as something that is fun and that she loves doing. The elves are real entities who pervade her life, and their antics show up everywhere, not just in the comic tale. The preliminary layout pages are not deadly serious but are approached with a giggle at the funny side of the situation. This keeps Wendy's attitude "up" and positive and keeps her from neglecting those delightful in-jokes that are so much a part of the comic. (Incidentally, I imagine they also keep her from going quietly bananas.)

The art of *Elfquest* can be summed up simply by saying that Wendy truly loves her elves and believes in the importance of the story she has to tell, so she tries to tell it as effectively as possible.

And her audience enjoys every minute of it. ✦

Elfquest: Fantasy Premise, Science Fiction World View

By J. J. Pierce

Elves are to fantasy as robots are to science fiction—how could anyone argue with that? "This is FANTASY we're doing here," avow the Pinis in response to a letter about the latest purported evidence for telepathy based on extra low frequency (E.L.F.) waves; how can anyone argue with them?

Nevertheless, it is possible to see *Elfquest* as science fiction—and for reasons that have nothing to do with the presence or absence of such science fiction trappings as robots (although the off-stage presence of the father of robots has a coincidental relevance). Or to be more precise, *Elfquest* can be seen as fantasy with a science fiction world view.

What is a world view, and what does it have to do with imaginative fiction? That takes some explaining indeed!

Next to arguing about what science fiction (or sf) is, the most popular pastime among sf fans is arguing about what the difference is between sf and fantasy. Most sf fans are also fantasy fans, so it isn't a question of trying to put "fantasy"—whatever it may be—beyond the pale.

It has often been argued that it is all simply a matter of trappings. J. R. R. Tolkien's *The Lord of the Rings* could easily be the post-holocaust sf a fanzine article once suggested (this was before Tolkien's *The Silmarillion* was available), if only the elves, hobbits, and orcs were defined as "mutants" and so on. "Magic" can always be explained "scientifically"—and no less plausibly—than old sf stand-bys like Faster-Than-Light (FTL) drive and time travel.

It is probably only coincidental that George Lucas has chosen to define the Star Wars saga, which involves not only FTL but the mystical Force, as "space fantasy" rather than science fiction (knowledgeable fans, of course, assign it to the space opera subgenre of sf), but the implied blurring of distinctions between sf and fantasy reflects the feelings of many fans and critics.

Elfquest, whatever else it is, is a created world story. Created worlds have a long tradition behind them in both sf and fantasy, and it is a tradition in which the distinctions between sf and fantasy have become especially blurred. Was there any more real "science" in Edgar Rice Burroughs' Barsoom (Mars) than in William Morris' worlds of fantasy? Is what sf writer Jack Vance does with created worlds different in any fundamental way from what Tolkien did?

There is a difference, and it is fundamental. But to appreciate it, we must look behind the created worlds them-

The shaman's complaint—one that was later to take on substance.

Compared to what they now face, their earlier crises begin to seem small.

selves. We must look at the world views they express.

In *The Silmarillion,* we learn that Middle Earth was sung into existence by Eru and the Ainur; that the world was once flat; that one of the silmarils, jewels wrought by Feanor, was set in the heavens and became a star. These are not mere myths or legends, but facts. Eru and Melkor are real. Magic is not the illusion of advanced science, it is magic.

In Burroughs' *The Gods of Mars,* we learn that Barsoom has its own creation myth: the various races of Mars sprang from the Tree of Life in the Valley Dor. But it is only that—a myth. Barsoom honors the cult of Issus, Goddess of Life Eternal, but the cult is a cruel fraud. What passes for science is fanciful, but it is treated as the workings of natural law in the common sense.

Middle Earth lies in the universe of Jehovah and Genesis, even if they are never given those names. Barsoom exists in the universe of Copernicus and Darwin, even if they are never invoked by name. The very nature and meaning of time and space are fundamentally different in Middle Earth and

Barsoom: in one, Creation, the Fall, and Salvation-Damnation are real; in the other, the Cosmos, Entropy, and Evolution.

Fantasy and science fiction in their purest forms reflect entirely different conceptions of existence—or world views. These conceptions are reflected not only in the details of their created worlds, but in the nature of dramatic conflict. Absolute Good and Evil are real in fantasy, as real as Eru and Melkor. In science fiction, by contrast, there may be good and evil, but they are not as easily defined, and absolutes are elusive, if they exist at all.

Melkor is not merely the enemy, but the Enemy. That he could ever be otherwise is inconceivable. In the context of Middle Earth, even a "good orc" would be a contradiction in terms. Moreover, there is only one kind of good and one kind of evil; circumstances are irrelevant. In the context of sf, however, circumstances can change; even on the relatively primitive Barsoom, one-time enemies could become allies. And there can even be conflicting ideas of what good and evil are.

Karel Capek will always be remembered for inventing the word *robot* in his play, *R.U.R.* But he ought also to be remembered for his conception of dramatic conflict in the play. In an interview for the *London Saturday Review* he called it a "comedy of truth," in which all the contending points of view were in some sense "right," and went on to say:

> *"Be these people either Conservatives or Socialists, Yellows or Reds, the most important thing is—and this is the point I wish particularly to stress—that all of them are right in the plain and moral sense of the word...I ask whether it is not possible to see in the present social conflict of the world an analogous struggle between two, three, five equally serious verities and equally generous idealisms? I think it is possible, and this is the most dramatic element in modern civilization, that a human myth is opposed to another truth no less human, ideal against ideal, positive worth against worth no less positive, instead of the struggle being, as we are so often told it is, one between noble truth and vile selfish error."*

What does all this have to do with *Elfquest?* As perceptive readers must have realized by now, Richard and Wendy Pini have created an epic that draws richly on the traditional elements of fantasy but in which the dramatic conflict and the world view behind it are essentially those of science fiction.

We know, of course, that the world of Cutter and Skywise is not our Earth—it has two moons, for starters. But it is nevertheless characteristic of fantasy worlds. Its humans are ordinary humans, its flora and fauna essentially those we know. The elves and trolls aren't Tolkien's elves and trolls, but they are elves and trolls, not aliens in the sf sense.

This "nameless world" may not, like Middle Earth, be the only one in its cosmos (we have yet to learn whence came the Fairy Castle); but certainly it can be considered the world for all practical purposes. The Cosmos does not intrude; and like nearly all fantasy worlds that express the world view of traditional religion, it is pre-scientific and pre-technological—evolution and entropy can also seemingly be disregarded.

Elfquest's setting then could easily have been the stage for an epic drama of Good against Evil in the tradition of Tolkien. Just turn the humans' false god Gotara into a real demonic being like Melkor or his minion Sauron, add an unseen but equally real Creator, stir in Rings or similar tokens of Good and Evil power—it isn't hard to imagine.

But *Elfquest* was never intended to be that kind of epic, and if some readers have thought it was, perhaps they have been inattentive—or have been overly ready to take some things at face value.

Knowledgeable comic fans, at least, should never have misled themselves. After all, they may remember that Wendy Pini first caused a stir in fandom

Fantasy and science fiction in their purest forms reflect entirely different conceptions of existence—or world views. In one, Creation, the Fall, and Salvation-Damnation are real; in the other, the Cosmos, Entropy, and Evolution.

with a letter protesting the absolutist morality in the *Silver Surfer* (ironically, some were nevertheless to fault her on the same grounds about *Elfquest*), and that should have been a clue towards how she would treat moral issues in her own work.

Although their family backgrounds were religious, neither Richard nor Wendy Pini took to their parents' faiths. Both grew up to become what the more alarmist apostles of the New Right would call secular humanists (Richard prefers "heathen.") But while they do not subscribe to morality in the authoritarian (and superficial) sense it is often preached, morality in its truer sense—and particularly the concept of moral integrity—is of paramount importance to them.

Art is often a means of discovering that within us to which we must be true, just as it later becomes a means to express that inner truth. C. S. Lewis' remark in *An Experiment in Criticism* that "scenes and characters from books provide [serious readers] with a sort of iconography by which they interpret or sum up their own experience," seems relevant here. And in their formative years, the Pinis each found works (not necessarily books) that spoke to them in this way.

Wendy's childhood discovery was *Alakazam the Great,* an animated Japanese fantasy rarely seen in this country. Richard's was Madeleine L'Engle's fantasy novel *A Wrinkle in Time.* They

Elfquest **was never intended to be an epic drama of Good against Evil, and if some readers have thought it was, perhaps they have been inattentive—or have been overly ready to take some things at face value.**

have little in common, it seems, except for heroes who must persevere against great odds—indifference, ridicule, and even malevolence—to achieve their goals, and most important of all, remain true to the best within themselves. This common theme struck deep emotional chords in the Pinis.

Another literary appreciation the Pinis found they shared was Shakespeare! They find his plays full of "marvelous wisdom and truth" but seem especially struck with the balance Shakespeare can show in treating contending personalities and viewpoints. Only in poor productions of *The Merchant of Venice,* for example, do they see Shylock portrayed as just a villain; in good productions, he is a man of integrity with his own view of the world which only *seems* evil to others.

Although he had been unaware of Capek's formulation for dramatic conflict, Richard Pini finds it applies to some recent work he respects, in particular a TV movie, *The Henderson Monster,* concerning an accident in recombinant DNA research. Many sf fans might have avoided it, expecting a simple-minded anti-science movie. What it actually was, Richard says, was a balanced and convincing portrayal of several points of view, each treated with both sympathy and antipathy.

How are such ideas of dramatic conflict worked out in *Elfquest?*

At first glance, it seemed they were not. In *Elfquest* #1, the origin of the conflict between elves and men is told in a prologue that suggests righteousness is totally on one side and iniquity totally on the other. All elves are seemingly as noble as Tolkien's—and the humans might as well be orcs. One might suspect the Pinis of playing the same game as some recent sf writers who pen moralistic tales of noble aliens and rotten Earthmen to make up for the sins of malevolent aliens past.

The ominous final scene of *Elfquest* #9.

The mistake was to assume that the prologue was true. Alfred Hitchcock found he had the same problem with *Stage Fright*, in which an account of a murder given by one of the suspects is shown on screen. It later turns out she was lying and was in fact the killer. But some moviegoers were annoyed; in a film, it seems, anything you see on screen must have really happened.

In the conventions of comics, panels with wavy edges imply a flashback or recollection, and the prologue in *Elfquest* #1 should thus be seen as what the elves of Cutter's tribe believe happened, not necessarily what did. The story of the origin of human–elfish hatred and warfare is their tradition, but is not necessarily the truth—and certainly not the whole truth.

Even in *Elfquest* #1, there were hints the elves were not, after all, perfect. Had Cutter been a bit more diplomatic in his dealings with the trolls, for example, perhaps the Wolfriders would never have been sent into the desert in the first place. And there was the shaman's complaint about the elves "twisting the shape of things with their foul magic." What things? Their arboreal home? Why would that bother anyone? Yet the shaman's complaint is later to take on substance.

In *Elfquest* #2, the Wolfriders' arrival at Sorrow's End sets the stage for another element of conflict: Cutter and his Wolfriders have always taken it for granted that their life is the elfish way of life. Now they are confronted with elves who "have no wolves, no tree houses and…live in the sun as men do." Their nearly disastrous first impulse is to treat the Sun Folk just like men.

But this is no conflict of good and evil; it is, to paraphrase Capek, that of an elfish truth opposed to another truth no less elfish. It might be mentioned in passing that the rivalry between Cutter and Rayek, while nothing startling in itself, is part of the same kind of conflict; in Middle Earth, such a rivalry would come about only through the machinations of Melkor or Sauron.

It is at Sorrow's End that Cutter must discover the true meaning of moral integrity, which involves not just the courage of one's convictions, but the courage to question one's convictions in the light of experience. This is very much in the spirit of sf, for the spirit of science itself lies in the quest for truth, not in blind loyalty to prevailing theory.

Cutter's decision at the end of *Elfquest* #3 to save Rayek is another sign of his spiritual growth, which has by this time become a major theme of the saga. Perhaps he realizes that in a sense he is as responsible for Rayek's enmity as Rayek himself. It is not a question of doctrinaire altruism, but of the recognition that actions have consequences which must be faced, that each of us helps make the world what it is, for good or ill.

As must often be the case, this conflict cannot be reconciled; the wound between Cutter and Rayek remains open, for now. Yet with the culmination of the romance between Cutter and Leetah (the notion that "Recognition"

> # Cutter must discover the true meaning of moral integrity, which involves not just the courage of one's convictions, but the courage to question one's convictions in the light of experience.

has a genetic basis, interestingly, is an sf element), one phase of *Elfquest* has been completed. Wolfriders and Sun Folk have embraced one another in elfish unity.

The stage for the next level of conflict, however, has already been set in *Elfquest* #4. The story of Madcoil, monstrous product of elfish magic gone bad, was necessary—as others have noted—to explain why so few Wolfriders were left even before they were burned out of their forest home. It should have occurred to readers, however, to wonder what other havoc Madcoil must have wreaked.

"You made monsters to prey on us," accuses Aro, head of the starving family of human refugees that approaches Sorrow's End in *Elfquest* #6, as he gives an account of human–elfish conflict and its origins that is quite at odds with that in the prologue of *Elfquest* #1. We know of Madcoil; we know, too, that Cutter's father, Bearclaw, did indeed steal human children for sport—perhaps Mantricker and those before him did worse.

Cutter cannot quite accept Aro's reproach, but he cannot quite reject it, either; else he would not stay what would once have been the unquestioned justice of slaying Aro's folk then and there. For the first time, doubt has been cast on all that the elves have always believed about themselves and their past. Compared to what they must now face, their earlier crises begin to seem small.

As the title of *Elfquest* #6 itself acknowledges, here is where "the quest begins." And here is where the series truly begins to take on epic proportions. Fundamental assumptions are challenged again and again as Cutter and Skywise pursue their search for the truth about their kind, not knowing they are followed by Leetah and the other Wolfriders on a parallel quest at least as important, and certainly more desperate.

Elfquest grows in complexity as the quest continues. Cutter and Skywise have already learned there are differences among elves. Now they must learn that there are differences among humans; and not only that, but that the relations between elves and humans don't seem to be the same anywhere. Among Olbar's people, the situation is still in a state of flux, while among Nonna's, elves are revered rather than feared.

The contrasts between Cutter and Skywise, too, begin to take on greater thematic significance. Skywise is the intellectual of the two and vital as such: without his discovery of the use of lodestones, the Wolfriders might well have perished in the desert, and in astronomy "he may get as far as Kepler," to quote Richard Pini. Yet Cutter has the greater moral imagination: "the ability not only to accept change, but to take advantage of it." It is as if Cutter and Skywise are the two halves of what the elves need to become whole.

Whatever qualities they, and the other elves, possess will be sorely tested in episodes to come. The shocks are far from over, as the ominous final scene of *Elfquest* #9 makes clear. The Wolfriders seem destined to learn some things about their distant kin that they would prefer not to know; what the outcome will be, we do not know. We do know that the elves' quest will be a slow and painful one, that their innocence can never be regained, and that they will have to assimilate and come to terms with more points of view than they now even imagine.

This kind of conflict, the interplay of a multitude of contending viewpoints, attitudes, and values, can be the stuff of epic drama just as surely as the Manichaean drama of Good and Evil. A number of sf works offer excellent examples—C. J. Cherryh's recent *Downbelow Station* is a case in point. In *Elfquest,* Richard and Wendy Pini have shown convincingly that the traditional science fiction mode of dramatic conflict can be equally valid for epic fantasy. ✦

The Woman Wolfriders

by Deborah Dunn

Six basic philosophical groups have emerged during the first twenty issues of the Elfquest series. These are the elves (divided into four distinct cultures: the Wolfriders, the Sun Folk, the Go-Backs, and the "High Ones" or Gliders of Blue Mountain), the humans, and the trolls. At this point let me say a few words about each.

The first two elfin groups tend to be close to the earth. Natural cycles are an intimate part of their lives. The Wolfriders were the first elves introduced, and their ranks provide most of the major characters throughout the series.

As their name implies, Wolfriders ride great wolves. They are hunters who come from a primeval woodland and who are very much in contact with the paradoxical forces of life and death in the natural world. Everyone in the tribe hunts, except for pregnant women and those with the very youngest of children. Yet rather than making them vicious killers, the Wolfriders' way of life reinforces an intense love of life and living. The Wolfriders are also close to their bodies and the sensual world, and much is made of their trust of their instincts. The night is their time, and physical exercise their joy.

The second elf tribe to be introduced, the Sun Folk, lives at Sorrow's End, an isolated village in the desert. They also look to the earth for their way of life. The Sun Folk are farmers, however. Their lives focus on different earth cycles,

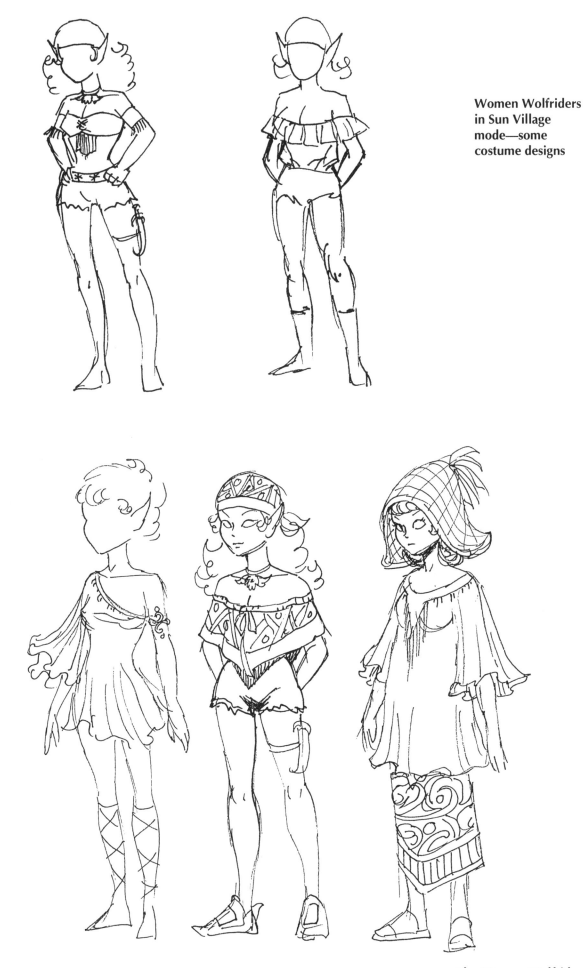

**Women Wolfriders
in Sun Village
mode—some
costume designs**

primarily those of day and night, and the seasons. The sun is their great symbol, the day is their time, and their activities tend to be mental rather than physical. They value the arts and elfin magic more than the Wolfriders do.

A least in the beginning, Elfquest's humans seem to represent all that humanity likes least about itself.

The third and fourth elf races are a startling contrast to the first two. The elves of Blue Mountain, the Gliders, claim to be the High Ones, the original elves to set foot upon the World of Two Moons, and the ancestors of all the other tribes. Like the Sun Folk, they have isolated themselves from what they consider to be a dangerous world. However, that isolation has been carried to such an extreme that it has proved to be nearly genocidal. Only a select few of these elves have ever left Blue Mountain. The rest are completely cut off from the natural world outside. Their great magical powers are wasted in a semi-utopian—or dystopian—society that is utterly devoid of love or creativity. Many of the Gliders, like the one called Door, have become so completely at one with their functions that they have ceased to exist as we understand the concept. This emotional barrenness is aptly symbolized by the fact that no children have been born in Blue Mountain for centuries.

A new look at elves and a leap of faith

Like the Wolfriders, the Go-Backs of the far northern mountains are a tribe at war with hostile neighbors. They are a hardy race of fighters who ride great elklike beasts. Constant battle has hardened them into a callous distortion of the close-knit Wolfrider clan. The Go-Backs have little patience with any way of life other than their own. For magic and the arts they show only scorn. Their rough-and-ready comeraderie is open only to those who fight as skillfully as themselves.

Wolfriders and Sun Folk compliment each other. Each group alone has fine qualities that are nonetheless sharply limited in expression. The Wolfriders are strong and vigorous but, for the most part, lack the use of magical powers. The Sun Folk possess much ancient wisdom but are far from being full participants in the life of the physical. The encounters between the two tribes continues to be an enriching and horizon-expanding experience for all.

Neither the Go-Backs nor the Gliders are able to accept the idea of change. They stubbornly keep to their own ways, rejecting outside influences. At times, this second pair of elf tribes seems to form a distorted reflection of the first pair. The heartless Go-Backs are to the Wolfriders what the sterile "High Ones" are to the Sun Folk: a warning of what the more vital groups might have become had they not had the courage to accept and learn from their differences.

By contrast, we humans tend at first to come off looking much less nice. At least in the beginning, *Elfquest's* humans seem to represent all that humanity likes least about itself. Following the dictates of an intolerant religion into endless racial warfare with the Wolfriders, the humans early on in the story would like nothing better than to practice genocide and have the world to themselves again. Dirty, brutal, strong rather than smart, superstitious rather than religious—as seen through the eyes of the elves—they are at once terrifying and impotent, blindly hating the elves, yet unable to do them any lasting harm. Humans fear the world around them (hence their concept of numerous nature spirits which at best are disinterested in human affairs), while still wishing to regard it as their own.

This dismal initial picture of humanity has lightened in later issues of the story. A new side to the humans emerged in issue #7 as we saw a human couple spared by the elves. In #8, another young human couple, Nonna and Adar, embrace the astounding assumption that elves are not demons, but godlings. They treat their elfin guests as objects of veneration and openly confess the humility they feel in the presence of the elves' beauty and grace. In #9, the humans' chief, Olbar the Mountain-Tall, shows the ability to face his superstitious fear and conquer it. Thus a new way of humans relating to the elves began.

Finally, there are the trolls, whom the elves seem to regard as only fractionally better than humans (and the trolls seem to return the sentiment). Sometimes it seems that the best thing one can say about the trolls, in fact, is that they are not humans! By the end of the series, however, we learn that the enmity between elves and trolls is ancient indeed. An alliance between the trolls and the elves proves short lived because of their insurmountable differences.

The trolls are, by our standards, phenomenally ugly; this applies to their personalities as well as to their warty hides. Their only emotions seem to be lust and greed, with fear thrown in upon occasion. Trolls are tried-and-true materialists. To them, love is a matter of wealth. "Any troll worth his hammer knows that a maiden's love is as true as

the gold he gives her," the troll Picknose tells us in issue #7, "and the more gold, the more true her love." Trolls live in underground caverns, trading wrought metal goods and weapons to the elves in exchange for fresh meat and hides. Like the elves of Blue Mountain, they have cut themselves off from contact with the natural world. The brilliance of sunlight is more than they can endure.

Again, humans and trolls seem to reflect each others' characteristics. The humans of Olbar's tribe make the first clumsy efforts to understand the elves, while the trolls reject the idea of any lasting alliance, choosing to keep to their own greedy and despotic ways. For the humans there is a hope of a better, less contentious future, but the trolls have condemned themselves to perpetual darkness.

The above sketches are great generalizations, of course. Each of *Elfquest*'s characters is an individual, acting as such. Time has wrought changes for all of them, some more than others. One of the Wolfriders, Rainsong, has become almost like one of the Sun Folk. Others, like Moonshade, continue to display a mild disdain for the peaceful ways of the desert dwellers. Most of the Wolfriders have managed to preserve their cultural integrity while keeping open minds toward the Sun Folk, attempting to learn from differences and similarities. Even trolls and humans are sometimes presented in a light which makes their unfriendly actions comprehensible, if not acceptable. There have been good humans and evil elves. This depth and variety of characteriza-

Through a glass darkly...

Roles, an early view: SunVillager vs. Wolfrider

tion is what gives *Elfquest* its special impact.

The main focus of *Elfquest*, within the context of these six groups, is on characters, and especially characters in relationships. The many and varied relationships, with their parallels and sudden interminglings, are the heart of *Elfquest*: parents and children; friends, male and female; lovers, mated or otherwise. There are more mated couples, family groups, and close tribal societies in *Elfquest* than in the rest of comicdom put together. The story at first focused on the Wolfriders, especially the two best buddies, Cutter and Skywise. The story then expands to include the first encounters with the Sun Folk, and Cutter's courtship of Leetah, his lifemate-to-be. (Let us pause for a moment at this point to talk about "marriage." Marriage in Elfquest jargon is called *lifemating,* which ought to say something about the kind of relationships elfin society is based upon. None of this equal-but-not-quite-equal husband-and-wife business for them! Both partners are truly equal in lifemating, a bond that means exactly what it sounds like. Lifemates mate for life, with all the long-term commitment that so often seems lacking in modern marriages.) Later in the saga the action grows again to include Cutter's quest for answers about who and what the elves were and are. The entire tale can be viewed as an expanding series of relationships.

But putting aside the philosophical implications of Cutter's quest and getting to the particular subject of this article, let's look at some of the common character types that appear in the series' development. First, there are the female leaders who appear among the Sun Folk, trolls, humans, Gliders, and Go-Backs. Each one of these figures is central to what we know of the tribal group and to how we feel about it.

Primary among these is Savah, Mother of Memory to the Sun Folk. I like the title "Mother of Memory" because it describes Savah's function so well. She is the keeper of lore and history for her tribe, their greatest magician, and (almost literally) the mother of them all as one of the two women from whom the entire tribe is descended. Savah is a living symbol of the past and a focus for the emotions of her tribe. Even the eldest of them can find a mother and wise counselor in her, if they so need. Her magical powers are all but forgotten by the tribe, but the wisdom of a very long life is available through her. Savah seems to assume this role, not as a social custom, but out of her own personal aptitude and choice. Often she helps the Sun Folk wrestle with their problems, and when an explanation of something is needed, everyone immediately turns to Savah. Without her, the Sun Folk are virtually helpless.

Savah's counterpart among the trolls is Maggoty, and her name tells it all. Maggoty is not quite as ancient to her small tribe of three as Savah is to the Sun Folk, yet in her distorted way she does mirror Savah's role with them. Maggoty is the oldest of the remaining forest trolls (the rest of their group lost a war and got marched away to the frozen north). She keeps most of their remaining lore and history, and all of the "magic" (actually, herb lore) is hers. It is Maggoty who mixes up the sleeping powders the trolls use to subdue their foes and who brews up the wonderful concoction called dreamberry wine. Maggoty is a reflection of the differences between elves and trolls in that she does not advise people what to do. No, she *tells* them, and her orders are generally obeyed (or else!)

A third female leader is the Bone Woman, whose rule of terror over the human tribe of Olbar the Mountain-Tall ends in issue #9. Like many of *Elfquest*'s humans, the Bone Woman seems to represent a negative extreme. Like Savah of the Sun Folk, she is a spiritual leader. But with the worst impulses of a religious institution, she uses her influence to maintain her power rather than enlighten her people. What knowledge she possesses is carefully kept to herself, to be used to her own best advantage. Though in magical terms she is far from a charlatan (her totemic bones do "speak" to her), much of her power, like Maggoty's, is concentrated in herbal preparations and a clever use of drugs. Unlike Maggoty, however, the Bone Woman manipulates instead of threatens. She is a very dangerous character, and her motives are very clear to the reader. She is greedy and selfish, but at the root of her dealings with the elves is the impulse for survival that motivates her. Her bones have warned her that the elves will be her downfall. Acting on this information, she actually creates her own fall from grace. But while we may disapprove of her actions, can any of us deny the reasoning behind them?

Winnowill of Blue Mountain is undoubtedly the most perplexing of all the characters in the series. The only other who even comes close to her is Two-Edge, her half-breed son. Like Two-Edge, Winnowill may be mad, but it is difficult to tell. If so, it is a dreadful madness, all the more because on the surface she seems completely sane.

Winnowill is not, throughout the original story, actually the leader of the self-named High Ones, yet her actions dominated the second half of the series. Some of *Elfquest*'s readers have compared her to Adolf Hitler, and not without reason. Winnowill possesses great healing powers, which she uses in a negative way to torture other elves. At one point she captures Savah's spirit and holds her prisoner for no reason except, it seems, to revel in her ability to do so. Winnowill has a cunning mind and an intensely magnetic personality. Her skill at manipulating others puts the Bone Woman's efforts to shame. She can attain anything she wants, whether by menacing, cajoling, or seducing.

Winnowill's motives are never clear. At times she professes to be motivated by concern for Lord Voll, the titular leader of the Gliders. At other times she speaks of him almost with contempt. Confronted by Leetah, whose own healing powers could have restored her twisted mind, Winnowill chooses to leap from a nearly fatal height. She is a character whose psychological depths have yet to be explored, and she remains a powerful, fascinating enigma.

Finally there is Kahvi, chieftess of the Go-Backs. Her function is to lead her tribe in battle, and she does this very well. Kahvi is gutsy and outspoken, but like all her people, lacks subtlety and compassion. When One-Eye of the Wolfriders is killed by trolls, her only comment is that now his widow will be

The Go-Back way: thick skins and blunt talk

a better fighter. Kahvi nearly leaves Cutter for dead on the battlefield as well, but the Wolfriders insist otherwise.

In her own way, Kahvi is as bigoted as the trolls. It seems that a lifetime of endless fighting has worn all the softness out of her, leaving only rough edges. She never wastes sympathy, even on herself. Kahvi does whatever she has to, to get her tribe to do what she wants, even resorting to mockery or blows. It is this that sets her as a leader so clearly apart from Cutter, whom she otherwise seems much like. The Wolfrider chief rarely must force his will on anyone in his tribe. Among the Wolfriders, even at the worst times, decisions are made by concensus. But the Go-Backs do things differently, and nowhere are those differences more plainly seen than in the personalities of the two leaders.

There is a certain category of heroine in popular literature with whom we are all familiar: the princess. Almost invariably, she is a helpless creature of delicate disposition, daughter of the local king (or duke, or what have you). She is the most stunningly beautiful woman alive, and incidentally, the male protagonist's love interest. She would be no one if she were not connected to some man (first her father, then her paramour), and her greatest talents lie in fainting, being captured, and/or dying. It's disquieting. Fortunately, there are none of these in *Elfquest*.

Leetah: a personality in flux

The few female characters who start out looking like they might be princesses end up being something else entirely.

Among trolls, Maggoty's granddaughter Oddbit is the Most Beautiful Woman. To us, she would seem almost unbearably ugly, with a huge frame, a nose like a limp sausage, a tiny, weak chin, warty skin, and small, squinty eyes. But to trolls, Oddbit is the most gorgeous creature in the world, and she knows it. She flaunts it, believing herself inviolable. She flirts unmercifully with the last surviving (she believes) male troll, her suitor Picknose, giggling, fluttering her eyelashes, cuddling up to him, and lounging with elephantine seductiveness. She is a great source of comic relief.

One is always aware of her canny mind beneath that preposterous beauty, however. It soon becomes clear to everyone, except for poor old Picknose, that she is only playing with him. Oddbit has no intention of marrying Picknose, even though he is literally the "last man on earth," unless and until he makes himself the World's Richest Troll. Nothing less will content this most practical of damsels. And indeed, it is not until the end of the quest, when Picknose becomes king of the trolls, that she gives in to him.

Oddbit's elfin counterpart is Leetah, Cutter's lifemate, the healer of the Sun Village, and daughter of the Sun-Toucher (the Sun Village's "high priest"). Just as Oddbit is Maggoty's granddaughter, so is Leetah descended from Savah. All these relationships do not define her character, however. They merely underline her crucial position.

In many ways, Leetah is the most complex and important of *Elfquest*'s female characters. Time and again the entire course of events pivots upon what Leetah does or does not do. The fact that she is not a simple character enhances her role, for one can never be certain what she will do. Part of the difficulty in understanding Leetah's actions is that she doesn't always behave in a rational, logical manner. In this she is much like most of us.

When we first see her in *Elfquest* #2, Leetah is flirting with Rayek, her first suitor, in a manner much like Oddbit's, although Leetah seems to be dangling Rayek more for the sake of fun than to get anything out of him. Then out of the blue, Cutter and the Wolfriders come swooping down upon the Sun Village. Compelled by Recognition, an irrestible mating urge, Cutter abducts Leetah.

This is the first of several shocks for Leetah. Like many modern women who believe themselves to be independent and "liberated," Leetah discovers that her society simply has not prepared her to defend herself in a crisis situation. Captured by the Wolfriders, she is incapable of doing anything more than to scream, "Rayek, do something!" Yet when Rayek is threatened, she folds like a house of cards and offers to do anything the Wolfriders ask to save him. And again, as soon as Cutter sets her down, she takes command, giving orders in the tone of an equal or superior. Clearly she very much likes to be in control of herself, and when control is taken out of her hands, she is at a loss.

How can we explain all of these changes and those that followed? It has been said that only in fiction are human beings expected to act in a reasonable manner. Only the best writing recognizes the essential changeability of human nature and can portray it in a coherent form. Like most of us at one time or another, Leetah does not always act rationally. At the same time, however, she never behaves as she does without a reason.

The key to understanding Leetah's personality is her love of freedom and her need of a stable base for her life. In a normal situation, where all is as it has been for centuries, Leetah is a confident, fearless person. But in an abnormal situation, or one in which her freedom is threatened, she either freezes up or acts irrationally. It takes several issues before *Elfquest*'s readers are allowed to see Leetah in a normal, nonthreatening situation, and so until then, we do not see her at her best.

The greatest threat to Leetah's freedom and her life order is her Recognition of Cutter. Recognition is another, particularly significant, piece of Elfquest lore. Briefly, Recognition is a genetically specialized form of love at first sight that takes place between two genetically ideal elves, binding them together in an intense, irresistible fashion for the purpose of producing extraordinary offspring. Once Recognized, the two elves cannot refuse each other, for if they do not mate, they will become deathly ill without each other.

Cutter the Wolfrider never questions Recognition, but Leetah does, resisting to the point where Cutter begins to fear death. Leetah's horrified denial of Recognition is perhaps understandable to us because most modern readers don't much go for the idea of biological predestination. To Leetah, Recognition is a deadly threat, both to her stable life and to her freedom to make her own decisions. It is the greatest challenge of her life to make a place in it for Cutter, and it takes four issues for her to accept Recognition as part of

At last, the acceptance of Recognition.

the natural order and not a violation thereof.

Leetah's next great challenge begins in issue #8. After Cutter embarks upon the quest named in the series' title, Leetah learns through Savah and her own son, Suntop, that Cutter is advancing toward a great, nameless danger. Savah has expended all of her psychic strength to obtain the meager warning and has implanted it in Suntop's mind, from which place only Cutter can release it. Leetah therefore has no choice but to venture into the vast, unknown world outside Sorrow's End so that Cutter and Suntop may be reunited and the danger made clear. If she refuses to leave her home, she knows that Cutter may die.

Humans *can* be kind.

We never see Leetah's struggle to decide whether or not to leave the comfort and security of Sorrow's End, the only place she has ever lived in all her life. From our knowledge of her, we can imagine this well enough. What we do see is that courageous moment when she leaves her home to seek and warn her lifemate. In the wide desert she faces the terror of the elements and finds that reality, though fearsome, is not really as bad as she had feared. The danger she imagined is more terrifying than reality itself.

Midway through issue #9, the skeletal remains of a solitary elf are discovered at the desert's edge. Leetah believes them to be those of Rayek, her former suitor and dearest friend. To her surprise, she discovers that the shock and grief do not kill her. From them, as from her fear, she draws the strength to turn away and continue her journey. And in issue #10, when she finally reaches both Cutter and the dreaded forest, she at last asks to be taught how to be a Wolfrider so she may move through the woods competently and meet the forest on its own terms.

Leetah faces many challenges in the issues that follow, but these are the ones that first try her character. The strength that she finds in meeting them sustain her through all other dangers.

There are a number of other interesting women characters who do not fall so easily into categories. For the sake of simplicity, I'll discuss them by racial groups, starting with the Sun Folk.

As mentioned earlier, *Elfquest* features a number of prominent family groups. The most significant of these in the Sun Village is Leetah's, which includes her parents and her sister. Toorah, Leetah's mother, is a delightful lady, as settled in life as Leetah, and of a greater serenity. She is close to her two adult daughters, yet not above teasing them at times. Toorah is also keenly aware of the purpose of the Sun Village as a human-free haven. Although she accepts her daughter's departure with as much grace as she can muster, it is clear she does not approve. Disapproval, however, only makes her concern show more clearly. It cannot banish her love for her daughter.

Leetah's sister is called Shenshen, and in their way the sisters are strikingly alike. Shenshen is lighthearted without being empty-headed, and she continues to enjoy the company of men, just as Leetah did before Cutter's arrival. She, too, has a personal skill: that of midwifery, a gift appropriately close to Leetah's healing. She relishes using her gift, just as Leetah enjoys healing, or perhaps even more, since she has few chances to employ it (elves have a very low birthrate). Sometimes antagonizing, sometimes teasing, almost always affectionate, Shenshen has had a rich relationship with her sister and is a major supporting character, representing perhaps, the Sun Folk at their most open and engaging.

There is also a trio of lovely ladies who are frequently to be seen with the dashing Skywise. After all, what's a comic book without some fellow who has women dripping off him all the time? In this case, his sex appeal is so exaggerated that it is impossible to take offense. Remarkably, there is never any animosity shown among Skywise's three paramours. Rather, they seem to have an informal agreement to share Skywise among themselves equally, enjoying him for what he is, rather than trying to possess him. This is a remarkably sensible attitude for them to take, considering how unlikely it is that Skywise will ever settle down.

Among humans, a grand total of four women (named, not background) characters have appeared. This places them just above the trolls, who are stuck at two. Of these four, the Bone Woman has already been mentioned. The first to appear as an actual character in the series was Thaya (*Elfquest* #6). She is an outcast travelling through the desert with nothing but her husband, her son, her crazed brother-in-law, and a pony. She plays mostly a supporting role to her husband, Aro, which is not surprising given the society she comes from.

The third human woman, who first appeared in Marvel Comics' *Epic Illustrated* #1 and who entered the main *Elfquest* saga in issue #9, is Selah, daughter of Olbar the Mountain-Tall. She is another princess type who breaks out of the mold. Though not an important character, she has been consis-

tently interesting. As befits the daughter of a great chieftain, she is strong willed and relatively fearless, carrying a flint knife and willing to use it. She is also first seen running away with her lover whom her father despises because he failed his test of manhood. What better guarantee is there of reader sympathy?

Most important of the human women is Nonna. She and her husband, Adar, lived alone in the forest until Cutter and Skywise helped them regain admission to Olbar's village in issue #9. Like Leetah, Nonna is (in her own quiet way) a healer, and like Savah, she dispenses a certain amount of lore as a symbol-maker. Yet unlike Thaya's people, she has been raised to accept the presence of elves (which she considers "spirits") in the world without panic. In later issues she even begins to lead Olbar's people toward her own reverent view of the elves.

Discovering Cutter in a fevered delirium, Nonna takes him in and attempts to cure him as she would a human child (*Elfquest* #8). This particularly alarms Skywise. There is a certain amount of hostility and confusion before the elves can accept the con-

Leetah's horrified denial of Recognition is perhaps understandable to us because most modern readers don't much go for the idea of biological predestination.

cept of friendly, helpful humans. Even when Nonna's good intentions have been proven, Cutter and Skywise have difficulty believing them. Yet it is her friendship that is crucial to both their quest and to the humans' change of attitude in issue #9.

Only one female character aside from Winnowill stands out among the

Blue Mountain elves. This is Aroree, one of the Chosen Eight. She serves as a hunter for her people, riding a huge hawklike bird and bringing in captured game. Of all her people, only Aroree is open enough to reach out to the Wolfriders. She quickly becomes friends with Skywise but is not able to escape the strictures of her society completely. Aroree is a troubled character, torn between her attraction to Skywise and her loyalty to Blue Mountain.

Likewise, only one Go-Back woman besides Kahvi really emerges as a character in her own right, and her story strangely parallels Aroree's. This is Vaya, a young warrior who becomes friends with Pike during the Wolfriders' stay with the Go-Backs. Her relationship with Kahvi is strained, however. The chieftess is especially hard on Vaya; nothing the girl does ever seems to be good enough. During the assault on the northern trolls' mountain fortress at the end of the quest, Vaya is captured, tortured, and killed. Only after her death do the Wolfriders learn that she was Kahvi's daughter.

Finally, we come to the women Wolfriders named in the title of this article. Despite the importance of the other elfin cultures, the Wolfriders remain the central group in *Elfquest*, supplying almost every major character throughout the series. In all, there are seven—hunters, lovers, mothers—plus several others mentioned as being deceased. Since the Wolfriders are a small, closed group, the incidence of interrelationships among them is high. This contributes to the atmosphere of extreme emotional closeness among the

Nightfall: a wellspring of love— and loving strength

Wolfriders and explains the fact that not a woman among them can be found who is not actively participating in at least one relationship of some kind.

The first woman, human or elfin, seen in *Elfquest* is Nightfall, and in my eyes she remains the most important of the woman Wolfriders. In many ways, Nightfall represents the very best that the Wolfriders can produce. She is strong and independent, giving an unshakable love to her lifemate, Redlance. Often, one discovers, love to the Wolfriders means protection of the beloved, be it parent, child, sibling, or mate. Just so, Nightfall insists upon remaining with her injured Redlance in the desert to defend him (*Elfquest* #2) even though there is a good chance this will mean her own death. Nightfall is also the first and almost only Wolfrider to reach out to Leetah during her struggle with Recognition, to try to help and understand. Later, she speaks in Leetah's defense before less tolerant Wolfriders. Knowing herself and her own value, Nightfall is not afraid to reach out to others. She has more courage than most, elf or modern human.

Each of the other characters is just as much an individual, with distinct strengths and weaknesses. Dewshine is Cutter's cousin, daughter of his mother's brother. She is perhaps best known for her skinny, flat-chested build (it is ironic that a comic book character should be considered unique for having an *un*-buxom body) but is a lively young lady nonetheless. Forever to be found at the forefront of hunt and battle, she risks her life with impetuous delight.

Clearbrook is the eldest of the female Wolfriders and was the lifemate of One-Eye who perished during the troll battles in the bitter mountains of the north. Taken in by the Go-Backs, she falls into a maniacal blood-lust, wanting nothing but revenge against the trolls. By the end of the series, however, a measure of peace has returned to her.

Rainsong is the Total Mother among the Wolfriders: the soft and retiring one who becomes so much at home among the Sun Folk. She devotes her entire being to the care of her family in a way that somehow transcends the stereotypical.

Moonshade seems to represent the "straight" Wolfrider with the fierce love of her people but less of their openness. Though certainly not an evil character, she is not always entirely positive. She is too much a Wolfrider, unwilling or unable to open her mind to the ways of the Sun Folk. Though she has lived in the Sun Village and knows their way of life, Moonshade does not truly respect it. To her, the Wolfriders' "Way" is the only way, and her impatience with Leetah on a number of occasions only underscores this intolerance.

Timmain is the ancient ancestress of the Wolfriders who suddenly—and shockingly—reveals herself to them at the very end of the series. A true High One, Timmain long ago took the form of a she-wolf and has lived as one for thousands of years. Although she can acknowledge the Wolfriders as her descendants, Timmain is not one of them. Her stay among them is too brief for that. She reveals the secrets of their past to the elves and then seals herself away forever within the palace that was the origin place of the High Ones. It seems only fitting, since she has been so much a part of the past, that she at the last join it physically as well.

Another woman Wolfrider, whose influence continues to be felt even after her death, is the chieftess Joyleaf, Cutter's mother. Actually, both of Cutter's parents were significant people. Their relationship was one of ideal mutual completion. Bearclaw, the chief, lived with a flair for enjoying the present that is typical of the Wolfriders, especially before the destruction of their forest home in issue #1. He gambled, drank, and stole the humans' children for sport. Joyleaf was exactly his opposite, a quiet person who knew how to enjoy life without being active every moment. Her specialty was wisdom, and her major task was restraining Bearclaw's hatred of humans. Together Bearclaw and Joyleaf created balance and order for the Wolfriders and themselves—no small task.

One last class of characters that is virtually unique to *Elfquest* is the children, generally a forgotten minority in comics (which is truly ironic, since children are comics' readers, at least in theory!) *Elfquest* regularly features five children, more than can be found anywhere else except the pages of *Richie Rich*. They are, not necessarily in order of importance, Suntop and Ember (Cutter and Leetah's twins), Wing and Newstar (Rainsong's two children), and Dart (son of Moonshade). All of them are portrayed with that mixture of innocence and wisdom typical of all but the youngest of children, and all possess the bouncy self-assurance of children who never doubt they are loved.

The farther I progress with this article, the more I realize the futility of trying to talk about *Elfquest* without talking about its men. It's true, a few names have crept in here and there: Cutter, Skywise, Redlance, Picknose, Rayek—fascinating names for fasci-

Joyleaf: a moderating influence.

"...IT WAS MY *GIFT* TO MY SON. HE WAS THE FIRST OF US TO HAVE THE RIGHT TO CALL THE LAND HIS OWN. IF YOU CHOOSE, WOLFRIDERS, YOU, TOO, HAVE THAT RIGHT — AND *NONE* CAN TAKE IT FROM YOU!"

SHADE AND SWEET WATER

nating characters. I'd like to give them the attention they deserve.

Unfortunately, I have to place a limit somewhere; one article can cover only so much. The male characters are a whole different barrel of monkeys, and this *is* about the females of *Elfquest*. Still, I hope it is clear that even though there are more, and better, women in *Elfquest* than in ten issues of the next best comic book title—and that is definitely not a statement I make lightly—no reading of *Elfquest* could ever be complete that did not take into account the men.

Having said this, I can go on to point out one final thing that, I think, accounts for the ultimate appeal of *Elfquest*. That is its treatment of the characters. A comic, or any other book, can have characters of every conceivable sort, but they would all be cardboard cutouts without the author's respect for each and every one of

them. In a letter to me, Richard Pini wrote, "It's not so much a case of sitting down one day and plotting it [*Elfquest*] as it is a case of knowing each and every character intimately and letting the story flow." It is that kind of care that makes *Elfquest* what it is.

With all the odd-type people in *Elfquest*, the men and women, the children and old people, the elves, trolls, and humans, there is hardly one of them that the reader doesn't come to know and respect as a person. The cast of *Elfquest* includes a tremendous variety, and yet each character is valued for what he or she is. Thus the full range of human experience and feeling, good, bad, and neutral, is acknowledged and approved. To be fully human is to have something of each character in us, and there is nothing wrong in that.

The "message" of *Elfquest*, if one must have one, is simply that very examination of the human character, in all of its manifestations; it is the recognition that this variety makes humanity what it is. *Elfquest* is about being human—what it means, how we do it, and maybe, just a little, an idea of what humanity could mean and be. ✧

This article, in shortened form, originally appeared in The Heroines Showcase #19, *published in 1983 by The Comics Heriones Fan Club.*

All together now! A gathering of many of the females of *Elfquest*.

Research into Elfquest

How to live like the Wolfriders (as closely as possible)

by Ree Moorhead Pruehs

Of course you know that no one is really thrusting swords through the magician's lovely assistant who is locked in a trunk onstage, no matter how convincing her screams or the blood gleaming upon the blades. In spite of that though, don't you feel a thrill of nervous anticipation until she emerges alive and whole? And wouldn't you feel cheated—even angry at the magician's incompetence—if the trunk were to fly open halfway through the trick, allowing you to see that it isn't real after all? Would you really want to watch the rest of his act?

If you are a creator, whether writer, artist, or gamesmaster, you have the same obligation to your audience as the above mentioned magician. Should the reader/viewer/participant catch an error in your creation, you run the risk of that trunk flying open—and along with it, a lost audience. "But it's fantasy," you say? So it is. But that simply means that by the laws of this world we live upon, the tale you're telling can't or likely won't happen. It does not mean you can allow your world to be internally illogical or inconsistent.

The first rule of writing is, traditionally, Write What You Know. But this isn't totally inflexible. You don't really have to be on personal speaking terms with a wolf, know a poultice from an infusion, or be able to *knapp* a razor-sharp knife from a couple of rocks to write about the subjects. Even if your honest-to-Gotara idea of "roughing it" is staying in an off-brand motel instead of the Hilton, there is hope for you. Behold the dread goddess who shall breathe life into your creations, and do not fear her: her name is Research.

"But research is dull!" you cry. Given the proper inspiration—your desire to write—and the proper material, it doesn't have to be. Let's head for the bookshelves, shall we? (If your shelves don't groan as heavily as ours, your local library, bolstered by interlibrary loans, can often produce an amazing amount of material on topics you'd never dreamed existed...outside the pages of *Elfquest*, that is.)

First of all, a caution: never lose track of the idea that if you're going to work with the World of Two Moons (hereafter WoTM), you are working within the confines of someone else's dream. "Improving" upon the original does not make for good pastiche; it isn't your world to improve upon. So go back to the source: the original *Elfquest* and its sequel, the novelization *Journey to Sorrow's End*, and published interviews with Wendy and Richard Pini. Of lesser importance and/or reliability (albeit still valuable for inspiration and background) are the Elfquest role-playing games and the *Blood of Ten Chiefs* anthologies.

Find yourself a good set of writer's tools—no, I don't mean the latest, gizmo-laden word processor on the market. Get a good dictionary and thesaurus. There are too many types of each to name. Browse in a bookstore until you find one or more of each that suit you.

Now, to WoTM specifics.

A quick, easy way to get another perspective on the right "word feel" is the excellent Earth's Children series by Jean M. Auel (published by Berkley Books). It's set in the right time and technology period, it's entertaining, it's accurate [*Well, reasonably accurate; some anthropologists roll their eyes up at the series—RP*]; Auel really makes the era, especially the crafts and skills practiced by her primitive humans, come alive. A warning: these are good thick books; don't get started on one if you have something else to do.

Do you want to learn the skills, crafts, and many of the philosophies of the WoTM elves for yourself? It isn't cheap—four to five hundred dollars a class as of mid-1987—but the classes exist. Tom Brown, Jr. began his "apprenticeship" in forest lore at the age of eight, guided by the Apache elder Stalking Wolf. After being featured in *People* magazine, he disappeared into the wilderness and spent a year there with only a knife for equipment. Today he runs the Tracking, Nature and Wilderness Survival School. [*Information about the school, and about any of the books and organizations mentioned in the rest of the article, can be found in the appendix, Sources of Information—ed.*]

Not that ambitious? Refer to Brown's excellent series of trade-edition paperback "Field Guides"; I find the complete collection the single most important set

WITHOUT BREAKING STRIDE, *CUTTER* SWEEPS *LEETAH* ONTO *WOODSHAVER'S* BACK!

NOW, MY GENTLE *LEETAH*—

—BE A *WOLFRIDER!*

of references for Elfquest writing, art, or gaming. In fact, if I were to name the single most helpful reference book for use in writing Elfquest stories, it would probably be *Tom Brown's Field Guide to Wilderness Survival*, with *Tom Brown's Guide to Living With the Earth* a very close runner-up (the first covers more subjects, the second explores its topics

Not the pause that refreshes? Oh, well...

in more loving detail and goes further into philosophy). Covered topics in *Wilderness Survival*, by chapter, are: Attitude, Shelter, Water, Fire, Plants (listing one hundred edible plants and a chart of general plant habitats), Animals (from hunting ethics to skinning, cleaning and utilizing the entire animal carcass), Cooking and Preserving, Tools and Crafts, Cautions and Suggestions (for the modern reader). These books do not exceed the given technology of the WoTM in any way (the only tool it is supposed you start with is a knife) and cover all aspects of "living with the earth." The books are simple

to read and understand, and are so beautifully told you're likely to forget you're doing research. They are also crammed with useful information, philosophy, and clear line drawings of the crafts, tracks, skills, or plants being spoken of. (The other books in the series deal with tracking, plant life, and nature observation; see the list in the appendix.)

In addition, Brown's autobiographical novels *The Search* and *The Tracker* furnish far more interesting scenario ideas than the standard Elfquest fantale of elves jumped by packs of random Gotara-worshipping humans.

There are other survival books readily available. Most of the following are easily located; generally you can find one or more in any given B. Dalton's or Waldenbooks store. All are paperbacks, some are mass-market editions: the *U.S. Armed Forces Survival Manual*, Bradford Angier's *Survival With Style*, Richard Graves' *Bushcraft: A Serious Guide to Survival and Camping*, and Larry Dean Olsen's *Outdoor Survival Skills*. None of these are as lovingly detailed or as entertaining to read as the Brown books, but all are handy, reasonably inexpensive one-book source guides. A caveat: use all of the above books with discretion as they utilize technology not yet developed on the WoTM; the "water stills" made with plastic sheeting are reasonably apparent as such, but other devices spoken of are equally unusable, but not as obvious. (A digression/commentary on *Elfquest Book One,* taken from *Outdoor Survival Skills*: "A cactus can be cut and peeled and the moisture sucked out, but this is not the same as drinking running water—it is more like drinking Elmer's Glue." Poor Wolfriders!)

Also available, if not completely useful, are the trilogy of books published by *Muzzleloader* magazine: *The Book of Buckskinning* Volumes I, II, and

III. Forget the gunpowder; it doesn't work on the WoTM anyway, by decree of the High Ones. Concentrate on the articles on brain-tanning buckskin, quillworking, horseback travel, and tomahawk/knife throwing. I've also found many interesting things in John Seymour's *The Guide to Self Sufficiency*. Many Elfquest writers seem to find the Foxfire series of books helpful; virtually every bookstore carries one or more of the volumes. Again though, these books utilize technology "outside the limits," and none of these volumes is comprehensive in and of itself.

As long as weapons have crept in here, let's talk about them. Weapons combat skill and hunting skill are different disciplines involving different motivations; an elf skilled in one may not be much good for the other! So far as weapons combat skill is concerned, many fantasy writers and artists—professional as well as fan—seem influenced by the Indiana Jones School of Swordplay (e.g., what they see on TV and in the movies) when creating scenes involving personal combat. Many sword-and-sorcery flicks are actually pretty laughable: all glitz, unusable weaponry, and little if any actual technique. (That the "thrust to the heart works every time equals instant kill" is one of the great fictional myths. It's actually pretty hard to hit the heart with a blade weapon, as a little thought and anatomy study will confirm. The breastbone and ribs tend to get in the way. The throat or the wrists are far more vulnerable targets on an unarmed person.)

Granted, I have certain advantages for weapons reference that many folks don't: my husband studies and teaches different forms of weapons combat, is an armorer and knifemaker by hobby, loves his crafts, and can happily give a twenty minute lecture/demonstration on such topics as "The Proper Use of the Spear in Troll/Elf Combat." You can get to know similarly talented people by contacting your local branch of the Society for Creative Anachronism, an international organization that specializes in medieval research and re-creation. The SCA has chapters in or near most good-sized cities and/or universities.

Roland Green (author, reviewer, and an *Elfquest* fan) once said that observing SCA fighting, combined with thorough research, is the best way to figure out how weapons combat "really works," and I've always found his advice sound. Re-creation of tournament combat is one of the things for which the SCA is best known, although SCA members also practice many other skills of the medieval/Renaissance time period—herbalism, dancing, illumination,

Don't get caught in this situation! Learn those herbs!

calligraphy, costuming, brewing, and feasting, just to name a few.

If research is all you're after though, ask the local group if you may attend a fighting practice. Tournaments are fun, but you can't really ask the fighters to "stop and do it again, would you?" Observe, take notes, and—if you've asked permission—take pictures. Be courteous and offer to bear water to hot, thirsty fighters. Wait until there appears to be a break in the action before asking questions of the person in charge. Most fighting SCA members, when not actually beating on each other, are more than willing to talk about the finer points of their hobby. Want to learn the arts of weapons combat for yourself? Go for it! In most cases, all you'll need to do is ask. The

Pharmacology, Bone Woman style.

other fighters will be glad to help you get started, and oh yes, in the SCA, women fight, too. I should mention, however, that for legal reasons most groups are prohibited from training minors in weapons combat.

Books on related subjects? Dan Inosanto's *The Filipino Martial Arts* and *Absorb What Is Useful* demonstrate many aspects of striking and defense. (Inosanto, a professional stuntman and protege of Bruce Lee, runs a school in California and teaches seminars across the country.)

Ignore the silly title and cover of *Traditional Ninja Weapons: Fighting Tech-*

niques of the Shadow Warrior by Charles Daniel, but don't ignore the book. Inside are clear pictures and accompanying descriptions of several forms of weapons combat, including knife, staff, and sword fighting. The SCA publication *The Fighter's Handbook* is also helpful to the novice, though it necessarily overconcentrates on shield work and armor requirements. The researcher can also look for other books about the Filipino martial arts *arnis, kali,* and *escrima* (stick fighting), as well as volumes that focus on the use of the *Bo* staff (similar to a quarterstaff). Some books on the latter are listed in the bibliography. A good basic book on the use of the bow and arrow is *Archery for Beginners* by John C. Williams, a gold medal Olympian and an Olympic archery coach. (Bow and arrow construction may be found in Brown's *Living with the Earth* mentioned above.)

The astute will notice that I've recommended no books on unarmed combat. It is my feeling that this type of combat—except for basic arts such as wrestling—is unlikely to develop in most WoTM cultures. On Earth, most of today's unarmed combat forms were developed in response to the needs of warrior cultures of a higher social and technological level than that of the average Wolfrider tribe. It would appear, too, that unarmed combat would do elves little good except against their own kind. Humans have a considerable reach and mass advantage over the elves, while trolls appear to have a lesser reach advantage and a greater mass advantage.

Don't go by what you see on TV or in some schlock kung-fu movie either. Movie combat is carefully choreographed to look good for the camera; it has little to do with "real life" fighting.

See the Inosanto book *Absorb What Is Useful*. If you are considering elf sans weapons against troll, think about a combat-trained man throwing kicks and blows at a sumo wrestler. The normal man bounces. Real life Bruce Lees are few and far between—and that sort of talent takes years of intensive study and discipline first to acquire and then to maintain. Survival, not warmaking, seems the elves' main goal on the WoTM. And unarmed combat is basically useless for hunting.

Unfortunately, the prime result of fighting is that someone usually ends up getting hurt. The result of blows or cuts to a given area of the anatomy may be found in or gathered from such books as Bruce Tegner's *Self-defense Nerve Centers and Pressure Points* or N. Mashiro's excellent *Black Medicine: The Dark Art of Death* series. Warning: the latter is very graphic and decidedly not for the squeamish. Symptoms and treatment of specific injuries, such as fractures or frostbite, can be found in any of a number of excellent medical guides on the mass market.

Do I hear a question about why elves would need to know first aid since they have psychokinetic healers? I ask in return: What happens when the healer is unavailable, exhausted, distracted, or nonexistent?

A good all-around first aid textbook is the American Red Cross's *Standard First Aid and Personal Safety*, readily available in most bookstores or as part of the package acquired by taking a Multimedia First Aid class at your local Red Cross center. A community service note: this course takes eight hours of your life, often less, costs under twenty dollars and could save someone's life. Wolfriders aren't the only ones who need to be prepared for the unexpected. Besides, didn't you need a break from that typewriter anyway?

Other books I continually return to are the American Medical Association's *Handbook of First Aid and Emergency Care*, John Henderson's *Emergency Medical Guide*, and Terry Brown and Rob Hunter's *Concise Book of Outdoor First Aid*.

While we're on the subject of medical reference, I shouldn't neglect *The Merck Manual*, one of the best-known and most readily available medical textbooks. Although it falls somewhat short on injury and shock reference, no other book really comes close on just about any other medical topic, particularly diseases. Unfortunately, even in paperback the book is expensive. Try to find a copy in a library or used book store. The manual also makes for dry, technical reading; you may want to have a medical dictionary handy.

Pharmacology on the WoTM is essentially herbalism. Billed as "the most complete catalogue of nature's miracle plants ever published," *The Herb Book* by John Lust is a six-hundred-page-plus paperback jammed with facts and more than 275 line drawings of plants. Most herb descriptions include the common name, medicinal parts, description, properties and uses, and preparation/dosage information. A separate section lists herbs that are used for natural dyes. *Living Medicine: The Healing Properties of Plants* by Mannfried Pahlow is not nearly as comprehensive but does have larger drawings than the Lust book and pretty color plates.

Other uses of plants are discussed in *Earth Medicine, Earth Food* by Michael A. Weiner which examines the plant remedies, drugs, and natural foods of the North American Indians. What is particularly fascinating about this book are the extra tidbits and anecdotes that make the herbal research more interesting for modern readers. For example, you may have read that primitive tribes drink willow-bark tea to cure fevers. Did you know that our modern-day aspirin is chemically related to the salicylic acid found in fresh willow bark? A different look at the same topic is provided in Frances Densmore's *How Indians Use Wild Plants for Food, Medicine and Crafts*. Information on dyeing processes may be found in Elijah Bemiss' *The Dyer's Companion*.

Of Wolves and Men has more than once been described as "the bible" of wolf books. I agree; if you only have one book on wolves, this should be it. This beautifully illustrated, comprehensive volume covers not only description, pack social structure, communication, and hunting habits of the wolves, but their relationship with man, and man's

Where there are elves, there are wolves.

The last two books mentioned are produced by Dover Publications which bears mention in its own right. Dover produces over two hundred books per year on a variety of topics and often publish facsimile editions of books long out-of-print. *The Dyer's Companion*, for example, was originally printed in 1815. Dover reproduces the original text intact, adding an introduction and appendices by the curator of the Smithsonian Institute's Division of Textiles. Nearly all Dover books are inexpensive, high quality paperbacks.

Quite often where there are elves, there are wolves. Barry Holstun Lopez's

attitudes towards wolves. It will inspire you. Be warned: it will also anger and sadden you. Also recommended: *The Wolf*, by Michael Fox, a narrative story about a pack and pack behavior that features excellent illustrations.

No, I'm not neglecting the trolls. Let's talk about blacksmithing and jewelry making. You may be able to meet a blacksmith through a horse farm, through the SCA, at a Renaissance Festival, or at some other site that stages historical reenactments. The last three may offer similar opportunities to let you speak with a jeweler. If none of these options are available, and you need to write about trolls, it's back to the bookshelf. Unfortunately, most modern texts on metalcraft presuppose the use of modern power tools, so we'll have to fudge where necessary. Modern books also tend to focus on toolmaking, not weapons-making. Many of the techniques will be the same, though.

The Practical Handbook of Blacksmithing and Metalworking by Percy M. Blandford is reasonably comprehensive and well illustrated. The first twelve chapters deal with ironworking, the last seven with metalworking. *Practical Projects for the Blacksmith* by Ted Tucker starts the reader at the forge, is well illustrated with sketches and photos, and features an excellent glossary of technical terms and a discussion of metallurgy. Alexander G. Weygens' *The Modern Blacksmith* is one of the easiest books for a novice to follow that I've found. Every page is illustrated by the author, and the margins bear clearly labelled, step-by-step instructions for the technique currently under discussion. The book also includes a good glossary and clear photographs of tools. Even the back cover is instructive: on it are color photos showing the hues that steel turns when exposed to different temperatures and heat-treating techniques.

Other books that may be of interest to troll fans are *Working With Metal* by Pamela Tubby which describes working soft metal (no harder than mild steel); simple jewelry-making questions may be answered in Garrison and Dowd's *Handcrafting Jewelry: Designs and Techniques* which features sections on casting, stone setting, and forging.

Finally, how about the world itself? You won't need to map out the entire world for your holt or campaign, just a small part of it. If you're an absolute tyro of a mapmaker (like me), perhaps you can find what you need in a commercially produced topographic map.

The Essential Whole Earth Catalog lists two sources of such products: Raisz Landform Maps and United States Geological Survey topographic maps.

There are several general field guides available in bookstores. Among these are the Audubon Society Field Guides (sixteen books as of late 1987), published by Alfred A. Knopf; and the Peterson Field Guides (thirty-five books) published by Houghton Mifflin. These cover a variety of animal and plant life and terrain types, and are illustrated with excellent photos and/or drawings. Select only the books you need.

It is important to remember, however, that WoTM exploits do not take place on our Earth; therefore, new and different forms of animal (and plant) life can be introduced as long as they fit into the ecology. (However, be real. There are no unicorns and dragons; no such critters exist on the WoTM, by creative decree. Remember?) One place to find what logical extensions of Earth-type creatures might look like is *After Man: a Zoology of the Future* by Dougal Dixon, a comprehensive field guide to one possible future of Earth animal life, with several chapters explaining how and why animal life evolves in response to specific circumstances. The book is fully illustrated in color with fascinating and beautiful drawings; it may even make you a little sad to realize that the animals depicted do not exist...yet.

These books are intended as starting points, no more, for your research. You will doubtless find even more inspiration in your local library or bookstore, or by browsing through a volume such as *The Essential Whole Earth Catalog: Access to Tools and Ideas* (a wellspring of source material!)

In closing, I would like to recommend several old friends that may influence more than your writing of Elfquest pastiche. The first is *People of the Lie* by M. Scott Peck. Written by a psychiatrist/minister, this book offers fascinating insights on the evil personality and the possible curing of same. Another resource is an essay by Poul Anderson, "On Thud and Blunder," which was most recently published in Anderson's collection *Fantasy!* and is a must-read for any budding fantasy writer. The third is the deceptively small and slender *The Elements of Style* by Strunk and White, a timeless commentary on the art of writing. (Most college courses should be as informative as that single book.)

A final word to those of you who want to write in the world of Elfquest: may your illusions be wondrous and unfailing.   ✧

The Universe Expands

Close Encounters

Over the years, *Elfquest* has produced varying responses from its readers, from imitation and flattery, to satire and parody. One of the first satires to be printed was a comic strip/column by Fred Hembeck. As Dwight Decker explained in the original introduction to the *Elfquest Gatherum* Volume One, "Fred Hembeck...[is] a perceptive commentator on the state of the art in comics and fandom, and his columns and articles appear as comic strips instead of solid blocks of prose....When *Elfquest* #1 appeared, Fred was writing and drawing (and starring in) a column called "Dateline @!?#!" for the weekly tabloid newspaper, the *Buyer's Guide for Comics Fandom*. It wasn't long before *Elfquest* was subjected to the inimitable Hembeck style, and that column is reprinted here."

But Hembeck's column was only the beginning. Here, along with Wendy's response to Fred Hembeck, are other versions of *Elfquest* you might have never seen before—at least, not in one place.

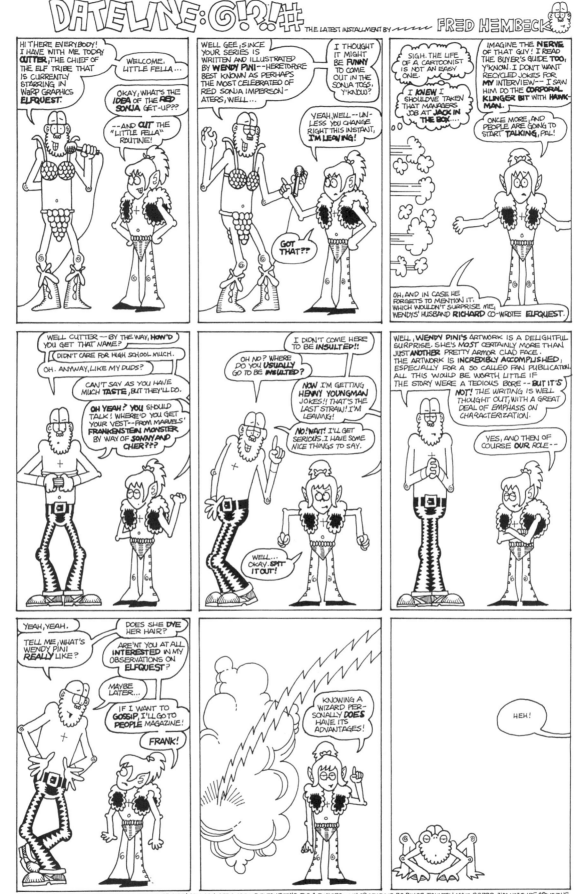

Right, Cutter the Slugrider makes a decision—
from *Normalman* #4
© Jim Valentino

Below, somewhere in the "real" world, a
rehearsal for "Sorrow's End: The Musical"—
from *Fantastic Four* #242
© Marvel Comics

Right, there's a new balloon in the Macy's
Thanksgiving Day parade—
from *DC Comics Presents* #52
© DC Comics

Potpourri

From the pen, pencil, and brush of Wendy Pini

From the cover of *Elf Wars*, a supplemental booklet for the Elfquest role-playing game

Concept drawings
of Scouter and
Dewshine for *Siege
at Blue Mountain.*

Early costume ideas for Cutter and Leetah, for the time that the Wolfriders lived in Sorrow's End.

Very first sketches
of Cutter's parents,
Bearclaw and
Joyleaf.

BEARCLAW

JOYLEAF

Skywise and Timmain—what does their relationship portend for the future of Elfquest?

Convention sketches

Left, Costume idea for Cutter for the Blue Mountain sequence in *Elfquest. Bottom,* costume ideas for *Siege at Blue Mountain.* When readers saw the *Siege* sketches (which admittedly were only first ideas), they thought the elves had gone punk!

This page, Ideas for
T-shirt designs—
before
Opposite page,
Ideas for T-shirt
designs—after

NEW
MOON

Women, Comics, and Elfquest

by Wendy Pini

When I go to the Marvel offices to deliver pages of art or to break down the next few *Elfquest* reprint issues with Mary Jo Duffy, I sometimes get that same queer feeling I used to get in high school—I guess everybody's had it—that uncertainty about one's status in the pack, that "am I in with the in-crowd?" anxiety.

It reminds me how much a creature of habit and conditioning I am. But it also makes me wonder if men and women in the work force, including myself, will ever rise above the pecking order of the pack system or if, indeed, they really want to. There is safety in the known, in the established norm. High school, for all its banality, prepares one for life in a way which can neither be forgotten nor escaped. I suspect that most people are what they are in high school and only continue to become more of what they are throughout their lives. I was an outsider. I still am.

High school and comic books: the mentality of one is ripe for the consumption of the other. In an industry which aims its product primarily at adolescent males, attitudinal changes toward the stereotyping of both male and female comics characters can only be hard won through long, yet subtle, combat. Many of those battles will be fought, unsung, by women—as artists, writers, editors and consumers. Inroads will be made quietly. Flamboyance is, for the most part, the province of the rooster, not the hen.

But sometimes the greatest changes are brought about by stealth, rather than by overt aggression.

The nature of the comic book audience has changed over the past ten years as much as has the medium itself. The most profitable change, artistically and commercially, has been the growing number of women, of all ages, who have swelled the audiences of such enduring series as *The X-Men, Star Wars,* and *Teen Titans* and have helped make the relatively new *Alpha Flight* a hit.

Elfquest boasts the highest percentage of female readers of any comics series currently on the market. I say this with ill-concealed pride and the results of a wide-sweeping demographic survey in hand. *Elfquest's* audience is, in fact, almost equally divided between male and female readers in their late teens and early twenties. Whether this trend will continue with *Elfquest's* newsstand distribution as a Marvel/Epic reprint remains to be seen, but I suspect the pattern will hold.

Tentative analyses and simplistic generalizations made by the industry and the fan press aside, what appeals to female comics readers is whatever turns them on, and that territory is still largely unexplored—even by women themselves.

It is a commonly and not incorrectly held view that women gravitate to stories which contain a high degree of "soap opera." Young girls are especially interested in relationships and in emotional interactions. They like stories about family-type groups. They are also attracted to slightly dangerous, youthful, androgynous male characters who, much to any hard-core Jungian philosopher's delight, would seem to represent the female *animus*

(or animating motive). *Elfquest* fills that bill on all counts, not because I deliberately set out to attract a huge female following, but because lurking not so deep within my own psyche is that same high school outsider who—horrors!—is a typical female adolescent.

One creates, after all, for an audience of one. But happily, times have changed so much that boys are now showing interest in those things that have been traditionally regarded as "girl stuff."

From my own experience and observations I have learned that many girls, and even women, spend time fantasizing, not just about connecting with males, but about being males. I remember discovering Michael Moorcock's Elric stories when I was sixteen. It mattered not a whit that the character was male: I identified because Elric expressed all the self-centered melancholy and anguish that most teenagers go through.

I was Elric mentally when I read the stories. I drew him, I wrote about him, I even corresponded with Moorcock and vented philosophical analyses of the character. Poor Michael! It didn't dawn on me until much later that I was obsessed with my own animus. At age sixteen I was simply thoroughly turned on, and because Elric was an effeminate character, it was that much easier to project myself into him.

Had he been a muscular Conan type, I doubt that identification would ever have taken place.

At about the same time I discovered Moorcock's writings, I began collecting Marvel Comics. I started with *The Avengers* and instantly loved Hawkeye, the loudmouthed misfit rebel.

Because the distinctly male slant of the writing had prejudiced me, my attitude toward the Wasp and the Scarlet Witch was just as sexist as that of any of the male Avengers.

I felt no obligation to those dippy female characters, did not even look for hidden depths in them, and continued to identify with the stronger, more interesting males. What teenager does not fantasize about being strong and effective? My experience was, and probably still, is shared by many girls. Young, impressionable, insecure: we become, vicariously, male heroes.

In one sense women's imaginations are more versatile than men's: to women, androgyny is not taboo. When a man dresses as a woman, he is, to straight society, ridiculous if not repellent. But when a woman dresses as a man, she does not seem to carry the same shameful stigma. The man risks being branded a wimp. The woman may be regarded as chic. This makes some women able to project themselves fearlessly into a male physique and frame of mind.

In 1982, Diane Venora, star of *Wolfen* (one of my favorite movies) played Hamlet off Broadway. She cut a dashing, persuasive figure in cropped hair, military uniform, and boots. By contrast, Robert Preston in *Victor/Victoria,* for all the poignance and gentle humor of his role, looked far more ridiculous in drag than did Julie Andrews.

Women have their own dignity which men, portraying them in any medium, seldom seem to be able to capture. Women, however, do not seem to be objects of derision even when aping male mannerisms and thought patterns. The deep-rooted misogyny of our society sustains the imbalance of image between the sexes—the male persona (the role he assumes to display conscious intentions to himself and others) is more respectable than the female— and those women with low self-esteem help to perpetuate it just as they help perpetuate bad pornography.

Many women buy into the supposed permanence of male-created female stereotypes because it is easier for them to accept someone else's definition of who they are than to discover their own identities. Women are conditioned by parents and peers to fear loneliness; there is no more lonely path imaginable than that which leads to the truth of one's own self.

Chris Claremont once said to me, "The reason why women often write better male characters than men write female characters is because women are taught not only to think for themselves, but to think for men, too."

Considering that, statistically employment throughout the entertainment industry is roughly 75 percent male to only 25 percent female, it is easy to understand why the increasing number of women breaking into the comics field do need to think like men in order to compete.

It is still commercially necessary for women to focus on those things that will interest male consumers, whether in storytelling, art style, or development of merchandising properties.

Given that the scope of the types of comics stories which are traditionally interesting to men is still rather limited, women now have a tremendous opportunity to enrich the medium with their insights and to promote new levels of understanding between the sexes. It is already happening, subtly, but still within the boundaries of the system.

Who, after all, wants the "mission

In one sense women's imaginations are more versatile than men's: to women, androgyny is not taboo.

impossible?" Who wants to be a crusader? No man or woman I know. Pioneers must be willing to be lonely.

Inertia is a ponderous thing. Having been pioneers of sorts, Richard and I, for all our knee-jerk "somebody do something!" reactions, are as shy of sticking our necks out as anyone. If we keep doing it, it's probably because we've rolled into a certain inertia of our own. One day we'll get off the merry-go-round and wonder how we ever rode it together so long.

Hey, it's only comics, after all.

Female comics characters, as portrayed by men, are sometimes seen only as vehicles of suffering. They exist to be put into peril and to agonize for men's amusement. Critics assert, rightly, that hostility to women has reached such perverse proportions in certain comics that women are often represented only as objects of rape or other forms of degradation. As it is now conceived, *The Savage Sword of Conan* is an outstanding example, and sales are reportedly healthy. But, whether the hostility is overt or merely the result of complacency, the representation of true femaleness, organic and psychological, has yet to come into its own in the graphic storytelling medium.

No matter what ideological gymnastics are required of women as they attempt to fit into an ever more rapidly moving technological society, the one act that remains intrinsically womanly is birth. Men can never really know what birth is like. Many can't even see it as a painful but fulfilling experience. Many men have great paranoia about retaining their physical identities, and the distortion of pregnancy coupled with the messiness of birth is more than some can cope with.

Consider: All splatter movies are made by men. Horror is gore and dismemberment. Consider too: Along with the mounting trend toward "goo" in horror films, many special effects monsters resemble embryos or aborted fetuses. *It's Alive, Prophecy, Humanoids From the Deep*—the examples are there.

And birth images themselves are given horrific stature, as in the chestburster scene in *Alien* or in the monstrous birth of *The Manitou.*

This is not coincidence. As male-dominated society grows increasingly coldly technological, the biological process of birth and death become at best remote, at worst gross and shameful. In the end it may be left to women to guard whatever remains of the human in humanity.

Whenever men depict birth in the comics, it seems as though the woman is always flat on her back, in extreme agony; there is usually associated violence or tension. The laboring woman has to be moved from point A to point B while the villain attacks, so her urgency is coupled with the anxiety of everyone whose life is in danger at the villain's hands. While this works dramatically, it is an overused device which portrays pregnant women as pains-in-the-neck. And the hero, whether it's his baby or not, is usually as fuddle-headed about it as Ricky Ricardo was during the birth of Little Ricky.

When Stan Lee and Jack Kirby brought Sue Richards to her "confinement" with Franklin in the '60s, the physical aspects of the birth were not dealt with at all. Yet it was a daring move for superhero comics at the time. In a *Killraven* story and more recently in *Sabre*, birth was represented fairly graphically with some focus on the woman's strained reactions to labor and, of course, with the aforementioned attendant violence.

It was with a certain self-consciousness that I approached the birth scene in *Elfquest* #20. Aware of what had been done before, I chose to portray the baby's birth as naturally as possible, without trauma. The mother was shown sitting up, which is how most women prefer to do it to take advantage of gravity. The father was right there with her, and the children were watching with fascination. The scene was a joyful one, and to the best of my knowledge, birth has never been handled quite this way in American comics. In addition, male elves can "lock-send" with their mates—that is, communicate telepathically in such a way that the male can actually experience the feelings of the birthing female. So the scene can be said to have added significance, done as it was from a woman's point of view.

Not so very long ago society ostracized women who refused motherhood. Now childlessness is an acceptable choice, but society still has difficulty embracing women who reject their other stereotypical roles: healer, nurturer, or mediator. The new breed of tough, independent superheroine that has emerged in various comics titles over the past few years, when not handled carefully, resembles in speech and mannerisms a man with breasts rather than a truly feminine woman.

As pointed out earlier, this does not necessarily make the character ludicrous; in fact, this breasted man is easy to work with in the violent superhero genre. She is uncomplicated. She takes her lumps alongside her male counterparts. But just to reassure the readers who represent society's standards (and society *must* be reassured) that she is, indeed, female, she is usually given some sort of romantic involvement which enables her nurturing side to show forth.

In some cases a fresh approach is taken. Ororo mothered Kitty Pryde early on in their relationship. And, though Mockingbird sparred several bruising rounds with Hawkeye (a daring scene in which man and woman were equal in skill if not in physical strength), she

later whisked him off to the Poconos for a honeymoon.

While I cannot deny the high entertainment value of these pairings, the message overall remains that the heroine who stands alone is not whole. Female readers cannot help but absorb this message, and many cannot help but buy it. A monthly dose of it from 80 percent of the titles on the stands, including alternative comics, has a numbing effect even on the most enlightened mind. True alternatives seem impossible. They are not. But they seem so.

Why do women read male-oriented comics? Partly because that is what is available. Options are currently limited. But there is another reason, the kind of secret vice that one takes a flashlight under the covers at night to indulge.

I hope I will be forgiven for spilling the beans, but some women actually *enjoy* seeing male characters injured or helpless, because they find emotional empathy with the pain to be stimulating. Sounds kinky? Maybe. But not only is it harmless, it may spring out of that same well from which a woman draws compassion and the desire to ease others' pain.

I wonder sometimes if women don't spend their lives waiting for explosions, for something cathartic to come along and blast them into a new state of being.

I used to go into rages as a girl because I didn't like where and what I was. But I wasn't ready to go somewhere else. If I wanted to draw something and hadn't developed the skill to do it, I wanted to explode. I wanted (figuratively) to be blasted apart to find that vision. Even now I feel that way at times.

That is the artist's point of view, but there are parallels in other areas of life. A girl refused a place on the soccer team by a repressive school system must want to put her fist through a wall in frustration. But she doesn't dare, because aggressive, violent females are too intimidating and seldom get their way in polite society. For such a thwarted individual, fantasy can be a form of escape—and violent fantasy can be cathartic.

Women as well as men are inspired by the "suffering hero" image. If the hero is down and out, the female reader feels sympathetic—drawn to the pain with a desire to make it better.

At the same time, she herself wants to be the recipient of that attention, to be down and out, and to have someone want to make it better for her. She projects herself into two roles, the healer and the healed. Perhaps she is also the injurer: Brahma, Shiva, and Vishnu all in one. The Dominatrix is a recurrent image in comics and a popular one with readers of either sex. Power is the name of the game: power to give life or to take it away, power to be the center of attention, power to explode.

There is a dignity to the physically wounded hero that is not accorded the heroine who goes through mental pain. Art reflects life, and life is not fair.

A woman might go through a great deal of anguish because she is being sexually harassed at the office. Hers is no less a battle than man against men with sword or spear—but her wounds are not so obvious or so easily bound, and she is not necessarily hailed for her courage.

When a woman draws attention to herself, she also draws attention to her so-called sisters, and they become uncomfortable. Subterfuge is a survival tactic, a la the Invisible Girl, and that requires a low profile. Real women's everyday triumphs and defeats are most often in the attitudinal area, not in hand-to-hand combat as depicted in the comics.

When the She-Hulk trashes a villain, a female reader can take it as symbolic of an ideological victory, but can she really identify in any other way with that kind of broad (pun acknowledged) violence?

How often are women arrested for acts of physical aggression? Not nearly as frequently as men are. Women's battles are usually cerebral, but just as brutal as any brawl.

The nobly wounded (as opposed to the tortured or abused) heroine is seldom seen in comics.

Red Sonja has taken some cuts in her day—in fact I used to take advantage of my appendix scar to illustrate that point when we were doing the "Red Sonja and The Wizard Show" at conventions years ago. And the Black Widow, under Gerry Conway's care, went through the ringer right along with Daredevil .

But nowadays, heroines seem to be getting wounded psychically rather than physically. Master of the psychic invasion, Chris Claremont delights in shocking his eager readers with the mental torment of his characters.

Yet he is conscientious enough that these writhings have symbolic validity. What he seems to be saying with Ororo, bizarre as she is now, is that the character is going through an explosion, suffering to reach a new state of being—like a birth. Birth as explosion. Women crave explosions. *X-Men* has an "X-traordinarily" high female readership. They are turned on. See the pattern?

I don't think men are comfortable with the thought of loss of identity through catharsis. Maybe that's why they depict birth as agonizing, because from their point of view it is necessarily an explosion, rather than a giving or an issuing.

How else does the suffering hero appeal to women? Young girls start reading superhero comics at just about the time they are discovering boys and their own sexuality. They're a little bit excited, and a little bit afraid.

In their fantasies, if the hero is helpless and hurt, he is harmless—approachable. This truth is dealt with symbolically in the otherwise wretched British film *The Company of Wolves*. Only after Rosalie shoots the wolf-man is he safe to touch. And oh, do the young girls want to touch the hero! They empathize. They, too, are helpless.

Some of the most romantic, lyrical scenes in comics concern the hero's fall. When Alicia Masters let the Silver Surfer recover on her apartment couch from The Thing's blow, there was certainly subtle, erotic interaction percolating beneath the surface of their conversation. The scene was both tender and a turn-on.

"Woman as healer" is a famous cliché. But underneath may be "woman as sexually awakening and vulnerable individual." We brought this out in our Elfquest novel, *Journey to Sorrow's End*. We examined Leetah's nature as a healer and tied it in with her sexuality. She had to make herself immensely vulnerable to go inside a person, find the injury, and work her healing magic on it. She had to share the pain to a certain extent. It drained her. So in compensation she could choose when to release forces in her that gave her great physical pleasure.

One assumes that a healer must know the secret sources of both pleasure and pain in the body. Leetah was balanced between them.

During the scene in which Rayek helped Leetah heal

Cutter (*Elfquest* #16) there was a strong undercurrent of the type of eroticism I call Liebestod: love and death.

Women find this terribly stimulating, yet it takes cold control to portray such melodrama without overdoing the mush. The Japanese use this type of thematic device in their romance, science fiction, and samurai comics, sometimes to an excess that even I, insatiable as I am, cannot tolerate.

American comics artists and writers are more reserved in their approach to this kind of all-or-nothing interaction between characters. The two most potent forces in human existence, sex and death, make dynamic dramatic storytelling when carefully blended. Comics that contain a heavy element of violence are more appealing to women when the aftermath of brutality is acknowledged with some kind of human empathy.

Obviously *Elfquest* contains many

Woman as healer. Leetah brings the four tribes together to help Strongbow.

elements that have attracted and held a strong female readership throughout the duration of the series. But it has also attracted an equally devoted male following, and that says more about the changing times, perhaps, than about *Elfquest* itself. Marriages have resulted from elf-fan meeting elf-fan. Richard and I smile at the poetic justice; we met through the letters pages of *Silver Surfer* #5, and why not? The Surfer had and has all the makings of the kind of vulnerable hero girls go for. I did. It wasn't fate. It was glands.

Whenever John Buscema and I meet, which isn't often enough, since I like the man and admire his work so much, he always busts my chops on the subject of women artists.

John asserts that women cannot draw truly masculine men, but men can draw women perfectly well. There is no debating with him because it's not really important to him, but it touches a nerve in me. Having been an animation-style cartoonist for more than eight years, I've almost forgotten many of the rules of anatomy that I've been breaking so merrily. And my male elves are nothing if not pretty.

It is some consolation that Warp Graphics does not receive letters from male fans complaining that the elves are effeminate. I have somehow managed to create believable male characters who do not trigger prejudicial responses in the men who read *Elfquest*. Though they could have been better drawn in some cases, the human men that I represented in the series were fairly rugged looking, so I did not shy away from tackling the artistic problem of rendering masculine figures. But I can do better.

Men deserve it; they're worth looking at and they're worth a truthful line on paper. So are women, you hear me, John? No more men with breasts!

Whatever the reason for male acceptance of my art style, I believe that Elfquest's audience was *conditioned* by Richard's and my pig-headed belief that our way was not just the right way to do the story, it was the *only* way.

The fan press jokes and says no one will ever figure out why Elfquest made it—it had everything going against it.

But quite simply, we created a market that did not previously exist for a look and a style of storytelling that was old-fashioned and yet had never been seen before. That bodes well for newcomers striving to tell their stories or to express their artistic styles in this highly competitive field, for the independent press is now as difficult to break into as the mainstream ever was. An audience will warm up to something new and different if the creators persevere. But some words to men and women, boys and girls alike: The quality of the work must merit the readers' time and money. Do it for yourself, but make yourself a member of your own audience. There is no other way to evaluate your own progress.

To women in particular, my only advice, which most of you have probably figured out already, is to channel your compulsion to meet others' expectations into the driving force behind your own creativity. Women are perfectionists, partly because of performance anxiety, partly because they are terribly competitive and don't like to be caught napping, but mostly because they put so much of themselves into what they do. Call it love, if it must be sentimentalized. The talent of women is an active volcano that the comics industry is just now beginning to explore. I'm enjoying the fireworks that I already see.   ✧

Elfquest Here, There, and Everywhere

Elfquest has gone international. If it isn't American enthusiasts recommending it to their overseas friends, foreign fans are discovering it on their own in European comic shops and dealers' listings—even if one German fan magazine referred to the creators as "Windy und Ralph Pini."

The international appeal is poignantly demonstrated by a letter from an American reader with a German girlfriend: "Just when I was pricing rings and making plans to pop the question the next time I saw her, she sent a 'Dear Hans' letter announcing that she had decided to marry someone else. But, she added, would I please keep on sending her *Elfquest?*"

Less pathetic but just as significant is this letter from a long-time South African comics fan (who published one of the first comics fanzines ever, in 1962), writing to an American friend who had sent him copies of the first nine issues:

> I was determined not to get involved with *Elfquest* until I had finished other work and other reading. Then I made the fatal mistake of paging through them...and everything else got shelved. In all honesty I can say it has been an awfully long time since any comic book has delighted me so. After the first few pages I was completely hooked—and remain so. (Good grief!—can it be so?—that a bunch of elves can excite me? Do I grow senile? Or have Warp Graphics come up with something which a lot of us have been hoping for, looking for, and never quite able to describe?)

Meanwhile, the first foreign edition of *Elfquest* appeared: *Elverfolket* (The Elf Folk) #1, a Danish translation of *Elfquest* #1 and #2 in one volume, published by Interpresse under the simple title "Ulverytterne" (The Wolfriders). The squarebound format and heavy, high quality paper stock are impressive, and the translation is generally accurate.

Since then, other foreign editions have followed. Here is a sampling of what you might find in other countries if you were to look for *Elfquest*.

Elfquest as it appears in Denmark...

...in Norway...

...in France...

...and most recently, in Russia.

Beyond the Printed Page

Games People Play

It was, perhaps, inevitable. The world of Elfquest is so well realized and its denizens so well fleshed out that it was only a matter of time before readers began to dream up their own adventures. Sometimes they would use the characters Wendy and Richard had already created; sometimes they would imagine their own elves and trolls, tribes and lands. By this time the phenomenon of role-playing games, usually exemplified by Dungeons & Dragons, was in full flower, and fans began to ask when an Elfquest game might show up. Since neither Wendy nor Richard are gamers, it became necessary for them to find people who had the ability and experience to take a world teeming with established characters and environments and boil them down into their component attributes. (What *is* Cutter's strength, numerically, compared to Picknose's, anyway?) Luckily the Pinis found not one, but two gaming companies that were more than equal to the challenge. One, Chaosium, turned Elfquest into a role-playing game; the other, Mayfair Games , developed a board game. On the following pages is reproduced some of the artwork Wendy has done for "what-if" tribes of elves that inhabit the World of Two Moons— if only in the imaginations of the players.

This page and the following two pages, scenes of plains dwellers and sea elves

WENDY
©85 PINI

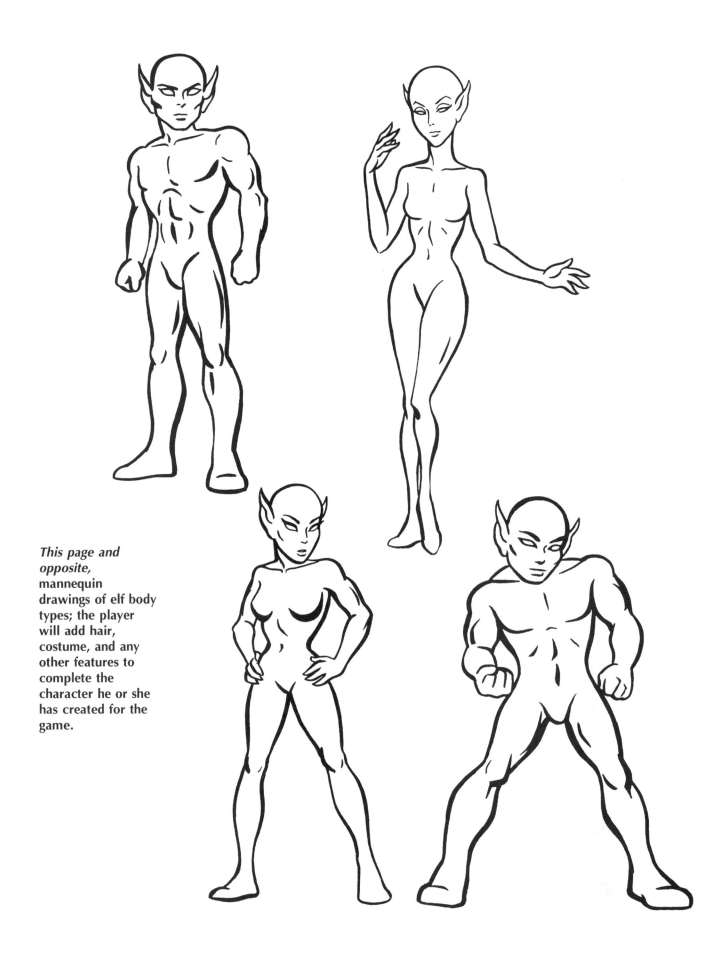

This page and opposite, mannequin drawings of elf body types; the player will add hair, costume, and any other features to complete the character he or she has created for the game.

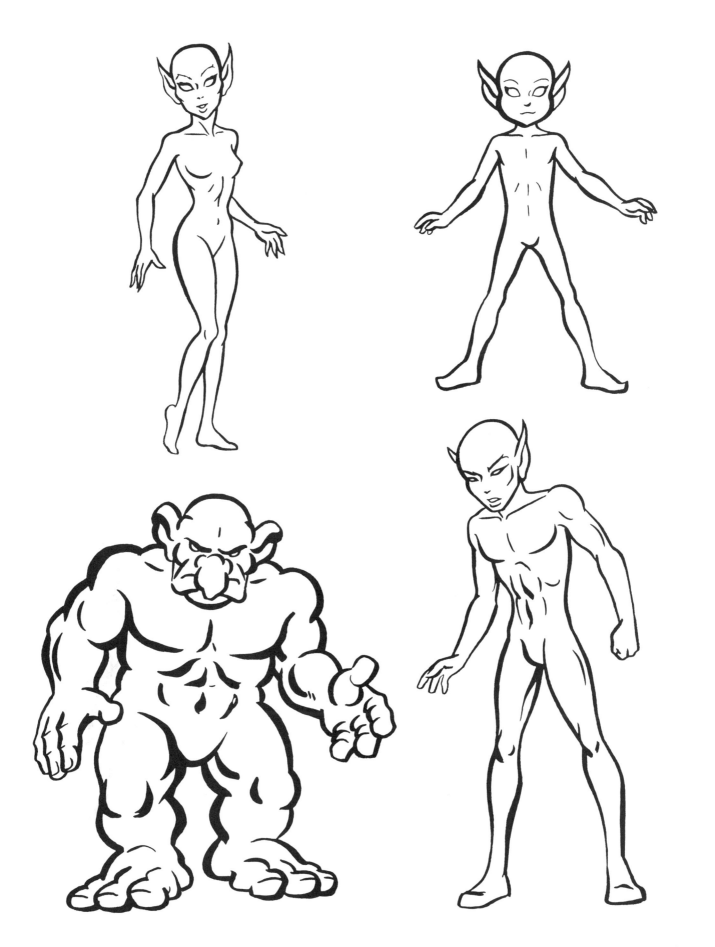

An Interview with Wendy Pini

by John Wooley

One of the true success stories in the field of fantasy is that of *Elfquest,* which began life as a small-run, black-and-white comic book in 1978. Unhappy with the quality of the first issue, creators Wendy and Richard Pini borrowed money and published the second issue themselves. The husband-and-wife team soon knew they had something. As Wendy says, "It just began to snowball from there." Circulation grew as word got around, and it wasn't long before *Elfquest* was established as a major hit.

Along the way, there have been color reprints (carried by the two largest bookstore chains in the nation), a novel from Berkley Books, and such spinoff material as a role-playing game, a fan club, T-shirts, and pewter figurines of the characters who populate the Elfquest saga. The story of an elf tribe's continuing adventures has also inspired near-fanatical devotion on the parts of many of its fans, whose numbers are now in the hundreds of thousands.

Perhaps it's only natural then that Elfquest would be making it to theater screens someday, and that day is rapidly approaching. In this interview, Wendy Pini—who draws, scripts, and co-plots *Elfquest*—talks of current plans for the Elfquest movie, plans that are being finalized even as you read this. [*This article appeared in late 1984—ed.*]

JOHN WOOLEY: *How did the idea of making a movie of Elfquest come about?*
WENDY PINI: It was there from the very beginning. Elfquest was conceived as a film before it was conceived as a comic, really. That's why the characters are drawn in animation style.

Elfquest received a lot of criticism in the early years, and right on up until now, from critics who couldn't accept the cartoon-ish, "too-cute" appearance of the characters. They simply refused to look deeper into the story and see

what those symbols meant. But Elfquest is designed the way it's designed so an animator can look at it and say, "*I can do this,*" which is exactly what's happening with the studios we've been showing it to. The first thing they say is, "Well, your characters are highly animatable." Of course they are. I've designed them to be.

I want to see them move. I have seen them move. Some animators have worked up some pencil tests that have just blown Richard's and my mind,

Elfquest— designed for animation.

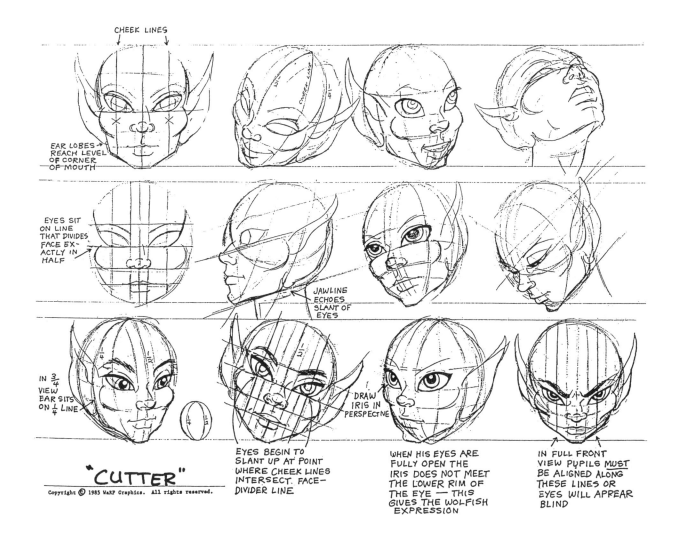

CHEEK LINES

EAR LOBES REACH LEVEL OF CORNER OF MOUTH

EYES SIT ON LINE THAT DIVIDES FACE EXACTLY IN HALF

JAWLINE ECHOES SLANT OF EYES

IN 3/4 VIEW EAR SITS ON 1/4 LINE

DRAW IRIS IN PERSPECTIVE

"CUTTER"

EYES BEGIN TO SLANT UP AT POINT WHERE CHEEK LINES INTERSECT. FACE-DIVIDER LINE

WHEN HIS EYES ARE FULLY OPEN THE IRIS DOES NOT MEET THE LOWER RIM OF THE EYE — THIS GIVES THE WOLFISH EXPRESSION

IN FULL FRONT VIEW PUPILS MUST BE ALIGNED ALONG THESE LINES OR EYES WILL APPEAR BLIND because it's one thing to see them on paper with incredibly lively drawings. It's another thing altogether to see them move.

WOOLEY: *I assume you want full animation.*

WENDY: Absolutely. What we're trying to do is reinvent the wheel with animation. We're not going to go for a lot of razzle-dazzle special effects or computer animation.

WOOLEY: *No rotoscope?*

WENDY: No rotoscope. This is going to be straight, on-the-board, back-to-basics animation. We're not looking to dazzle the public with something they've never seen before. What we're looking to do is to remind the public that animation is a good storytelling medium, and when you have a solid story and animation that complements it rather than overwhelms it, you're going to have a classic film. And that's what we're aiming at.

WOOLEY: *Did the studios contact you, or did you contact the studios?*

WENDY: In the beginning, we were with Nelvana in Toronto, Canada. They had contacted us and said they wanted to do it. We were thrilled because they had the best quality animation as far as we were concerned. We'd have gone to them if they hadn't come to us.

But they just sort of jerked us around for a couple of years. Their first feature film, which they were finishing up at the time, *Rock & Rule*, bombed miserably during its premiere. I'm not saying it was a bad film from an animation standpoint—it was exquisite animation—but the storytelling was a complete failure. I mean, they were editing it right up to the last minute and they didn't even know what they were after with the story.

We didn't mind this. We knew their reputation for bad storytelling, but we didn't mind because we felt that if they were willing to work closely with us on the story, I mean, how could they lose? They had the animation. They had the pen.

But they weren't willing to work closely with us at all. They wanted us to turn over the property, say, "Bye-bye, visit us a couple of times and we'll show you around," and that's that. It just did not work out. So, after that, we went scouting around for studios who would be willing to essentially let us be the executive producers and co-directors.

Let me singularize that. Richard is involved in the financing and business end. The artistic control would be mine. That's my job. Each studio that we are considering now is willing to give us that input and that control. My function will be as art director, co-director of the script and so forth, and key animator. I would provide the key scenes and then the animators would fill them in.

WOOLEY: *It takes a lot of clout to work a deal like that, doesn't it?*

WENDY: It takes money. And fortunately, we're in that position right now.

WOOLEY: *By the time you left Nelvana, your circulation had grown and I assume you had more leverage.*

WENDY: Oh yes. Losing Nelvana was not a blow to us because we were ready to go on from there. It did not put that much sand in our gears at all. We just simply went scouting for other studios right away.

WOOLEY: *When do you think the movie will be out?*

WENDY: Our most optimistic projections is three years for the release of the film. And the timing would be terrific, because Marvel plans to reprint *Elfquest* as a color series in spring of '85. If all goes well, their reprints will take about three years. So, ideally, the film could come out then and the audience would be hungry for the next Elfquest thing, because through the Marvel reprints we're hoping to triple our audience.

The newsstand is the one market

we've never been able to reach. There are only about three thousand direct sales shops in the country, and that's where people have been getting the black-and-white comics, either there or through subscriptions. But where a lot of people have been discovering *Elfquest*, people who don't ordinarily read comics, has been in Waldenbooks or B. Dalton's with our color volumes. That was another groundbreaker, because Waldenbooks and B. Dalton's were very leery of putting what was essentially a glorified comic book on the stands. But when they saw how it sold, they even began to be interested in other titles besides *Elfquest*.

So, because *Elfquest* came in first and was successful, now things like *Beowulf* and *Lightrunner* can come in and have their shot. I hope that trend continues, and I'm very proud *Elfquest* was the first. In Europe, graphic novels are the norm, but here in America they're just getting started.

WOOLEY: *You've said that you plan to use full animation in the film. Isn't that going to cost a lot more?*

WENDY: Well, it costs more in time than in money. Full animation, limited animation, whatever, it's more the time factor than the money factor. Animation is still a much cheaper way to go than live action.

WOOLEY: *Then why can't we have good Saturday morning cartoons on television?*

WENDY: You don't even want to talk about the factories that crank out the Saturday morning cartoons. They are not animation studios. They are, you know...ciphers. I can't say enough negative things about them.

WOOLEY: *Were you influenced by any television cartoons?*

WENDY: "Jonny Quest," which was designed by Doug Wildey and came out in 1964, was a tremendous influ-

ence on me. I was a tremendous "Jonny Quest" fan. I could quote you all the titles and some of the dialogue. And I had the great pleasure of meeting Doug Wildey a couple of years ago, and I've been corresponding with him since. He's very much behind *Elfquest* and very eager to see it become a film, and I'm just thrilled because it's like a full circle. He was so very inspirational to me, and to have him pat me on the back and say "go for it" is really exciting.

"Jonny Quest" was a very noble experiment. It sort of elevated the art of TV animation about as far as it could go. It was limited animation, but it was extremely expensive and it did not go over well with the public. The public wasn't ready for it.

WOOLEY: *Originally, it was a prime-*

When "Quests" collide, courtesy of Doug Wildey.

time show. But it later reran on Saturday mornings. A couple of years ago, when it ran network on Saturday mornings, many of the more violent scenes were cut.

WENDY: Yes, they sanitized it completely.

WOOLEY: *How do you feel about that "sanitization"? Not just with "Jonny Quest," but also with the Warner Bros. cartoons and even the newer stuff?*

WENDY: Oh, I think it's vile. I think it's vile. I don't think they have any idea how children's minds work at all. I think the more you take away the effects of violence, the less you show how violence can really hurt someone, the more detached from reality the observer becomes, whether it's a child or an adult.

I think it's a completely vile practice, and I think it's hypocritical as hell. And I've written letters of complaint to networks until my hand's about to fall off. Richard and I both have. I remember when Filmation brought out a thing called "Black Star," which is apparently still running in reruns. Richard and I sat down, and we wrote a letter, and we said, "Don't you realize that all the corny special effects in the world, all the hypocritical allusions to extant fantasy like Trobbits, for god's sake, are not going to nourish a child's mind one bit? If you are going to tell a fantasy story, you've got to realize that fantasy is truth in symbols. You've got to feed their minds. Don't just give them batwing dragons and light sabres with no motivation, no good dialogue, no good direction, no plot to speak of whatsoever. Don't rip kids off."

We got no reply, of course. We sent it not only to the director of the show, but also to the children's programming department. But it didn't do any good at all, but at least we launched our protest.

WOOLEY: *You began a trend with your successful self-publishing venture. You started another trend when your comic book reprints were picked up by the major bookstore chains. Do you hope to start another trend with the Elfquest movie?*

WENDY: Absolutely. What we're hoping is that, if nothing else, Elfquest will be a renaissance in storytelling for animation. All the major animated films that have come out in the past ten years have more or less bombed at the boxoffice, or only made back a little more than they cost. *The Fox and the Hound* was a success. It didn't make much money, but it was dubbed a success. It was good storytelling. *The Last Unicorn* did fairly well. It was pretty sophisticated storytelling for an animated film, and I think it's the most recent feature film that I admire. I think it was a very noble effort and I think the script was good, and if the animation had been full and a little less cheap, it would have been a classic, I think.

But what we're hoping for with Elfquest, which will have full animation along with a mature but not overblown script, is that we'll bring in a wide general audience, that parents will feel comfortable taking their children to see it. We will be frank about the eroticism, we will be frank about the violence, but in perspective. We want to show the results of each. I mean, you can't hide your child's head in the sand any more. They see too much on TV and read too much in newspapers to believe that the world is pretty and all right. It's not, and I think that Elfquest reflects a lot of the tension of our times today. It's a fantasy for the time.

WOOLEY: *What have you done to prepare yourself for filmmaking?*

WENDY: Richard and I are reading like crazy. We recently made a trip to the Anaheim [CA] area for the World Science Fiction Convention, and we stopped off in Hollywood and bought books and books and books on animated feature film making and how to write a screenplay, and we're just loading our heads with all kinds of information.

I think that we both have pretty good instincts for visual storytelling, but there's an awfully big difference between telling a story cinematically and telling it in the linear fashion you use in a comic book. Even though a comic book looks like movies on paper, it's quite different. People say, "Well, you've always done the storyboard in your eight years of working on *Elfquest,* by doing all twenty issues of the book." Hardly. We're approaching it from an entirely different angle. The dialogue has to be different, the pacing of the scenes has to be different, and—once again—we're learning as we go. But fortunately, we'll be working with some really good people.

WOOLEY: *One of the most impressive things about the Elfquest story is how you've beaten the odds so many times.*

WENDY: I think a lot of what's helped us is the fans. *Elfquest* has always sold itself by word of mouth. We've hardly had to do any advertising at all. The fans went into Waldenbooks and B. Dalton's and bought, and then other people who weren't fans started discovering it and bought. The incredible interest in the film the fans have been showing has been a good motivation for us and the studios, because we've done surveys and so forth and we can show them figures that say, "You really ought to..."

You couple strong characterization with a strong plot, and I really believe you're going to get a following because the fans tend to gravitate to a story that has a real strong vision behind it. They can tell when they're getting garbage, and they can tell when they're getting something that the artists and writers believe in. ✧

A Brief and Personal Reminiscence

by Richard Pini

Elfquest was made for animation. This is literally as well as esthetically true. Two people may be said to be "made for each other" if they discover themselves to be compatible, but that discovery is made long after their birth. *Elfquest* was born to be animated.

Elfquest was a gleam in its creators' eyes well before its first appearance as a comic book in early 1978. Wendy Pini, the scripter and artist of the series, had already been a professional fantasy artist for a decade; I was writing professionally for the planetarium field; and we both were avid fans of comics and film. The basic ideas for a tale of elves and wolves had been percolating in Wendy's mind for several years when we drove from our then-home in southeastern Massachusetts to Boston in April, 1977, to see a newly released animated film by Ralph Bakshi called *Wizards*.

This film was a revelation, in that it was the first "not necessarily kiddie" fantasy animated feature to come down the pike. It had grit and darkness—hallmarks of Bakshi productions—and yet unlike his earlier "street" films, *Wizards* contained all the elements that Wendy had already been drawing since she was two years old: elves, pixies, magical creatures. Seeing *Wizards* did not give us the idea for *Elfquest,* but it did say to us, "Look, a big, rollicking fantasy story can be done and make it to the silver screen. Give your own idea a shot."

Thus, *Elfquest*—always envisioned as an animated adventure—achieved

its first incarnation, took its first karmic steps, as a black-and-white newsprint "independent" comic, hitting the shelves of the (then) few existing comics shops in March 1978. This was a necessary step, for there was no way for two people to produce, from whole cloth, an animated feature-length film out of dreams. *Elfquest* had to become known, to show itself as something more than just an idea, to attract outside interest. And so, the adventures of Cutter, chief of the Wolfriders, and his tribe of forest-dwelling elves were committed to paper. The characters, drawn deliberately in a rounded, easy-to-animate style evolved, as did the story. Over the next nearly seven years, *Elfquest* the comic would go on to become the best-selling "indy" title, reaching a per copy sale of nearly one hundred thousand copies, and demonstrating itself something of a cult phenomenon.

Animated films are almost always (these days) done in color—rich, vibrant color—and so the next step in *Elfquest*'s evolution was to attempt a color version of the black-and-white tale. And while we could manage and afford the publication of a one-color comic book, color was a quantum leap beyond our means. However, early in 1981 the Donning Company, located

in Virginia, got wind of *Elfquest*'s popularity within the comics-buying audience and offered to publish compilations of the saga. Wendy and a small team of assistants painted copies of the original art, and over the next four years, four volumes of full-color *Elfquest* adventures appeared and sold, not only in the comics shops, but also in mainstream bookstores as well. This was the trigger, the exposure to get *Elfquest* noticed.

I recall I was at a science fiction convention in November, 1981, when I got a phone call from Nelvana, an animation studio in Toronto, Canada, expressing interest in optioning *Elfquest* to produce as an animated feature film. Up to this point, Wendy and I had only begun to think about trying to sell *Elfquest* as a film property and were just starting to do our homework. We'd looked at the work of many studios, large and small, and had, quite by coincidence, discovered that we enjoyed the short films Nelvana had done to that time, seasonal and holiday offerings for television like "The Devil and Daniel Mouse" and "Romie-O and Julie-8." When Nelvana's call came in out of the blue, we were excited. We were on our way!

Little did we know.

Artists and creators should never

Wendy's notes on Skywise: "Impish, cheeky, sly. Eyes are narrower than Cutter's, pupils small. Slightly downturned nose, overbit, soft jawline, chin rounded in profile, pointed in full-face view."

Opposite, Trinket preening for the cameras

get directly involved with the process of negotiating and producing films. This we now know very well, but at the time we were fill of beans and vinegar, rearing to go. We made several trips to Toronto to sit with the Nelvana people—mostly our conversation was with Michael Hirsch, one of the founders of the company—and batted ideas back and forth. One point that we made abundantly clear to the producers was that we Really Wanted to Be Involved. With everything, from script to character design to storyboarding to... It was pure naive hubris on our part, but we felt certain that a film could only benefit from the input of its creators. Michael and his associates nodded and smiled.

Two years went by in this manner, with little more than conversation between us and them. The initial one-year option was renewed for another year, and we kept the faith.

Little did we know.

Finally, we got word from Nelvana that they were changing course and planning to do *Elfquest* as a live-action film. We were stunned. *Elfquest* was made for animation! How could anyone possibly even entertain the idea of live action? Our characters are four feet tall and they ride wolves. No problem, the reply came back, we'll use children and put them on big dogs. We asked for and received story treatments which struck us at the time as a Frankenstein patchwork of bits and pieces from our

> # We were stunned [at] the idea of [Elfquest as] live action. Our characters are four feet tall and they ride wolves. No problem, the reply came back, we'll use children and put them on big dogs.

story stitched haphazardly together. We said, wait a minute, our agreement with you is for an animated film only. They said no, they could do whatever they wanted. Things went downhill from there, and it took lawyers and time and money to get *Elfquest* back from them. We learned afterward that for much of the two years that we were cooling our heels, Nelvana had been finishing up their own first animated feature, *Rock and Rule*. Due to some very botched marketing by the distributor (I believe it was MGM), the film died at the theaters, was yanked out of release, and was shelved until it could be re-released on video. However, the experience had soured Nelvana on animation; thus, their attempt to do *Elfquest* in live-action.

In retrospect, it was probably a reasonable reaction for them. However, we were not having any of it, and so once again *Elfquest* was looking for a home. For the next year or so, we dabbled with the dream of opening up our own animation studio. Why not? When we'd begun the comic book, we'd tried to entice Marvel or DC to publish it for us, been turned down, and rediscovered the wisdom of the old saying, "if you want something done well, do it yourself." But while we could start a publishing company with a couple thousand dollars and two people, an animation studio, we knew, was at least several orders of magnitude more costly and complicated to achieve.

There is a word that, to this day, I can only hear as spoken with a particular accent, and that word is *investors*. That word was said to me many, many times by an individual who presented herself to us as a financial consultant to help us raise the capital it would take to start up, outfit, and staff an animation studio. This person had many investors, *about* whom we heard often but *from* whom we never heard a word. We went round and round on just how a

Sketches of Cutter
showing his
adaptability to
animation.

financial deal was to be set up between Wendy and me, and whatever entity would provide the cash to get the studio project going, and what we accomplished was a good deal of frustration. That relationship came to an end when it became clear that the consultant wanted a much bigger piece of *Elfquest* than we felt was warranted; finder's fees are one thing, but equity—actual ownership of some aspect of what we'd created—was another. However, it was the start of our education in how money people look at properties and the people who create them. Properties are good things, if they can be milked, but artists and writers are to be avoided at all costs.

Of course, we ignored that.

Somewhere in there, if memory serves, a phone call came in from Rankin-Bass wanting to know if *Elfquest* was available. By this time we'd moved to Poughkeepsie, New York, and since Rankin-Bass' office was located in New York City, it was easy to catch the commuter train in for meetings. "Thundercats" had just made a decent-sized splash in the syndicated cartoon market, and R-B was looking for other interesting properties. There was even talk of letting the triumvirate of Rankin-Bass, Telepictures (the distributor), and LCI (a licensing entity) handle Elfquest from beginning to end, with the prospect that we'd make lots and lots of money. This time, however, it only took a short while to recognize the signs of "We want *Elfquest,* not you," and we said thanks but no thanks. Sometimes we still wonder...

If we can be said to have done one thing wrong in this entire ongoing process of getting *Elfquest* animated, it is that we have cared too much.

We began to perceive a pattern in our own behavior. From the beginning we'd wanted to be closely involved with whoever and whatever was going to transform *Elfquest* to the large or the small screen. We wanted approvals, we wanted say-so. And absolutely no one on the production side wanted us anywhere near the process. We knew it wasn't personal, that all creators of licensed properties are very low on the totem pole, but it galled us. Still, we decided to try to swallow the bitter pill.

Our next dance with wolves was with CBS, starting in 1985. We got word through an acquaintance in the animation community in New York City (and a large community it is, with a great deal of commercial work being done there) that CBS was looking to develop shows for the upcoming Saturday morning season, and someone had brought *Elfquest* to their attention. Well! Network television! If it wasn't the most artistically respectable avenue in the world, it was certainly one that would get *Elfquest* seen by lots of people.

We resolved that this time we would do things differently. We knew that CBS would not want to work closely with Wendy and me directly, so we put together a team that would act as a buffer. We made an arrangement with an animation studio in New York to be our representative to the network. Since CBS doesn't do any of its own animation but farms it out to other studios, we figured this would be the best way to let "the suits" have their way in dealing directly with a production entity and yet be able to sit in on the actual work as it was being done.

Elfquest actually made it into pre-production. CBS ordered up storyboards and pre-production drawings and a bible and some script ideas, which we delivered through our animation connection. We—the two of us and the studio folks—even got to make several trips to California to sit with the heads of Childrens' Programming to talk about the proposed show and the directions it might take. Wendy and I shook hands all around, dutifully sat by, and nodded and smiled at all the right places. Things seemed just peachy.

Little did we know.

At the time this was going on, CBS had on the air, at 11:30 on Saturday morning, a decent little show called "Dungeons and Dragons." It was an adventure show, and it seemed to all concerned that "Elfquest" might make a good back-to-back offering with it. So we began to mold our thinking along those lines—something with adventure, a villain or obstacle to overcome each episode. We knew we'd have to pare down the cast list; *Elfquest* has dozens of characters and the show and the animators could only deal with a few, but that was all right, we could do it. We'd stick to the core family of Wolfriders and things'd be fine.

Then we began to get the requests for more changes. Example: the main character, Cutter, has a mate, Leetah, who is from a desert tribe of elves. She has dark skin; desert-dwellers do. The dark skin had to go; the network was uncomfortable with the idea of a "mixed marriage." Example: Cutter and Leetah have twins, a boy and girl. The girl is a real scrapper and will be chief someday; the boy is a gentle mystic. Nope, won't do. Can't have a wimpy boy character and a strong girl; change them. Leetah is a healer, she uses magic to knit wounds and heal ills. Nope, can't have that, it's laying on of hands and the Fundamentalists will complain.

And we tried to comply! We really did! We found ways to fudge around CBS's requests and to keep a certain integrity in our story and characters. But then they decided to move "Elfquest" earlier in the morning, to about 9:30 A.M., which meant that we

had to retool everything for a younger audience. And we checked our creative egos at the door and managed that as well. Then Pee-Wee Herman came along and bumped us out of that time slot, so CBS said "How about eight in the morning or so?" and we realized that they were asking us for the Elfquest equivalent of "The Muppet Babies." We finally had to say no, and the project was left to die when the development period was over—April 15, 1986, as I recall. Another reason, in addition to the filing of income taxes, to love that date.

There is a secret to success—however one measures that—in this endeavor. Ernest Hemingway articulated it decades ago when he said that the way to deal with Hollywood is to take your book to the Nevada-- California border and toss it over toward the movie studios. They will toss some money back at you. Take the money and forget about your book or anything else. If we can be said to have done one thing wrong in this entire ongoing process of getting *Elfquest* animated, it is that we have cared too much. We have not let go, the way Eastman and Laird were able to do with their *Teenage Mutant Ninja Turtles.* Letting go is not in and of itself a bad thing. It gives those to whom you have licensed your work the freedom to do what they think is best, and that is something they need to feel and have. And if the end result is not something you're in love with, so what? With luck, you've made some money from the work you've done, and you can always continue to tell your new stories your way.

The (animation) quest goes on. ✧

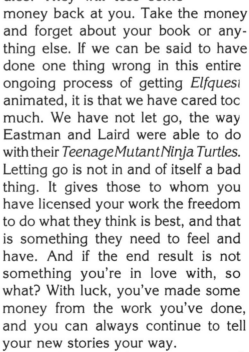

From Elfland to Tinseltown

In 1981, the Canadian animation studio Nelvana approached Wendy and Richard with a proposal to produce an *Elfquest* animated film. They had the story for two years and ultimately decided they wanted to do a live-action film instead. The Pinis said no to that and turned to a smaller animation studio in Pennsylvania. Things looked promising there until it became apparent that the studio wanted a much larger share of the pie than they originally indicated. So it was back to square one. Wendy and Richard began to investigate opening a studio right in Poughkeepsie where they live. It's still an attractive idea—the next five million dollars that comes by that isn't doing anything, they'll no doubt start groundbreaking.

'Round about 1985–86 the CBS television network made interested noises, looking to develop *Elfquest* into a Saturday morning adventure cartoon series. It was a good idea at first. Then the network kept moving the potential show to earlier and earlier in the morning, which meant the stories had to be aimed at a younger and younger audience. Pretty soon *Elfquest* had become "Elf Babies," and neither CBS nor the Pinis were happy. So long, CBS.

However, in the development process, a lot of artwork was done—character charts, concept paintings, storyboards—and a selection has been reproduced here. In the meantime, Wendy and Richard are still plugging away at bringing the adventures of Cutter and company to a theatre near you.

What an animated Elfquest could look like. A production cel drawn by Wendy, inked and painted by Chelsea Animation of New York, with background by Johnnie Vita.

Wendy's anatomical
model chart for
Cutter—preliminary
sketch showing
body proportions.

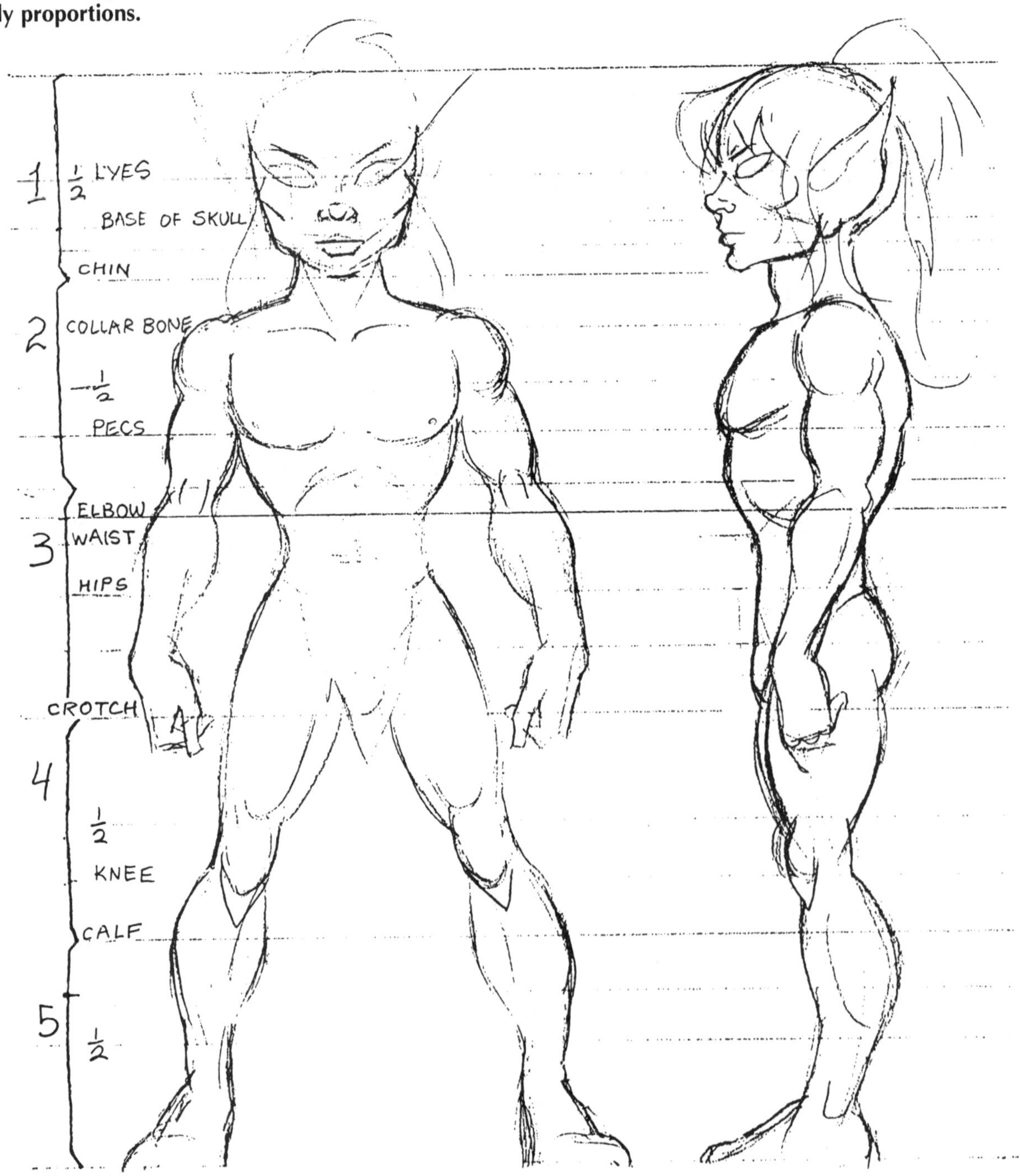

1 1/2 EYES
BASE OF SKULL
CHIN
2 COLLAR BONE
1/2
PECS
ELBOW
3 WAIST
HIPS
CROTCH
4
1/2
KNEE
CALF
5 1/2

CUTTER ～   HEIGHT: 4 feet
WEIGHT: Approx. 60 pounds

FIG. 1   FIG. 2

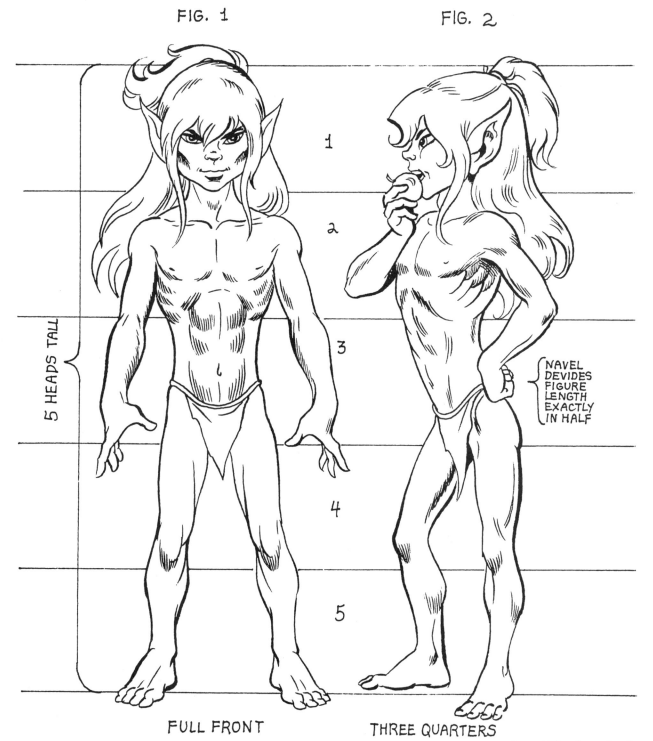

5 HEADS TALL

1

2

3

{ NAVEL
DEVIDES
FIGURE
LENGTH
EXACTLY
IN HALF

4

5

FULL FRONT   THREE QUARTERS

One of the first to attempt to animate *Elfquest,* animator Dan Haskett made these sketches of Cutter.

© 1979 WARP GRAPHICS

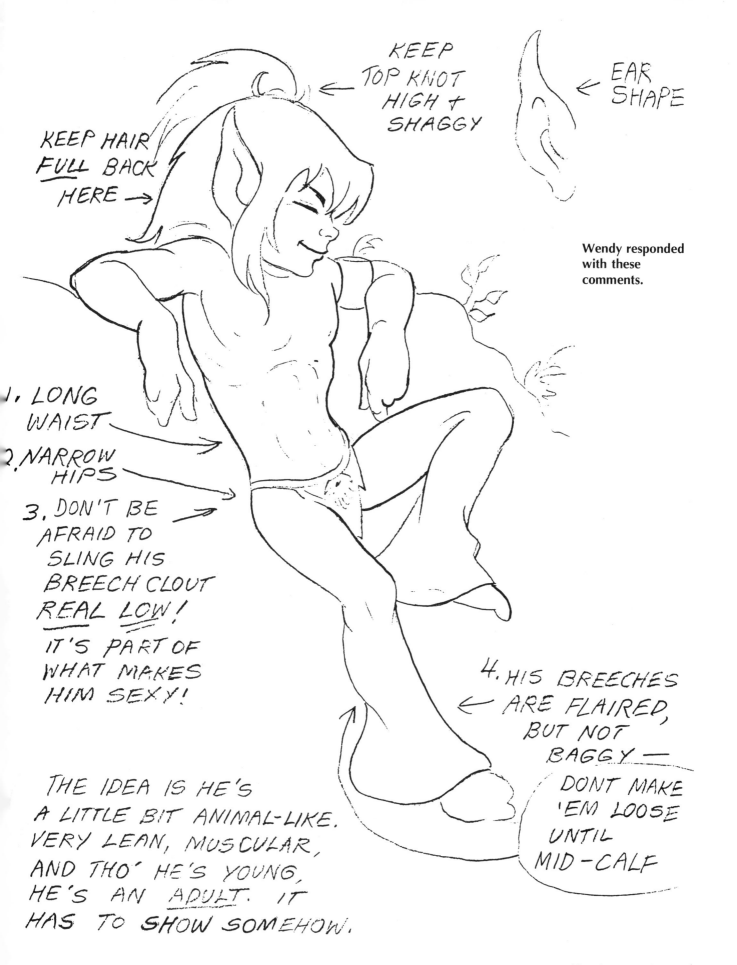

KEEP TOP KNOT HIGH & SHAGGY

EAR SHAPE

KEEP HAIR FULL BACK HERE →

Wendy responded with these comments.

1. LONG WAIST
2. NARROW HIPS
3. DON'T BE AFRAID TO SLING HIS BREECH CLOUT REAL LOW! IT'S PART OF WHAT MAKES HIM SEXY!

THE IDEA IS HE'S A LITTLE BIT ANIMAL-LIKE. VERY LEAN, MUSCULAR, AND THO' HE'S YOUNG, HE'S AN ADULT. IT HAS TO SHOW SOMEHOW.

4. HIS BREECHES ARE FLAIRED, BUT NOT BAGGY — DON'T MAKE 'EM LOOSE UNTIL MID-CALF

Haskett made these facial sketches.

©1979
WaRP
GRAPHICS

CUTTER HAS NO
OVERBITE AND
HIS UPPER TEETH
AREN'T AN
EXAGGERATED
LENGTH

Wendy made these
corrections.

This page and opposite, more examples of Haskett's drawings compared to Wendy's. All in all, they show the difficulty even professionals have in drawing the Elfquest elves.

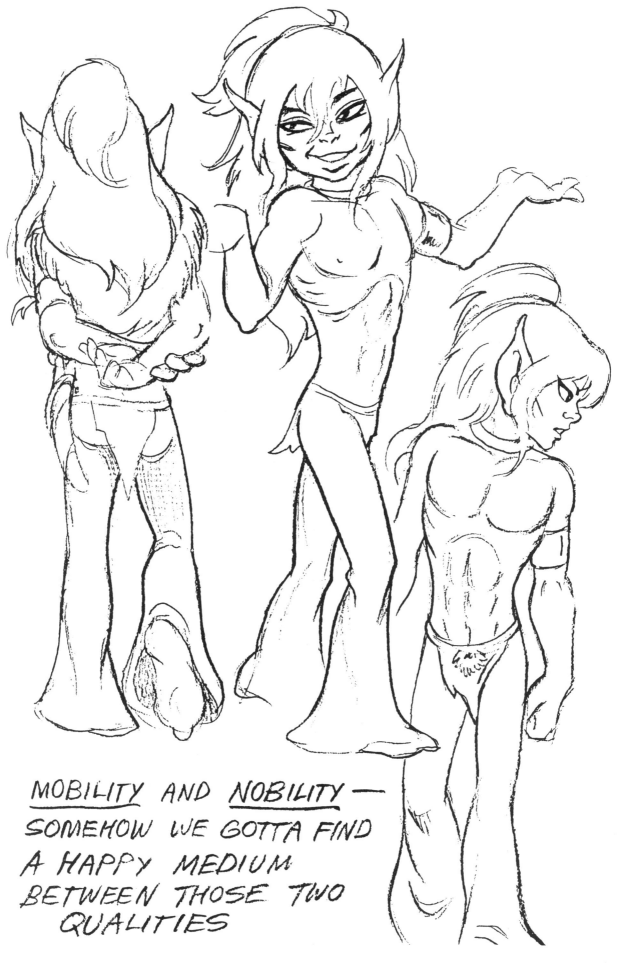

MOBILITY AND NOBILITY—
SOMEHOW WE GOTTA FIND
A HAPPY MEDIUM
BETWEEN THOSE TWO
QUALITIES

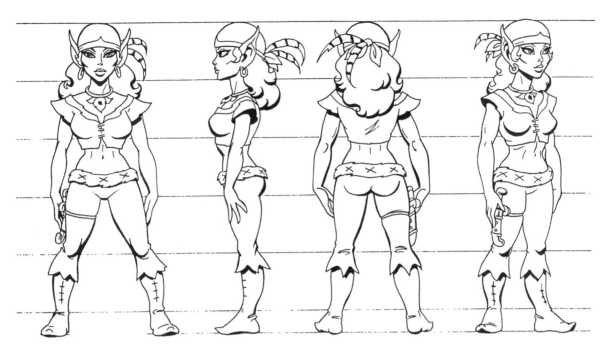

NIGHTFALL

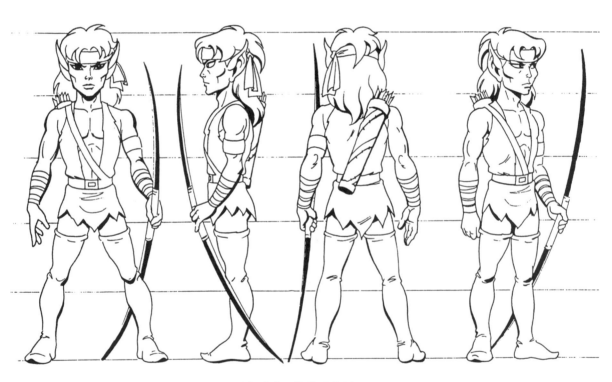

STRONGBOW

This page and opposite, model charts for several characters

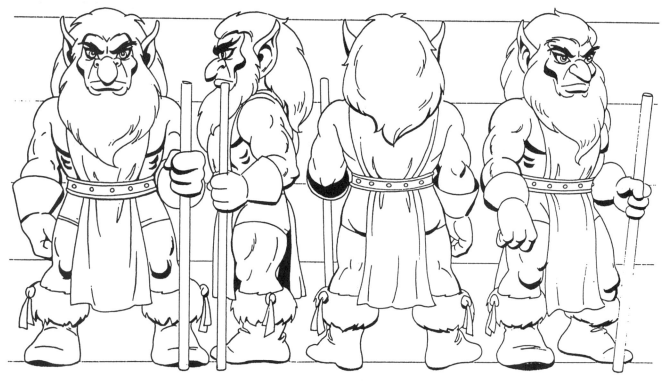

TWO-EDGE

OLD MAGGOTY

"DOMESTIC BLISS"

This page and opposite, concept paintings illustrating episodes and events from a proposed CBS animated television show.

"ELVES' BEST FRIENDS"

"CHILDREN OF THE HIGH ONES"

"LITTLE TROLL LOST"

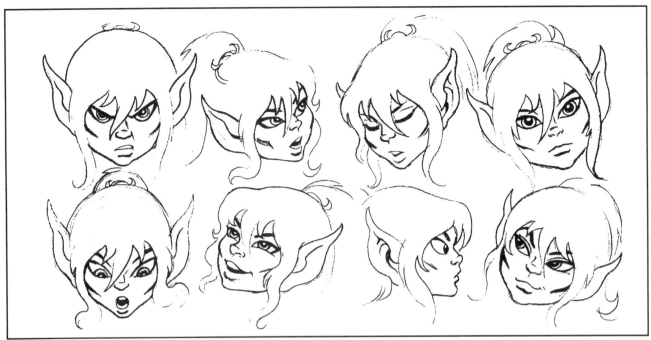

Wendy's notes on Cutter, *above:* "Square face and strong jaw softened by general suggestion of graceful curves surrounding his face. Pupils are always large. Must have a romantic, heroic quality."

Leetah *above:* "Heart-shaped face, straight nose with slightly uptilted tip, flexible, expressive. Not so sexy or pretty that it gets in the way of her personality showing through. Charmingly huffy when she blows her cool."

Beyond Elfquest

Beauty and the Beast

Interview by Peter Sanderson

Beauty and the Beast, as any kindergartner will tell you, is a fairy-tale love story about a beautiful woman and an ugly beast of a man, and of the troubles they must endure because of their love. It is a basic theme as old as the hills and one which has been rendered into the folk tradition of, probably, every society that has ever existed on the face of the Earth. And in whatever form taken, it is marvelous and endearing and magical and reassuring. Thus, it should come as no surprise that these same qualities are to be found in the CBS television program named "Beauty and the Beast." That this show is such a startling, poignant, moving, and potent realization of the basic theme, however, is another matter. In some manner which can only be described as a kind of magic, all of the perfect elements came together at just the right time, in just the right place, in just the right way, and something truly unique unto itself emerged.

And now, Wendy Pini, famed co-creator of *Elfquest* along with her husband Richard, has turned her skills toward creating a graphic novel derived from that television show...

PETER SANDERSON: *So, how did this project come about?*
WENDY PINI: Well, it's kind of a neat story. This all started in the spring of '88. I was out in California for a month, just doing some work, visiting relatives, and so forth. I was in the Los Angeles area, and I called up George R. R. Martin.

In *Portrait of Love,*
Vincent initially
fails to capture
what he feels for
Catherine.

We had spoken previously; I had called him up out of the blue to tell him how much I liked "Beauty and the Beast," because I was sure I had bumped into him at one or two conventions, he looked so familiar when I saw him on a CNN interview. And he knew me, he knew *Elfquest,* and so we had a nice conversation. So when I was in Los Angeles he said, "Let's have lunch, and I'll take you on a tour of the set." I was delighted. While I was on the set, seeing just how beautifully conceived the whole thing was and how dedicated the

actors and the crew were and everything, I got a very strong feeling that the show had a life of its own beyond television.

So, I spent about three hours with George, and at the end of that I asked him if he thought that Ron Koslow might be open to the idea of a graphic novel based on the show. George wasn't sure, but he said, "Hey, go ahead and give it a try." Some months later I sent in a proposal package. It was at the San Diego Con that summer that I found out that First Comics was also in the process of negotiating for "Beauty and the Beast" as either a comic or a graphic novel property. Olivia De Berardinis apparently is quite good friends with Ron Koslow, and she had a lot to do with interesting First in the property. So, the whole team started to come together at that point, because I let Rick Obadiah know that I was very, very interested in doing this graphic novel. I visited First Comics and showed them the package that I had sent, and one thing led to another, and I struck the deal with First.

Then it was kind of a long, slow process of getting everything in place, in terms of getting approval from Ron Koslow. He is extremely protective of "Beauty and the Beast"; that's why you haven't seen too many properties at all that have been licensed off the show.

SANDERSON: *What is Ron Koslow's connection with the show exactly?*

WENDY: Ron Koslow is to "Beauty and the Beast" what Gene Roddenberry is to "Star Trek." He is the executive producer; he is the *creator* of the show. Apparently somebody from on high at CBS asked him to develop "Beauty and the Beast"—taking inspiration from the Cocteau film, it's my understanding. Ron Koslow wrote the pilot episode, "Once Upon a Time in New York," and things took off from there. He's really like the heart and soul of the show. Everything goes through him.

SANDERSON: *And George R. R. Martin is the story editor?*

WENDY: George R. R. Martin is a producer, or *also* an executive producer,

"**I** think when the idea of a graphic novel was proposed, [Ron Koslow] probably felt, 'Oh, god, my show is going to be a comic book? What are they going to *do* to it!'"

and he is chief story editor and writer for the show.

SANDERSON: *What made you decide not to go after the rights yourself once you heard First was—*

WENDY: Well, at first we didn't know exactly what the situation was going to be because Father Tree Press had also expressed interest, but so many things were in place already with Olivia and First Comics. It just so happened that things fit together in that way. For me, ultimately, I think it was a good situation because it kind of put me down in the trenches. For ten years I have been totally spoiled! [*Laughs.*] You know, having my own company, and having my own editor and publisher right here, and just being able to have total freedom, and not have to wait on anybody's mercies. But through working with First, I have had a real education in what it's like to have one's fate in someone else's hands and require approval from them before you even make a move. I feel like it's a really good life experience for me that it turned out this way.

SANDERSON: *Not that you've had any trouble with First?*

WENDY: Quite the contrary. From the beginning everyone has been extremely enthusiastic about this project. The team that's been put together, my editor Laurel Fitch, my art director Alex Wald, and Rick Obadiah and everybody else involved, have just been incredibly supportive. They are very, very excited about the project, and I think they really started getting excited when all of the final approvals came through. It's kind of difficult to describe the stress of the stop and go. First of all, it took a long time to get approval on a story. I think originally Ron Koslow wanted us to just adapt an episode that had already been done, but the people at First were against that. So was I, on the grounds that, you know, the audience has already seen this story, and when you have it on TV, why have it in a glorified comic book?

SANDERSON: *Especially when a lot of them have already recorded it on their VCRs.*

WENDY: Oh, I'm sure. [*Laughs.*] But again, this goes back to Ron Koslow's protectiveness. He has such a clear and such a strong vision of what he wants for the show that he was concerned, because he really doesn't know from comics, he's not a comics reader. I think when the idea of a graphic novel was proposed, he probably felt, "Oh, god, my show is going to be a comic book? What are they going to *do* to it!" There were some natural and very understandable reservations there.

SANDERSON: *But you can understand that, having been in the opposite position: "Oh, no, my comic books are going to become a TV show" or a movie or whatever.*

WENDY: Yeah. That's a very keen insight, Peter, because I think it's because I have been on the other side of that, that I was able to tolerate whatever delays came up. I felt that Ron Koslow was entitled to be as involved and to have as much say-so as possible, so that the project would be as true to his vision as possible. And I think that once we gained his trust... First, it took, like, four stories. I submitted three different plots before he finally accepted a fourth plot. The first three plots were more or less based on the formula of the first season which was kind of violent and cops 'n' robbers and that sort of thing—it was a little bit darker. This was in October when the second season was just starting, and they were going in a softer direction.

So I spent a couple of days on the set out there, and I had a chance to talk with the cast and crew and with George R. R. Martin, and I really got a strong feeling for what it was Ron Koslow was looking for. That's when I was able to write *Portrait of Love,* and that was the story that he accepted. But that took a long, long time to push through, and then after that he had to see the script, he had to see full layouts of the artwork; and, actually, real steady work on this project didn't begin until sometime in January. It was a *long* wait.

The process of getting all of the approvals was so hard, and yet I understand that—and this relates very much to Richard's and my experience with *Elfquest.* Fantasy is very

> "**F**antasy is very fragile. It exists in your head; there isn't any other point of reference outside that."

fragile. It exists in your head; there isn't any other point of reference outside that. So, Mr. Koslow is, like, the main protector of the vision. I think it's only natural that he would want everything that he sees, in terms of licensing, to be true to that vision. And it's awfully hard to *talk* about what that vision is. If you are a fantasy artist or writer, or a combination of both, it's really very difficult to explain what it is you're doing, and why you're doing it. And so if someone comes to you and says, "Oh, I want to do a comic book based on your show," and you've got this very delicate, fragile thing that is very difficult to talk about, very difficult to do interviews about, a really weird concept that's *very* hard to explain, and that met with a lot of resistance before it actually got on the air, then the reserve about having any kind of adaptation done from it in another medium is entirely understandable.

It's so fragile that it could come apart at any point, and I think the main thing in pushing this project through was to prove ourselves, in that the project would not come apart, the vision would not suffer as a result.

SANDERSON: *So, that's what you did, obviously.*

WENDY: I think so. The final verdict isn't in yet. I am happy with what I've done. I feel satisfied with the work. I know that everyone in Hollywood seems to be satisfied with what's been done. When the book is finally out and people hold it in their hands and see it, the final verdict remains to be seen. But I have a good, positive feeling about it. I think it will do well, and I think that everyone involved will feel the tribute. Those are my hopes, at any rate.

It was a moment of great delight to me when Ron Koslow called me and gave me his final blessing on what I had done. He said—I'm not quoting him exactly—but he said something to the effect that I had gotten all of the voices right. In other words, each character that appears in the graphic novel speaks in the recognizable or identifiable way that they speak on the show. I was extremely pleased with that, extremely pleased that he was comfortable. The last thing I wanted to do was worry him, what with everything else going on in the hectic second season. I wanted the graphic novel to be a project that would make him feel positive, not like it was something he had to worry about.

SANDERSON: *Well, tell me more about your visit to the set. What was it like?*

WENDY: Oh, there are so many terrific little stories! I had the best time! I was treated so beautifully, it was a very welcoming experience. The first day I came on the set—my guardian angel on the set was David Schwartz, who is the set producer, and he basically oversees everything that goes on for the day's shooting—he took me in and he sat me down because they were filming a scene for "Chamber Music," the first episode of the second season. The room was full of smoke and people, and one of the cameramen came by and looked at me and said, "Are you trying out for the prostitute?" [*Laughs.*] And I said, "No, I'm not an actress," and he said, "Oh, damn. We need a prostitute." [*Laughs.*]

SANDERSON: *My gosh, whatever were you wearing?*

WENDY: I—well, you know, I'm sure actresses don't necessarily totally dress the parts. Actually, I was wearing roses, a rose print jacket which I call my "Beast jacket" because roses are such a strong image in the show. I don't know why he asked me that. But anyway, basically I just kind of stayed in the background and stayed as quiet as possible and just sketched anything that came into view. It's very, very eerie when Ron Perlman comes on the set in full makeup, because the makeup is so convincing, and in fact the closer you get to it, the more convincing it is—it's absolutely seamless!

SANDERSON: *Is it eerie for other people, too? Is there, like, a calm, a quiet, that comes over the set? Or was it just because you were new to this?*

WENDY: Well, I would have to say that there is an aura of deep respect among the cast and crew for this product that they are producing. One of the most enjoyable things that happened to me on the set was I had a very long conversation with Roy Dotrice, who plays Father in the show. I asked him at one point, "Is it just me, or is this an unusually happy set?" He said, "This is an unusually happy set; there is very much a family feeling here." And that is the truth. My impression was that everyone

"**T**he first day I came on the set...the room was full of smoke and people, and one of the cameramen came by and looked at me and said, 'Are you trying out for the prostitute?'"

cares very, very deeply about what they are doing. Everyone seemed to share Ron Koslow's vision, particularly David Schwartz—it's like from Ron's mouth to David's ear. Just the general feeling about the show is that everyone cares deeply about it, they respect what they're doing, and they take it very seriously.

And I had so much fun visiting the set. The set is wonderful; everything is just as you see it on TV. The tunnels are all built, you walk through yards and yards of them, and they are extremely realistic. Oddly enough, they're made of wood, but they certainly don't look it—they look like old, rusty metal, and the pipes are there and everything. And the entire set is full of smoke, constantly, and it's this absolutely vile chemical smoke. I had only been there a couple of hours and my eyes were watering, it was just terrible. I can't imagine how it must feel for Ron Perlman to work in all of that makeup *and* have to work in that smoke. But I saw some wonderful things while I was there.

The first time I saw Linda Hamilton they were going to do a balcony scene. She was the last actor that I met because, I guess, she was all over the place and very hard to spot. So, she came on the set in this adorable, satin pink bathrobe, but I noticed that she had these *enormous* black fuzzy slippers on. [*Laughs.*] Which I thought was really cute. Of course the camera wasn't picking those up in the balcony scene, but they looked really cute.

The first night I was there, David Schwartz took me around. The set is bilevel, and it's all in this great big warehouse, and they have some of the tunnels and some of the pillars and outdoor stuff downstairs. And then upstairs they have more tunnels and Cathy's bedroom and the DA's office and Father's den. Father's den was just out of this world. Everything was de-

signed by John Mansbridge, who, as I understand it, did the sets for *20,000 Leagues Under the Sea* for Disney. So the *detail:* there is just stuff and stuff and stuff there. David Schwartz took me up there, because they weren't filming that particular night, and he lit all of the candles on the set of Father's den, sat me down on a piano bench, and I just sat there sketching for two hours and barely made a dent because

IMPRESSION OF RON PERLMAN AFTER MEETING HIM IN FULL MAKEUP AS "VINCENT"
2/24/88

there's so much detail to capture. But it was eerie and wonderful because I was the only person up there at the time, and everything else was quite dark and the tunnels were all around me. I truly felt that I was down in the tunnels, the atmosphere is just amazing.

SANDERSON: *Was that frightening?*

WENDY: Not in the least. I felt very much at home. And every once in awhile someone would come up and chat with me and see if everything was all right. The thing that amazed me the most was the way that I was accepted. I was definitely not an intruder in the tunnels. [*Laughs.*] You know, people would come up to me and grab my arm and say, "Come over here, you've got to sketch this!" They are all extremely proud of what they've done.

SANDERSON: *And nobody obviously was condescending to the idea of a comic book being done. Were they excited about this comic book artist being on the set who was going to do something with their show?*

WENDY: Absolutely. They were excited and flattered, and I don't think they were thinking in terms of comic books. I don't think they really knew what a graphic novel was. Some of the people among the crew knew what *Elfquest* was, and they were pretty excited, and it was kind of nice to have that point of reference with them. But most of the people were new to the idea of a graphic novel, and so they were asking a lot of questions like, "What is this, some kind of illustrated book with text?" I did a lot of explaining about

what the format was like and so forth, and of course passed out copies of *Elfquest Book One.*

As a matter of fact there is a copy of *Elfquest Book One* somewhere in Father's den now. Owen Marsh is one of the head cameramen, and he and I were talking in the DA's office set as I was sketching, and I said, "Gosh, there's just so much incredible stuff in Father's den, it looks like very expensive antiques from all different eras, and it's such an interesting hodgepodge. And he said, "Oh, yeah, whenever one of us finds some neat little article or chatchka, we bring it in and stick it on the set." So I said, "Oh, books, too?" And he said, "Yeah, any interesting old book, we just bring it and stick it in." So I said, "Would you put a copy of *Elfquest* in there?" [*Laughs.*] And he said, "Sure." So he took a copy and sprayed it with hair spray to age it down, and it's somewhere stuck behind a candle.

PETER: *What is the single strangest thing that happened to you on the set?*

WENDY: Well...[*Laughs.*] Apart from being asked if I was trying out for the prostitute? [*Laughs.*] Well, I wouldn't apply the word *strange* to it, but most of the interesting things that happened had to do with Roy Dotrice. He was in the process of telling me a story about how when he was a boy he decided to raise hamsters in his basement, and meanwhile he was trying to get his robe on—he had a ceremonial robe of some kind, and it was all kinds of patchwork and quilting, and it was difficult to find the sleeves or know which was the top and which was the bottom of it. He was telling me how the hamsters in his basement got out of hand and before he knew it, he had thousands and thousands of these little things in his basement, and so he had to get rid of them rather quickly.

Below and opposite, **character studies of Catherine (Linda Hamilton) and Vincent (Ron Perlman)**

[*Laughs.*] Marvelous Father is telling me about these hamsters down in his basement, and I'm trying to help him on with his robe, we're trying to find the sleeves and so forth—that was a great deal of fun. I took that away as a very fond memory.

SANDERSON: *What was the single most delightful thing that happened?*

WENDY: That has to be when I met Linda Hamilton—she called me! She said, "Oh, I've heard all about you, but I haven't had a chance to meet you yet." So I

came over, and I was agog. You know, she's a tiny, delicate, elfin—if I can use that adjective—woman, and just extremely warm. So, I told her how much I admired her work, and I showed her some of the sketches that I had done during the day, and we discussed how close my likeness of her was and so forth. I gave her a Xerox of one of my sketches of her and said, "Would you be so kind as to autograph this for me?" She said, "Wait a minute. Let me go get a pen." So she left, and I was talking to Margaret Beserra, and all of a sudden there were these two little arms around me from behind, and my autograph was there before me—Linda was hugging me from behind! So I turned around and I hugged her, and I said, "Look, I'm not a man, but I'm in love with Beauty! I think you're just exquisite!" And she seemed to enjoy that very much. So I gave her a big hug, and she went off to film a scene. I would say that was the most delightful, because she really is something special.

Well, so is Ron Perlman. There's no choice between the two of them, they are an incredible team. The show would not work without the two of them together—it could never be an all Catherine show or an all Vincent show. And he was exhausted—most of the time when I saw him he was either resting or engaged in other conversations. I went over to him to say good-bye, and I said, "Look, you are the thing around which this show resolves. It's very important that they take care of you." And he kind of laughed and said, "Well, it's important they take care of me anyway." [*Laughs.*] So, that was my farewell. It was a wonderful experience. For a couple of days I really felt like family.

SANDERSON: *What were your impressions of Mr. Koslow and the major actors on the show, having met all of them?*

WENDY: Well, actually, when I was on the set I didn't get a chance to talk to Ron Koslow directly. He was really, really busy. The only time I saw him, he popped in and out on the set during the filming of a scene, and he was surrounded by about ten people. They were in the process of trying to cast a show that they were already filming, and my impression was that things were a little bit tense at that point. I knew he was aware of me, because I was sitting there sketching, but we really didn't speak at that point. I've only really spoken to him on the phone. He's a very soft-spoken man—as a matter of fact he has a voice as nice as Vincent's. He sounds like a very imaginative person, someone who likes to use words beautifully, and I can't wait to meet him in person.

George R. R. Martin is a very interesting guy. He's funny. He's got a very wry sense of humor, very droll. And he's extremely sharp. He's been very helpful to me so far. When things were beginning to look a little bleak, in terms of whether or not Ron Koslow was going to accept the story that I had submitted, George was the one who kind of set me on the right track as to what Koslow was looking for.

It's hard to talk about Ron Perlman because you're really talking about two people. He literally seems to be channeling Vincent. [*Laughs.*] Vincent is just such a powerful entity on his own. I have never met Ron Perlman out of the makeup, I've only met him in full makeup. It's startling. It unsettles you because Vincent is extremely real. The makeup is just so superior. To have Vincent walk up to you, or to hear him bitching loudly about the Mets, or to see him eating Chinese food, it kind of puts a little sand in your mental gears. [*Laughs.*]

> "To have Vincent walk up to you, or to hear him bitching loudly about the Mets, or to see him eating Chinese food, it kind of puts a little sand in your mental gears."

My impression of Ron Perlman is that he is a very regular guy, that this has not gone to his head at all, that he works under tremendous stress and he gives 110 percent of himself, and that he's kind of reserved. In that manner he is a little bit like Vincent. I'm sure he didn't quite know what to make of me, because every once in awhile I would bump into him or he would see me sketching, and at one point he asked me, "What exactly is this for?" I tried to explain it to him as best I could. So, I gave him a sketch of himself, and he gave me an autographed picture of himself, and that was very nice. But I don't really think he'll know exactly what this is all about until he actually sees the book.

Linda Hamilton is absolutely wonderful. She has got this explosive laugh, and she's very funny and warm and natural. The funniest incident that happened with her was about Vincent's cape. It was my second day on the set, and I was actually just about to leave because it was quite late—they all work up until midnight and beyond, they literally are tunnel people, they don't see the sun. [*Laughs.*] So, one of the technicians got Vincent's cape for me—Ron wasn't wearing it at that point—and put it on a coat hanger and hung it up on a piece of the scenery so that I could sketch it. One of the difficulties that I've had in this book is trying to find a way to be truthful to the costume design, and yet at the same time sort of whittle down some of the detail, because there is just fringe and stitching and patches and so forth *everywhere*. My general rule of thumb for drawing "Beauty and the Beast" is "when in doubt, stick a candle on it or put fringe on it." [*Laughs.*]

So, I'm sketching the cape, and Linda Hamilton and Margaret Beserra are sitting together nearby, and I come to a part of the cape that I don't quite understand because it looks like a long, thin lump of leather with fringe attached to it. I held it up and said, "What's this?" And Linda and Margaret looked at each other and started cracking up, and Margaret goes, "Oh, that's the 'Vincent sausage'; she plays with it all the time!" [*Laughs.*] So there was a little bit of ribaldry there.

SANDERSON: *Well, it's nice to know they don't take themselves too seriously.*

WENDY: No, they don't. There's a wonderful balance of humor. As I said, the thing I heard Ron Perlman talk about mostly was the Mets, because apparently it was the night after the game with the Dodgers and the Dodgers had won, and he was rather vociferous about that.

SANDERSON: *So, I take it he only channels Vincent when he's actually playing the part, doesn't do this all the time when in makeup?*

WENDY: He does not stay in character the whole time; I don't see how he would be able to stand it. I would think that that would be just too stressful, to be in that character all of the time.

SANDERSON: *But one does read about actors who try to stay in character as long as they can when in costume.*

WENDY: Yes. Well, there appeared to me to be always an element of Vincent's reserve and shyness, but I don't know whether that simply is a part of Ron Perlman's character or what. The first time I met him, in the spring of '88, the first time I visited the set—that was not the same set that they're on now—it was kind of neat because he had his full mask and makeup on, but he didn't have his costume on, he was wearing khaki pants and white sneakers. I just happened to turn around and here was Vincent coming toward me in these khaki pants and sneakers; and right away I got a dose of his sense of humor. He was very mischievous and quite friendly.

At one point while we were talking, we heard these gunshots go off, and there was a guy up in the rafters shooting blanks through the ceiling because there were pigeons on the roof and the microphone was picking up their cooing. So Ron, wearing the Vincent makeup, looks up and goes, [*Goofy voice*] "Is that 'fire in the hole?'" ([*Laughs.*]) There are these wonderful moments of humor all of the time.

SANDERSON: *And Mr. Dotrice?*

WENDY: Oh, he is an absolutely delightful person. He is a cross between a very cultured English gentleman and a bit of a rake. [*Laughs.*] He's a little bit ribald. But of course we had something in common right away, because both he and I have had extensive hip surgery. The first part of our conversation was mainly in swapping doctor stories. Just seeing him scoot around, vital and vibrant as he is, he is just wonderful fun to watch. And he is just full of stories. I get the impression that if he gets on a roll he can go for six hours straight. And he was very generous with his time and particularly helpful to me in consolidating my ideas about *Portrait of Love.* As a matter of fact, he himself had just finished contributing to the teleplay for an episode called "Ashes, Ashes," so he was able to give me a lot of insight on just exactly what it was they were looking for, in terms of tone and content, and again, the voices of the characters. So that was extremely helpful. And oh, he was so funny, just full of all kinds of gossip and everything.

SANDERSON: *Gossip?*

> "**M**y general rule of thumb for drawing 'Beauty and the Beast' is 'when in doubt, stick a candle on it or put fringe on it.'"

THE MAN ONCE CALLED JACOB WELLES HAS SEEN HIS BEST-LOVED SON COME STAGGERING HOME. BONES BROKEN, BLINDED, HALF DEAD FROM THE FEAR AND ABUSE OF THE WORLD ABOVE.

BUT HOW CAN A FATHER SHIELD A SON FROM THAT WHICH RISES IN HIS OWN MATURING SOUL?

VINCENT...?

WENDY: Oh, yes, lots of interesting gossip—and I'm not going to give you any! [*Laughs.*]

SANDERSON: *Well, I didn't expect you to, but it's another sign of how well you were welcomed to the set.*

WENDY: I felt very much at home. I truly did. I don't know why it happened. Again David Schwartz, I would have to describe him as my guardian angel. Whenever I was at a little bit of a loss of where to go or what to sketch next, he would show up and either introduce me to someone or say, "Hey, Cathy's set is empty now, do you want to come and sketch her bedroom?" And you're going to see the result of that in the graphic novel, in the sense that there is a very, very strong sense of place in the graphic novel, a strong atmosphere, a

feeling that the objects that are being drawn and represented all have a place and purpose. Again, as I said, I had to whittle down a lot of detail because it's very difficult to represent all of that detail panel after panel. But all in all, to people who are really devoted to the show and who know the sets very well, they're going to look at it and say, "Yeah, that's the way I know it." They're going to recognize a lot.

SANDERSON: *Which I expect is important to the audience of the show.*

WENDY: Yes, because I think that part of the romance of the show, part of the character of the show, is in the wonderful attention to detail that has been paid to the set—particularly down in the tunnels. It would not have the same romance and atmosphere if there wasn't this layer upon layer of detail, whether it's in the costuming or in the environment. But that is not to disparage the above-ground sets. Cathy's apartment, the DA's office, everything is very, very impressive in its detail. Cathy even has diplomas and newspaper articles pinned to a bulletin board, which is very realistic and adds to the realism of her world, as opposed to the fantasy of Vincent's world.

SANDERSON: *And if readers who pick this up pick up on this detail, it will convince them that this is something that a lot of thought has gone into.*

WENDY: Yes.

SANDERSON: *I know that often when I see adaptations of properties in other media, they don't go to all the trouble of getting everything right.*

WENDY: Well, I think it all depends on the property. One of the adaptations that I admire the most is Walt Simonson's adaptation of *Alien*. I'm still inspired by that because...I would not say that he went for photographic detail in that, but what he did was absolutely capture the spirit of the film.

SANDERSON: *Well, the actual details of all of the rooms in that spaceship don't matter as much in that.*

WENDY: Well, even as to the likeness of the characters, I think that there was some leeway for exaggeration for effect and so forth. But to me Walt Simonson's adaptation of *Alien* stands out as one of the most *exciting* and—I don't know whether I want to use the word *reverent* or *respectful*—respectful of its source adaptations that's ever been done. I often thought of that, as I was working on "Beauty and the Beast," and wanted to give that kind of respect for the source in what I'm doing.

SANDERSON: *Are you going to be able to do exact likenesses of the various cast members, or do you have to pretty much make them up?*

WENDY: No, I'm not making them up. Richard has helped me considerably. We set it up so that he could take a great deal of photo reference for me off of the television—I taped a lot of the shows, and Richard took many, many photos. I would tape specific episodes where I knew there would be certain facial expressions or certain full figure shots that I might be able to use, and Richard took them right off of the screen. Republic Pictures did not really supply me with any photo reference, and all of the stills that I have seen so far are too posed, too artificial. It's much better to catch the figures in mid-motion: it gives a truer likeness.

So I have scads and scads of photo reference to work from, but what I'm trying to do is create what I like to call transcendent likenesses. Even though I'm using a specific photo reference, I might take a head shot and change the angle or the facial expression or move the eyes, in order to make the expression better fit whatever dialogue is taking place in that particular panel. One of the things that I find to be kind of awkward about adaptations done in graphic novel form is that when the artist uses photo references, they sometimes are so true to the photo references that it comes across as a bit stiff on the page. The image in the photo may not necessarily relate to what's going on in the story.

> "**I** have scads and scads of photo reference to work from, but what I'm trying to do is create what I like to call transcendent likenesses."

So, I'm taking the likenesses, but I'm adding extra movement and depth according to what's needed in a given panel.

SANDERSON: *Now, what can you tell us about the story?*

WENDY: [*Laughs.*] Well, as I said, this grew out of my experience on the set. At the time, what they were looking for was something softer, more sentimental, more poetic, and a lot less cops 'n' robbers. But in any good story there has to be an element of conflict, so it was suggested that I include the villain Paracelsus in this story. So after visiting the set, I got the idea for *Portrait of Love,* and the basic plot is that Vincent and Catherine share a very special moment, a moment of triumph, and Vincent sees something in Catherine that he never saw before. It's so special to him that he wishes he could capture it in some way, and after some encouragement from another artist down in the tunnels, he makes an attempt at doing a portrait of Catherine.

But he can't *quite* get it right! Something's missing. So he goes to

Father's library, looking for inspiration, and he happens upon one of Paracelsus's old journals, and in the writings of Paracelsus before he turned evil, Vincent finds the inspiration that he needs. He decides to follow the advice of what he's read, goes off by himself to paint the portrait, and nobody in the tunnels knows where he is or what he's doing or how long he'll be away. But when the portrait is finished, Vincent has accomplished what he set out to do—it's kind of a one-shot labor of love, he could *never* do it again, and it's truly a thing of beauty.

The interesting thing is in the story you never see the portrait because I'm leaving it to the reader's imagination just what it is that Vincent has captured, because to each person it might be something different. But in any case, he gets what he wants. And there comes a point in the story where the portrait is left for a moment, and Paracelsus discovers it and decides to use it against Vincent, to lure him away and destroy him once and for all. And that's all I'm gonna tell ya! [*Laughs.*]

SANDERSON: *Besides Vincent and Catherine and Paracelsus and, I take it, Father, are there other familiar characters from the show who turn up?*

WENDY: Yes, I tried to work in as many as possible. There's Mary and Jamie and Mouse and Elizabeth and Narcissa and...let's see...that's all that come to mind right now. There are also various tunnel people. I invented one, a little girl named Emily Anne.

SANDERSON: *Now, it seems to me that since this is a story about, in part at least, being an artist, that this must have some sort of special resonance for you.*

WENDY: Absolutely, especially right now because I'm in my most intense period of working on the book. All of the final go-aheads, every last approval, came toward the middle of March, and that's when I really started

to get going on the painting. The full layouts, the full script and everything, had been done. We decided to do the pages bypassing pencils, believe it or not. I'm using a coloring process which is mostly watercolor, but I did my layouts in Prismacolor pencils, which is really neat because it doesn't erase, so it creates a nice, solid drawing that you can Xerox—this is what Ron Koslow saw and approved—but it also leaves a nice terra-cotta color on the page, and that is my base color. Over that I'm doing watercolor paintings. So essentially, I bypassed the pencils altogether and went directly to color. But even with that timesaving step, it's just kind of been murder since March. [*Laughs.*] Right now this is about all I do: I eat, I sleep, and I paint. I'm expecting to finish the book at the end of April. But I feel very much like Vincent now: I'm off by myself in a little cave. [*Laughs.*] I'm concentrating on finishing this thing, and I won't come out until I'm done.

SANDERSON: *Trying to capture—*

WENDY: I'm trying to capture the feeling I got when I first discovered the show. I came to it a little bit late; it had been on the air for a few episodes, and...I wouldn't describe myself as a fan of the show. I would say that I have a great respect for the show. I totally agree with the show's politics. When I saw it, I saw that the show dealt with so many themes that we had been dealing with in *Elfquest* for so many years, and I just kind of went, "Oh, this is completely familiar ground, I agree with this completely!" And that's what I am trying to capture in the book, my feelings of the rightness, the solidity of the concept, the dedication of the actors themselves.

I think one of the most amazing things about this show is the personal commitment and involvement of the actors, particularly Ron Perlman. I have a little trouble understanding how he does it. He is in that makeup up to eighteen hours a day! When I saw him, he was filming three different episodes at once, because things were just starting up after the writers' strike and they were really rushing to get as many episodes out as quickly as possible. He seemed exhausted, but at the same time he was absolutely right there, and when he had to be Vincent he was Vincent. To me this is extraordinary strength of character, extraordinary commitment to one's profession—and apart from that, he is, quite simply, a superb actor.

Also, Linda Hamilton is absolutely fascinating to me, because she is not one of these "window mannequin" beauties, she does not *look* like every other actress on the screen. It makes her particularly interesting to draw because she has an extremely mobile, emotional face, and her eyes are extremely expressive. I really love drawing her; I

think she's probably the only actress who could possibly upstage Ron Perlman in makeup. [*Laughs.*] I find her just as interesting to draw as Vincent.

SANDERSON: *What specifically do you see as the themes that* Elfquest *and "Beauty and the Beast" have in common?*

WENDY: Well, first and foremost, the element of "don't judge by appearances," the element of how different people react to the strange and the unknown, the magical, and the concept of tribe and family, which you find in the tunnels—these folk who have isolated themselves from the mainstream of society in order to build a better world for themselves, one that they can cope with. These are gentle people, *shy* people; they are perhaps not all that functional in the difficult, stressful society of the world up above, but they have found peace and harmony and family down below in those tunnels. I find that very similar to what we did with the Wolfriders, in terms of their holt, their safe place, their desire to just live and let live, and really to have a life that is as easy as possible, and only fight when they have to.

Vincent himself is a very magical character. He's very powerful, very archetypal, and there are a lot of things about him that I can relate to. He is an artist, he is a poet, he's soft-spoken, reserved, and doesn't necessarily have all that hot a self-image. But he's overcome a great deal and has tremendous inner strength. There just seems to be a wealth of interesting possibilities in these characters.

SANDERSON: *How long is this novel that you're doing right now?*

WENDY: The actual story itself is forty-eight pages long.

SANDERSON: *Are there possibilities for sequels?*

WENDY: Well, we've already talked about that. As I said, all of the people at First are extremely supportive of the project, very excited about it, and they are anticipating good sales. As a matter of fact, there are a number of trade shows that are going on right now, and word has been coming back to me through Richard and through Rick Obadiah that the response to the artwork has been very good. I suppose that I'm saying that with a little bit of a wry sense of humor, because some of the responses have been, "Wendy Pini didn't do this, that can't be her artwork, I thought she only did elves." You know, for ten years I've tried to prove that I am capable of doing things other than elves by

doing other projects, but I guess a lot of distributors and store owners have it very firmly in their minds that all I do is elves.

SANDERSON: *I had heard you were doing this in a very different style than you are known for.*

WENDY: Yes. It's extremely realistic, the lighting and the settings and everything. You will feel like you're holding an episode of the show in your hand. This is an art style that I have been capable of always, but just haven't had that much opportunity to make use of. It's wonderful! It's refreshing and revitalizing to me as an artist to have a chance to use this particular style.

SANDERSON: *Have you other projects in your future?*

WENDY: Well, obviously there is always something to do with *Elfquest*. *Elfquest* is an ongoing thing.

SANDERSON: Elfquest *is eternal.*

WENDY: [*Laughs.*] *Elfquest* is eternal, yes. But as far as "Beauty and the Beast" goes, there are a number of possibilities; one that I'm not really at liberty to talk about, but what I can say, is that there is a possibility—assuming that the show is renewed this fall—that my connection with the show may be something else besides a graphic novel. That's all I can say. There have been some conversations in this direction.

SANDERSON: *Does that mean you actually will get to play the prostitute?* [*Laughs.*]

WENDY: Who knows? I'll tell you, I wouldn't mind being a tunnel person, that might be kind of fun. I like the clothes they wear.

SANDERSON: *Is there anything in the future besides* Elfquest *and "Beauty and the Beast"?*

WENDY: To tell you the truth, all I really want to do is put this thing to bed and enjoy the summer and enjoy people's reactions to it. I would be better able to tell you what's going on in the fall. There are a number of options open to me, and I kind of just want to get through the summer and make my choice after that. I'm going to take the summer off, definitely. This has been an enormous project. Essentially, it began last July when the wheels were put in motion, and it's been a hurry up and wait situation until, actually, January—the work came in stops and starts. That was kind of stressful. So, actually, when I finish this it will be about seven months that I have spent on the project, so I'm looking forward to taking a break.

SANDERSON: *What do you hope the effect of your graphic novel will be on people who aren't already acquainted with "Beauty and the Beast"?*

WENDY: I'm glad you asked that question, Peter. When I first saw the show, my reaction to it was much the same as you would have to an endangered species—said to myself, "This thing is so good, it's got to be in danger of being canceled!" I started to think right away about what I might be able to do to contribute some positive energy to it in some way as a professional. I hope that the show is renewed. It had a rocky second season, and I think the voice and vision of the show got tangled up in the effects of the writers' strike and so forth. I think that the episodes that they've been showing towards the end of the second season have shown that they've gotten their voice and vision back, but it's a tough recovery and the ratings aren't terrific right now.

So, the people at First and myself, and I guess everybody who is rooting for the show, we're just crossing our fingers and hoping that it's going to be renewed. From what I heard from Ron Koslow, they're expecting to be renewed, but who knows? We just keep thinking positive. I think the show is very important, (1) because there is nothing else like it on the air, and (2) because its values are very important right now, the emphasis on family and caring and being sensitive to others' feelings, being in touch with someone else—it's anything *but* a cold show. It's a very warm show. And I feel that since there is nothing else like this on television right now, it's definitely contributing something special to the world, and I would like to see it continue.

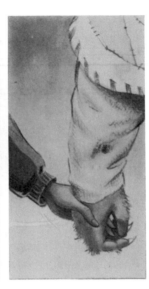

So what I'm hoping is that when someone walks by the graphic novel in a Waldenbooks who may never have seen the show, and they get intrigued by the artwork or whatnot and flip through it, they'll say, "Oh, I better catch this and see what it's all about." I just hope that it brings more support, more positive energy to the show. I hope it contributes to the possibility of the show being renewed.

SANDERSON: *But of course by the time the graphic novel comes out that decision might already have been made.*
WENDY: Well, I'm hoping that CBS's awareness that this product is being turned out contributes to their feelings that the show does have a life beyond this season.

SANDERSON: *It also occurs to me that since "Beauty and the Beast" is unique for network television, the property is also unique for comics—maybe more so because there aren't that many romances, in the traditional sense of the word, being published in this grim and gritty comics market of today.*
WENDY: Well, I think if any ongoing comics series fills the bill of fantasy/adventure/romance, you know which one I'm thinking of. [*Laughs.*]
SANDERSON: *Yes.*
WENDY: *Elfquest,* of course.
SANDERSON: *But this is a minority of the comics being published today.*
WENDY: Absolutely. I think it's a natural progression that I should slip into doing "Beauty and the Beast" from having done *Elfquest,* because the politics are similar, the values are similar, the sensitivities are similar, and I feel very much as if I am on my home ground. I feel extremely comfortable working with the characters. And yes, I definitely do think it will be an unusual thing in the comics market, and for that reason I hope it does very, very well. I hope a lot of women get out there and buy it, and turn their boyfriends on to it. I hope people sit by the fire and read it together and get all mushy and gooey. [*Laughs.*] I hope it does bring a little romance into comics readers' circles.

It's kind of interesting: at the San Diego Con last year there was a panel of women in comics, and one of the women on the panel—I was in the audience—asked me if I was going to be doing a romance comic any time in the near future. At the time we were still in the process of negotiating, so I couldn't say anything. So, I just sort of sat there and grinned like I had something up my sleeve. [*Laughs.*]   ✧

Elfquest Profiles

by Deni Loubert and Wendy Pini

When Wendy and Richard expanded the *Elfquest* universe to include other writers and artists, they knew they would need a guide for those who couldn't identify every elf or remember every detail about them. This guide, the *Elfquest Bible,* contains information on the various character groups in *Elfquest*—elves, trolls, and preservers—as well as individual character biographies. Even though the guide doesn't list every character—any who are dead at the end of the quest, such as One-Eye, are omitted—we thought the readers of *Elfquest* might find it interesting and could possibly learn something new about a favorite character.

The Elves

The Wolfriders

The Wolfriders, being mortal, are different from all the other elves. Timmain, the High One, sought to gain survival for her people by shape-changing to hunt as a wolf. Her cub was a half-elf/half-wolf called Timmorn Yellow-Eyes, the first chief of the Wolfriders. All Wolfriders are his descendants, though their blood is mixed with that of pure-blooded elves too. Because of that dollop of true wolf blood, Wolfriders must all die of old age, if not from mishap.

The Wolfriders are hunter-gatherers who have only recently begun to climb out of their Stone Age by trading the animal skins and meat for troll-forged metal weapons and ornaments. While any elf may have the power to establish a bond with an animal, the bond between Wolfrider and wolf is especially intense. Wolfriders live by a code of conduct called "The Way." It is based on the natural cycle of the wolf: it glorifies the wild, free hunter's life and the "now" of wolf-thought.

The Sun Folk

As Timmorn led the Wolfriders on their path, another small band journeyed across the southern desert. In an oasis beyond a far mountain range they founded a village called Sorrow's End. Savah, the Mother of Memory, is the oldest of her tribe. Many children were born to her and others. The Sun Folk of Sorrow's End can work soft metals, such as copper, silver, and gold. They are excellent weavers and are capable of building elaborate homes of sun-dried clay. Their culture is largely agrarian, though they do supplement their diet with small game. Their semi-domesticated beast of burden is the camel-like Zwoot. Rayek was the Sun Folk's chief hunter until the Wolfriders came across the desert and changed everyone's lives.

The Gliders

First born of the High Ones, Lord Voll led a party of young elves to Blue Mountain to create a safe haven from the humans. There they remained, honing their abilities and skills. They bred a race of giant hawks to bear them through the skies and came to be worshiped by a human tribe dwelling at the foot of Blue Mountain. The Chosen Eight were the elfin messengers who bore gifts to the humans, received tokens and live offerings of tribe members, and flew the great hawks to hunt for the Gliders. Because they had lived so long in claustrophobic isolation, the Gliders ceased to Recognize and therefore ceased having children. They convinced themselves they were sterile and that all their elfin kin had died in the terrible "outside." The tale of their fall can be found in *Book Six*.

The Go-Backs

The ancestors of the tribe to become known as the Go-Backs sheltered in the snow, just as the Wolfriders' ancestors sheltered in the forest, surviving where humans could not. Their life was short and harsh, and they opted not to use magic because it made life deceptively soft. The Go-Backs also developed two survival tactics unique to them, the first being the domestication of giant elk as mounts. The other adaptation was quite drastic. Early in their history, it became obvious their harsh environment made the low birthrate tied to Recognition a path to their eventual extinction. Recognition was suppressed so that its pangs were no more than those of human desire, thus allowing the Go-Backs to produce children from any mating. The resulting offspring were not genetic works of art, but they were numerous and allowed the tribe to survive.

The Go-Backs believed, and still believe, in quantity, not quality. About one hundred years before Cutter's arrival, the Go-Backs began to feel a call deep within their psyches from the Palace. Uncovered by the retreating glaciers, it was broadcasting its message of home and refuge to its runaway children. Being the closest to the Palace, the Go-Backs were drawn to the call but were unable to approach because the trolls, who had found the Palace first, defended their possession. Until the Wolfriders' arrival, the Go-Backs waged an ongoing war with the trolls, stealing their weapons, learning to work troll metals to some extent, and continually trying to get over or around the mountain, back to the Palace.

Humans, trolls, and other assorted players

The High Ones

The High Ones came from a distant star where they evolved beyond the need for physical existence. As they multiplied beyond the land's ability to support them, they discovered their inner magic and learned both to change shape and to send their spirits out. Even with the ability to abandon their physical bodies, they chose to keep a physical form and traveled frequently to the stars. In time they left their dying planet permanently behind, taking with them small burrowing apes and winged insects. In their travels they found they were unique among life-forms; they yearned to communicate with others of their kind. The preservers cocooned them for their lengthy travels so they could navigate their vessel without need of sustenance. As they traveled, the burrowers and winged ones evolved, changing into humanoid beings. In time, the High Ones came upon a planet with two moons. In the legends of its human population were beings much like them, and they wondered, "Could these be our brothers?" Taking the shape of elves, trolls, and wood sprites, they prepared to enter the double-mooned planet's atmosphere. But the rebellious trolls revolted and slashed open the guiders' cocoons, hurling the Palace into the planet's prehistoric past.

Trolls

Unlike the elves, the descendants of the trolls grew in size and weight since the time of the Firstcomers. While the elves took to the woodlands, the trolls forged their survival by moving underground where they developed bulky bodies, pale skin, and a propensity for working rock and metal. Trolls can work pure metals and smelt unusual alloys; they are capable of making sophisticated traps and special doors, as well as weapons, hinges, gears, etc. Two troll communities have been described, but others may occur as well. They are definitely xenophobic, but they will deal with elves to obtain the fancy furs and meat from animals which can only be caught and cured by elves. In return for these items, the trolls trade metal weapons, tools, and ornaments to the Wolfriders. Trolls have developed the fine art of fermenting dreamberry wine and the vice of gambling.

Humans

At the time of the original quest, perhaps through the example of the elves, humans have slowly developed their culture to what one would call a Neolithic level, with the most advanced tribes capable of working soft metal and sewing clothes. The humans with the best standard of living are the pampered servants of the Gliders of Blue Mountain; they are totally devoted to their protectors and receive fine metal weapons and other benefits in exchange. The descendants of the Neanderthals who first confronted the elves spread across the continent and remained dedicated enemies of the elfin interlopers. These fanatical servants of Gotara spied on the Wolfriders, ambushed them during hunts, and methodically tried to exterminate them. Eventually, hostilities drove Gotara's servants to set the entire forest afire, destroying the Wolfriders' holt. Other human tribes know of the elves through legends but maintain a distance between themselves and the "forest spirits." Some humans secretly suspect that elves don't exist. Ten thousand years have passed since the original quest. The humans have evolved and now live in towns, with a culture close to that of medieval earth. Although there is still no real technology, the use of metals has advanced, and there has been an evolution in mathematics and language. The Wolfriders hide from these humans and cannot speak their tongue.

The Preservers

The most enigmatic of the creatures to accompany the elves to the World of Two Moons, they are asexual, seemingly immortal, and are intelligent, though their intelligence is strictly channeled into certain areas of activity. All preservers know instinctively the direction of the Palace. They can spit out webbing which obscures the vision of living victims and entangles them. If the preservers completely encase a victim in their webbing, the victim will go into suspended animation. The original value of this was to "preserve" the elves on their travels through the stars. More mundanely, preservers' webbing keeps animals alive for future use as food. Long ago, most of the known preservers were tricked by Winnowill into leaving Blue Mountain and going to the Forbidden Grove. Their leader, Petalwing, was told they had to catch and store food for the Gliders future use. Once there, they encased every living thing in their webs and gave the grove the reputation of being haunted. Indeed, nothing that entered returned, and humans learned to avoid it. For centuries the preservers held on, waiting in vain for their masters to come and claim the food.

THE WOLFRIDERS

CUTTER

Hunter, warrior, "kinseeker"; Chief of the Wolfriders

Cutter

Age: Around 500 years, mortal
Soul Name: Tam

Cutter became leader of the tribe as a teenager following the death of his chief-father, Bearclaw. Initially a young visionary whose seat-of-the-pants style of leadership was formed by a rapid succession of extraordinary events, Cutter is now confident and decisive in most matters. He has the flashes of temper and humor of his father, but his ability to get himself centered and clear comes from his mother, Joyleaf. Nowadays he perceives the simple Way of the Wolfriders as being threatened by a shrinking habitat and by a marked increase in usage of the "old powers" by such gifted elves. When confronted with a new situation (an almost daily occurrence for him in his perpetually tumultuous reign), Cutter will consult the tribe, then take his best guess as to how to proceed. Only major mistakes make him beat himself up. He's a classic "responsible child" ACOA type. In his immediate family, Cutter finds both his greatest strength and his Achilles heel. Parted from them, he feels not quite whole and will move heaven and earth to be reunited with them. Although his devotion to the Wolfriders has only increased over the years, he is not quite as democratic and people-pleasing as in his youth. This causes occasional friction with other assertive tribe members. His lifemate, Leetah, can usually wrap him around her little finger.

SKYWISE

Skywise

Stargazer, keeper of the lodestone; brother in all but blood to Cutter
Age: Technically somewhere in his 40s, immortal (genetically altered)
Soul Name: Fahr

Orphaned at birth by the death of his parents, Shale and Eyes-High (see *Hidden Years* #5), Skywise is our resident Peter Pan. While his tribe has aged some five hundred years (see *Book Eight*), to Skywise less than twenty years have passed since the first quest began. Alone among the Wolfriders to choose immortality, he is feeling his first "outsider" twinges. Yet he happily knows that he now has an eternity in which to exercise his most outstanding trait (yes, *that* one too!): curiosity. Cheerful, witty, devil-may-care most of the time, Skywise has a dreamy, thoughtful side when he contemplates the stars. Though he has made remarkably scientific observations about how the universe works, he still thinks it's all "magic" because it's more fun that way. Once a little older than Cutter, Skywise served as advisor, confidant, and close friend to his chief. Now, due to their substantial age difference reversal, Skywise is still Cutter's cherished sidekick and advisor—but more like a clever younger brother. Skywise has yet to experience Recognition and doesn't relish the prospect, for true parenthood represents a bit more responsibility than he fancies. (One child of his produced outside of Recognition, Yun, is known—see *Hidden Years* #2. Others are highly likely.) His closest bond is with Cutter with whom he shares soul names.

LEETAH

Healer, gatherer; Cutter's lifemate, Sun-Toucher's daughter
Age: About 600 years old, a young immortal

Born in the idyllic, Shangri La-like Sun Village, Leetah's rather smug and safe existence was permanently altered by Recognition with Cutter (see Book One). Sharing her lifemate's rugged lifestyle has changed her from a coquettish, willful princess to a conscientious and loving spiritual leader. While her potent healing powers are often in demand, given the Wolfriders' dangerous environment, she has learned not to overdo it as she once did with her own Sun Folk. Still exploring the unknown limits and moral ramifications of her powers, Leetah helps when asked or when it's a matter of life and death. Otherwise she checks her natural compassion with the knowledge that a certain amount of hardship builds strength and character. She is an intensely sexual presence, flirtatious and sensuous—every inch the classic elfin nymph who dances by moonlight. Retaining much of the gracious and refined manner of the immortal Sun Folk, she's accepted "The Way" and become a peaceful warrior, knowing that her beloved Cutter and tribe are mortal by choice.

SUNTOP

Son of Cutter and Leetah, twin brother to Ember
Age: 15 years old, immortal

Suntop was born in the Sun Village and might as well have grown up there, so little has the Wolfrider lifestyle rubbed off on him. Though he has been well loved, he has never been well understood, even by his own father. Consequently, Suntop has taken after Leetah in most respects. Shy, soft-spoken, and gentle, he dwells in the inner world of the mystic, seeing and hearing things

Leetah

most others cannot. If any elf can be said to have a destiny, it seems Suntop is fated to unite his race in a way that goes beyond even Cutter's most ambitious questing. Until recently, Suntop has been more at the mercy of his own mysterious powers than in command of them. But with Savah's training and support, he is finding out just who he is and what he can do. Suntop's psychic bond with his twin sister, Ember, might have been phenomenal had

Suntop

Ember

they been identical. But despite the fact that Ember is pure Wolfrider and Suntop is immortal, he does share a special emotional and spiritual link with her. Suntop doesn't require Ember's presence to mindlock with her, and he can sense her ups and downs from afar. There is a slight aura of sadness or loneliness about him, as if he's too sensitive for his own good.

EMBER

Daughter of Cutter and Leetah, twin
sister to Suntop
Age: 15 years old, mortal

Gamin, pixie, sprite—mix these in a pot with a dash of *hellion* and you've got the spicy brew that is Ember. Just recently initiated into the pleasures of joining by Mender, the Sun Folk's healer, Ember is at that delicious teenage stage where all of the joys and none of the burdens of young adulthood are hers. Always an upbeat, cocky, and playful kid, she's "Daddy's girl" all the way. Ember is destined to be chief of the Wolfriders someday and tries to emulate Cutter in many ways. She

tends, however, to be thoughtless and careless at times, which causes the Wolfriders some inconvenience. Ember has never been shy about speaking her mind, even when she hasn't had that much to say. She can be goofy and distracting during council meetings, causing the Wolfriders to take her less than seriously—which is a mistake. Surprisingly, Ember has a high degree of deductive reasoning. But she tosses off her observations so casually that it's easy to overlook the wealth of logic hidden in that apparent bubble-brain. Without realizing it, she's a good detective and puzzle-solver. Her sense of humor leans toward the mischievous, and she's every bit as hot-tempered as Cutter. In fact, father/daughter clashes are commonplace these days. Ember is like a yearling wolf testing just how far she can push the *alpha* male. She knows her aggression is OK, that the whole tribe, including Cutter, subtly encourages it for it is part of her preparation for leadership. There is not, however, a mean bone in Ember's body. She would not willingly injure anyone, physically or emotionally, and she would go to the limit to defend loved ones from harm. Ember always sounds a positive note, even when things look blackest.

REDLANCE

Tracker, gatherer, tree-shaper;
    Nightfall's lifemate, Tyleet's father
Age: About 600 years old, mortal
Soul Name: Ulm

If there were railroad tracks on the World of Two Moons, Redlance would inevitably end up tied to them by a villain. Sweet-natured and vulnerable, he tends to need looking after. Not that Redlance is muddleheaded; he's just not naturally aggressive. He tends to think well of everyone and everything

Redlance

and be a bit too trusting. It would seem his mildness might make him a low-ranking member of the Wolfrider pack. In fact, he ranks quite high, for he is one of their few magic-users. His plant-shaping powers emerged during the seven years he lived in the Sun Village. Insecure up until this "blossoming," Redlance knows he's absolutely vital to the tribe's welfare and comfort. In a pinch, this gentle gatherer can hold his own in a fight—which is why his tribe-name was changed by Bearclaw from Redmark to Redlance (see *Book Five*). But at heart he's a true pacifist and nurturer. He has one daughter, Tyleet, by induced Recognition with Nightfall. Their love story is the stuff of legend to the Wolfriders.

NIGHTFALL

Huntress, warrior, scout, guard; Redlance's lifemate, Tyleet's mother, probable daughter of Brownberry and Longbranch (deceased)
Age: About 500 years old, mortal
Soul Name: Twen

How such a bundle of yang impulses could come in such genuinely feminine wrappings is one of Nightfall's pleasant paradoxes. She wouldn't think twice about downing a bear with only a dagger in hand. Yet this is the maiden who dances naked by moonlight with Leetah and any other Wolfriders who care to join in. This is the maiden who yearned so for motherhood that she had Leetah induce Recognition with Redlance. As a warrior, Nightfall is trusty, uncomplicated, brave to a fault, and highly aggressive. As a nurturing influence, either to Redlance or to her hard-won daughter, Tyleet, Nightfall is tender, tolerant, and encouraging. She allows her loved ones to be what they must and does not tout her way as the only

Nightfall

way. In her greatest act of love, Nightfall was able to lower the last of her personal barriers and give her soul name to Redlance, calling his forth in return. Nightfall is definitely alpha to her lifemate. When she says "frog," Redlance jumps. However, Tyleet and Nightfall's age difference is now so slight that their bond has changed from one of mother/daughter to one of deep friendship. Born almost at the same time as Cutter, Nightfall is more than her chief's closest female contemporary. She truly adores him and, for a while, she, Redlance, and Cutter were a threesome when Cutter's family disappeared into the future (see *Book Eight*).

TYLEET

Gatherer, scout, guard; Nightfall and Redlance's daughter
Age: About 500 years old, mortal

Tyleet

First, and as yet, only child to be born to the Wolfriders in the New Land (see *Book Eight*), Tyleet herself acknowledges that she's been spoiled rotten; but if she is, she's "rotten" like a persimmon, which just gets sweeter with age. Gentle, brave,

Strongbow

and self confident, innocent, but not gullible, Tyleet is always on center with her emotions. Nothing rattles her. This is why she always gets her way when she wants something—no one can resist her calm, determined persuasiveness. Tyleet once raised a human baby to adolescence, whereafter the boy returned to his birth-tribe (see *Hidden Years* #3). Of all the Wolfriders, Tyleet, with her affinity for humans and her gift for animal sound mimicry, now has the greatest potential to learn the language of the medieval-period humans. If she accomplishes this feat, despite the personal risk, it will give her tribe an invaluable survival edge.

STRONGBOW

Hunter, warrior, scout, guard, tribal
    elder; Moonshade's lifemate, father
    of Dart
Age: About 900 years old, mortal

Moonshade

If political parties existed in the holt, Strongbow would be the staunchest of Republicans. An arch (archer?) conservative, his adherence to "The Way" is as straight and narrow as one of his arrows. Being a tribal elder, Strongbow doesn't care for his younger chief's new-fangled ideas and always challenges any procedure he thinks will disrupt the natural order. He's stubborn, not stupid, and knows in his heart that change is part of nature. Damned if he'll kowtow to it like some panty-waist, though! He's one of the most intensely monogamous Wolfriders, deeply devoted to his Recognized lifemate, Moonshade. The fact that he communicates with her solely by sending is a sign of his great desire for intimacy. To Strongbow, words just muddy things up. If he talks at all, he's either addressing a non-sender or he's so emotionally overwhelmed he can't get his thoughts straight. However, Strongbow is not the cliche dark, silent type who can't express his feelings. He has one son, Dart, of whom he is very proud—and shows it. As a rule, Strongbow hates humans, fire, lies, waste, extravagance, and folly—which means he detests Winnowill and Rayek. Though he himself is one of the more strongly gifted Wolfriders, he mistrusts overuse of the old powers and thinks all elves would be better off if they'd just follow "The Way." First of his tribe within memory to kill a fellow elf, Strongbow agonized over the deed until he received forgiveness from the slain one's spirit. Strongbow has a thoroughly good heart encased in somewhat thorny wrappings.

MOONSHADE

Tanner, maker, gatherer, huntress,
    tribal elder; Strongbow's lifemate,
    Dart's mother
Age: At least 900 and possibly older
    than Strongbow, mortal

In Moonshade's case, artistic temperament tends to leave the accent on "temper." At her worst, somewhat timid and prejudiced, at her best, a no-nonsense practical type, she's easily peeved by others' unpredictable behavior. Her mind is set on certain "oughts" and "givens," which leaves her free to concentrate on her work. Watch out, women's libbers! Moonshade gladly defers to Strongbow on most issues and usually sticks up for her lifemate, even when he's wrong. As far as she's concerned, that's part of "The Way." Though she makes no overt effort to be charming, she is naturally womanly, sexy, and mysterious. The type of clothing and accessories she designs are an ideal blend of utility and esthetics. Each outfit suits its wearer perfectly which means, despite her guarded air, Moonshade *groks* her tribefolk well. During peaceful times her more decorative flair emerges. But she will not dress her tribe only for vanity's sake, exposing them to danger with garish colors that stand out in the woods. That's not the Way. As a mother she has tended to stay in the background, letting Dart and Strongbow work things out between them. She's not easy to get close to, but she's true blue, unshakeable in her convictions, and always rises to the occasion.

PIKE

Hunter, gatherer, warrior, guard; son of Rain the Healer (deceased), brother of Rainsong (deceased), Skot and Krim's lifemate
Age: Over 600 years old, mortal

It seems Pike was born to bug conservative types like Strongbow and Moonshade. He was, in fact, Rain the Healer's first experiment in induced Recognition, but he is considered to have been born *outside* of Recognition. Even Pike jokes that the experiment went awry. Pike is the Wolfrider pack's omega in the sense that the others can't help picking on him for laughs—after all, he gives them so much to work with! Everybody's comic relief, Pike

Pike

lives for pleasure, play, and getting high on fermented dreamberries. Never mind that he's managed to live long enough to see his own face-fur come in; Pike is an eternal adolescent who constantly needs to be told what to do. Once told, he's obedient. But he won't initiate ideas or go out of his way to implement them—unless it has to do with sex, a good joke, sex, filching dreamberry wine from the trolls, sex, a good game, sex, partying, fighting or, oh yes, sex. Pike is currently part of a three-mating with the two transplanted Go-Backs, Skot and Krim. Regarding them as lifemates, Pike identifies closely with them, for all Go-Backs are born outside of Recognition. Since the first quest began, Pike's had the occasional heartache (the death of Vaya—see *Book Four*; the loss of Krim's baby—see *Book Eight*), but these things don't stay with him. He truly lives in the now of wolf thought. Pike doesn't drink to forget, but he never forgets to drink!

TREESTUMP

Hunter, warrior; father of Dewshine, uncle to Cutter
Age: Over 1000 years old, the eldest Wolfrider, mortal

Treestump

Clearbrook

Born under Bear-claw's leadership, brother of Cutter's mother, Joyleaf, Treestump is a loveable father figure to his tribe-folk. Gruff, kindly and wise, he's a warrior not a "worry-er." The Way is all he knows, and he takes it one day at a time. Tree-stump is not a deep thinker or tactician, but he's as solid as his name suggests and tireless when it comes to defending his territory. With all the changes that have taken place since Cutter became chief, Treestump is glad he doesn't have the job and is more than willing to let Cutter deal with the complexities of post–Palace War life. However, because of his down-to-earth wisdom, Treestump is usually Cutter's first choice to speak for him in council. Treestump is currently *treeing* with Clearbrook. He has one daughter, Dew-shine, born of Recognition with the long-dead Rillfisher. He's had lovemates and lifemates in the distant past, and it's likely he's been Recognized more than once. Few Wolfriders have ever lived to be his age and he has forgotten much. Yet he is not re-garded as over-the-hill by any of his tribemates. Like good ale, he gets stronger and has more charac-ter with age. Tree-stump has a comical side and can take as much teasing as he dishes out.

CLEARBROOK

Huntress, gatherer, warrior; lifemate to One-Eye (deceased), Scouter's mother
Age: Over 1000 (slightly younger than Treestump), mortal

As the eldest female Wolfrider, Clear-brook is in many ways the most re-spected. Normally calm, level-headed, and thoughtful, she has a truly wom-anly and dignified presence. One-Eye's murder in battle brought out the grim, avenging angel in her. But coming at last to terms with her lifemate's death lifted her onto a higher spiritual plane. She is now an advocate of forgiveness and letting go of the past. No Wolfrider lives more in the now of wolf thought than she. As her name suggests, Clearbrook is the mirror in which the Wolfriders can see the wholeness, right-ness, and even the beauty of their own mortality. She is both mother figure and warrior. Her quietly offered advice is not a gift to be disregarded. On the lighter side, she has let her braid grow long again, a sure sign that she has rediscovered her sexuality and sense of fun with Treestump. Clearbrook has one son, Scouter, born of Recognition with the slain One-Eye. Though little has been said of it, she had a daughter long ago, probably by a different Rec-ognized lifemate. Her instincts tell her she's past bearing more children. If that is so, then the elfin equivalent of meno-pause has less to do with biology than psychology.

SCOUTER

Hunter, scout, warrior, guard; son of Clearbrook, Dewshine's lifemate
Age: About 500 years old, mortal

Scouter

Scouter has always been the chivalrous sort, dutiful, loyal, and generous. He has a big heart and tends to put his own wishes on the back burner if it will serve his loved ones in some way. Like Cutter, he lost his father young. But unlike Cutter, he also had to cope with Dewshine's Recognition of another and the child that resulted. His anger a thing of the moment, Scouter holds no grudges and always gives others the benefit of the doubt. He readily adopted Windkin, showing he possesses a clarity of heart-vision that corresponds to his superb eyesight. Scouter is the Sir Galahad of Wolfriders, watching over the tribe, protecting and defending. Should he ever Recognize another, it will cause *him* more angst than Dewshine.

DEWSHINE

Huntress, gatherer, guard; Treestump's daughter, Cutter's cousin, Scouter's lifemate
Age: About 500 years old, mortal
Soul Name: Lree

Dewshine is a sylph in the classic sense. She weighs next to nothing and, with every step, seems ready to leave the ground in flight. Her personality is equally light, airy, and elusive. She's extremely feminine and girlish with hidden strengths. An Armani porcelain comes to mind. She has one son, Windkin, born of Recognition with Tyldak, the winged Glider. Choosing to stay in the Sun Village with Scouter to raise Windkin, Dewshine was forced to dwell there for hundreds of years due to the disappearance of the Great Palace. Making the best of her lot, Dewshine cultivated her gift for mimicking birdsong, bringing the remembered music of the forest to the Sun Folk. She and Scouter are still loving

lifemates, but she is less monogamous than he. Dewshine does not as yet yearn for a second Recognition. But who knows what urges this spunky lass will rediscover upon her return to the Wolfriders' holt?

Dewshine

THE TRANSPLANTED WOLFRIDERS

SKOT

Warrior, hunter, guard, former Go-Back; Pike's and Krim's lifemate (a three-mating)
Age: About 500 years old, a young immortal

Give Pike a mean streak, an attitude and a few less gray cells, and you've got Skot. Born in the Frozen Mountains to the hardy Go-Back tribe, Skot is much older than he ever expected to be. He finds the Wolfrider lifestyle rather plush compared to how he grew up. But he still lives as if every day were his last, just out of old habit. He's really fond of Pike and Krim and beats them up regularly to prove it. To Skot a punch in the gut is a sign

Skot

Krim

of affection. He prefers not to make decisions—prefers not to think at all if he doesn't have to. As cannon fodder he's ideal: just point him at the enemy and turn him loose. He's absolutely fearless in battle and would require being hacked to bits to be stopped. Skot's sense of humor leans toward the sadistic, but he's not completely stupid. The stunts he pulls stop just short of doing real harm. And though he never did get the hang of riding on wolfback, he actually has some respect for the Wolfrider elders; to him they're like High Ones. He thinks Cutter is an OK chief but wishes he wouldn't be so careful of everybody's welfare. Like all Go-Backs, to whom immortality is meaningless, Skot doesn't see the value in living as long as possible and is even looking forward to some gloriously appropriate demise. He'd like to sire a few children first and keeps trying with Krim, since he knows Recognition is probably not in the cards for him. Skot considers Pike and Krim lifemates but likes to dally outside the group when he gets the chance. For him, pleasure is where you find it, and any partner, male or female, could make his last hour sweeter

Venka

KRIM

Hunter, warrior, guard; Pike's and Skot's lifemate

Age: About 500 years old, a young immortal

Like Skot, Krim is surprised to still be alive after all her years dwelling with the Wolfriders. Kahvi, chief of the Go-Backs, was a role model for Krim who has hung onto her tough, ornery, "F—you!" manner. Even so, there's a warmth that can be kindled in Krim if you can make her laugh. Probably that's what keeps her bonded with two jokers like Skot and Pike. She's a bit wicked and mean-tempered, which lends her a certain fascination. One gets the impression she's murder in the furs, leaving Skot and Pike staggering around the next day. She is known to have had—and lost—one baby since joining the Wolfriders; whether the sire was Pike or Skot is unclear. She seemed to take the loss in stride and does not come across as the type that knits little booties. If she has any care-taking qualities at all, they are channeled into her tribal duties, which she takes seriously. Of the two, it was probably Krim who convinced Skot to leave the Go-Backs and go exploring the world. She likes the wolves and admires the Wolfriders' style—they appeal to a wild, romantic streak in her. Combat is a source of joy to Krim, and she yearns for more of it than she gets. She doesn't fully understand Cutter's style of leadership but keeps cool about it, for it's not a warrior's place to question too much.

VENKA

Huntress, gatherer, guard; daughter of Rayek and Kahvi

Age: About 500 years old, a young immortal

Cool, calm, and aloof, the Greta Garbo of elves, Venka is as mysterious as she is attractive. Hers is the path of subtlety. Hers are the arrows that fly true and hit home when nobody's looking. She can deck you with a few quiet, well-chosen words and leave you wondering what hit you. Not that Venka is cruel; she is, in fact, quite compassionate. But like her mother Kahvi, Venka tells the truth whether others are ready to hear it or not. Raised by the Wolfriders in the New Land, Venka regards herself as one of them and, despite her lack of wolf blood, follows "The Way" willingly. However, since meeting her father, Rayek, Venka has become newly fascinated with her desert heritage and has visited the Sun Village at least once. Her relationship with her father is odd, to say the least, for the Wolfriders depend on her to "keep him in line." She completely disapproves of many of the choices Rayek has made in the past, yet she behaves respectfully toward him and is clearly drawn to him by the deep blood ties they share. For as long as she can remember, Venka has protected the Wolfriders from the invasive psychic probings of Winnowill. Since this is relatively easy for her to do, Venka doesn't fully realize the enormous service she performs for the tribe that adopted her. She takes her "jamming" power for granted and has never experienced, as others have, the full force of a black sending by Winnowill. The day may come when Venka's powers are tested beyond their current limits. Living in the "now" of wolf thought as she does, such a test may catch her unawares and shatter, for once, her characteristic serenity.

ZHANTEE

Hunter, gatherer, scout, guard; former
    Sun Villager
Age: Unknown, immortal

Zhantee's life as a Wolfrider began in the Sun Village when he became one of Dart's jack-wolf riders to help protect Sorrow's End. Always an admirer of Rayek's, Zhantee has more spunk than the average Sun Villager and a willingness to try new things. He never knew a psychic shield-throwing power slept within him until his first encounter with the Palace of the High Ones. Timmain herself selected Zhantee to travel with the Wolfriders to the New Land; since then he has more than proved his worth. It's no secret he carries a king-sized torch for Leetah—he all but sacrificed his own life to rescue her from Winnowill. And he has shielded others from certain death, including Cutter. Zhantee is a shy, day-dreamy type, content to worship Leetah from afar, innocently proud to be regarded as a tribal hero. His lovemates have included Venka and Shenshen, but like all elves, he has no taboos about same-sex partners. If he has internal conflicts or secret sorrows, he keeps them to himself. Mild as his mentor, Redlance, Zhantee doesn't usually speak up in council. One learns more about him through his actions than his words. And what one learns is that Zhantee is touched with grace: unselfish, present to others' needs, and cheerful.

Zhantee

Aroree

AROREE

Glider, scout, teacher, hunter, gatherer; Sky-wise's non-exclusive lovemate

Age: unknown, immortal

"Sad Eyes." So Kahvi nick-named Aroree and it stuck. Aroree has lost something—she's not sure what. She has no idea where to find it, so she just keeps looking. At first she regretted losing her status as one of the Chosen Eight. But that status came at the cost of being a minion of an increasingly insane and abusive Winnowill. So that can't be what Aroree misses now, can it? Then she thought she missed her friend Skywise. But he told her what she really needed was the Palace (see *Book Five*). So she went seeking it but was frightened away by the Go-Back's violence. After that she lost all her people in the fall of Blue Mountain. They themselves meant little to her at that point, but her resulting loss of identity was overwhelming. When she finally found Skywise again, after his eons of sleep with the Wolfriders, she was still no closer to finding herself than before (see *Book Eight*). It may be that Aroree is the sort who always requires others to tell her who and what she is. In her role as teacher to the Wolfriders, recounting her memories of Lord Voll's founding of the Blue Mountain realm, Aroree seemed to find a measure of contentment. She abhors loneliness and prefers to be part of a family—any family. Perhaps what draws her to Skywise is his very oppositeness, his fearlessness. She who can control the flight of the giant hawk and soar above the clouds, cannot, for reasons that deserve exploration, let her own heart soar without fear.

THE SUN FOLK

SAVAH

Spiritual leader of the Sun Folk, founding mother of Sorrow's End, Mother of Memory, former "Rootless One," grandchild of Firstcomers

Age: Well over 10,000 years old, immortal

Savah

Mother Goddess, High Priestess, Sacred Sage, Guardian Angel: humans would bestow such titles upon Savah, Mother of Memory. She is almost beyond comprehension in human terms. So ancient, so advanced, so pure in thought, word ,and deed is this regal elf woman that if it weren't for her sense of humor, she'd be impossible to relate to! What keeps her in her body after all these thousands of years? Why doesn't she "go out" and stay out in the cosmos where such a transcendent being as herself belongs? Her children—the Sun Folk, the Wolfriders, the Go-Backs, the Gliders, and all those elves yet to be found—*they* keep her wrapped in her fleshcoat. As long as they need her guidance and her memories, she will stay. Savah's love for her own kind is unconditional and all-forgiving. She loves to teach; and even when a pupil such as Rayek goes off the path of right action she will not blame or reject but merely attempt to redirect. Never forgetting Suntop who, from her point of view, was gone for thousands of years, Savah called him to the Sun Village to complete his training. Possibly she sees Suntop as her successor, or at the very least, one who will become her equal in power, authority, and wisdom. It's said that Savah doesn't sleep. Not even those closest to her, such as Ahdri, Sun-Toucher, or Suntop, have a clue to her innermost thoughts. Perhaps she dreams of a future in which elves and humans dwell together in peace. At any rate, her memories apparently do not give her that gnawing homesickness for the stars that has caused aberrant behavior in the likes of Rayek and Winnowill. Savah is a touchstone, an eternal presence, a continuity, and a comfort to her fellow immortals.

TOORAH

Sun-Toucher's lifemate, Leetah and Shenshen's mother, Suntop and Ember's grandmother
Age: Over 10,000 years old, immortal

Perhaps Toorah can provide the answer to the question posed in Ahdri's personality profile. We first met Toorah during the Trial of Head, Hand, and Heart (see Book One). At the time, she seemed motherly yet quite willing to poke gentle fun at her uptight elder daughter Leetah. It's to be assumed that Shenshen is the product of a repeat Recognition between Sun-Toucher and Toorah (an unusual phenomenon which deserves exploration). Since we know so little about her, what Toorah herself is like now and how her lifemating with Sun-Toucher has evolved after thousands of years is open to speculation. When love endures that long, does it become so rarefied as to be an unrecognizable emotion to us poor humans? Does it revitalize in endless cycles, or does it turn purely platonic?

SUN-TOUCHER

Environmental and emotional sensitive, day-to-day leader of Sun Village activities; Leetah and Shenshen's father, Suntop and Ember's grandfather, Toorah's lifemate
Age: Over 10,000 years old, immortal

Toorah

One of the eldest elves born in the Sun Village, Sun-Toucher, like Savah, has probably forgotten which of the immortal villagers he sired in his youth. He does remember that Leetah and Shenshen are his daughters by Recognition with Toorah, but he hasn't a shred of fatherly possessiveness; too much time has passed. Sun-Toucher's perpetual goal is harmony: balance between the land and the population of Sorrow's End. Blinded thousands of years ago by staring too long into the sun's rays, he never sought healing from Leetah for fear of losing the compensating powers that awoke within him. Deeply reverent and deferential toward Savah, Sun-Toucher nevertheless keeps her in touch with the realities of daily vil-

Sun-Toucher

Shenshen

lage life. It would never occur to him to be other than what he is. He enjoys his role, the services he performs, and his involvement with all the villagers' trials and tribulations. Perhaps the loss of his sight makes life extra interesting to him and therefore helps him maintain contentment with his own unending existence.

SHENSHEN

Midwife, herbalist, gatherer; Toorah and Sun-Toucher's daughter, Leetah's sister

Age: Over 800 years old, a young immortal

Shenshen used to get a kick out of being the much younger sister who teased and tormented Leetah. Now that because of the time paradox (see *Book Eight*) she is a couple of hundred years older than Leetah, Shenshen doesn't quite know what to do with herself. Stranded in the New Land with the Wolfriders after the Great Palace disappeared, Shenshen did her best to fill Leetah's shoes and was the closest thing to a healer the Wolfriders had. She fell in with Pike, Skot, and Krim (well,

Dart

Pike always did have a soft spot for her), and treed with them for a long time. The passage of five hundred years has hardly dampened Shenshen's bubbly personality. She's still the spicy coquette, the tease, and the troublemaker, but living in the woods has made her somewhat tougher and more self reliant. She can never go back to being the fluff-brain we met in *Book One*. Just as Scouter and Dewshine never intended to live so long in the Sun Village, Shenshen never dreamed she'd spend more of her life in the green-growing place than in the desert. It's been hinted that she had something of a mentor/pupil relationship with Old Maggoty, the trolls' resident hag and brewer of strange potions. Gaining that ancient crone's trust, however slight, would take spunk, ingenuity, and patience. Shenshen clearly has qualities that elevate her above airhead status. But most often, like her dear friend Pike, she's an amusing, comical character: flirtatious, frisky, and prone to huffs if slighted.

DART

Hunter, warrior, scout, guard, founder and leader of the jackwolf riders; Strongbow and Moonshade's son

Age: Over 600 years old, mortal

Dart was just four years old when he came with the Wolfriders to live in Sorrow's End. He never left. At eleven he chose to remain behind in the village when the Wolfriders went in quest of Cutter. Even that young, Dart committed himself to becoming the Sun Folk's protector, as Rayek once was. But unlike Rayek, Dart had no ego-need to do it all by himself. Slowly, patiently, with the help of fellow transplants Woodlock, Rainsong, Wing (now all deceased), and Newstar, he trained those Sun Folk who had the aptitude to become pseudo-Wolfriders. Dart prefers to see others working together in a harmonious and active group. A natural leader, he's inspired by his father Strongbow, who always sticks to his guns, and by Cutter, who became chief at a very young age. While his loyalties are mainly with the Sun Village, Dart hasn't forgotten his true heritage. The Little Palace is very important to him; it enhances his sending abilities enough that he can contact his parents an ocean away. After five-hundred–plus years of being the Sun Village's protector, Dart opted to have himself preserved in long distance fellowship with Cutter's Wolfriders. Mortal, he probably wanted to survive to see his birth tribe again. However, since he instructed the Sun Folk to release him from his cocoon whenever they needed his help, his ten-thousand-year sleep was often interrupted, which accounts for his additional aging. While cocooned, he was Recognized by a young village maiden (a story yet to be told). He is also known to have had a soul brother/lovemate, Shu-shen, killed in battle with the Go-Backs (see *New Blood* #11 and #12).

WINDKIN

Glider, ex-Wolfrider, hunter, scout, explorer; Tyldak and Dewshine's son by Recognition, Ahdri's unRecognized lifemate
Age: Several thousand years old, genetically altered immortal

A very new character, Windkin is a blank slate waiting to be written upon. We know he's spunky and very loyal to the Sun Village. He's met Tyldak and is absolutely clear that Scouter, his foster dad, is his only dad. He tried sleeping in wrapstuff along with Scouter, Dewshine, Dart, Mender, and Newstar, but his immortal life screamed to be lived, so he sent telepathically to have someone cut

him free. It was probably Ahdri. Because he can fly so far, it's likely that during peaceful times he has left Sorrow's End to find out what the rest of the world looks like.

Windkin

AHDRI

Rock-shaper, handmaiden to Savah; Windkin's unRecognized lifemate
Age: Over 10,000 years old, immortal

A relatively minor character so far, Ahdri has constantly been seen at Savah's side, worrying, fussing and attending to her every need. Having come into her rock-shaping power due to the presence of the Little Palace, Ahdri has very likely come into her own in other ways as well. The villagers obviously rely on her spectacular magic, so her status has elevated accordingly. Her long-term relationship with Windkin, barely hinted at, has yet to be explored. What does happen to love over the course of ten thousand years?

Ahdri

Newstar

NEWSTAR

Weaver, seamstress, gatherer, water-bearer; daughter of Woodlock and Rainsong (deceased), sister to Wing (deceased) and Mender

Age: Less than 500 years old, mortal

Picture an unearthly, beautiful maiden with yards of shimmering blonde hair flowing behind her as she rides in the light of double moons on wolfback. You don't need to know very much about her. In fact, no one should ever know very much about her because she's an elf—one of the "elfiest" elves we have! Newstar epitomizes elfness! She has always seemed sweet and gentle and "not all there." No one should ever try to get her "there" (meaning dissect her) because we need her to remind us all just what it is about elves that make us poor humans love them, hate them, envy them, and fear them all at once. Consider her an archetype. Rackham has done her. Kay Nielsen has done her. Erte has done her. Disney has done her. She's just that simple and just that classical. Yes, she Recognized a Sun Villager and had a son named Kimo. Her lifemate was killed in the battle for the Little Palace, and

Mender

she had herself preserved along with her mortally wounded son so that she could be there to see him healed by Leetah someday (see *Hidden Years* #4). That's a very elfin thing to do. Time means very little to her. She's a mortal with an immortal mind who cares nothing that a huge chunk of her life was spent in suspended animation. She's starting from now...the "now" of wolf thought.

MENDER

Warrior, healer, hunter, gatherer; son of Woodlock and Rainsong (deceased), brother of Wing (deceased) and Newstar

Age: Over 600 years old, mortal

You are what you eat, and Mender is just about as schizoid as elves come. Fortunately, having a split personality hasn't driven him bonkers as it did poor Two-Edge. A pure-blooded Wolfrider, Mender is a throwback to Bearclaw's time when life was risky, short, and violent. Fighting turns Mender on (and with a healer's hormones that means *really* turned on!) But as a native Sun Villager, raised in the placid, agrarian atmosphere of Sorrow's End, Mender can't help having developed a gentler side. The battle for the Little Palace, probably the most glorious event of his life (see *Hidden Years* #4), divided him so that he ended up healing wounds that he caused. Yet Mender shows pride rather than guilt for his violent streak. He would never give it up. He doesn't have a firm personal philosophy, which is why he had himself preserved under conditions identical to Dart's. Mender slept in order to meet Cutter and Leetah, seeing them as role models who could help him balance his warrior and healer self. In the normally peaceful Sun Village where a healer's duties run toward minor gardening or hunting injuries, Mender's real chance to shine has been in his role as sexual initiator. A pretty boy and a dandy, he ought to have face fur at his age. But he's obviously using his powers to retard beard growth. His history of initiations and teachings (including Ember) is elaborate enough to make even Skywise drool with envy. But has Mender ever loved? Has he ever felt anything so deeply that it has shaken him to his very soul?

THE TROLLS

PICKNOSE

Former guardsman of Greymung the Shiftless (eaten), former king of the Frozen Mountain trolls; patriarch of extended, inbred family including Trinket, Oddbit's mate, Old Maggoty's grandson-in-law
Age: Who knows, immortal

As trolls go, Picknose has some fairly admirable qualities. He's got... perseverance. He's a doting Papa and a faithful mate in his own disgusting way. Picknose has always had ambitions to be a great monarch, but any time he's actually achieved the position of wealth and power he craves, he's managed to blow it (see *Book Seven*). He's the Fred Flintstone of trolls, family man, loudmouth and fall guy. But is he altogether a loser? Well, he's had a degree of success in establishing his own "mini" underground empire in the New Land. His descendants are numerous and heavily inbred, but this may not be the genetic problem for trolls that it is for humans and animals. His grandchildren and great-great-grandchildren are also his subjects, and he works them hard. Picknose spends his time overseeing the design and construction of his kingdom while underlings bring reports of production in the forges and

mines. Picknose knows he can't always trust these reports and has spies to spy on his spies. It's all in the family after all. He's a complete softie for his daughter, Trinket, newly returned to the fold (see *Book Eight*). He showers on the brat all the attention and affection that seems lost on

Picknose

the aged, but still-vain Oddbit. Picknose is easily brow-beaten by his ever-demanding mate and even moreso by Old Maggoty, who believes the only way to handle a male is to stomp on him regularly. Why he doesn't just haul off and belt them both is a mystery. Is he a wimp? Or is he really the trollish equivalent of a gentleman? In many ways Picknose is a credit to his kind: greedy, treacherous, cowardly, sadistic, smelly, utterly materialistic, and short-sighted. So why is he so damn loveable? There's more here than meets the nose!

OLD MAGGOTY

Old Maggoty

Great-great-great-great-great-(etc.)-grandmother of just about every troll on the World of Two Moons; cook, gatherer, teacher, medicine hag, power behind the throne

Oddbit

Age: Beyond reckoning, immortal

The image of the withered crone cackling over her bubbling cauldron is always compelling. Old Maggoty is a hag's hag and therefore rather fascinating. Older than old, she lives by her own rules and answers to no one. She is the popper of foolish balloons, the deflator of overlarge egos. She calls it as she sees it. And no one dares sass her back! She is a healer without sentiment, treating the ailment 'til she conquers it, giving not a hang for her patient's physical or emotional pain. Maggoty believes in "boot-strapping" and will not tolerate sloth. She's the one who deals most often with the Wolfriders, haggling over furs and game to be traded for troll-forged blades, tools, jewelry, and of course, her delicious dreamberry wine. She doesn't like elves but has a grudging respect for the Wolfriders' sense of family. Maggoty raised her granddaughter, Oddbit, to embody all the maidenly virtues: greed, deception, opportunism, manipulativeness, coyness, vanity, and fickleness. In the highly sexist troll society, Maggoty believes a successful female plays the game better than those who make up the rules. Unfortunately, once mated to Picknose, the indolent Oddbit did not live up to Maggoty's expectations. So the crone is now concentrating on Trinket who pursues her lessons much more diligently than her mother ever did. Though she constantly bitches and scowls, Maggoty relishes her role and life in general.

ODDBIT

Matriarch; Old Maggoty's granddaughter, Picknose's mate, mother of Trinket and many, many others
Age: The mind boggles, immortal

Oddbit's personality is...oh, brother! Scarlet O'hara on steroids? Nope, not that bright. Betty Boop with a gold-digging streak? Getting warmer. Madonna without the class? Well, you get the idea. Oddbit doesn't think she's aged a bit in several thousand years; her figure's just as bountiful as it ever was—and how lucky for Picknose! Other girls don't hold up nearly as well, you know! If only Trinket weren't always stealing the show, the nasty little twit! But that's okay. Just keep the furs, the jewels, and the food coming. After all, a girl's got to maintain her image! Perhaps Grandmama has a potion for hair loss? And maybe a potion that cures a mate's loss of...um...interest?

TRINKET

Picknose and Oddbit's daughter, Old Maggoty's great- something-grand-daughter
Age: About ten years old, immortal

Remember the bad little girls who always got their come-uppance from Shirley Temple in those treacly thirties movies? Well, Trinket would make goose pate out of Shirley and walk away with the film! Indomitable, a force of

Trinket

nature, such is the brat-hood of Trinket the troll. She yowls and mountains tremble. She whines and rivers change course. She blubbers and flowers wilt. It's a lot of fun being Trinket; she's in her power and she doesn't hesitate to use it. Ethnic groups aside, she's most certainly a "princess." The only ones who can control her at all are her friend Ember, Old Maggoty, and Ekuar.

RATS, WILD CARDS AND LONERS

RAYEK

Former chief hunter and protector of the Sun Village, master of the Palace of the High Ones; Venka's father
Age: Over 600 years old, a young immortal

"Nothing is ever enough" should be tattooed on this lonely elf's chest. If he loves, he must also possess. If he accomplishes a feat, he must top it. If he's praised, he can't accept it gracefully but says, "I can do better." Is this so bad? It is when pride makes you unable to receive what's offered or appreciate what you already have. Rayek is "star struck"—always has been. Even before he saw the Scroll of Colors, Rayek believed that he was too good for the World of Two Moons. He could do better and so could all immortal elves—or so he thought. Despite his disastrous efforts to prove his point (see *Books Seven* and *Eight*), he still thinks so. The racial memory of the High Ones is strong in him, which makes him homesick for a place somewhere "out there" where he and all others like him belong. The Wolfriders' love for the World of Two Moons and acceptance of their own mortality baffles and hurts him. He's ashamed of the limitations forced on him by this planet of exile and aspires to nothing less than becoming a High One.

WINNOWILL

Ex-Lord of the Gliders, anti-healer; one-time lovemate and advisor to Lord Voll (deceased), Two-Edge's mother
Age: Probable contemporary of Savah, immortal

Rayek

Why did the Gliders need stairs in their Blue Mountain domain? Because one among them couldn't float. Dragged down by her own inner darkness, Winnowill walks where others fly. She is the Shadow, the Dark Mother, the Loveless One. She is power turned in upon itself when others have no use for it. As the centuries passed, the Gliders became so safe and so passionless within their stony stronghold that there was nothing for Winnowill to do. She could not heal, force Recognition, or act as sexual initiator. So she festered and finally went mad. Torture and enslavement became diverting pastimes for her. She learned to feed off the dreams of her people and continued the practice with humans.

Winnowill

Ekuar

Winnowill is attracted to humans because it's so easy to introduce the element of fear into their dreams, which provides her with spectacular entertainment. She "protected" Lord Voll, and ultimately, almost all the Gliders to death. Because she can't tolerate her own company, she's always messing about with others' lives. Somewhere under her layers of darkness is the same homesickness which makes her Rayek's natural soulmate. She yearns to be cleansed by travel to the stars. Partially healed by Leetah, Winnowill no longer has the luxury of madness and must recall her evil deeds—especially her extreme cruelty to her half-troll son, Two-Edge. Rather than complete her own healing, Winnowill has retreated to a catatonic state in the Palace of the High Ones where she waits...and plans.

EKUAR

Rock-shaper, Rayek's mentor, firstborn of the High Ones
Age: Beyond reckoning, immortal

Ekuar is a perfect example of suffering turned to transcendence. A slave to trolls for untold thousands of years, Ekuar experienced systematic torture, mutilation, and amputation designed to crush his spirit. Certainly he still shows the effects of this abuse, even apart from the obvious missing arm, leg, and finger. He often forgets his name or what he came into a chamber

to do. He talks to himself. Depending on one's point of view, he's either serene or not "with it" when it comes to crises. He's seen it all and nothing fazes him much. Yet despite these weirdnesses, Ekuar operates almost exclusively from love. No one can enter his space without immediately falling under the spell of his warmth, his impish humor, and his kindness. He bears no ill will toward trolls; possibly he has voluntarily erased those memories from his mind. He adores children and those, like Two-Edge, with childlike qualities. He loves Rayek like a father and will overlook almost any shortcoming in this arrogant youth who saved him from the pit. Nevertheless, Ekuar will not go along with acts of harm and will simply withdraw himself, which is usually enough to bring Rayek around. Though Leetah has offered to attempt limb restoration, Ekuar, for his own mysterious reasons, hasn't taken her up on it as yet. Having once been essentially *dead* to the world, the body must mean something to him. But he seems content with himself as he is and has been known to enjoy the occasional dance of joining.

TWO-EDGE

Troll/elf halfbreed, craftsman and weapons-maker supreme; Winnowill's son
Age: Born sometime after Greymung's rebellion, immortal

The ultimate abused child, poor Two-Edge's identity crisis is of cosmic proportions. In his youth his mind was split by Winnowill to prevent him from going to Voll and exposing all her perverse activities. From his prison cell, he saw his mother blast his troll father apart, which drove Two-Edge further into madness. It is not known how he escaped Winnowill's clutches, but he did remain bound to her in a sick pas de deux wherein he became a disembodied voice that pursued and tormented her constantly. He engineered the troll–elf war for the Palace just to resolve his identity problem. Clearly, he has no sense of proportion. The consequences of his actions concern him only insofar as they concern his own welfare. Ekuar did befriend Two-Edge and had a calming influence on him for a few brief years. And Leetah did lay hands on Two-Edge long enough for his inherited elfin sending power to awaken (see *Book Six*). Yet this is but small ground gained. He's still a child twisted by hate and fear, looking for the mother he never had. Two-Edge survived the collapse of Blue Mountain and has continued his long duel with Winnowill. He talks to her when she's not there—but she's always "there." Near or far, she is his constant dark companion.

KAHVI

Chief of the Go-Backs, warrior, huntress, guard; Venka's mother, Tyldak's lovemate
Age: unknown, immortal

Here's a dame who's got a lot going for her. But loveable she's not! It's tempting to try to see a heart of gold under her hard exterior, but Kahvi is interesting precisely because she has few redeeming qualities by most human societies' standards of female behavior. "Well, OK, she's tough, but at least she's honest, right?" Hardly! When it suits her purposes, Kahvi will lie through a smile. She knows she seems plainspoken, not really bright enough to be a clever deceiver, and she uses that appearance to her advantage. "OK, so she fibs. But when she really cares about someone...?" Sorry. You're looking for depths that just aren't there—deliberately! Yes, she shed a tear when

Two-Edge

her daughter, Vaya was killed in the Palace War; Kahvi's not made of stone after all! But she danced the grief out quickly (see *Book Four*). And she let Venka be raised by the Wolfriders mainly to vex Rayek; she's not above using her kids as pawns. As for lovemates, Kahvi's a great pal, promiscuous as a bunny, and has no idea which of the Go-Backs fathered most of her kids. She had a thing for Cutter once but lost interest when his fire didn't match hers. Does she love Tyldak? Close, but not like he loves her. He's useful for long-distance travel and surprisingly good in the furs, which is all Kahvi requires in a male companion. "So she's a slut, a bitch, and a liar. Why isn't she a villain?" She can be, sort of. But she's also a chief. Most of her actions, ethical or not, are geared toward keeping the Go-Back's numbers up and seeing they're in great fighting fettle. If they're living and dying well, she's doing her job.

Kahvi

Tyldak

TYLDAK

Glider; Windkin's sire by Recognition with Dewshine, Kahvi's lovemate
Age: Younger than Winnowill, immortal

"Be careful what you wish." Tyldak begged Winnowill to give him wings and she sure did—along with an aerodynamically redesigned physique and one hell of an eating problem! Little is known of Tyldak before Winnowill flesh-shaped him. But he was clearly willing to risk everything in order to realize his dream of pure flight. Tyldak has been one of Winnowill's flunkies and a bit of a sourball at times, but he never quite made it to villain status. He's basically a nice guy, even chivalrous in a strange way. Life in Blue Mountain corrupted him, as it did most of his people. His Recognition with Dewshine was the first crack in his shell. Later, he escaped Winnowill's enslavement, and he's been flying free ever since. Tyldak was so disturbed by Dewshine's wolfishness he chose to have nothing to do with raising Windkin. Whether or not he and Windkin ever established a father/son relationship is doubtful, but open to speculation. What now draws Tyldak to Kahvi is his sense of her as a kindred spirit. He values freedom more than anything else; he would die for it. And Kahvi is nothing if not free, a law unto herself. He loves her ardently, has sworn to defend her—even from herself—but resists pinning her down. Precisely because he is not obnoxiously possessive, she stays. So it works very well.

PETALWING

Preserver, arrived on the World of Two Moons with the original High Ones
Age: Beyond reckoning, immortal

Happy happy, joy joy! Oh, what fun it is to be a complete airhead! Let's face it, preservers are fairies and Petalwing is a prime example. Generally, Petalwing hasn't a care in the world. It's bossy, prankish, sassy, affectionate, and just plain silly. Yes...*it*. Preservers are sexless (though they're quite the little voyeurs), and their personalities are almost interchangeable. Somehow Petalwing stands out as their leader—possibly because it has the biggest mouth. Preservers make great watchdogs; they delight in foiling and humiliating intruders. But they are also capable of tuning in when there's serious trouble. Preservers love elves and have an instinctive need to take care of them. The form of their caretaking can sometimes be a complete nuisance but try telling that to Petalwing. One might as well try to move a mountain as contradict a preserver that has made up its little mind. Petalwing loves to sing. But if you've heard fingernails on a blackboard, you will know why it won't be winning any Grammys real soon. ✧

Petalwing

Appendix: Sources of Information

Research into Elfquest

Tracking, Nature and Wilderness Survival School. Send a SASE (self-addressed stamped envelope) for information to: The Tracker, PO Box 318, Milford, NJ 08848

To locate the SCA group nearest you write: Registrar, Society for Creative Anachronism, Inc., Office of the Registry, PO Box 360743, Milpitas, CA 95035-0743. Enclose an SASE.

For a free Dover catalog, write to: Dover Publications, Inc., 31 East 2nd Street, Mineola, NY 11501

Raisz Landform Maps, 130 Charles Street, Boston, MA 02114

For information on United States Geological Survey topographic maps, send an SASE to: Map Distribution, US Geological Survey, PO Box 25286, Federal Center Building 41, Denver, CO 80225

A Selected Bibliography

Blacksmithing, Metalcraft and Jewelery Making:

Blandford, Percy W.
The Practical Handbook of Blacksmithing and Metalworking
TAB Books, Blue Ridge Summit, PA, 1980.

Garrison, William E. and Dowd, Merle E.
Handcrafting Jewelry: Designs and Techniques
Contemporary Books, Inc., Chicago, IL, 1972.

Tubby, Pamela
Working With Metal
Thomas Y. Crowell, New York, NY, 1972.

Tucker, Ted
Practical Projects for the Blacksmith
Rodale Press, Emmalus, PA, 1980.

Weygens, Alexander G.
The Modern Blacksmith
Van Nostrand Reinhold Co., New York, NY, 1974.

Herb Reference and Natural Dyes:

Bemiss, Elijah
The Dyer's Companion
Dover Publications, New York, NY, 1973.

Lust, John
The Herb Book
Bantam Books, New York, NY, 1974

Pahlow, Mannfried
Living Medicine: the Healing Properties of Plants
Thorsons Publishers Ltd., Wellingboro, Northamptonshire, England, 1980.

Weiner, Michael A.
Earth Medicine, Earth Food
Collier Books, New York, NY 1972

Medical Reference:

American Red Cross
Standard First Aid and Personal Safety
American Red Cross, 1979.

Berkow, Robert (ed.)
The Merck Manual of Diagnosis and Therapy
Merck and Company, Rahway, NJ, 1982.

Brown, Terry and Rob Hunter
Concise Book of Outdoor First Aid
Gage Printing, Agincourt, Canada, 1978.

Franks, Martha Ross
The American Medical Association's Handbook of First Aid and Emergency Care
Random House, NY, 1980.

Henderson, John
Emergency Medical Guide
Mc-Graw-Hill, New York, NY, 1978.

Medical Reference (cont.):

Mashiro, N.
Black Medicine: The Dark Art of Death
Paladin Press, Boulder, CO, 1978.

Tegner, Bruce
Self-Defense Nerve Centers and Pressure Points
Thor Publishing Company, Ventura, CA, 1978.

Survival Skills and Everyday Life in the Woods:

Angier, Bradford
Survival with Style
Vintage Books/Random House, New York, NY, 1972.

Brown, Tom Jr.
Tom Brown's Field Guide to the Forgotten Wilderness
Berkley Books, New York, NY, 1987.

(with B. Morgan) *Tom Brown's Field Guide to Living with the Earth*
Berkley Books, New York, NY, 1984.

(with B. Morgan) *Tom Brown's Field Guide to Nature Observation and Tracking*
Berkley Books, New York, NY, 1983.

Tom Brown's Field Guide to Wild Edible and Medicinal Plants
Berkley Books, New York, NY, 1985.

(with B. Morgan) *Tom Brown's Field Guide to Wilderness Survival*
Berkley Books, New York, NY, 1983.

(with William Owen) *The Search*
Berkley Books, New York, NY.
(as told to William Jon Watkins) *The Tracker*
Berkley Books, New York, NY.

Boswell, John (ed.)
The U.S. Armed Forces Survival Manual
Rawson, Wade Publishers Inc., New York, NY, 1980.

Graves, Richard
Bushcraft: A Serious Guide to Survival and Camping
Warner Books, New York, NY, 1978.

Olsen, Larry Dean
Outdoor Survival Skills
Pocket Books, New York, NY, 1976.

Weapons Combat:

Daniel, Charles
Traditional Ninja Weapons: Fighting Techniques of the Shadow Warrior
Unique Publications, Burbank, CA, 1986.

Demura, Fumio
Bo: Karate Weapon of Self-Defense
Ohara Publications, Burbank, CA, 1976.

Inosanto, Daniel (with George Foon and Gilbert Johnson)
The Filipino Martial Arts, as taught by Dan Inosanto
Know Now Publishing Company, Los Angeles, CA, 1980.

Inosanto, Daniel (with George Foon)
Absorb What Is Useful
Know Now Publishing Company, Los Angeles, CA, 1982.

Williams, John C. (with Glenn Helgeland)
Archery For Beginners
Contemporary Books, Inc., Chicago, IL, 1976.

Yamashita, Tadashi
Bo: The Japanese Long Staff
Unique Publications, Burbank, CA, 1986.

Wolves and Zoology:

Dixon, Dougal
After Man: A Zoology of the Future
St. Martin's Press, New York, NY, 1981.

Fox, Michael
The Wolf
Lorgman Canada Ltd., Toronto, Ontario, Canada, 1973.

Lopez, Barry H.
Of Wolves and Men
Charles Scribner's Sons, New York, NY, 1978.

Games People Play

The Elfquest role-playing game is available from: Chaosium, 950-A 56th Street, Oakland, CA 94608.
The Elfquest board game is available from: Mayfair Games, 5641 Howard Street, Niles, IL 60714

The Elfquest Glossary

Many people contributed to this glossary, but John C. LaRue Jr. got the ball rolling in the *Elfquest Gatherum* Volume One. Since then, the following people have helped expand the glossary to its present size: Katerina M. Hodge, Benjamin Urrutia, Vince Mora, Eliann Fensvoll, Brad Johnson, Linda Woeltjen, and Anne McCoombs.

A note on pronunciation: Rather than using standard dictionary notation, pronunciation of certain names here is indicated phonetically.

A

Adar: (AY-darr) Human, male; mate of Nonna; son of Tolf, the Wood-Cleaver; exiled and returned member of Olbar's tribe; skeptical guide of Cutter and Skywise, he later helps them free Winnowill's human captives.

age-mate: A friend about the same age.

Ahdri: (AH-dree) Elf, female; Sun Villager; Savah's handmaiden and a rockshaper.

airwalker: Used to refer to one who levitates, particularly Rayek.

Alekah: (ah-LECK-uh) Elf, female; Sun Villager; Savah's granddaughter; a rockshaper who formed the Sun Symbol at the end of the Bridge of Destiny.

allo: A large, carnivorous dinosaur, packs of which still roam the world.

always now, the: The state of mind that exists in a perpetual present; the "now" of wolf thought.

anti-healing: The opposite of healing, the power to inflict pain; used by Winnowill.

Aro: (AH-row) Human, male; refugee from the holt fire whose life is spared by Cutter at Sorrow's End; tells the human myth of the elves.

Aroree: (uh-ROW-ree)Elf, female; one of the Chosen Eight from Blue Mountain, rider of the great hawk Littletrill; loves Skywise; survives the downfall of Blue Mountain and joins the Wolfrider tribe.

arrow whip: A weapon consisting of a flexible stick with a sling on the end to shoot arrows; used by Dart in the Sun Village.

Ayoooah!: Wolfrider shout derived from a wolf's howl; a general tribal cry of the Wolfriders.

B

babah: Wolfrider baby talk for "father," equivalent to "Dada."

bagfrog: A large frog with an air pouch at its throat.

barbarian: Sun Folk term (derogatory) for Wolfriders, used particularly by Leetah and Rayek for Cutter.

bearberry: An edible berry used by the Wolfriders to supplement their diet.

Bearclaw: Wolfrider elf, male; tenth chief of the Wolfriders; Recognized lifemate of Joyleaf; father of Cutter; a reckless, fierce, dreamberry-loving elf.

beesweets: Preserver name for honey.

bellow torches: Used by the trolls to heat their forges to high temperature.

belonging-time: Preserver term for the period when preservers dwelt with elves in the Palace.

Berrybuzz: Preserver, neuter.

big belly pictures: Fertility symbols.

Big Moon: The larger of the two moons that orbit the world; has a period of roughly sixteen days; also called the Greater Moon or Mother Moon.

bigthing: Preserver term for a human.

bird elf: Wolfrider term referring to Tyldak.

bird riders: General term of the **Wolfrid-**

ers for the Chosen Eight of the Gliders of Blue Mountain.

bird spirit: Term of the Hoan G'Tay Sho (Nonna's tribe) for the Gliders, later all elves.

birdbasket: Preserver term for a bird nest.

Black Hair: Wolfrider term for Rayek, used also by Kahvi.

black sending: The pain-filled telepathic attack of an antihealer such as Winnowill.

black snake: Wolfrider term for Winnowill.

Blackfell: Bearclaw's wolf.

Blood of Ten Chiefs: Honorific, used in referring to Cutter.

blood-bat: A parasitic bat, equivalent to a vampire bat

Blue Mountain: The home of the Gliders far to the west near the Vastdeep Water.

Bolli: (BOW-lee) Human, female; lives in the medieval-type village near the Wolfriders' reunion with the Palace.

bond-bird: One of the great hawks ridden by the Chosen Eight.

bonding: The process by which an elf and an animal become attuned to each other, not as master and subordinate, but as equals; technically, only the Wolfriders with their wolf blood can truly bond with wolves.

Bone Woman: The foul shamaness of Olbar's tribe when Cutter first encounters them.

bow-harp: A musical instrument based on a hunting bow but with more than one string.

Brace: Blue Mountain elf, male; tranced rockshaper who maintains the stone structure of one of Blue Mountain's arches.

branch-horn: A deerlike animal with

Aroree (with Petalwing)

spreading antlers.

Bridge of Destiny: A high stone arch overlooking Sorrow's End; a natural formation that is used as the site for the Test of Heart (see Trial by Hand, Head, and Heart).

Briersting: (BRY-er-sting) Strongbow's wolf.

bright-metal: Light, silvery, troll-made metal of which Cutter's sword New Moon is forged.

bristle-boar: A burrowing swine found in the desert near the Sun Village.

Bristlebrush: Scouter's wolf.

Brownberry: Wolfrider elf, female; killed by Madcoil in the first attack.

Brownskin: Name used by the Go-Backs and Ekuar for Rayek.

Bruga: (BROO-guh) Human, male; a member of the Gotara tribe, he captures Skywise, who escapes and cuts off some of his fingers; later helps hunt the "demons."

buck: Go-Back term for father.

bug: Term used by Cutter to refer to Petalwing.

Bumper: Scouter's and Dewshine's nickname for Windkin.

Bundles: Tyleet's wolf.

Burning Waste: The Wolfrider name for the desert between the Tunnel of Golden Light and Sorrow's End.

burrowers: The original chimpanzee-like creatures that evolved into the trolls.

busyhead highthing: Petalwing's term for Cutter.

C

cave slug: A wormlike creature found in troll caverns. Trolls consider them a delicacy.

Challenge Wand: Golden carved dagger used among the Sun Folk to ritually challenge a rival to the Trial of Hand, Head, and Heart.

Cheipar: (CHAY-par) Go-Back/Wolfrider elf, male; son of Krim by Skot and/or Pike; died in infancy.

Chiad G'Cho: (CHEE-ad guh-CHO) Hu-

The Bridge of Destiny

man, male; member of the Hoan G'Tay Sho tribe who joins the war party against the "wolf demons" and tries to start the forest fire.

chief-friend: An affectionate term used by Nightfall and others to refer to Cutter.

chief's lock: A bound lock of hair (ponytail) worn only by the chief of the Wolfriders.

Child Moon: The smaller of the two moons that orbit the world; it has a period of roughly eight days; also called Lesser Moon or Little Moon.

Children of Gotara: One human tribe's name for itself.

Choplicker: Ember's wolf.

Chosen Eight, the: Elves of Blue Mountain who ride the great hawks and do all the hunting for their people.

clap rocks: A musical instrument played during festivals at Sorrow's End.

Clearbrook: Wolfrider elf, female: lifemate of One-Eye; mother of Scouter and a deceased daughter; later becomes close to Treestump.

clearstone: A colorless, transparent mineral similar to mica; used as ornamentation by the Sun Folk.

cloud tree: A desert plant whose blossoms look like puffs of smoke.

Coneheads: Informal term used to refer to the High Ones because of their elongated skulls before taking the form of elves.

council: A formal meeting of all the Wolfriders, usually to consider a major decision.

cub: An affectionate name for a Wolfrider child.

cubling: An affectionate name for a very young Wolfrider child.

Curlneck: Wolf (rider unknown).

Cutter: Wolfrider elf, male; eleventh and current chief of the Wolfriders; son of Bearclaw and Joyleaf; Recognized lifemate of Leetah; father of Suntop and Ember; called Kinseeker by Two-Edge during the quest.

D

Dark Sister: Term used by Winnowill to refer to Leetah.

darks: Preserver term for nights.

dark-robed one (var.: **dark-robed mother**): Human term for Winnowill.

Dart: Wolfrider elf, male: son of Strongbow and Moonshade; during the Quest, remains in Sorrow's End and leads the jackwolf riders as the village's protector.

daystar: Sun Folk name for the sun.

death sleep: Wolfrider term for autumn.

Death Water: A waterfall of the Great River, near Olbar's tribe, which flows into the Valley of Endless Sleep.

deer-sloth: Scouter's name for a zwoot.

demons: Human term for elves.

den-hide: A practiced, coordinated defensive action of the Wolfriders, in which all members of the tribe hide and keep silence on command.

Dewshine: Wolfrider elf, female; daughter of Treestump and Rillfisher; cousin to Cutter; lovemate to Scouter; mother of Windkin through Recognition with Tyldak.

dig-digs: Preserver term for trolls.

Dodia: (doe-DEE-uh) Sun Villager elf, female; a jackwolf rider who participates in the rescue in the Forbidden Grove.

Door: One of two Blue Mountain elves, one male, one female; tranced rock shapers that secure the entrances to Blue Mountain.

double-shell nuts: An edible nut whose meat is enclosed in two tough shells.

dreamberry: A berry that causes intoxication in elves when eaten fresh; fermented, it is hallucinogenic; can be poisonous to humans.

dreamberry talk: Drunken babbling.

dreamberry vision: An hallucination.

dreamberry wine: Fermented product of dreamberry juice; first concocted by the trolls living under the original holt, a tradition kept up by Old Maggoty.

Dreen: Elf, male; one of the Rootless Ones; adopted as a child by Hassbet.

Dregg: Northern troll, male; one of Guttlekraw's guards who detects the elf army's approach.

Dro: (Drow) Human, male; Aro's insane brother; a refugee from the Holt fire who dies of illness at Cutter's feet at Sorrow's End.

Drub: (drubb) Troll: one of Picknose's progeny.

E

Egg: Blue Mountain elf, male: a tranced rockshaper who levitates the Great Egg and adds to its carvings.

eight-of-days: Elfin unit of time, equivalent to a week.

Ekuar: (ECK-wahr) Firstborn elf, male; a rockshaper once enslaved by trolls since childhood who was later befriended and freed by Rayek; now living with the Wolfriders.

elf: One of a number of different groups of beings, all descended from the original group of High Ones, who now inhabit the World of Two Moons; most known elves—Wolfriders, Sun Folk, Go-Backs—are shorter and hardier than their forebears, though some—Gliders—are still tall and delicate.

elf-friend: A wolf's particular Wolfrider.

Ember: Wolfrider elf, female: daughter of Cutter and Leetah, twin sister of Suntop.

F

Fahr: (farr) Skywise's soul name.

Father Tree: A great tree, shaped by generations of tree-shapers, home of the Wolfriders from Goodtree's time until

The effects of dreamberry wine.

burned down in Cutter's time by humans; also the new dwelling tree within Forbidden Grove.

fawn: Go-Back term for their children.

Festival of Flood and Flower: Annual celebration held by the Sun Folk at the end of the rainy season.

fever dream: A delirium.

fire eyes: Gems used as currency by the northern trolls.

The Great Egg being tended by Egg.

Firecoat: Redlance's wolf.

firemaker: One whose magic talent is the starting of fires.

firstborn: Early Wolfrider name for the immediate descendents of High Ones.

firstcomer: Early Wolfrider name for those who appeared with the Palace, i.e., High Ones.

First Dance: The oldest of the Sun Folk celebration dances, it tells of the Rootless Ones and the founding of Sorrow's End.

fisher bird: A water bird similar to a kingfisher.

five-fingers: Wolfrider term for a human.

fixed star: Skywise's term for the star which never seems to move that is located nearest to the Hub of the Great Sky Wheel.

Flam: Troll; one of Picknose's progeny.

flesh-shaping: An elfin magic power to shape flesh into any form, natural or unnatural; healing is a form of flesh-shaping.

floater: Term for an elf who has the power to levitate, but unlike Gliders, lacks propulsion.

floods-and-flowerings: Sun Folk expression for a year.

flyhighbaby: Preserver name for Windkin as an infant.

flyhighthing: Preserver name for Tyldak.

Forbidden Grove: A dense, wooded area in the Valley of Endless Sleep west of Olbar's village and east of Blue Mountain; home of the preservers after Winnowill sent them there from Blue Mountain; feared by Olbar's tribe as a dwelling place of evil spirits; the Wolfriders establish a new holt there.

forest brothers: Wolfrider term for wolves.

Foxfur: Wolfrider elf, female; lovemate of Skywise; killed by Madcoil

Freefoot: Wolfrider elf, male; sixth chief of the Wolfriders; father of Tanner.

Frosty Mane: Go-Back women's nickname for Skywise.

Frozen Mountains: The great mountain chain that lies to the north of Blue Mountain, beyond which lies the Palace of the High Ones; home to the northern trolls.

fur flower: Forest plant with puffy white petals.

fursoft cradlebaby: Preserver name for a mouse.

fursoft yapthing: Preserver name for a wolf cub.

G

Geoki: (gee-OH-kee, hard "g") Human, male: young hunter of the Hoan G'Tay Sho who joins, then opposes the war party against the "wolf demons"; befriends Dart.

Geru: (GEH-roo, hard "g") Human; one of three adopted children of Adar and Nonna.

Gliders: Self-levitating elves, especially of Blue Mountain.

go out: Term used to describe when an elf such as Savah, Winnowill, or Suntop travels outside the body in a type of astral projection.

Go-Backs: Elf tribe living just south of the Frozen Mountains near the Palace of the High Ones and the Northern trolls; a tribe of hunters, led by Kahvi, who have given up the use of magic; they were the first to feel the pull of the Palace when it was freed from its glacial tomb.

Goodtree: Wolfrider elf, female; eighth chief of the Wolfriders; Recognized mate/lifemate of Lionleaper and Acorn; mother of Mantricker; established the holt where Cutter was born.

Goodtree's Rest: Constellation named by Skywise.

Gotara: (go-TAH-rah) Supreme spirit worshipped by the tribe of humans who burned the Wolfriders out of the original holt.

Graysha: (GRAY-shah) Human, female; Olbar's latest mate.

Great Egg: A huge egg-shaped sculpture inside Blue Mountain that contains within its concentric layers the pictorial history of the Gliders.

Great Ice Wall: Go-Back term for the glacier that until recently hid the Palace of the High Ones.

Great River: A westward-flowing river that leads from the Death Water waterfall near Olbar's tribe to the Valley of Endless Sleep and on to Blue Mountain.

Great Wolf: A constellation named by Skywise.

Great Sky Wheel: Skywise's term for the entire sky, which seems to wheel overhead as time passes.

Greater Moon: *See* Big Moon.

green growing place: Leetah's term for the forest or woods in general.

Greymung: Troll, male; king of the holt trolls until killed in the war with the invading northern trolls.

ground-quake: An earthquake.

growler highthings: Preserver name for Wolfriders.

growler: Preserver term for a wolf.

Guiders: The Coneheads who were responsible for navigating the palace ship on its voyage through the stars.

Guttlekraw: Troll, male: king of the northern trolls; killed by Cutter and Kahvi in the final battle of the quest.

H

Halek: (HAHL-eck) Sun Villager elf, male: trained in the use of the arrow-whip by Dart.

hand, head, and heart: *See* Trial of Hand, Head, and Heart.

hangey-down: Preserver term for the cocoon they encase a living creature in to "preserve" it; it is suspended from a branch.

healer: An elf who has healing powers.

healing: The power to shape flesh to close wounds, knit bone, cleanse the body of poisons, and so on; a kind of psychokinesis.

High Ones: General elfin term for the beings who first came out of the Palace when it crashed on the World of Two Moons; the ancestors of all elves.

Greymung

highthing: Preserver term for an elf.

Hoan G'Tay Sho: (hone guh-TAY show) Tribe of humans living at the base of Blue Mountain who worship the Gliders; the name means "favored of those who dwell on high"; Nonna's tribe.

holt: Generally any place where the Wolfriders live, particularly their current home.

Holtfinder: Moonshade's wolf.

holt trolls: Trolls who lived beneath the Wolfrider's original forest holt; a splinter group from the northern trolls.

homeplace: Preserver name for the Palace.

hometrees: Preserver name for the holt in the Forbidden Grove.

Honored Ones: Human (Hoan G'Tay Sho tribe) term for the elves of Blue

Mountain.

hood spider: A desert spider that hides under the sand.

hoof-dog: A desert animal similar to a boar.

Hotburr: Pike's wolf.

howl: A Wolfrider ritual; a gathering of the tribe to celebrate or mourn a person or event. There may be storytelling or simply a howl to the sky.

A Howl.

Hub of the Great Sky Wheel: That part of the sky around which the stars seem to rotate; the north sky pole.

Human Hunter: A constellation named by Skywise.

human: General term to describe the original inhabitants scattered throughout the World of Two Moons. Some groups are at the same stage of development as Neanderthals, others at that of Cro-Magnons.

hummer: A bird similar to a hummingbird.

hunt, the: (1) Early Wolfrider term for the offspring of Timmorn and the she-wolves; (2) any elf with very strong wolf characteristics.

Huntress Skyfire: Wolfrider elf, female; fifth chief of the Wolfriders; Recognized mate of Dreamsinger; mother of Freefoot.

I

Itchback: Troll, male; young scout and guard in Guttlekraw's army; killed by Cutter and Rayek before the great battle.

J

jackwolf: A jackal-wolf hybrid, ridden by Dart and others in the Sun Village.

joining: The physical act of lovemaking.

Joyleaf: Wolfrider elf, female; Recognized lifemate of Bearclaw; mother of Cutter; killed by Madcoil.

juiceberries: Succulent berries that grow in the forest.

K

Kahvi: (KAHH-vee) Go-Back elf, female; chief of the Go-Backs; mother of Vaya and of Venka by Rayek.

Kakuk: (KACK-uck) Human, male: old member of the Hoan G'Tay Sho; serves and is imprisoned by Winnowill; freed by Adar, Nonna, and the Wolfriders.

kill-hunger: A frenzy.

Kinseeker: Name given by Two-Edge to Cutter.

kitling: Sun Folk term of affection, especially for a child.

Kiv: (KIVV) Go-Back elf.

Kohahn-Chief: (KOE-hahn) Human, male; leader of the Hoan G'Tay Sho.

Krim: (KRIMM) Go-Back elf, female; joins the Wolfriders after Quest's End; a lovemate of Pike and Skot.

Kureel: (koo-REEL) Glider elf, male; one of the Chosen Eight; loyal to Winnowill and hate-filled toward Wolfriders; dies when shot by Strongbow.

L

Leetah: (LEE-tah) Sun Villager elf, female; Recognized lifemate of Cutter; mother of Suntop and Ember; daughter of Sun-Toucher and Toorah; a powerful healer; is learning the ways of the Wolfriders.

Lesser Moon: *See* Child Moon.

Lifebearer: Name sometimes given to Woodlock.

lifegiver: An honorific title given to Leetah by the Sun Folk and Wolfriders.

lifemate: (1) An elf who has consciously and freely made a commitment to another to bond for life (or at least a very long time) in a pairing equivalent to marriage. (2) to make such a bond (*see* lovemate).

Lift-Leg: Human male; he inadvertently showed Tanner one way to cure animal hides by urinating over the pit where Tanner had buried some skins.

Lionskin: Treestump's wolf.

little bear-stabbers: Krim's name for Go-Back children.

Little Moon: *See* Child Moon.

Little Silver-hair: Savah's nickname for Skywise.

Little Spitface: Two-Edge's name for Petalwing.

little star cousins: Skywise's name for fireflies.

little winged ones: Human term for preservers.

Littletrill: Aroree's great hawk.

lock-sending: A kind of telepathic communication that is closed to all but the sender and the intended recipient(s).

Lodestone, the: The fragment of magnetic stone that Skywise wears as an amulet around his neck; also the magnetic meteorite from which the fragment came.

Longbranch: Wolfrider elf, male; formerly called Longreach; One Eye's brother; Wolfrider storyteller; killed by Madcoil.

Longreach: Old tribal name for Longbranch.

Longspear: Constellation named by Skywise.

longtooth: A large, wild cat resembling a sabretooth.

Lord Voll: (VAWL) Glider elf, male; one of the firstborn of the group of High Ones who fled the Palace and ended up at Blue Mountain; killed by Frozen Mountain trolls.

Loveless One: Name used by Savah and Leetah to refer to Winnowill.

lovemate: (1) An elf who joins with another for the pleasure involved but who has not made a stronger commitment. (2) To engage in lovemating (*see* lifemate).

Lree: (l'REE) Dewshine's soul name.

M

Maalvi: (MOLL-vee) Elf; one of the Rootless Ones; cousin to Hasbet.

Madcoil: A monstrous creature born of the magical mutation/combination of a longtooth cat and a giant snake.

Maggoty: *See* Old Maggoty.

magic: General term used to describe various elfin abilities or powers; not a supernatural power, but rather a form of energy that can be used and stored and refers to powers of the mind such as telekinesis, telepathy, pyrokinesis, and so on.

magic feeling: Suntop's term for the feeling he gets whenever he is around magic or a place where magic has been used.

Malak: (MAH-lack) Human, male; a member of Olbar's tribe who incurred the wrath of that leader by becoming the lover of the chief's daughter Selah and running away with her.

Mantricker: Wolfrider elf, male; ninth chief of the Wolfriders; a merry trickster.

marsh-piper: A singing bird.

Mekda: (MECK-dah) Firstborn elf, female; rockshaper enslaved by Frozen Mountain trolls since childhood and forced to work for them; called Sack 'o' Bones by the trolls; dies of exposure during the war between the Northern trolls and the Go-Backs and Wolfriders.

Mender: Sun Villager/Wolfrider elf, male; son of Woodlock and Rainsong; a healer.

metal shaper: One who has the power to shape metals that have been refined or found in a relatively pure state such as gold.

Minyah: (MIN-yuh) Sun Villager elf, female; an expert gardener who witnesses Redlance's emerging plant-shaping abilities.

moon madness: Insanity, crazy ideas.

Leetah

moons: Unit of time equivalent to months.

Moonshade: Wolfrider elf, female; lifemate of Strongbow; mother of Dart; quiet traditionalist; tanner and seamstress.

moonsword: Sometimes used to refer to New Moon because of its shape.

moss mush: Troll baby food.

Mother of Memory, the: *See* Savah.

Mother Moon: *see* Big Moon.

mother-mother highthing: One of Petalwing's names for Timmain.

mountain thing: Human term for the fallen Palace of the High Ones.

mud rat: A small animal that hibernates.

mump: Troll name for their children and youngsters.

N

nastybad dig-dig: Preserver name for trolls.

nasty bad high dig-dig: Preserver name for Two-Edge.

near-wolf: Cutter's term for a dog.

Nestrobber: One Eye's third wolf.

new green: Wolfrider term for the season of spring.

New Moon: Cutter's sword, forged by Two-Edge of brightmetal, with a key to Two-Edge's armory hidden in the handle; first owned by Bearclaw.

Newstar: Wolfrider elf, female; daughter of Woodlock and Rainsong; settles with her family in Sorrow's End.

Nightfall: Wolfrider elf, female; lifemate of Redlance; archer and huntress.

Nightrunner: Cutter's first wolf.

Nima: (NEE-mah) Human; one of three adopted children of Adar and Nonna.

nohump: Elfin term for a pony.

Nightfall and Redlance

noisybad bubblebangs: Preserver description of the Tunnel of Globes, a passageway to Winnowill's private chambers in Blue Mountain that is lined with explosive globes.

noisybad: Preserver description of anything they find disagreeably loud.

Nonna: (NAWN-ah) Human, female; mate of Adar, adoptive mother of Nima, Tenchi, and Geru; symbolmaker of the Hoan G'tay Sho who settles with Olbar's tribe; closest human friend of Cutter.

northern trolls: Trolls who live beneath Frozen Mountain.

now of wolf thought, the: *See* the always now.

nut-mash: (1) Gruel. (2) Metaphorically, weakened to the point of uselessness.

O

Oddbit: Holt troll, female; mate of Picknose; mother of Trinket; granddaughter of Old Maggoty; an opportunist who bestows her affections to her own advantage.

Olbar the Mountain-Tall: (OLE-barr) Human, male; superstitious chief of the tribe that lives by the Great River.

Old Maggoty: Holt troll, female: grandmother of Oddbit; herbalist with the knowledge of dreamberry brewing; first discovered by Bearclaw which revealed the existance of trolls.

old old highthing: Petalwing's name for Lord Voll.

One-Eye: Wolfrider elf, male; lifemate of Clearbrook; father of Scouter and a deceased daughter; falls in battle with Northern trolls; his body is preserved in Preserver wrapstuff while his spirit inhabits the Palace.

Orolin: (OH-roe-lin) High One, male: a Conehead who was keeper of the Scroll of Colors; died in the Palace's fall when his wrapstuff was torn.

Osek: (OH-seck) Firstcomer elf, male: a rockshaper enslaved by trolls since childhood who escapes with Ekuar and Mekda during the holt trolls' rebellion and dies in the desert near the Tunnel of

Golden Light.

owl pellet: General Wolfrider curse or insult, derived from the result of an owl's regurgitation.

P

Palace: Also called Palace of the High Ones, Lost Dwelling of the High Ones, and other names. The starship the High Ones (as Coneheads) shaped to resemble a castle; crashed on the World of Two Moons, stranding the High Ones.

Petalwing: Preserver; "leader" of the preservers until Quest's End, then stayed with Rayek in the Palace; guides the elf army during the troll-elf war.

Picknose: Holt troll, male; originally, one of Greymung's guards; later is briefly king of the Northern trolls, during which time he takes Oddbit as mate and fathers Trinket; subsequently establishes his own kingdom.

Pike: Wolfrider elf, male; son of Rain out of Recognition; overly fond of dreamberries; trainee storyteller of the Wolfriders under Longbranch.

preserver: A sexless, butterfly-like creature shaped by the Coneheads that can spit a kind of webbing, wrapstuff, which preserves whatever it completely enwraps. It also has a keen directional sense and can be used as a kind of living compass to locate the Palace.

pretty was-growler highthing: One of Petalwing's names for Timmain.

Prey-Pacer: Wolfrider elf, male; third chief of the Wolfriders; son of Rahnee the She-Wolf and Zarhan Fastfire.

puckernuts: Very bitter nut-like fruit; an exclamation of distaste.

punkin: A type of gourd.

Pusgums: Troll, male; one of Guttle-kraw's guards; killed by Rayek and Cutter.

Q

quill-pig: A type of porcupine.

R

Rahnee the She-Wolf: (RAHH-nee) Wolfrider elf, female: second chief of the Wolfriders; daughter of Timmorn Yellow-Eyes and Murrel.

Rain, the Healer: Wolfrider elf, male: father of Pike and Rainsong; healer under Bearclaw's chieftainship; killed by Madcoil.

Rainsong: Wolfrider elf, female; Recognized lifemate of Woodlock; mother of Newstar, Wing, and Mender; a nurturing elf devoted to family; settles in the Sun Village and becomes virtually a Sun Villager.

Rayek: (RAY-eck) Sun Villager elf, male; strong user of levitating and hypnotizing magic; prideful; loves and loses Leetah at which point he leaves Sun Village; befriends Ekuar, later loves Winnowill.

Recognition: A mental and genetic imperative that produces an irresistible mating urge between genetically compatible elves that guarantees offspring with superior qualities.

Redlance: Wolfrider elf, male; lifemate of Nightfall; a gentle plantshaper.

Redmark: Redlance's childhood tribe name.

Reevol: (REE-vole) Glider elf, male; one of the Chosen Eight.

Rillfisher: Wolfrider elf, female; lifemate of Treestump; mother of Dewshine; deafened by a fever; killed in an accident.

rock-shaping: An elfin magic power

Preservers (Petalwing is on the left)

that enables the possessor to mold rocks and minerals (as opposed to refined metals).

Rootless Ones: Name of one group of High Ones who escaped from the Palace and wandered for generations before settling at Sorrow's End.

rosynose highthing: Petalwing's name for Pike.

round-ears: Elfin term for humans.

run-rabbits: Dart's playfully insulting name for his jack-wolf riders.

S

Sack 'o' Bones: Troll name for Mekda.

sand flea: A biting desert insect.

Savah: (SAHH-vah) Sun Villager elf, female; oldest of the Sun Folk and revered by them as the Mother of Memory; has virtually all the elfin magical powers including the ability to "go out" (astral projection).

Scouter: Wolfrider elf, male; non-Recognized lovemate and later lifemate of Dewshine; adoptive father of Windkin; son of One-Eye and Clearbrook.

Scroll of Colors: An extremely high tech, i.e. magical holographic device in the Palace that contains a record of the High Ones' history.

Savah

Scurff: Holt troll, male; the keeper of the door that led from the tunnels to the original holt.

seek-root: A tiny-blossomed desert flower.

Selah: (SAY-lah) Human, female; daughter of Olbar who ran away with her lover Malak.

self-shaper: One who can manipulate their own physical body in a more advanced way than mere flesh-shaping. Timmain was the last elf to be a self-shaper.

Self-without-image: Savah's term for her astral being which she can project for short distances.

sending: Telepathic communication; a power that is well developed in some elfin tribes such as the Wolfriders and rare or unknown in others such as the Sun Folk. Sending can be open (broadcast to all in range) or locked (limited to specific elves). *See* lock-sending.

shade and sweet water: Common Sun Folk greeting.

shadow beast: Human term for a wolf.

shaky-shake: Preserver description of an earthquake.

sharpdark highthing: Petalwing's name for Rayek.

She-Wolf: *See* Rahnee the She-Wolf.

Shenshen: (SHEN-shen) Sun Villager elf, female; daughter of Sun-Toucher and Toorah; sister of Leetah; midwife; joins Wolfriders.

shinysword highthing: Berrybuzz's name for Cutter.

showing throat: Wolfrider expression for backing down in a confrontation, derived from wolf pack challenges.

Shyhider: Moonshade's wolf that died in the desert.

Shu-Shen: (SHOO-shen) Sun Villager elf, male; jack-wolf rider who goes on the rescue to the Forbidden Grove.

Silvergrace: Rainsong's wolf that died in the desert.

silversoft highthing: Petalwing's name for Clearbrook.

six-sided stones: A dice game of chance played by trolls.

skeleton weeds: Desert plants resembling tumbleweeds.

Skimsand: Dodia's jack-wolf.

Skot: (SCOTT) Go-Back elf, male: joins the Wolfriders; irreverent; a friend of Pike who joins with him and Krim to form a threesome.

Skyfire: *See* Huntress Skyfire.

skyfire storm: A lightning storm.

Skywise: Wolfrider elf, male; soulbrother of Cutter; loves the stars and the company of elf maidens; abhors humans.

sleep dust: A powder concocted by Old

Maggoty that puts animals (and by virtue of the wolf blood, Wolfriders) into a deep sleep.

Sleeping Troll: Wolfrider name for an active volcano visible from the original holt.

Slidderback: Zhantee's jack-wolf.

Smoketreader: One Eye's wolf.

Smoking Mountain: A not-quite-dormant volcano near Sorrow's End.

snow bear: Similar to a polar bear.

snows: Human term for years.

softpretty highthing: Petalwing's name for Leetah.

Sorrow's End: The Sun Folk's oasis village founded by the Rootless Ones. It was discovered by the Wolfriders after their desert trek.

soul name: A word/sound/concept that embodies all that an elf is mentally and spiritually. It is both a door to and contents of the innermost private core of the mind. It is sacred among Wolfriders, but for elfin tribes that do not send, such as the Sun Folk, it has neither meaning nor use and has disappeared.

Spirit Man: Human, male; shaman of the human tribe that burned the Wolfriders from their original holt; killed by Strongbow.

Spirit Slayer: Name taken for himself by the thief Cutter killed.

square-eye: A goatlike animal domesticated by some early groups of elves.

squatneedle: A type of cactus resembling a barrel cactus.

Starjumper: Skywise's wolf.

sticker plants: Wolfrider name for cactus.

stillquiet: Preserver term for sleep.

stingtail: Desert creature similar to a scorpion.

strangleweed: A dangerous vine which twines rapidly around anything that touches it.

striped doe: A deer known to the Sun Folk.

Strongbow: Wolfrider elf, male; lifemate of Moonshade; father of Dart; strong-willed traditionalist who seldom

speaks aloud; one of the Wolfrider elders.

Strongest Man: Early human who was the first to kill a High One when the Palace crashed onto the planet.

Sun Folk: A tribe of elves descended from the Rootless Ones, living in the desert village of Sorrow's End (also called the Sun Village).

Sun Symbol: A figure carved into the stone at the end of the arch of the Bridge of Destiny.

Sun Village: *See* Sun Folk.

sun-comes-up (or **sun-goes-up**): Elfin term for east.

sun-goes-down: Elfin term for west.

sunnygold highthing: Petalwing's name for Dewshine.

Suntop: Wolfrider elf, male; son of Cutter and Leetah; twin brother of Ember; a mystic often distressed by his own powers.

Sun-Toucher: Sun Villager, male; mate of Toorah; father of Leetah and Shenshen; blind interpreter of the ways of the sun and the earth to his village.

Sur: (SOOR) One-Eye's soul name.

Symbol Maker: (1) Shamaness who uses drawings to work magic; (2) Nonna's title in the Hoan G'Tay Sho.

Skywise

T

taal: (TAHL) An elfin child's game similar to hide and seek.

taal-stick: A wand used by children playing taal to touch each other, each touch counting a point.

Timmain being
wrapped by a
preserver.

A treewee

Tabak: (TAH-back) Human, male; killed by Cutter as he was about to sacrifice Redlance; his death triggers the burning of the forest and the original holt.

tall one: Elfin term for a human.

talon-whip: The hunting weapon carried by the Chosen Eight, consisting of grasping claws at the end of a coil of rope.

Tam: Cutter's soul name.

Tanner: Wolfrider elf, male; seventh chief of the Wolfriders; father of Goodtree.

Tenchi: (TEN-chee) Human; one of three adoptive child of Adar and Nonna.

Tenspan: Greatest of the Glider hawks; flown by Lord Voll; killed by northern trolls.

Tenspan's Hall: The great aerie in Blue Mountain from which the Chosen Eight fly their hawks.

thaw-time: Trollish term for spring.

Thaya: (THIGH-yah) Human, female; refugee from the Holt fire; mate to Aro.

Thief: Human, male; exiled brother of Olbar whose name was taken from him; killed by Cutter while attempting to kill Skywise.

think-do magic: Preserver term for the magic practiced by the High Ones while suspended in the timelessness of a Preserver cocoon.

thornbush: Prickly plant known to Wolfriders.

three-mating: A menage a trois where three elves bond and choose to live together.

Timmain: (tim-MAIN) High One, female; the only one of the High Ones who remained a selfshaper; she became a wolf and bore Timmorn to save her people and begin the tribe of Wolfriders.

Timmorn Yellow Eyes: (TIM-morn) Half-wolf son of Timmain; the first chief of the Wolfriders.

Tolf, the Wood-Cleaver: Human, male; father of Adar.

Toorah: (TOO-rah) Sun Villager elf, female; mate of Sun-Toucher; mother of Leetah and Shenshen.

toss-stone: A Sun Villager child's game; also a trollish gambling game.

touch-me-touch-you: A child's game similar to tag.

treehorn: An animal with antlers similar to a deer.

tree-shaper: One with the magic ability to accelerate plant growth and direct the shape of that growth.

Treestump: Wolfrider elf, male; lifemate of Rillfisher; father of Dewshine; eldest Wolfrider in Cutter's time; becomes close to Clearbrook after One-Eye's death.

tree-walker: One who is at home in the tops of trees and can move easily from branch to branch.

treewee: A small, timid arboreal animal that resembles a perpetually miserable tarsier.

Trial of Hand, Head, and Heart: A Sun Village rite between rival suitors. The Trial of Hand is a test of physical ability; Trial of Head, a test of mental ability; and Trial of Heart, a spiritual test.

tribe name: Generally, the public name by which an elf is known and which can be changed, as opposed to the soul name which is eternal and private.

Trinket: Troll, female; daughter of Picknose and Oddbit; bratty friend of Ember.

troll: Beings who have evolved from small, apelike, burrowing creatures used by the Coneheads as servants and mechanics on the Palace-ship; it was a rebellion by the troll precursors that caused the ship to crash on the World of Two Moons. There are two known groups of trolls: the holt trolls and the northern trolls.

Trollhammer: Dewshine's wolf.

Tunnel of Globes: One of Winnowill's

defenses; a tunnel containing spheres that explode when touched.

Tunnel of Golden Light: A passage from Greymung's caverns to the desert at the base of a sheer cliff.

Tunnel of the Green Wood: Tunnel from Greymung's throne chamber to the site of the original holt.

turn of the seasons: Wolfrider season corresponding to a year.

Twen: Nightfall's soul name.

Two-Edge: The abused half-breed son of Winnowill and a troll father; an advanced smith whose mental imbalance causes him to precipitate the troll-elf war; later, partially healed by Leetah, he participates in the downfall of Blue Mountain.

Two-Spear: Wolfrider elf, male; fourth chief of the Wolfriders.

Tyldak: (TILL-dack) Glider elf, male; his arms are flesh-shaped by Winnowill into wings; Recognizes Dewshine and fathers Windkin; later escapes Blue Mountain's downfall.

Tyleet: (tih-LEET) Wolfrider elf, female; daughter of Redlance and Nightfall by "forced Recognition" (aided by Leetah); her name means "healer's gift."

U

Ulm: Redlance's soul name.

Urda: (OOR-dah) Go-Back elf, female; Kahvi's second-in-command.

V

Valley of Endless Sleep: A wooded valley west of Olbar's tribe and east of Blue Mountain that contains the Forbidden Grove.

Vastdeep Water (or **Vastdeep Sea**): Glider term for a great ocean to the west of Blue Mountain.

Vaya: (VIE-yah) Go-Back elf, female; Kahvi's daughter; killed by Guttlekraw's guards in the troll-elf war.

Venka: (VEN-kah) Elf, female; daughter of Rayek and Kahvi; has the ability to cancel Winnowill's magic; has joined the Wolfriders.

Voll: *See* Lord Voll.

Vok: (VOCK) Go-Back elf, male.

W

wackroot: An analgesic plant known to Olbar's tribe.

Wadsack: (WODD-sack) Northern troll, male; one of Guttlekraw's guards; killed by Cutter and Rayek.

Warfrost: Cutter's second wolf.

Way, The: The Wolfrider philosophy, traditions, and codes of behavior, derived from wolf pack law.

whistling leaves: A purgative medicinal plant found in bogs and known to Wolfriders. Its perforated leaves make a whistling sound when the wind blows through them.

Whitebrow: Clearbrook's wolf.

whitecold (var. **season of the white cold**): Wolfrider term for winter.

whitestripe: An animal similar to a skunk.

Wile-Eye: Troll; one of Picknose's progeny.

Windkin: Elf, male; son of Dewshine; sired by Tyldak but adopted by Scouter; a floater.

Wing: Wolfrider elf, male; son of Woodlock and Rainsong; settles in Sorrow's End with his family.

Winnowill: (WINN-oh-will) Glider elf, female; mother of Two-Edge; evil schemer; powerful antihealer; mind-invader and flesh-shaper; she gave herself the title of lord of Blue Mountain.

Winnowill

wobble-wobble: Preserver description of the effects of drunkenness.

wolf children: Sun Folk term for the Wolfriders.

wolf demons: Human term for the Wolfriders.

Wolfriders: Tribe of wolf-blooded elves descended from the High One Timmain and a true wolf who are currently lead by Cutter. Of all the elves on the World of Two Moons, they are mortal because of the wolf blood that runs in them.

wolf-friend: Wolfrider term for their bond wolves.

wolf-send: A Wolfrider's method of communicating telepathically to his or her wolf.

wolfsong: A state of mind without past or future; also known as the "now of wolf thought" or the "always now."

Wood of Dreams: Another name for the Forbidden Grove.

Woodlock: Wolfrider elf, male; Recognized mate of Rainsong; father of Newstar, Wing, and Mender; settles in Sorrow's End.

Woodshaver: Nightfall's wolf.

woodworms: Tree-boring insects.

World of Two Moons: The planet on which the Conehead's palace-ship crashed and on which Elfquest takes place.

World's Spine: A mountain range near Sorrow's End.

worm-root: An edible, but bitter plant liked by the holt trolls.

wrapstuff: Preserver term for the webbing they spit to form cocoons.

Y

yapthing: Petalwing's name for Choplicker.

Yellow-Eyes: *See* Timmorn Yellow-Eyes.

Yif: Go-Back, male; dies in the troll-elf war.

Yurek: (YOO-reck) Elf, male: one of the Rootless Ones, he was Savah's lifemate; a rock-shaper who created the Bridge of Destiny and died by leaping from it when it was finished.

Z

Zhantee: (ZHON-tee) Sun Villager elf, male; becomes a jack-wolf rider and later a member of the Wolfrider tribe.

zwoot: A rather stupid creature resembling a cross between a horse and a camel; used as a pack and draft animal by the Sun Folk.

A Zwoot with rider